# THE COLUMBIA GUIDE TO

# Modern Chinese History

THE COLUMBIA GUIDES TO ASIAN HISTORY

# THE COLUMBIA GUIDES TO ASIAN HISTORY

Gary D. Allinson, *The Columbia Guide to Modern Japanese History*

# THE COLUMBIA GUIDE TO

# Modern Chinese History

R. Keith Schoppa

COLUMBIA UNIVERSITY PRESS

NEW YORK

Columbia University Press
Publishers Since 1893
New York    Chichester, West Sussex
Copyright © 2000 Columbia University Press
All rights reserved

Library of Congress Cataloging-in-Publication Data

Schoppa, R. Keith, 1943–
The Columbia guide to modern Chinese history / R. Keith Schoppa.
p. cm. — (Columbia guides to Asian history)
Includes bibliographical references and index.
ISBN 0–231–11276–9
1. China—History—19th century. 2. China—History—20th century.
I. Title. II. Series.
DS755 .S635 2000
951.05—dc21
99–053420

Casebound editions of Columbia University Press books are printed on permanent and durable
acid-free paper.
Printed in the United States of America
c 10 9 8 7 6 5 4 3 2

*To the memory of three master teachers at Valparaiso University*

*Willis Boyd*
*Daniel Gahl*
*Paul Phipps*

# CONTENTS

# ACKNOWLEDGMENTS

I owe much to Loyola College in Maryland and to their bestowal of the Edward and Catherine Doehler Chair in Asian History in 1998; this position allowed me to work more quickly on this book than first projected. For their generous support of the chair itself and their special kindness to me, I want to thank Edward and Catherine Doehler. For various kinds of support during my first year at Loyola, I am grateful to my colleagues in the Department of History, especially to Professors Charles Cheape and Thomas Pegram, who repeatedly offered sound advice when I struck various snags along the way. Special thanks should go to my editor at Columbia, James Warren, who invited me to write the guide and was always eager to discuss the project, offering sage words of advice on many occasions. Finally, to my wife, Beth, who continually offers love, support, and encouragement, and to Kara, Derek, and Heather, who through each stage of growing up and maturing have offered new joys and challenges, I say my deepest thank you.

June 1999
Valparaiso, Indiana
Baltimore, Maryland

# INTRODUCTION

*The Columbia Guide to Modern Chinese History* is an introduction to major features of modern Chinese history and a reference for general readers interested in pursuing certain topics. This introduction points first to the importance of understanding Chinese history, as it sets forth some of its distinguishing aspects; it then explains the guide's approach to the history of modern China.

At the heart of modern Chinese history have been the efforts of the Chinese people to transform the traditional polity into a modern nation-state, the Confucian orthodoxy into an ideology that could help shape the process, and an agrarian economy into an industrial one. The result has been the largest revolution in world history in terms both of the radicalism of the changes and of the numbers of people affected. The revolutionary twists and turns have brought alternating cycles of hope and despair to the world's most populous country. At the opening of the twenty-first century, as the search for a new definition of modern China seems to be quickening, the United States, like the rest of the world, ponders whether the China coming into being will be friend or foe, challenger or collaborator. Hence, the need for an up-to-date understanding of the history of China.

Embedded in the effort to understand modern China are significant difficulties. On the surface and simplest level is the fact that there are many Chinas. Though a standard geographical division is between north and south China, the reality is much more complex. The standard dialect taught in schools is Mandarin, but there are more than 250 dialects, many of them as different as different languages. Traveling from mountain valley to mountain valley, one encounters these different dialects, each used to carry its own cultural traditions and practices, its own patterns of social and economic life.

Such diversity makes it extraordinarily difficult to generalize about the Chinese experience and the Chinese past.

At a deeper level, also contributing to the difficulty of understanding modern China are gulfs in historical perspective. Beginning in the early nineteenth century, the once mighty and glorious Chinese state was set upon by the West and turned in degradation into a semicolony. China's struggle to emerge from Western-imposed humiliation continues, from the Chinese perspective, until the present. In this historical experience, the United States and Western European nations that provided the more powerful imperialist force generally have never known the long-term subordination and the problems of identity and self-concept thereby produced. The West cannot easily appreciate the historical memory of the Chinese. The problem of historical perspective is made even more difficult by the polarized Chinese political situation that has left China's modern identity still unsettled. With the People's Republic (PRC) on the mainland and the Republic of China on Taiwan each claiming to speak for China, the history of the revolution itself becomes hostage to particular political stance. One goal of this guide is therefore to deconstruct the historical interpretations attached to polarized politics in order to appreciate the diverse realities of the revolution and therefore of modern China.

At the deepest level in difficulty of understanding the dynamics of the Chinese past is the cultural chasm that exists between the West and East Asia. Though evident in a myriad of ways, two social-ethical realities are perhaps most stark in contrast. Whereas Western society is focused on the individual, China's basic social unit is the group. The group, the most important of which is the family, is conceptualized as existing prior to the individual; therefore, the individual does not have *rights* over and against the group, but rather *responsibilities* to the group. In addition, while the West has developed a universalistic ethic, ideally treating all members of society with the same ethical standards, the Chinese ethic has tended to the particular. Certain members of society—for example, members of one's group or those to whom one has connections—are therein shown special ethical consideration and treatment. Both of these practices make it difficult for Westerners to appreciate the sources and dynamics of Chinese life and history.

We study modern Chinese history in order to understand the Chinese people's memory of the past and understanding of themselves. We also study the Chinese past to derive for ourselves a foundation for comprehending the present in as full and accurate a context as possible in order to act responsibly as citizens of the world and as citizens of the United States. But a study of

China, with its diversity, its varying historical perspectives, and its sharply different cultural values, very importantly provides a mirror through which to see ourselves more clearly. Through a study of the modern Chinese past, the historical development and culture of our own society stands in contrast, and our own, ordinarily submerged political, social, and cultural assumptions come into clear view.

The focus here is "modern" China. By the word *modern*, I do not mean to imply some judgment about the nature or extent of economic or political development; nor do I intend to imply some developmental teleological goal. In other words, in using this word, I am not entering the social science controversies over the wisdom and appropriateness of the use of *modern*, or its noun form, *modernization*, in analyzing societies. The use of *modern* is simply a way to differentiate the period from about 1780 to the present from the era of the Chinese traditional imperial-bureaucratic state. Why begin our study about 1780, when that traditional state was still very much alive? In the past, Western studies of modern China frequently began with the Opium War (1839–42), the rationale being in part that it was a clear demarcation of the beginning decline not only of the Chinese state but also of traditional Chinese civilization, as well as the inauguration of the search for a new Chinese way. Recently, historians have come to argue that taking the Western impact as the point of departure for modern China distorts the reality of the past and places far too much importance on the role of the Western nations. Such an approach in effect deemphasizes the part that China played in its own development. Recent work has shown that some "modern" elements that have developed in the nineteenth and twentieth centuries had their origins in the 1770s and 1780s, suggesting that Chinese society was beginning to change well before the full impact of the West was felt. A date around 1780 as the beginning of modern China is thus closer to what we know today as historical "reality." It also allows us to have a better baseline to understand the precipitous decline of the Chinese polity in the nineteenth and twentieth centuries, for in 1780 the wealth and power of the mid-Qing state was as yet generally unscathed, despite various indications that severe problems were beginning to emerge.

Finally, a word about the history treated in this book: the subject of history is what human beings have said and done, but a volume of this length cannot presume to be so all-inclusive. My coverage includes developments and change in five main arenas of action: domestic politics, society, the economy, the world of culture and thought, and relations with the outside world. It will not focus on the arts, theater, science and medicine, and sports—except when these subjects impinge directly on the larger picture of change in modern China. Despite these omissions, the material presented should provide a comprehensive overview of the major developments in the history of modern China.

Four parts comprise this volume. They are a Historical Narrative; a Compendium of Key Figures, Events, and Terms; an annotated Resource Guide; and Appendices. Readers using this guide may do so at various levels of focus, depending on their purposes and interests. The following brief descriptions of each part of the guide will suggest to the reader the various ways that this book may be used.

Part I, the Historical Narrative, provides a comprehensive overview of Chinese history since about 1780, in five main arenas as listed above: domestic politics, society, the economy, the world of culture and thought, and relations with the outside world. This overview also attempts to offer the best contemporary historical interpretations of the dynamics of developments and events. The narrative focuses on the evolving forms of the Chinese nation, state, and society and the ideas that shaped and infused them. It is organized chronologically, with the length of each chronological period determined by theme. Thus, chapter 1 charts the decline of the traditional Chinese state from the height of Qing dynasty power to its nadir in the Boxer Protocol of 1901. Chapter 2 explores efforts of Manchus, Republicans, Nationalists, and Communists to begin to restructure state and society (1901–28) and to build the nation amid a cultural revolution. This time of great change included the abolition of the traditional civil service examination and the monarchy and the radicalism of the May Fourth Movement. Chapter 3, covering the years 1928 to 1960, presents the Nationalist and Communist alternatives for structuring state and society, the meaning of the nation through the war against Japan, and especially the travail of some of the most violent and unsettling days in one of history's most shattering social revolutions. Chapter 4, on recent historical development from 1960 to the present, looks at the effects of ideology and economic developments (disasters in the Great Leap Forward and the Cultural Revolution and recent prosperity both in the PRC and on Taiwan) on the state, society, and the sense of nation. Depending on their purpose, readers may read the entire narrative, read for similar themes or about similar topics in each chapter, or read for specific events and developments. Names and terms that appear in boldface at their first appearance in the narrative can also be found in part II, the Compendium.

The Compendium describes key figures, events, and terms. It can be used to access more specific information on these matters than is available in the Historical Narrative. The 250 entries of the Compendium are divided into eleven sections: events and movements; terms; institutions and organizations; treaties; emperors; Qing dynasty government leaders; leaders of dissent, rebellion, and revolution; Nationalist Party leaders; Communist Party leaders; military figures; and intellectuals, writers, and artists. Some party and government leaders were, of course, previously, or even concurrently, leaders of revolution and/or military figures; in such cases, I give priority to their party affiliation, and hence the section listing leaders of rebellion and so forth contains mostly pre-1920 figures and dissenters under the Nationalist and Communist regimes. Entries in the section on writers name major publications that are available in English translation. For ease of reference, each entry can be found in the index, and entries within each section are alphabetical.

The Compendium thus provides mainly reference material that the reader can find quickly and use briefly. Part III, the Resource Guide, by contrast offers direction to sources that will enable readers to explore modern Chinese history more widely and deeply. It is divided into three sections. The first is an annotated bibliography of sixty-one general works and more than 430 of the most authoritative books in English, many of which have been used in the writing of the Historical Narrative. In the annotations, I have strived for succinctness in pointing out the strengths or other nature of each work. The second section of the Resource Guide deals with documentary and feature films that offer information and insight into the developments and changes in modern Chinese history. Each annotated entry includes the film's name and date, its applicability and usefulness for specific age groups, and its distributor. Thirteen documentary titles and twenty feature films are listed. The Resource Guide's third section annotates electronic resources available for probing more deeply into modern Chinese history and today's China. Electronic media are rapidly developing and changing in both format and content, and the information in this section is likely soon to be superseded. The information therein is therefore in large part suggestive—pointing to the kinds of opportunities available for utilizing this type of source.

Part IV of the guide, Appendices, offers material supplementary to the Historical Narrative and the Compendium. Appendix 1 is a chronology of key events in the period 1780 to the present; it essentially presents events from the narrative in tabular form. Appendix 2 contains excerpts from twenty key documents from modern Chinese history. Brief essays introduce each document's context, issues, and import. The documents, which date from 1839 to

1993, range from government and party documents to editorials from the May Fourth period, the Marriage Law of 1950, and a wall poster from the 1989 Beijing Spring. Their inclusion in this appendix is noted in relevant places in the Historical Narrative. Appendix 3 presents key information on the major party congresses of both the Guomindang (Nationalist Party) and the Communist Party from their formation in the 1920s into the mid-1990s; the dates of meetings and details of major party decisions, often related to party leadership, are presented. Appendix 4 provides key quantitative data on twentieth-century demographic and social trends and patterns; it also includes economic information.

In sum, the guide serves a number of learning functions. For readers seeking a quick answer to a question or concern about the Chinese past or about a personage or institution, it provides that answer in parts I, II, or IV (or perhaps in all of these parts) and thus can be the end of the search. In its versatility, the guide also serves as a vehicle for further study and research on the Chinese past, part III being especially designed to facilitate that goal; however, the Historical Narrative, the Compendium, and the Appendices may also stimulate new ways of looking at the Chinese past and raise new interests in the reader's mind. It is the hope of the author and publisher that the reader will find the guide a helpful, accessible, and reliable reference to modern Chinese history.

# PART I

# Historical Narrative

The following narrative offers a chronological overview of key arenas of Chinese history since about 1780: each of the four chapters discusses domestic politics, social and economic developments, the worlds of thought and culture, and relations with the outside world, though historical development, trends, and themes determine the extent of particular coverage in each. Trends and themes from the saga of Chinese history also shape the length of each of the four chronological periods as well as the chapters that discuss them.

Chapter 1 studies the decline and collapse of the traditional Chinese state from its acme of power and wealth in the late eighteenth century to the humiliating 1901 Boxer Protocol. Chapter 2 charts the efforts of various political groups from 1901 to 1928 to reconstruct the polity and erect a nation amid the turmoil of warlordism and both cultural and political revolution. Chapter 3 analyzes the differing policies established for the structuring of state and society by the Nationalist and Communist Parties from 1928 to 1960, a period that saw war between China and Japan, civil war, and one of history's most violent revolutions. Chapter 4 brings the narrative from 1960 to the present, focusing first on the tragedy of ideology run amok in the disasters of the Great Leap Forward and the Cultural Revolution and then on the economic revolution that at century's end has raised national hopes but also many questions about future directions and policies.

Readers wanting an overview of the key elements of Chinese history should read the entire narrative. A reader interested in a particular theme or topic, like the role of nationalism or the treatment of intellectuals by the state, may use the index to mine each chapter for the relevant material. If interested in a particular event (say, the May Fourth Period) the reader can go directly to the indicated chapter (in this case, chapter 2) for detailed coverage.

Boldface type in the narrative indicates that the names and terms so marked are included in part II, the Compendium.

# CHAPTER ONE

# The Decline of the Traditional State, 1780–1901

## CHINA IN 1780

### The Standard View of the State of the State

First, a freeze-frame as a baseline to understand the context of modern Chinese history. The date 1780 is a somewhat arbitrary choice, selected to represent in general the last years of the eighteenth century. From the beginning, it should be understood that the meaning of a nation's past is relative—relative to, among other things, the present, the perspective of those trying to understand it, and the arena of the past that is in particular focus. The standard view of China's late eighteenth century, relative to state and society *as a whole*, is that traditional China reached its apogee of wealth and power during the reign of the **Qianlong emperor** (1736–95). Indeed, there is much to recommend and support that view. In the middle of the century, triumphant military campaigns extended Chinese control into the central Asian Tarim Basin, bringing six million square miles of new territory into the empire. Three interventions in Tibet from the 1720s to the 1750s made that state a Chinese protectorate. With peace and prosperity the order of the day within China, peripheral states in South, Southeast, and East Asia sent missions bearing tribute in what is generally known as the tributary system. This act, which dated back many centuries, the Chinese understood as a younger brother's recognition, as it were, of China's superior, elder-brother status. Underscoring their subordinate status was the central ritual performed before the emperor by mission leaders on reaching Beijing—the kowtow (*ketou*), three prostrations, with three pressings of the forehead to the ground with each prostration, a ritual traditionally performed by children before their parents on New Year's Day.

Efficient and effective government in the reigns of the Qianlong emperor's father and grandfather (the Yongzheng emperor and the Kangxi emperor) had created a situation in which economic prosperity could flourish. In 1736, the state treasury had a surplus of twenty-four million taels of silver; fifty years later, the surplus was more than triple that. Four times the Qianlong emperor canceled the collection of annual taxes because of the state's remarkable fiscal status. The growing significance of regional cash crops—cotton, tea, and tobacco—underscored the expansion of interregional trade; southeastern coastal provinces carried on a thriving trade with Southeast Asia and Taiwan; the availability of silk, tea, and porcelain brought Europeans and Japanese to the Celestial Kingdom. The importation of new crops from the New World—sweet potatoes, maize, peanuts—allowed the cultivation of previously unarable sandy or mountainous land.

Agricultural commercialization and diversification helped fuel an economic boom that had a great impact on Chinese society. Historians have noted the increasing importance of money and markets; taxes were now generally paid in money rather than, as in previous dynasties, in kind. Native banks and new fiscal institutions were developed because of the credit and transfer needs of long-distance interregional trade. Important social changes were stimulated by the new prosperity: wealth became increasingly significant for elite status; new opportunities arose as occupational differentiation grew greater; markets linked village farmers to towns and the world beyond in new commercial relationships.[1] The general scene is one of economic well-being and plenty. An eighteenth-century writer described it: "Houses cluster together like fish-scales and people are as numerous as ants. Since local administration is simple, the district is often quiet. While everywhere on the fields mulberry, hemp, and various cereal crops are grown, the streams abound with carp and other fish."[2]

An extraordinarily significant social product of economic growth was a huge increase in population. Although traditional population figures are notoriously unreliable, we can get some idea from those that are available: the population was said to have soared from more than 177 million in 1749 to more than 301 million in 1790, an increase of 70 percent in only four decades.[3] The New World food crops and such techniques as widespread double-cropping helped support this increase, although the dynamics of the surging population are still not clear: there may have been both a declining mortality rate and a rising birth rate during these years. The increase's positive results were as a stimulus to "internal colonization, diffusion of technology, and maximization of yields," making "possible the remarkable territorial extension of the empire."[4]

It is perhaps not surprising that in the late eighteenth century the glories of China were celebrated in the West. Many things Chinese were increasingly sought after, and in Europe even became the rage: Chinese interior decor and furniture were imitated; Chinese gardens with Chinese pavilions were created at the homes of the elite in Potsdam and Versailles; "enlightened" or "benevolent" despotism, the perceived Chinese model of rule, was championed by European royalty and by Enlightenment philosophes. In the United States, Benjamin Franklin marveled, "Could we be so fortunate as to introduce the industry of the Chinese, their arts of living and improvements in husbandry . . . America might become in time as populous as China."[5] It is indeed likely, as an American historian suggested, that "literate Westerners knew more about China in the eighteenth century than they do in the twentieth."[6]

## The Complexity of Chinese Reality

This generalized macropicture of China at the zenith of its traditional strength must, however, be modified by the environmental and historical complexities of Chinese reality. Anyone who travels to the various regions of China—say, to the mountains of eastern Sichuan or the loess landscape near Xi'an, to the flat ricelands of northern Zhejiang or the surrealistic karst topography of Guilin—will recognize that the functionings of daily life, society, and politics had to have been substantially different in each place, if only because of the natural environment. Jonathan Spence has summarized it succinctly: "China's vast expanses allowed for endless variation in such areas as pace of economic change, types of lineage organization, efficiency of transportation, religious practices, sophistication of commerce, and patterns of land use and landholding."[7] Dialect (as different as different languages) and culture might vary from river valley to river valley. Obviously, the realities of eighteenth-century life varied tremendously across the Chinese landscape.

In the face of such diversity, in the last two decades efforts have been made to analyze Chinese developments in late-traditional times on the basis of regions of economic integration rather than administrative categorization (provinces, prefectures, counties). Nine **macroregions** have been described (see map 1). They bear little relationship to provinces: some include a number of provinces; some provinces are divided into different macroregions. Sometimes macroregions are structured around important river valleys bounded by mountains; transportation and communications networks as well as social and political connections within macroregions are denser than those between macroregions. Macroregions have been divided into *cores*—zones of denser population and urbanization, greater commercial activity, and higher levels of economic development—and *peripheries*—zones of less dense population, urbanization, and commercial activity. Thus, in the generalized prosperity of the Qianlong period, it is likely that macroregional cores experienced greater economic well-being than peripheries.

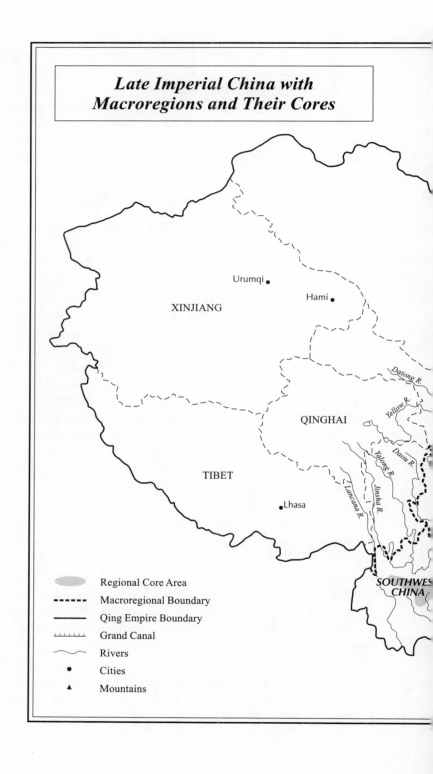

# Late Imperial China with Macroregions and Their Cores

XINJIANG

Urumqi•

Hami•

QINGHAI

TIBET

•Lhasa

Datong R.

Yellow R.

Daou R.

Yalong R.

Jinsha R.

Lancang R.

SOUTHWEST CHINA

Regional Core Area

Macroregional Boundary

Qing Empire Boundary

Grand Canal

Rivers

• Cities

▲ Mountains

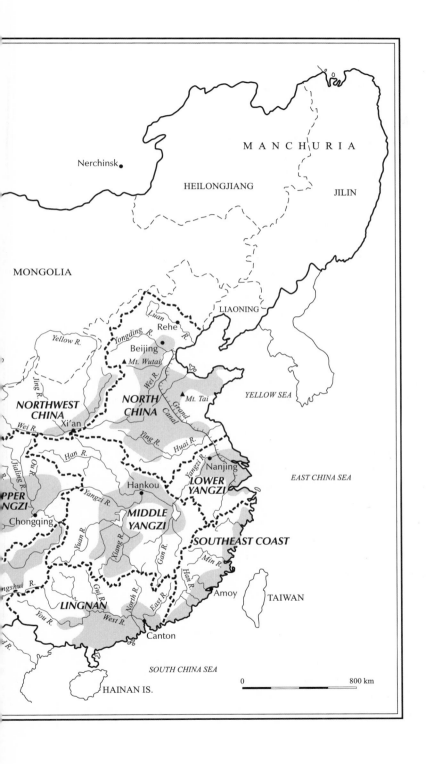

Further, it is important to see that the nine macroregions themselves varied substantially from each other. Zhejiang Province, along the southeast coast, is split into two macroregions, the Lower Yangzi and the Southeast Coast; I will use them as a case in point to underscore the different macroregional environmental, historical, and social realities. The Lower Yangzi's level plains, crisscrossed by numerous canals and waterways, made it one of the "rice baskets" of Chinese agriculture; it was also an important tea and sericulture region. In the eighteenth century, it was China's most economically developed region, with the highest degree of urbanization and the highest density of population. Its importance in interregional trade meant the presence of large numbers of merchant sojourners from around the country. Large numbers of successful candidates in the **civil service examination** came from the Lower Yangzi, and it was a center for art, culture, and learning. In its historical role, it was preeminent in the seventeenth and eighteenth centuries but fell on harder times in the nineteenth.

The Southeast Coast, in contrast, was largely mountainous, divided into four major subregions structured around four river valleys. Seaports at the mouths of the rivers were heavily involved in trade with Taiwan and Southeast Asia. These ports were generally prosperous, but the mountainous interior remained in poverty. The region was known for its social instability, with the presence of feuding lineages (some of whom lived in walled settlements during a general militarization of the region in the eighteenth century), Triad brotherhoods, and maritime pirates. This region had the dubious distinction of introducing opium into China. Historically, it suffered in the early Qing because of its proximity to Taiwan, a Ming dynasty loyalist stronghold; in contrast to the Lower Yangzi, it had a better time in the nineteenth century, facing outward to the sea with great intensity. Thus, each macroregion had its own physical, economic, social, and cultural characteristics. Given such diversity and the country's immense size, it is not surprising that centrifugal forces sometimes spun the empire apart: after its establishment in 221 B.C.E., the empire twice broke up for lengthy periods (220–589; 907–60) during which China was split up into a number of regimes.

## Sources of Chinese Unity

Perhaps, indeed, the generally persisting unity of the Chinese state is the surprising reality. There are several likely explanations. Most basic is the written language. Though there are more than 250 dialects, they are all written using the same characters, which were generally standardized in the Qin dynasty

(221–207 B.C.E.). Thus, a traveler from Hangzhou, the capital of Zhejiang Province, to Wenzhou, in the southern part of the province, may communicate with Wenzhou natives by writing, even though Wenzhou dialect is generally unintelligible to natives of Hangzhou. Such a common written language created substantial cultural unity.

Another source of unity is the thought and ritual of Confucianism that became the orthodox state ideology, primarily through the jewel in the Chinese crown of government: the civil service examination system. The **civil service examination**, evolving over a number of dynasties and ascendant in the dynasties from Song (960–1279) through Qing, provided political, social, ideological, and cultural unity amid the diversity of regional and local cultures. The examination was based largely on Confucianism and commentaries on Confucian texts. Thus, all who studied to take the examination and all those who passed were trained in a common orthodox way of thought and action; this common background did not, of course, mean that there were no disagreements among scholars, but the parameters of political correctness were indeed set and understood.

In addition, the three-tiered examination provided the vehicle for the emergence of the political and social elite that managed the empire through the vast bureaucracy; members of this elite are usually called scholar-gentry, or literati. Only those who attained the highest degrees at the second and third levels of the examination had any chance of becoming an official. Held at the provincial capital (for the second level) and the national capital (for the third level), these essay examinations, which lasted several days, had pass rates that varied, it is estimated, from less than 1 percent to about 3 percent. Obtaining the second-level degree might help one become a magistrate (the key official in county government), a prefect (the next higher level, in a prefecture), or possibly an imperial appointee in an official management position. For those who passed the highest examination, thereby receiving the *jinshi* degree, the greatest career possibilities opened up; they could be governors of provinces, governors-general of several provinces (in the Qing), ministers in the government, or participants in the **Hanlin Academy**, the government policy brain trust. In traditional China, generally only intellectuals became the officials and politicians. A father who passed the examination could not pass his status on to his sons; the degree redounded to the standing of the family, but each individual had to climb the ladder to success alone.

Those who passed the first (i.e., the lowest) level of the examination, generally held at administrative levels above the county but below the province, were rarely entitled to official positions. But attaining the first-level degree brought status in the local community. The degree holder could set up a flag-pole in his compound and fly a flag; parades might be held in his honor; like upper-level literati, he could wear a cap and garb marked by special insignia. He was respected throughout his county as a member of the elite, important in local decision making, during local crises, and potentially as a teacher, mediator, and funder and administrator of public works and charity. Having studied for the exam within the boundaries of Confucian orthodoxy, he at least theoretically brought to his local leadership those values that penetrated communities in every macroregion in the country.

Those values provided a social and political glue that held the civiliza-tion together. They were Confucian values—humanistic, familial, and pre-sentist. Human beings were the measure of things; what mattered most were social connections and relationships. Confucian ethics were particu-laristic; that is, one treated family and those to whom one had connections more favorably and conscientiously than those to whom there were no social connections. The most important of the relationships were familial, and included ancestors. As set forth in the so-called Confucian bonds, the important family relationships were framed in categories of superior and subordinate, with father, husband, and elder brother having responsibilities of leadership over and against son, wife, and younger brother. The latter tri-umvirate must show respect and obedience to the former. The son's special relationship to the father and to ancestors in the patriarchal line was known as filial piety. Marriages were arranged, and they often were painful psy-chological experiences for women. But recent study has shown that in the eighteenth century, in some regions, literate women were able to create spaces for themselves within the patrilineal system through their writing.[8] As in the emphasis on male education for the examination, highly valued literacy and learning under Confucian ideology provided a separate identi-ty for some women.

A fourth Confucian bond was that between ruler and ruled, again with an obvious superior/subordinate dynamic. People must respect the emperor, who was called the Son of Heaven. Although never as explicitly stated as in Japanese political theory concerning the emperor, the family model was never very far beneath the surface of Chinese political reality: the magistrate of the county, the people's closest representative of the emperor, was called the "father-mother official." In return for their respect and even as a prerequisite to ruling, the emperor must rule benevolently for the people. Since the Chinese conceived of the worlds of heaven, earth, and human beings as being intimately interconnected, if the emperor should fail to rule benevolently or be negligent in performing necessary state rituals, natural disasters would occur. If the situation became unbearable enough, people, through whom Heaven made known its will about the fate of its Son, could legitimately rise up against the emperor to overthrow him. Heavy indeed was the responsibility of the emperor.

In the Qing dynasty, the relationship between ruler and ruled was made more difficult because the rulers were Manchus, a confederation of tribes from beyond the Wall, who seized power in 1644. They were the last in a series of outsiders who had taken over part or all of China beginning in the tenth century. For such outsiders, a continual crucial issue was finding an acceptable compromise between adopting sufficient Chinese ways to be accepted by the masses and yet retaining their own identity. Through various policies and political gestures, the Qianlong emperor and his father and grandfather were able gradually to assuage elite fears following their bloody conquest and to gain sufficient acceptance by most scholar-gentry. But throughout the dynasty, as various events would show, the Manchus' outsider identity was never deeply buried within the consciousness of many Chinese elites.

## Thorns Amid the Fruit of Late Eighteenth-Century Prosperity

If, in general, the last half of the eighteenth century, from the point of reference of the state as a whole, was traditional China's most glorious period, there were also numerous thorns amid the fruit of prosperity—or, put more directly, many danger signs that all was not well as China headed, unknowing, into confrontation with the West. The successful military campaigns in central Asia and a series of generally successful police-type actions dealing with problems on the country's periphery had begun to erode the once-abundant treasury. When put to renewed tests in dealing with domestic rebellion in central China, the Chinese military was tentative and ineffective, taking eight long years to put down the **White Lotus Rebellion** (1796–1804). Reportedly the state spent one hundred million taels (or 30 percent more than the government's annual revenue) in dealing with this threat.[9] A weakening economy and military did not bode well.

To make matters worse, in his declining years the Qianlong emperor had entrusted much power to a handsome court favorite, **He Shen**, who was able to parley the emperor's patronage into great personal power. He was able to appoint men to whom he was personally connected to key bureaucratic posts around the empire; he and they engaged in many corrupt activities whereby they took millions of taels of government money for themselves. When He Shen was forced to commit suicide by the Qianlong emperor's son in 1799, he was found to have in his possession the equivalent of two years' revenue of the realm. Corruption had a way of metastasizing like a cancer on the body politic, proliferating far beyond He Shen and his cohorts, ultimately affecting the people themselves as each level of the bureaucracy took more from the levels below. It ultimately not only robbed economic resources but undermined the respect that the populace ideally should have had for those who ruled.

The population surge itself, indicative of the general prosperity, was undoubtedly the greatest long-term danger. Although new land had been brought into cultivation for new crops, the increase in population far outran the possible land increase. Some estimates suggest that from about 1680 to 1780, the population tripled, but land in cultivation only doubled. Even without the Chinese partible-inheritance system, whereby land was divided among all the sons, land per capita was shrinking dangerously; when coupled with the inheritance system, the likelihood of once economically viable farmers falling into bankruptcy and poverty escalated sharply. Even though certain regions of the country were affected more than others by the population increase, since demographic growth occurred at different rates, the larger population put greater strain on a fiscally weakened government to provide those services, especially charitable relief, that were necessary for the government to give evidence of the benevolent rule that holding the Mandate of Heaven implied.

It is likely that the effects of the problems were more serious in the peripheries, which had far fewer human and natural resources, than in the cores. In his study of the eighteenth-century sorcery scare, Philip Kuhn notes that "one did not have to travel far from the commercialized cores to find abject poverty, unemployment, and disorder."[10] These problems led Kuhn to explicitly question the standard positive view of the widespread prosperity of state and society, posing in essence the "glass half full or glass half empty" conundrum. Focusing on the problems of "overpopulation . . . worsening ratio of resources per capita, and . . . declining social mobility," he claims that "China entered her modern age crowded, poor and with little awareness of the real forces that were eroding ordinary people's life chances."[11] Such a view must surely be tempered by our knowledge of the variety, diversity, and complexity of China's macroregions, cores, and peripheries.

## THE FACES OF WESTERN IMPERIALISM

### *Evolution of the Canton System*

The drive of European states to build their empires was fueled by merchants, missionaries, and the military, the first two evidencing historical and cultural developments in the early modern West—that is, the rise of capitalism and the Western drive to compel others to be like itself. In 1600, the British government granted the East India Company a monopoly on trade east of the Cape of Good Hope to the Straits of Magellan; the monopoly, made perpetual in 1609, lasted until 1834. Others had come to China before. In 1517, the Portuguese made a disastrous start when they followed their African practice of seizing adolescents to take as slaves; they were forbidden by the Chinese to return. The Spanish arrived in the 1570s, trading along the southeast coast and building a base in Taiwan. The Dutch arrived in 1604, displacing the Spanish in the 1640s and introducing the mixing of tobacco with opium. The Jesuit missionary Matteo Ricci made it to Beijing in 1601, to be followed by a series of Jesuit priests who conducted a quite successful mission operation until a papal bull ended it in the 1740s over the issue of ancestral rites.

Much of the West's most active early phase came at a chaotic and disorienting time for the Chinese state—the ignominious last days of the Ming and the bloody Manchu conquest. Fear of Ming loyalists, based in Taiwan, led the Qing to close coastal ports in 1662, but when the domestic political threat was put down, four ports were reopened in 1685. Traditional state cultural and economic attitudes had frowned on merchants and trade; in the state's self-conception, China was "everything under Heaven" (*tianxia*), and almost by definition self-sufficient, with no need of goods from outside. China's allowing trade probably stemmed to some degree from the country's traditional paternalistic outlook toward outside "barbarians," but in the main likely from a government desire to profit from the trade even as it scorned it. Much of the trade gravitated to Canton; and in 1759, after Englishman James Flint defied Chinese rules and made it to Tianjin, near Beijing, the court in retaliation decreed that Canton was the only open port. It was there that the court made the trade on the Chinese side a monopoly under the control of a superintendent of maritime customs (the "hoppo") and a group of thirteen **hong merchants** (the Cohong), who served as his agents. The government profit came from the hong merchants, who had to both buy their positions and make extensive annual presents and contributions.[12] Corresponding to the number of hong merchants was the number of Western trading posts, or "factories," located on an island in the Pearl River.

Over the years, a Chinese system of trade and barbarian management evolved at the city. Called by the West the **Canton system**,[13] it was essentially a Chinese attempt to place Western merchants into the traditional Chinese tributary-state framework, where China set various restrictions that the outsiders had to obey. All goods had to be paid for in cash. Foreigners could not enter the Canton city walls, could not ride in sedan chairs, could not learn Chinese, could not bring weapons or women to the factories. They could deal only with hong merchants and could have no direct communications with Chinese officials; any communication with officials had to go through the Cohong, and the paperwork had to display the character for *petition*. Finally, if there were problems, trade was stopped, as in the traditional tributary system, until the outsiders handled any difficulties as the Chinese prescribed. The Westerners were generally willing to play by the Chinese rules and thus were able to continue to buy the silk, teas, and porcelains that European and American consumers desired. Trade continued to expand: by 1833, the tonnage of foreign ships had increased to more than thirteen times what it had been in 1719.[14] The increase did not, however, enable Westerners to change the terms of trade: in 1793, Lord Macartney made an unsuccessful effort to extend and expand the trading relationship; his effort was treated by the Qianlong emperor as a tributary mission.[15] Another mission in 1816 was not even received.

## *The Opium Problem*

From the perspective of Western merchants, the serious trade problem was that they had nothing that the Chinese wanted to buy; British woolens hardly appealed to Chinese in tropical Canton and its environs. The consequence was a severe trade imbalance: European ships arrived in Canton with 90 percent of their stocks composed of bullion. The problem was lessened somewhat by the **country trade**, carried on British ships between India and China; through the country trade, the Chinese could buy camphor, tin, cotton piece goods, birds' nests, and spices. But it was not until Western merchants discovered the Chinese yen for opium that their trade problem was solved.

The widespread allure of the drug that Jean Cocteau described as "the only vegetable substance that communicates the vegetable state to us" is somewhat mysterious.[16] Its consumption across the social spectrum, from rich to poor, from officials to merchants, from soldiers to coolies, meant that there were many different motivations for its use. Smuggled into the country (because there were frequent imperial edicts against the drug), the numbers of chests imported grew dramatically, from four thousand to five thousand chests around 1820 to eighteen thousand in 1828, and to forty thousand in 1839.[17] Estimates of numbers of smokers vary widely; about 10 percent of the population was a commonly accepted figure. Addicts may have comprised 3 to 5 percent of the population.[18] There were many sides to the developing tragedy; the most ironic was that the economic well-being of large numbers of people, both Chinese and British, came to be dependent on the drug. As the numbers of chests increased, so did the numbers of foreigners and Chinese with vested interests in the trade. Other countries joined in; while the British brought in Indian opium, U.S. firms, for example, imported Turkish opium.

Now silver bullion left Chinese coffers to pay for opium. This development destabilized the Chinese economy, based as it was on a bimetallic (silver and copper) system. As silver left the country, it became more expensive in terms of copper. Although daily purchases were made in copper and may have remained initially unaffected, those coins had be changed into silver for the payment of taxes. Thus, taxes in the form of necessary coppers were driven up by the outflow of silver. This growing economic pressure was exacerbated by years of bad harvests in the first half of the 1830s, a situation creating food shortages and rising prices.[19] A crisis of international relations and the demoralization of a portion of the Chinese populace thus created and exacerbated economic troubles.

After much uncertainly and debate over policy (including the possible legalization of the drug), in early 1839 the emperor appointed **Lin Zexu**, an experienced official with the highest credentials and a reputation for incorruptibility, as imperial commissioner to suppress the opium traffic (see document 1, appendix 2). Lin dealt harshly with Chinese dealers and smokers, arresting many and confiscating their opium and pipes. He ordered the British to turn over their opium stocks; they first ignored the order, then refused. Following the logic of the tributary system. Lin halted all trade and instituted a siege of the factories and their 350 foreigners. For six weeks, until mid-May, the foreigners held out, considering the action a "piratical act against British lives, liberty, and property."[20] When the British finally delivered their stock to Lin, he mixed it with salt and lime and flushed it out to sea, having won what seemed a moral victory over the foreigners.

But it was Pyrrhic: the siege was treated by the British as a national affront and a cause for war. Tensions were ratcheted up in the summer when drunken British sailors beat a villager to death in Kowloon and the British refused to turn over the guilty men for Chinese justice. The dynamics involved in this episode—the conflict over law and its administration—would become issues in treaties that followed the war. The war itself was an on-again, off-again struggle against a backdrop of almost continual negotiations between the two sides. For the Chinese, fighting the most powerful nation in the world, it was military disaster.[21] The Central Country surrendered to the English barbarians, the terms spelled out in the **Treaty of Nanjing** in August 1842.

The **Opium War** opened a century of aggression by Western nations against China, a century of clashes between very different cultures with different worldviews. Some conflicts may have been inevitable, but it was particularly tragic that the war centered on questions of interstate morality— specifically, England's insistence on its "right" to smuggle opium into China with no heed in the least about what it was doing to China or many of its people. One of the consequences of the war was that foreign nations could legally import opium into the country. Thus, whereas the number of chests smuggled into China in 1839 was about forty thousand, by 1884, the number had reached eighty-one thousand.[22] Another consequence for some Chinese was the linking of immorality with the foreigners.

## The Unequal Treaty System

The freedom to import opium into China was only one of the gains that foreign nations made as a result of the war. The Treaty of Nanjing was the first of many treaties between China and foreign nations. Between it and the **Treaty of Tianjin** in 1858, following another war waged by England and France, a series of treaties, called unequal because China did all the giving and received nothing in return, began to chip away at China's sovereignty. In the beginning, China rationalized that its "generosity" followed the precedent of its tributary generosity. It was only over time that the insidious nature of the treaties began to be felt.

The treaties opened up more ports for trade. The Treaty of Nanjing, for example, opened up four new ports (Xiamen, Fuzhou, Ningbo, and Shanghai) to join Canton as sites for foreign settlements and continuous trade. Other treaties opened more places, first along the coast, then in inland rivers, especially the Yangzi (see map 2). Foreign settlements were areas carved out of the existing Chinese city, where foreigners now called the political and economic shots. They decided on taxes and collected them; they policed the area; their troops could patrol there; their law held sway there— all in areas where many Chinese still lived. Thus, Chinese residents in the foreign settlements were uprooted from their native state without moving an inch, and Chinese sovereignty over these former citizens was erased.

# Nineteenth-Century Foreign Encroachments

### The Treaty Ports

⊙ *Canton* — The original 5 ports opened in 1842–1844
● *Tianjin* — The 9 additional ports opened in the 1860s
○ Aigun — Ports opened by 1911 (the names of some are omitted on this map)

## ■ Foreign Leased Areas, 1898

Port Arthur and Liaotung Peninsula (Kwantung)(Russian)
Weihaiwei (British)
Jiaozhou (German)
Kowloon New Territories (British)
Guangzhouwan (French)

## Tributary States Lost 1870s–1890s

RUSSIAN
EMPIRE

Aigun

*Russian Sphere of Influence*
Manzhouli

MANCHURIA

*Japanese Sphere of Influence*
Harbin  Suifen
Changchun  Hanjun

Mukden
Nuchuang
Beijing  Andong
Tianjin  Port Arthur  Dairen
Yantai  KOREA  JAPAN
Weihaiwei

Qingdao  Jiaozhou
*German Sphere of Influence*

Old mouth of Yellow R.

Jinjiang
Nanjing  Wusong
*British Sphere of Influence*  *Shanghai*
Hankou  *Ningbo*
Chongqing  Yichang
Jiujiang
Yuezhou
Changsha  Wenzhou

*Fuzhou*
Dengyue
*French Sphere of Influence*  Danshui
RYUKYU IS.
Simao  Mengzi  *Amoy* Taiwanfu
*(Xiamen)*
BURMA  Nanning  *Canton*  Swatow
Kowloon  (Shantou)
Beihai  HONG KONG (Br.)
FRENCH  MACAO (Port.)
INDOCHINA  Guangzhouwan

HAINAN

SIAM
PHILIPPINES

Another treaty "right" established by the West was that of **extraterritoriality**—a system of consular jurisdictions wherein a foreigner accused of a crime would be tried not in a Chinese court but in one in which his national consul presided. The Western rationale was that Chinese law was uncivilized. This Western attitude stretched back at least to 1784, when a round from a salute fired by a British gunner from the *Lady Hughes*, a country-trading ship, killed two Chinese. When the gunner was turned over to the Chinese after a tense and lengthy standoff, he was strangled, in accordance with China's eye-for-an eye homicide law. His death underscored in foreign minds the barbarism of the Chinese legal system; it was the reason for the British refusal to turn over the sailors who had killed the villager at the Opium War's beginning in 1839. The Western position was that extraterritoriality was necessary until the Chinese amended their legal system.

Initially, there was no great Chinese reaction to the loss of control over foreign citizens. For one thing, the Chinese did not have to burden themselves with learning the languages of these barbarians. China could also find a precedent for such an arrangement: Arab traders in Canton during the Tang dynasty had held extraterritoriality. But the rub came when Chinese citizens also gained the right. This happened when Western business firms and Western missionaries offered such protection to their protégés, respectively Chinese middlemen or compradors and Chinese converts, individuals whose lives were deemed crucial by some Westerners. Essentially, there came to be a category of Chinese who were more privileged than others, a galling situation for the Chinese. When, as happened more than once, missionaries were able to have their consuls dispatch gunboats to force the issue of extraterritoriality for their protégés, this treaty "right" became not simply a legal dispute but a matter of brute force.

According to the treaties, China also lost its sovereign right to control and collect its own tariffs. These were set at about 5 percent ad valorem, again not notably out of line with traditional tariff rates. But the times were not traditional. One of the legacies of the Opium War was China's coming face to face with modern technology in the form of ships and weapons. The early Chinese effort to establish their own modern technology and industry was hampered by the low and unalterable tariff, which meant that China could not protect its nascent industry nor keep out unwanted items like opium. In addition, in the 1850s, in the midst of the turmoil of the **Taiping Rebellion** in the vicinity of Shanghai, the British began collecting customs duties to ensure their collection. This practice became institutionalized in the **Imperial Maritime Customs Service**. Despite the effectiveness and dedicated commitment of long-time director **Robert Hart**, who essentially saw himself as part of the Chinese bureaucracy, the collection of customs for one country by another bespeaks a humiliating loss of sovereignty. Yet another loss of sovereignty, according to the treaties, was that China could not make any inland waterway off-limits to foreign ships.

An important aspect of the tributary system had been to set ports of entry far away from the capital so as to keep foreigners at bay. Visitors would be escorted to the capital and, following the prescribed rituals, would be allowed to remain in Beijing for only a specified period. There was no ongoing presence of foreigners in the capital or the rest of China. Now, according to the Treaty of Tianjin, ambassadors of foreign states would reside permanently in Beijing. With this stipulation and with its underpinning in the Western state model of equality among nations, the traditional tributary system was, for all practical purposes, dead. This treaty also allowed anyone with a passport to travel anywhere in the country, and passports were not even required for travel up to thirty miles from treaty ports. The treaty called for the opening of ten new treaty ports. Although China never became a "colony," its loss of sovereignty and control over its own territory and people transformed it into what has been called a semicolony, subject to the demands and pressures of many foreign nations.

One other crucial "right" gained by Western nations in the Treaty of Tianjin was that the open propagation of Christianity was guaranteed. Coupled with the treaty's open-travel stipulations, this meant the missionaries could go anywhere, could purchase property for church and school, and could proselytize at will. The story of the impact of nineteenth-century missionaries is complex: each missionary naturally had his or her own motives and outlook. Missionaries came from a variety of countries, each one with its own approaches to China and attitudes toward the mission enterprise. On the whole, the story is not a happy one. The political and social landscape of the last fifty years of the dynasty is studded with episode upon episode of unrest and violence sparked by the actions of missionaries in communities across China. In essence, at the core of the difficulties were mirror images: the cultural imperialism of the missionaries and the cultural chauvinism of the Chinese. The missionaries were convinced of their own superiority; educated Chinese saw all non-Chinese and their ideas as barbarian. The missionaries saw their teachings as Truth and the Chinese as benightedly superstitious; the Chinese saw themselves as grounded in realistic pragmatism and Christian teachings of a virgin birth or a father allowing his son to be crucified as scandalous and worse than superstitious. The missionaries saw the Chinese as greedy and materialistic; the Chinese saw missionaries maneuvering to purchase the best sites for their churches and pronounced them materialistic and greedy.

The missionary could rely on the support of his national consul, who had the treaties behind him. In extreme situations, gunboats could be called for a show of force or firepower if a missionary was being thwarted by local officials from gaining what he wanted. Chinese elites did not possess such instruments of force; but they did wield the writing brush, and they often felt directly threatened by the missionary's work. In many cases products of the civil service examination, they were the locality's teachers, mediators, authorities, and charity providers. Missionaries performed the same functions for their congregations, thereby separating out some Chinese from others, just as the treaties had done with foreign settlements and extraterritoriality. Their roles directly threatened, the literati wrote propaganda tracts about missionaries and their work with the intent to tar them with a broad brush of sexual immorality, a tactic that was standard in the Chinese inventory of political attack. These tracts, which were widely circulated among both elites and nonelites, painted pictures of despicable depravity and perversity. Certainly they helped fuel the violence that frequently flared up against missionaries and their converts.

The June 1870 clashes in Tianjin pointed to the cultural gulf and the fragility of relations that existed between foreign missionaries and Chinese; the incident often stands as a symbol of the deeply troubled relations between these two sides. French Catholic nuns operated an orphanage in the same compound as a large new church; they especially wanted to be able to baptize sick children who might be near death. The orphanage thus saw a higher mortality rate than normal. Rumors spread that orphans were being killed, with their body parts being used for aphrodisiacs before sex play between priests and nuns. The fact that the nuns had been giving a small amount of money to people who turned in orphans to the orphanage helped fuel the rumor that scoundrels were kidnapping children to make some cash. As rumors swirled, Chinese demanded a search of the orphanage and agitation in the city grew. The search of the premises by a high local official and his announcement that all seemed to be in order did nothing to quiet the increasing disturbance.

In the midst of the crisis, the French consul, carrying two pistols, accompanied by his chancellor with drawn sword, charged into the office of the county magistrate, demanding that the official break up the growing crowd of angry Chinese. Losing control, he shot at the magistrate, missed him, but hit and killed his servant. Transformed into an angry mob, the Chinese then killed the consul and his officer and seventeen others, including twelve priests and nuns. The church, along with four U.S. and British churches, was burned. French demands followed. The settlement included a large sum for reparations, the execution of eighteen mob leaders, hard labor for twenty-five others, the exile of the prefect and magistrate of Tianjin, and the sending of a mission of apology.[23]

If the various faces of imperialism in its onslaught of the three Ms—the merchants, the military, and the missionaries—differed as to motive, approach, and national and individual purpose, they shared a common feature: they all saw what they had to offer the Chinese as infinitely better than what the Chinese already had. The merchants, acting for the increasingly capitalist countries of the West, could pull China out of what the Western countries considered its self-sufficient dream world into the world system of international trade. The military, with its power, could blast what Western countries considered the Neanderthalic and outmoded regime and culture and thus make possible the expansion of a more "enlightened" Westernism. The missionaries were assured that they had the Truth to save Chinese from eternal damnation. But Westerners were dealing with a culture with a long history and vaunted traditions, with an educated elite that was absolutely convinced of the superiority of its culture. In terms of commitment to their respective civilizational goals, China and the West were seemingly two immovable forces. What made the difference in this gargantuan confrontation was the West's military power, which arrived in force at a time when China's military fortunes were sinking to a low ebb. But . . . *what if?* (the historical game of *What if?* is frequently instructive). *What if* the West's military had come during the military heyday of the Qianlong emperor? Obviously, we cannot know, but it is safe to say that the course of world history would have certainly been different, and it is likely that the story of modern China would not have been so tragic.

## DOMESTIC REBELLION AND THE DEVOLUTION OF POWER TO THE LOCALITIES

If the nineteenth century was born amid expanding opium smuggling and an emerging foreign threat, it was also born in domestic rebellion. Millenarian Buddhism gave rise to the White Lotus Rebellion, a movement that straddled the turn of the century (1796–1804), and to the 1813 rebellion of Lin Qing, which reached the Forbidden City in its aim to assassinate the **Jiaqing emperor**. Though there was, as Jonathan Spence suggests, "simmering discontent" in both northern and southern society—often expressed in the north through religion-based organizations and in the south through blood brotherhoods like the Triads—there was no direct line to the major conflagrations of midcentury rebellion that threatened to destroy Chinese culture.[24] Though general contexts—perhaps an agrarian crisis as in the early 1830s, or the loss of a war—may have favored certain social or economic or political developments, we must understand the particular contexts of rebellions or other social movements to appreciate its dynamics and import.

## The Taiping Rebellion (1851–64)

The Taiping Rebellion, the largest, most destructive such explosion in world history, devastated much of east central and southern China and reached militarily into sixteen of the eighteen provinces within the Great Wall. A half century after the end of the bloodshed that killed an estimated twenty million people, once-prosperous commercial districts of Lower Yangzi regional cities were still in ruins. The rebellion was the brainchild of **Hong Xiuquan**, an erstwhile but failed degree candidate, whose sickbed visions left him with the conviction that he was the younger brother of Jesus Christ and that he had a mission to accomplish. The historical and spatial contexts provided him with the people and the support that made his movement a threat not only to the ruling Manchus but to traditional Chinese civilization as well.

The Taiping Rebellion was born in the Canton area in the years following the Opium War (1839–42). Destabilized before the war because of the opium smuggling and currency fluctuations, this area had then seen the pitiful performance of the Chinese military when it was beaten handily by the British. Doubtless, in some elite quarters in a region that perhaps had never fully reconciled itself to barbarian Manchu rule, there was talk or at least thought about the Mandate beginning to slip from the dynasty's grasp. Certainly, as Jonathan Spence notes, China's defeat began "to divide the Chinese against themselves. For as a result of the fighting the belief [was] growing that the country [was] full of traitors. . . . New kinds of angers flare[d] as the blame for humiliation and defeat [was] parceled out among the vanquished."[25] Manchus, their military, and their bureaucrats could become obvious targets.

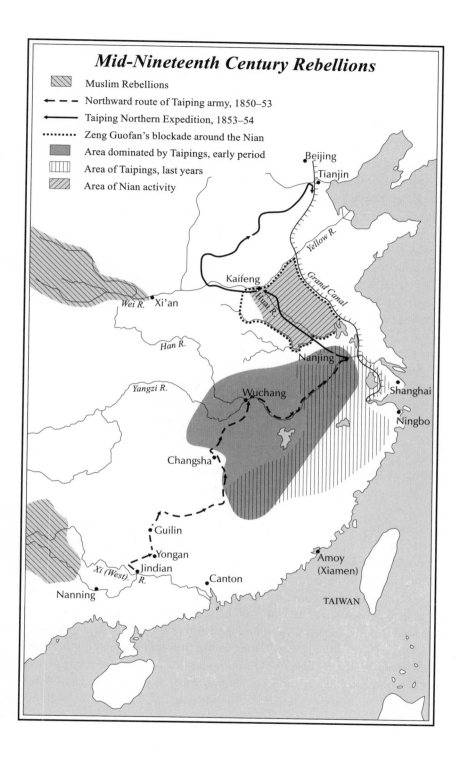

# Mid-Nineteenth Century Rebellions

Muslim Rebellions

←--- Northward route of Taiping army, 1850–53

←--- Taiping Northern Expedition, 1853–54

·········· Zeng Guofan's blockade around the Nian

Area dominated by Taipings, early period

Area of Taipings, last years

Area of Nian activity

Beijing

Tianjin

Yellow R.

Grand Canal

Kaifeng

Wei R.    Xi'an

Huai R.

Han R.

Nanjing

Yangzi R.

Wuchang

Shanghai

Ningbo

Changsha

Guilin

Yongan

Amoy
(Xiamen)

Xi (West).    Jindian

R.    Canton

Nanning

TAIWAN

The peace itself contributed to the destabilization of the region. In the seventy years when Canton was the only open port and silk and tea were the prime objectives of Western merchants, overland and riverine trade routes had developed from the main silk- and tea-producing regions in Zhejiang, Jiangsu, and Fujian Provinces to Canton. Involved along these routes were shippers, brokers, and toughs who protected the expensive commodities and drew their livelihood from the trade. With the opening of the treaty ports of Ningbo and Shanghai in the Treaty of Nanjing, these trade routes dried up, no longer needed, since the silk and tea could much more easily be taken to the closer new ports. Men who had by the nature of their occupations been able to deal with dangerous situations and handle themselves amid potential violence and criminal behavior were now unemployed. Their frustration and need for new sources of revenue for daily living created new, potentially destabilizing forces. To make matters worse, with the new ports opened along the southeast coast, the British began a policy of suppressing pirates, endemic to the region. Reportedly, the pirate suppression campaign was generally successful, forcing these men and women into the interior, where, as land-based bandits, they now preyed on inland Chinese.

In addition to these new forces, old ethnic rivalries tore at the region's social amity. There were Hakkas, "guest people," immigrants from north China centuries earlier, who had remained separate from the locals, speaking their own dialect. They were known to be industrious; both male and female Hakkas worked the fields—often the poorer land since the area had been settled when they moved in. Hakka women did not have bound feet as any "respectable," sophisticated Han Chinese woman would have. Yet even Hakkas fit in more easily with the Han Chinese than the Miao, another ethnic group.

Hong Xiuquan was a Hakka. A precocious child, he had been primed to take the civil service exam. But repeated efforts to pass the examination brought only failure. After one such experience, he returned home, fell deathly ill, and had a vision. Only after his recovery and his looking over a book of Christian sermons and tracts, which had been thrust into his hands when he was in Canton to take the exam, did he realize the meaning of his vision. A venerable old man was God; standing nearby was someone Hong surmised was Jesus; and God addressed Hong as the heavenly younger brother. God told Hong to slay the demons. Given the historical context of the region (as not especially strong supporters of the Manchus) as well as the recent disturbances and upheavals of war, it is not surprising that Hong soon began to see that the demons were Manchus and that ultimately a crusade of sorts would have to be launched against them.

The next few years were remarkable for the speed with which Hong's message spread and with which a movement grew—from the early conversions of friends and relatives to the participation of tens of thousands of down-and-outers and even some social elites. The movement became known initially as the God-Worshippers. The message was millenarian: realizing the Heavenly Kingdom on earth now. Incipient dynastic pretensions came fully grown in January 1851 with Hong's declaration of the Heavenly Kingdom of Great Peace (*Taiping tianguo*). In little more than two years, Hong's forces took the city of Nanjing, following an amazing series of military victories in their march north. Historians speculate whether the Taiping could have swept the Qing away if they had kept their remarkable military momentum; but they did not know where to proceed, so Nanjing remained their capital as they made forays out in all directions. In the end, in 1864, Nanjing became their tomb. During their eleven-year stint in the city, they tried to implement their vision of politics and society, even as they wreaked havoc and destruction on the Lower Yangzi region.

Taiping ideology was a mixture of traditional Chinese ideals, Christian (especially Old Testament) doctrine, and Buddhist practice—all filtered through Hong's derangement. The blueprint for the new society came from the ancient idealistic vision of the *Rituals of Zhou*. It established a primitive communist society in which groups of twenty-five families shared a common treasury and daily life under a "sergeant," who performed religious, judicial, educational, and administrative functions (see document 2, appendix 2). It is perhaps not surprising, given its communelike structure and primitive form of economic communism, that twentieth-century Communists have seen the Taiping in a positive light.

The eventual collapse came for a host of reasons. This was a fanatical, totalitarian religious movement that promised utopia but delivered nothing except enforced sexual abstinence: until the complete realization of the kingdom of heaven on earth, all sexual relations, including those between married couples, were forbidden. Once the promises were not forthcoming, support among the masses declined. The movement was directed from the center by five "kings," each jealous of his own position and some of whom claimed to speak for persons in the godhead. When jealousy escalated to episodes of violence and outright butchery, the center collapsed and the movement began to disintegrate. Other contributing causes were faulty military strategy, inability to link up with other rebellions or secret societies, lack of foresight in trying more directly to curry favor with Western missionaries and merchants, and in the end, a successful mobilization of anti-Taiping sentiment by the Qing government among the Chinese literati, who saw Hong's movement as a threat to traditional culture. At the behest of the Qing, key Chinese officials formed regional armies (see below) that took on the role that the Manchu **banner** forces (the imperial army) and the **Green Standard** (the constabulary forces) could no longer fulfill, leading those new armies to victory over the Taiping.

The destruction wrought by the rebellion is almost unfathomable. Population estimates for the Lower Yangzi macroregion alone suggest that the population in 1843 had reached sixty-seven million, but that fifty years later in 1893 it had fallen to forty-five million.[26] And the rebellion destroyed more than people's lives, having "even altered the face of the country; destroyed its communications; deflected its rivers; broken down its sea defenses . . . smiling fields were turned into desolate wildernesses; 'fenced cities into ruinous heaps.' The plains . . . were strewn with human skeletons; their rivers polluted with floating carcasses; wild beasts descending from their fastnesses in the mountains roamed at large over the land, and made their dens in the ruins of deserted towns."[27]

### The Nian Rebellion (1853–68)

The **Nian Rebellion**, which developed in the bleakly poor Huaibei region of north central China, was the only one of the four major midcentury rebellions that did not have a religious dynamic. Following the collapse of key Yellow River dikes, it developed from being "a local struggle for scarce resources" into a major peasant movement.[28] Although the etymology of the word *nian* remains somewhat unclear, the term came to be applied to groups of bandits with a blatantly Robin Hood approach. Existing as bands from the early nineteenth century on, the rebels developed into a large-scale movement only in 1853. Structured in the beginning mostly around families and lineages, the bands conducted mobile guerrilla strikes, plundering for their livelihood and in the process depriving government troops and others of food supplies and other necessities. Coupled with predation was the protection and fortification of their home communities. In 1856, an alliance among various bands produced a banner system that brought greater coherence to the movement, though some Nian bands in Henan Province did not join the federation. Most of the rebellion's plundering occurred in Shandong, Henan, and northern Jiangsu. In the end, the Qing, again in armies led by Chinese scholar-officials (**Zeng Guofan** and **Li Hongzhang**), defeated the Nian rebels by turning the tables and adopting the strategy that the Nian had used so successfully— scorched-earth tactics and fortified settlements. The scorched-earth approach denied the rebels their resources, and by building fortifications, troops made settlements "safe" by registering inhabitants and then protecting them from rebel seizure.

## The Muslim Rebellions

Two bloody rebellions waged by Muslims ravaged southwest and northwest China concurrently with the Taiping and the Nian. The southwest rebellion in Yunnan Province grew from a mix of ethnic, religious, and economic rivalry. Long-term friction between Muslims and non-Muslim communities was exacerbated by competition over control of mineral resources. Beginning in 1855, the rebellion was led by a devout Muslim, based in eastern Yunnan, who believed that Islam was incompatible with Confucianism; he was, however, induced to agree to terms and peace in 1861. The rebellion continued in the western part of the province until 1873. Led by another religious figure, in the west it was marked by siege warfare, waged around the more than fifty walled cities he controlled. Most of the seizures of the cities resulted in massacres by Qing troops.

In the northwest, the rebellion began in 1862 in Shaanxi Province and spread westward to Gansu. The arena of this rebellion, also led by a religious partisan, was of greater strategic value than that of Yunnan, located as it was between Mongolia and Tibet and reaching to the Russian border. The campaigns of both the rebels and Qing troops were marked by widespread slaughter of the denizens of walled cities. Eventually, another Chinese scholar-official, **Zuo Zongtang**, led the suppression of the rebellion, advancing slowly in a bloody, five-year campaign.

With the exception of the southwest Muslim rebellion, the midcentury rebellions were suppressed not by Qing generals but by scholar-officials, civilians who had upper degrees in the civil service system. They were military generalists, not professionals, who applied Confucian moral and political principles, insisted on serious training for and discipline among their troops, and used some Western technology, particularly modern guns and ships. They faced toward both the Chinese past, trying to save their culture from the Taiping version of Christianity, the Nian plunderers, and the Muslim crusaders, and the Chinese future, gingerly taking the first steps toward what became known as "**self-strengthening.**" In one sense it was a case of ethnic Chinese saving Manchu overlords; but more accurately it was an effort of scholar-administrators imbued with Chinese culture aiding rulers also committed to that culture. All in all, the rebellions created vast devastations in six of the nine macroregions, killed tens of millions of people, and destroyed hundreds of towns and cities.

## The Devolution of Power

A continuing tension in Chinese political life, a legacy from the Zhou dynasty (1122–256 B.C.E.) and the Qin dynasty (221–207 B.C.E.), existed over how much power was to be wielded by the center and how much by the localities. Zhou feudalism had by definition functioned as a decentralized system, with considerable power going to vassals in localities. The authoritarian Qin regime had in contrast instituted a strongly centralized government. In subsequent times, despite the fact that the state remained centralized, the issue of the best mix of the alternatives continued, in part because of Confucian antipathy to the legalist Qin and its centralization and in part because of the Confucian idealization of Zhou feudalism. In the midst of the mid-nineteenth-century domestic upheaval, foreign threat, and a weakened central regime, the question of the role of localities and their leaders emerged as significant. It came to the fore primarily as the result of Qing policies and of local elites acting when the center could not or did not. A first point in looking at the devolution of power is the relativity of the meaning of *local* in the Chinese context: local could be any arena from the province down to the prefecture or county or township.

Policy decisions by the Qing government regarding the quelling of the Taiping Rebellion contributed directly to the question of the center and its power. In 1852, the **Xianfeng emperor** named some militia commissioners whose job was to bring together gentry-led local militias into federations that could protect local society from the rebels. The above-mentioned Zeng Guofan, an important official, took the appointment and, with Qing permission, ran with it straight to the formation of his own provincial (Hunan) force, recruited from networks of gentry connections. Throughout the chain of command, Zeng's army was built on Confucian principles—"duty to one's neighbors, piety to one's family, and personal loyalty to one's commander."[29] It was largely funded by a new tax, the **lijin**, collected on shipped commercial goods at customs barriers along key routes. Zeng's protégé Li Hongzhang set up a counterpart provincial army in Anhui Province. Thus, in turning the handling of the crisis over to provincial forces, the Qing was in essence subverting central power through the devolution of military force to the provinces. The degree of localism in these armies is underscored by the fact that initially the lijin was collected by local commanders for their own troops; eventually Zeng's and Li's headquarters centralized the collection under their control.

The government's appointment of militia commissioners points to the existing initiative of local leaders in organizing community militia for local defense. As Frederic Wakeman has noted, such organizing and leadership allowed local elites to wield new fiscal powers (to fund the units) and judicial powers (to deal with captured prisoners).[30] When the rebellions ended and the tasks of reconstruction weighed heavily upon an impotent center, local elites emerged as key managers for reconstruction and reform in their communities. The composition of these managerial elites varied according to location. In core areas, they were more diverse; they were composed of both degree holders (upper and lower) and people without degrees. In these areas, merchants played a key role. In less developed areas, at least in the Lower Yangzi region, the managerial elites tended to be upper-degree holders. Their arenas of action included welfare and relief, charity, education, public works, and in some cases conservancy work.[31]

The role of local elites in governing functions had been a subject of discussion among Chinese political philosophers of the so-called statecraft school since the early nineteenth century. The dominant philosophical focus of the eighteenth century had been evidential research, "a mode of empirical scholarship that sanctioned new, precise methods by which to understand the past and conceptualize the present."[32] In actuality, this school of evidential research had developed into one that emphasized philology and linguistic issues. The crises of the nineteenth century brought a reaction against what was perceived as such a narrow focus and a call for applying scholarship to deal with the current pressing problems. Recalling the late-Ming, early-Qing statecraft writer Gu Yanwu, scholars argued that learning must have some practical use for society. Gu had advocated using local elites as hereditary local officials; in the 1850s, **Feng Guifen**, a Hanlin Academy scholar and local administrator, began to call for local elites to play a greater role in local governance. The stumbling block to such a development had been the law of avoidance, which theoretically applied only to the county magistrate, forbidding him to serve in his native county for fear of ready-built connections that might bring into question the fairness of county government. Feng asserted that local gentry should not be bound by the law of avoidance. He argued that local elites would have a greater interest in solving the problems of their native areas, that, on the whole, local governance would benefit, and that the administration of the country would be improved. The readiness of many elites to step into managerial positions during the rebellions as militia leaders and afterward in a whole array of public arenas suggests that Feng's prescription was not misplaced. Feng's ideas would continue to be significant as China moved into the twentieth century.

## MILITARY DEFEATS AND THE LOSS OF TRIBUTARY STATES

### Self-Strengthening

Feng Guifen was also one of the strongest proponents of and perhaps the first to use the term *self-strengthening*: that is, strengthening China with a view to fending off Western imperialists.[33] While it involved a multipronged effort in the spheres of diplomacy, education, technology, and the military, advances in military technology were usually taken as a yardstick of successful self-strengthening since they were most clearly related to defense.

Though self-strengthening did not call for institutional change, emphasizing instead already existing institutions and policies, an important institution was established in 1861. Ostensibly formed to deal with foreign policy, the **Zongli Yamen** (Office for General Management) oversaw many of the self-strengthening efforts; foreign policy crises were, like the 1830s opium crisis, usually placed into the hands of ad hoc commissioners.

In the sphere of diplomacy, the Zongli Yamen sponsored the establishment of a school to train diplomats to handle the world "after the tributary system": the Tongwenguan (Interpreters College) became in 1869 a school with an eight-year course of study. Headed by American missionary W. A. P. Martin, the school offered a curriculum of languages and science. Most of China's diplomats were trained there. Martin also cotranslated a major work on international law by which diplomats and the Zongli Yamen could begin to become acquainted with Western concepts and practices of international relations.

The major diplomatic step managed by the Zongli Yamen was the sending of diplomats abroad — not a small accomplishment given the shame, even contamination, that many Chinese associated with dealing with Western "barbarians." Zongli Yamen members were frequently referred to as "devil's slaves"; and when the first ambassador to England, **Guo Songtao**, returned to China after filing dispatches praising British technological and industrial advances, he was reprimanded and publicly humiliated. In the same vein, Mongol Woren, who wept when appointed to the Zongli Yamen, argued, "Why must we learn from the barbarian foreigners? . . . They are our enemies."[34] China's first ambassador abroad was an American, Anson Burlingame, sent around the world in 1868 with Chinese and Manchu co-envoys going along as observers. Guo was the first native Chinese to serve as full ambassador, taking his post in 1877, fully sixteen years after Western ambassadors had begun to live in Beijing, a time gap that underscores the difficulty of the undertaking.

In his arguments about self-strengthening, Feng Guifen asserted that "what we then have to learn from the barbarians is only the one thing, solid ships and effective guns."[35] The first steps toward attaining Western military technology came about through the Zongli Yamen with the establishment of arsenals, shipyards, and machine shops. Key here again were the scholar-administrator heroes of rebellion suppression. In 1865, Zeng and Li established at Shanghai the **Jiangnan Arsenal**, which produced ships, ammunition, tools, and machinery; also, Western scientific and technological works were translated. The following year, Zuo built the **Fuzhou Shipyard**, at which 2,000 Chinese workmen and an administrative staff of 150 labored to produce larger ships than the Jiangnan Arsenal. Attached to the shipyard was a naval academy for cadet training. The educational aspect of many of these undertakings is noteworthy.

## The Loss of the Ryukyu (Liuqiu) Islands

In the twenty-one years from 1874 to 1895, China lost its three most important tributary states, the Ryukyu Islands (Liuqiu, in Chinese), Vietnam, and Korea (see map 2). Aggressive actions by Japan in the islands and Korea and by France in Vietnam pointed to a new wave of imperialism in the closing quarter of the century. The first two cases resulted from China's naïveté and inexperience in managing foreign relations in the system of Western international law.

China saw the Ryukyus as an important tributary state; the islands had regularly sent tribute missions to China since 1372. China did not know that in 1609 the feudal lord of the Japanese domain of Satsuma, on the southeast coast of Kyushu, had conquered the islands and ruled the northern part of the islands outright, with the rest under the titular control of the Ryukyuan king. From that time the islands paid tribute to Satsuma, and even to the shogun in Edo. Since Satsuma wanted to participate in trade with China, it ordered the

Ryukyus to continue the tribute system with China as well. China remained completely unaware of the dual status of the islands.

Late in 1871, more than fifty shipwrecked sailors from the Ryukyu Islands were killed by aborigines on the east coast of Taiwan. Two years later, the Japanese asserted that they had the sole right to speak for the islands, and in 1874 they undertook a naval expedition to Taiwan to punish the aborigines. When China responded in amazement, claiming that both Taiwan and the Ryukyus were Chinese, the Japanese argued that the aborigines' action was evidence that the Chinese did not in fact exercise sovereignty over the island. Thus Japan claimed it had to act. When head-to-head diplomacy failed to solve the dispute, the British minister mediated. In the end, China paid 500,000 taels for the victims of the killings and for some Japanese barracks erected in Taiwan, promising as well not to condemn the Japanese expedition. Both actions pointed to diplomatic obtuseness: acquiescence in the expedition was in reality a recognition of Japan's position (and control) over the Ryukyus, and the payment to Japan amounted to a "willingness to pay for being invaded."[36]

## The Loss of Vietnam

Vietnam, the northern part of which China had controlled outright from the Han through the Tang dynasties (roughly 100 B.C.E. to 900), was a close tributary in the Ming (1368–1644) and Qing (1644–1912) dynasties. Though it rejected Chinese political control, it lay tightly in the Chinese cultural orbit, borrowing central political and cultural institutions and approaches. From the Chinese perspective, the tributary relationship—which included Chinese investiture of Vietnamese sovereigns as well as sending troops at the behest of its tributary "younger brother" when there was civil disorder in Vietnam—was a crucial reality. There were, in addition, statements in the 1880s that indicated China was also aware of the strategic importance of the country: "The border provinces are China's gates; the tributary states are China's walls. We build the walls to protect the gates, and protect the gates to secure the house. If the walls fall, the gates are endangered; if the gates are endangered, the house is shaken."[37]

French interest in Vietnam began in the seventeenth century with Jesuit missionaries, but development was slow. The French Revolution and the Napoleonic Wars put East Asian expansion on hold. But in the late 1850s, the French took military action in southern Vietnam as revenge against antimissionary riots; by 1862, the French had taken, through cession, Cochin-China, the southernmost section of the country. A treaty between France and Vietnam in 1874 expanded French influence, allowing French shipping on the Red River in the northernmost section, Tongking, and taking control of Vietnamese foreign relations. Part of the function of this treaty was to establish the independence of Vietnam from China; a precondition of taking control of Vietnam's foreign affairs was the recognition of "the sovereignty of the King of Annam [Vietnam] and his complete independence of all foreign powers."[38] The Chinese response to this treaty was to assert that Vietnam had for centuries been a tributary state of China and that China would investigate the matter; but it did nothing to follow up that statement. When the Chinese response was translated into French, "had been a tributary" was translated into the past perfect tense, which the French took as Chinese acquiescence in what was in essence a French protectorate—a recipe for trouble. The French stepped up their aggressive actions in northern Vietnam as the Vietnamese government, functioning as the tributary "younger brother," asked the Chinese for help. The Chinese responded with irregulars, known as the Black Flags, who began to skirmish with French troops in 1882; regular troops were sent in 1883.

The **Sino-French War**, which would rage for three years, had begun. Like in the Opium War, negotiations and military action played out concurrently. Two potential peace treaties were scuttled, the first by the French, the second by the Chinese. The Chinese situation was made more complicated by the emergence of a group known as "the party of the purists" (a rough translation of **qingliu** *dang*), who stressed China's moral superiority and power in comparison with that of France and argued that China should continue the fight until victory. They were opposed by "realists" like Li Hongzhang who contended that self-strengthening had not yet reached the point where the country could fend off France. The persistence of the purist party in pressing the vacillating empress dowager for the continuation of the war helped to scuttle the second treaty; the consequent delay in ending the war made possible an event that not only justified Li's position but was a disaster.

In summer 1884, with the war on the southeast coast on a hiatus (unlike the war that continued in Vietnam), the French had begun to sail ships up the Min River to the port of Fuzhou, home port of one quarter of the Chinese navy and site of the Fuzhou Shipyard. On the morning of August 23, their largest ship in Chinese waters sailed up the twenty-mile reach of river. Other ships followed, sailing past numerous Chinese batteries armed with modern guns and cannon purchased from European firms—exhibits of the self-strengthening program. Early in the afternoon, the French fleet made target practice of the Chinese fleet and the shipyard. Within fifteen minutes, all but two of twenty-three Chinese war junks and men-of-war were sunk or were burning; the shipyard was leveled. Approximately three thousand Chinese were killed. In one afternoon, the hollowness of the self-strengthening efforts was revealed: without proper organization, coordination, and leadership, all the modern machines and weapons, manufactured or bought, proved ineffectual. The sad irony was that the court had tried to coerce two of China's other fleets to participate in defense against the French, but their leaders, one of whom was Li Hongzhang, refused. The presence of the French fleet at Fuzhou at a time of increased likelihood of war in the area should have alerted Chinese authorities to the danger.

The end of the war came with an agreement in mid-1885 by which China recognized French control over Vietnam, thereby ending its centuries-long tributary relationship. To this point the self-strengthening movement had failed: China was clearly not capable of fending off aggressors. It had not been able or willing to make the institutional and personnel decisions that would provide the proper context for self-strengthening success. The principal decision makers did not, however, take institutional and personnel changes as the main lessons of the war; rather, they believed that there had simply not yet been enough self-strengthening. Therefore, the decade following the loss of Vietnam saw an expanded scope of the self-strengthening policy, including the establishment of more arsenals, iron foundries, and some industries. Some institutional initiatives did, however, portend greater changes to come: military academies were established, as were schools for industrial arts, mining, telegraphy, and railways, and at least the façade of a centralized navy was set up, functioning under a Board of Admiralty.

Navy-related problems pointed to the realities that would render this latest round of self-strengthening ineffectual. The Board of Admiralty was soon a dead letter because of the system of personal connections and corruption that entangled any efforts to change. Further, in a story that has become classic in its bitter irony, many of the appropriations that were earmarked for naval expansion were used by the empress dowager for repairing the Summer Palace, which had been sacked and looted during the Arrow War. The story goes that part of those naval appropriations funded the renovation of the infamous Marble Barge, the vessel on which the empress dowager liked to picnic—at a time when there were no ships whatsoever added to the main Chinese fleet.

## The Loss of Korea

Korea was one of China's closest tributary states. In the Han dynasty (202 B.C.E.–220) China had occupied the northwestern part of the peninsula and had tried unsuccessfully in the Sui (589–618) and Tang (618–907) dynasties to seize the country. Even with that history of aggression, the Koreans modeled their cultural and political institutions on those of China; by the Yi dynasty (1392–1910), Korea's was in many ways, though smaller, a replica of the Chinese system. Its geographical position has led repeatedly to tragedy. Caught between Japan and the mammoth land powers of China and Russia, Korea has been the bridge of land powers to Japan (as in the thirteenth-century Mongol invasions) and of Japan to the land powers (as in Hideyoshi's late sixteenth-century invasion). It is not surprising that Korea tried to close itself to foreign aggression, turning itself into the "hermit nation."

In light of potential threats from the mainland, Japan saw Korea as a "dagger pointed at its heart." In the early years after the overthrow of the Tokugawa shogunate, some government leaders in the new Meiji regime saw Korea as an opportunity as well—a chance to let erstwhile samurai get fighting blood out of their system in retaliation for a Korean rebuff to Japanese vessels. Though that plan was quashed, Korea—only a hundred miles across the Japan Sea—began to play an important role in Japan's conception of its role in northeast Asia. Well aware of the special relationship that existed between China and Korea, Japan sent emissaries to China to test the waters for greater Japanese involvement in Korea. Li Hongzhang's tributary-framed response was that "though Korea is a dependent country of China, it is not a territorial possession; hence in its domestic and foreign affairs, it is self-governing."[39] Bolstered by China's implicit permission to approach Korea about opening trade with Japan, the Meiji government proceeded in the "opening" of the hermit nation to trade by the signing of a treaty in 1876. As to Korea's status, the treaty stated that "Korea, being an independent state, enjoys the same sovereign rights as does Japan." While China interpreted *independent* as *autonomous*, it is clear from subsequent events that Japan saw things differently.

The treaty inaugurated a decade of increasing tensions between China and Japan on the Korean peninsula; both countries kept some nationals in Korea, and the situation was always ripe for problems. In 1882, a mutiny in the Korean army over better treatment of a small elite Korean military unit being trained by the Japanese led both countries to send forces "to restore peace." The upshot was that the Japanese maintained a permanent guard at their legation in Seoul; the Chinese kept three thousand soldiers in the country, sent arms and Chinese instructors to the Korean military, and posted advisers to the Korean government. The Chinese would have explained their actions as in accord with the traditions of the tributary system. Then in 1884, young Koreans, having returned to the country after study in Japan and having drunk the heady wine of Japanese Meiji reformism, attempted a coup against what they perceived as the troglodytic Korean regime. Chinese forces, though weakened by the withdrawal of three divisions to serve in the war against France, were able to quash the coup effort. But Japan sent forces and demands both for an indemnity and an apology for damage to the Japanese legation. Ito Hirobumi was sent to China, where he negotiated an end to the crisis with Li Hongzhang, eager for a solution in light of the war over Vietnam. Each country withdrew its forces and promised to notify the other if it was planning to send forces in the future. Presumably, in that case, joint consultations would mean that cooler heads would prevail and another crisis could be averted. This Li-Ito convention brought another decade of peace, in which China's resident general, **Yuan Shikai**, sought to preserve the forms of Chinese suzerainty.

Beginning in the 1860s, an eclectic religion called Tonghak (Eastern learning) began to sweep across southwest Korea. In many ways, especially its leaning toward millenarianism, it was reminiscent of the Taiping movement. In the 1890s, it shaped a rebellion that grew out of the mix of political, social, and economic problems enervating the Korean countryside. As the rebellion spread, the Korean government, still operating under its tributary mentality, asked the Chinese government to send troops in summer 1894 to help quell the unrest. Under the Li-Ito convention, the Chinese government notified Japan of its intentions to send fifteen hundred troops and to withdraw them once the rebellion was put down. The Japanese responded by sending some eight thousand troops. When the Chinese then sent reinforcements, the Japanese sank a British steamer that had been chartered by the Chinese, drowning almost a thousand Chinese. On August 1, both countries declared war.

The war was the first test for the Chinese military after a decade of what might be called advanced self-strengthening. The results were no different from those in the war with France a decade earlier: utter and humiliating defeat on land and sea. Japan, a nation comprised of what earlier Chinese had contemptuously dismissed as "dwarf people" and itself a former tributary, had smashed its former suzerain; many nations were shocked by the outcome, having assumed that the land giant would overwhelm the upstart island-nation. But the outcome should not have been surprising. Japan had been rapidly modernizing since the 1870s and its war effort was national in scope. China's efforts at modernizing had been marked by fits and starts—counterproductive policies that in reality enervated the effort; when war came, it was fought mostly by Li Hongzhang's Beiyang fleet and Anhui army. As Immanuel Hsu put it, "China had no clear demarcation of authority, no unity of command, and no nationwide mobilization. Conflicting advice from the Tsungli [Zongli] Yamen, provincial authorities, and irresponsible Ch'ing-liu [*qingliu*; purist party] officials rendered the court indecisive."[40] The postmortem is a déjà vu, recalling the denouement of the Sino-French War.

The settlement (1895) might have been much worse from the Chinese perspective had two contingencies not intervened. When peace envoy Li Hongzhang was shot in the head by a Japanese fanatic, the Japanese, horrified that the insane act might jeopardize their victory booty, withdrew some of their most expansive demands—specifically, that they be allowed to control three cities in the Beijing area. Then after the conclusion of the **Treaty of Shimonoseki** ceding Taiwan and the Liaodong peninsula in southern Manchuria to Japan, the so-called Triple Intervention, involving Russia, Germany, and France, returned the Liaodong territory to China. Nevertheless, the Chinese lost Taiwan outright and had to forfeit forever any tributary-related claims to Korea. Though there were protests in China against the treaty by provincial graduates who had come to the capital to take the *jinshi* degree examinations, they were to no avail. They might be seen, however, as the incipient expression of a nationalism born out of an abasing shame.

## THE CULTURAL, IDEOLOGICAL, AND POLITICAL NATURE OF CHINESE RESPONSE TO CIVILIZATIONAL CRISIS

For a culture so rooted in the glories of the past, the bloody and violent nightmares of the middle and end of the nineteenth century were powerfully disorienting: they seemed such a marked break from the past. Chinese culture had always been fixated on the past. For Confucius, the golden age was in that past—a time when society functioned harmoniously and the country was at peace. Throughout history, the goal of statesmen was to try to restore something of that glorious time, but there remained a strong sense that it could never really be done. The past framed and constrained the present so that every change in state and society had to be rationalized in terms of it, whether that past was the policies of a former emperor or one's ancestral traditions.

China had faced foreign invaders before, but they had come by horseback, on land, and had wielded bows and arrows. Generally, China had been able to deal with them, to a greater or lesser degree, bringing them into the Chinese cultural sphere. But now the foreign invaders had come by ship, with powerful cannons and other armaments, and there was no indication that they would ever accept the Chinese cultural tradition. The disjuncture with the past was evident. The crises of the nineteenth century thus presented Chinese leaders with a dilemma: how to overcome their obvious military and strategic weakness so that they might deal with these foreigners from a position of some strength.

Chinese leaders came up with a range of responses. Some saw China's saving strategy in the revivification of its culture: traditional culture was incomparably great; it had fostered the glories of the past; it should be the vehicle to China's restoration. Above all, these culturalists argued, barbarian weapons and machines were not the answer. The use of such implements of war would sully the Chinese hands that wielded them. If tools of war were to be part of the answer to China's problems, then the Chinese should use those from the Chinese repertoire of warfare from the past.

Others contended that Western weapons and ships were simply inanimate machines—culture-neutral, as it were. These self-strengtheners argued that foreign weapons and ships could thus be bought or manufactured without cultural contamination. Indeed, they argued, what they were doing was protecting traditional Chinese culture (the *end* that must be preserved) with foreign military implements (the *means* to do that) under the dire circumstances China faced. Said another way, Western guns and ships were the techniques by which the substance of Chinese civilization could be preserved. By this formula, self-strengtheners could rationalize change only through the guise of protecting the past. Even for these "reformers," the past was the lens making possible change in the present.

On its face, this formula seemed innocuous, but a serious logical fallacy lurked beneath. While foreign machines might look culture-neutral (after all, anyone can turn on a switch, pull a trigger, or pilot a ship), they came with a host of culture-specific worldviews and scientific views. To build ships and weapons at the Jiangnan arsenal or Fuzhou shipyard likely required the study of engineering and technical manuals, an endeavor that could bring the student into a new world where old assumptions about the natural world might be challenged. Once a Chinese entered that world and then returned to the

Chinese classics, he would likely ask new questions of those classics and see them in a broader context. For that student, the meaning of those classics—indeed, the meaning of Chinese culture—had been changed: in short, means did affect ends.

Or, on more practical issues, when arsenal and shipyard had been established with collateral engineering and foreign-language courses of study, how could they attract able young men to study "barbarian" things when the ladder to success in imperial China remained the civil service examination? One answer was to open up the traditional degree system to a new kind of degree earned through these courses of study. But that strategy would open the possibility that a traditional-type degree could be earned outside the classical tradition. Clearly, in such a case, the practical requisites for successful self-strengthening meant that the means had come to have a huge impact on the ends. The logical fallacy of the self-strengtheners would begin to open up China to new, not always predictable, forces and would be replayed more than a century later as China opened itself up to computers and high technology in the 1980s and 1990s.

In addition to self-strengthening, there were other, more mechanical, ways of rationalizing change in the name of the past. One argument, based on patterns of cyclical change, posited that two thousand years had intervened between the time of the ancient sage kings of Yao and Shun and the establishment of the empire in 221 B.C.E. And now, since the late nineteenth century was roughly two thousand years after that momentous event, it was cyclically proper that a new great change could occur. Another argument suggested that Western science and technology could be legitimately borrowed because mathematical and chemical ideas that were being used in the West had first appeared in ancient China. This we-had-it-first approach opened the Chinese to the questions of why, and how, if these ideas were so important in the development of modern science, China had lost them.

### The Ideology of Kang Youwei: Giving the Chinese the Idea of Progress

One of the motive forces in the modern Western world, emerging in the Enlightenment in the late eighteenth century, was the idea of progress. Using their brains and the wonders of modern technology and science, humans had the power to progress in a view of history that was ever onward, ever upward. The Chinese view of history, in contrast, was a trend cyclically downward from the golden age, a worldview marked by what Westerners have often interpreted as a pessimistic acceptance of fate. In the 1890s, schol-ar **Kang Youwei**, a *jinshi*-degree holder, gave to the Chinese intellectual world its idea of progress, building a rationale, as always based upon the past, for major institutional change. Notably, his prescribed changes were not to preserve traditional Chinese culture but, more fundamentally, to preserve China as a country.

Long concerned for the nation, Kang had been one of the provincial graduates who had called in 1895 for the Chinese to continue their fight against Japan. He had already, by that time, begun to construct his impor-tant ideological edifice. In 1891, he published a book claiming that textual criticism showed that the basic texts of the school of Han Learning (that is, those that had been used by the most important "school" of Confucian thought since the seventeenth century) were really forgeries. The true Confucian teachings were to be found not in these ancient texts but rather in what were called the "new texts," from the earlier Han dynasty. Kang's point was to undercut the "socio-moral indifferentism" of the school of Han Learning, which had focused its attention on textual and philological work, in order "to reaffirm political concern and institutional reform as the cen-tral orientation of Confucianism."[41] Though today Kang's interpretation is not seen as credible, its impact on the intellectual world of the 1890s was shattering, already buffeted as it was by realities of foreign military superior-ity, the bitterness of imperialism, and the experience of heterodox rebel-lions. With the central canon shown to be false, there was no firm intellec-tual ground on which to stand—indeed, no firm past to rationalize in the name of.

But Kang himself would provide the more accurate intellectual ground, the more appropriate past. In 1898, he published *Confucius as a Reformer*, a work that argued that Confucius, far from simply being the "transmitter" that he himself claimed, was a great innovator, "a messianic, forward-looking 'sage king,' " a man who used the past to call for major institutional change. Kang then set forth his rationale for progress, using, according to one historian, mainly ideas from the West, but framing them in categories that he found in the so-called new texts, *the* proper Confucian texts according to Kang.[42] His ideas were similar to the unilinear view of history in the post-Enlightenment West. He found three axial ages through which history moved: the Age of Disorder, the Age of Approaching Peace, and the Age of Universal Peace. He argued that the world had been mired in the Age of Disorder but that it could enter the next axial age, that of approaching peace, should Kang's ideas about reform be adopted. His ideas went farther than any others in using the past to break away from the past. His reform proposals called for basic institutional change, including a state constitution and assemblies where popular sovereignty might be exercised.

Even if many in the intellectual and political worlds judged him to be heretical, his calls for institutions undergirded by and infused with Western ideas began to stimulate as nothing had before an interest in Western things beyond guns and ships. As such, Kang's works began to prime the pump of greater change. Perhaps even more important, Kang's interpretation of Confucianism had a major impact, the reverberations of which would continue for decades. For Kang's treatment of Confucius and his thought had the effect of changing Confucianism from "what so far had been the unquestioned centre of faith into an ideology, the basic character of which was problematic and debatable."[43] Once Confucianism became simply an ideology, for example, it could be seen as a tool elevating certain social types (say, fathers, husbands, parents, elder brothers) and demeaning other social types (sons, wives, children, younger brothers). Kang's work was, in essence, the first step, however little he intended it, in the dethronement of Confucius and his thought as the basis of Chinese culture.

## The Reform Movement of the 1890s

Kang, however, was not the sole voice calling for a reevaluation of the Chinese political and cultural situation. Most influential was his disciple **Liang Qichao**, who had been with Kang in Beijing at the time of China's surrender to Japan and who in his writings proposed solutions for the desperate plight of the Chinese nation. Liang is important because many elements of his thought would remain in the discourse of change throughout much of the twentieth century. Liang believed that the self-strengthening efforts had focused too narrowly on technological innovations and that the times necessitated political reforms. His avenue for such change was the traditional cultural approach of educational reform. A crucial vehicle for saving the nation was the spread of literacy. Since this could not be accomplished through the traditional examination system and since it was clear that so long as the examination system remained in place no other system could be successfully implemented, Liang favored abolishing the examination and establishing a national school system. In that system, both intellectual development and political consciousness would be raised as students studied both ideas from the West and Chinese traditions.

Liang supported Kang's idea that significant institutional change was the motive force propelling history's unilinear progress. A central concept in his thought about the changes China needed to make was "grouping"—an idea that involved several aspects of change.[44] At its simplest level, it meant the formation of gentry associations that would meet to study and discuss the political and social changes that must be undertaken; in a real sense, "grouping" would mobilize the intellects and energies of China's leaders. But the concept also had a deeper, more revolutionary thrust. China's plight required national solidarity and a commitment of the people as a whole to solving problems. Implicit in his arguments was that traditional Chinese political culture and institutions inhibited both solidarity and an energetic commitment. The traditional state was authoritarian, constraining the populace through repressive policies and by denying the free flow of information. For China to be able to compete with the West, such constraints had to be broken so that Chinese political culture could develop an essential "collective dynamism."

Certainly there is the strong flavor of nationalism here, even if Liang did not use the term. And Liang's call for a new political community as the center of a reconceived state for the first time brought democracy into Chinese discourse. For the new state was not to be based on the powers of a monarch over his subjects but on participation of both rulers and ruled—indeed, by what might be called popular sovereignty. The concept of grouping then encapsulated in a basic way ideas of political community, the nation, and democracy. Liang's radical political discourse—mobilization of the people, the collective and the community, popular sovereignty—would be the watchwords of later Chinese reformers and revolutionaries from Sun Yat-sen through Mao Zedong.

The efforts of institutional reformers, led by Kang and Liang, began with the establishment of "groupings," in particular study societies. Reformers intended them as vehicles to bring together official and nonofficial elites with the goals of stimulating greater social integration among policy makers and potential policy makers, and of educating and, through the study process, mobilizing elite energies for the remaking of China. The first study societies were formed in Beijing and Shanghai in the summer and autumn of 1895. According to Manchu policies, they were illegal, for the Manchus had proscribed the formation of private societies since the 1650s. By the spring of 1896, then, both study societies were banned. But in late 1897, in Hunan, central China, a reform-minded provincial administration gave rise not only to industrial and commercial innovations but also to the establishment of educational institutions with teachers from among the reformers (including Liang) and the formation of study societies.

The most famous was the Southern Study Society, founded by the more radical reformist gentry, at its height having more than twelve hundred members from both official and nonofficial elites. In name a private voluntary organization, it avoided being banned because the provincial government had supported its formation and participated in its functioning. Proposals of its members on matters of public policy were, for example, sent from the society to provincial officials for consideration and possible implementation. Liang, commenting on the society after it had closed, noted that "though nominally a study society, the Southern Study Society had all the makings of a local legislature."[45] In 1897 and 1898, there were, in addition to this society, thirteen other study societies operating in Hunan.

Another important aspect of this reform activity was the publication of newspapers. In the coming decades, newspapers—most of them short-lived, but in prolific numbers—would play a key role in reshaping thoughts about the new China. They were initially published by the early Beijing and Shanghai study societies, as well as those in Hunan. Most of Liang Qichao's essays appeared in these newspapers. Distributed mostly free of charge, the papers kept reformist ideas alive in Hunan and along the southeast coast, publicizing and propagandizing goals.

## 1898: The Reform Movement Collapses

In the Hunan reform movement, the teachings of Liang Qichao and various writings in the Southern Study Society's newspapers became increasingly radical in early 1898, taking on not only Chinese nationalistic positions but also anti-Manchu overtones. Moderate reformers and even conservative men who had been associated with the provincial reform activities became alarmed. A bitter struggle between the reformers and the more conservative forces erupted; for the latter, the issue was simple and central: the necessity of defending the very heart of Chinese cultural values against the heterodox views of the reformers. The power of the past was at work overwhelming possibilities of institutional change. The attack on Kang and Liang spread as various impeachments poured into the court, denouncing their ideology and reform agenda. By the summer, most reformers were expelled from Hunan, with most Hunanese gentry mobilized not for the building of a new state and society but against the reformers.

It is ironical that at the very time when Kang and company were being attacked in and then driven out of Hunan, Kang was to come closest to holding substantial national power. With the help of **Weng Tonghe**, the reform-minded tutor of the emperor, Kang was able to reach the ear of the twenty-seven-year-old **Guangxu emperor** (see document 3, appendix 2). From mid-June to mid-September, in what has come to be known as the **Hundred Days**, the emperor, with Kang providing the agenda, issued more than a hundred decrees calling for institutional reforms in almost every policy arena. In this remarkable period and its tragic denouement, the temporal and political contexts played crucial roles.

In many ways, the birth of the reform movement at the court at the very time it was receiving the excoriations of reformers from Hunan and elsewhere was made possible because of a new crisis between China and the foreign powers. In November 1897, Germany, using as a pretext the killing of a German missionary, occupied Qingdao. In March, it leased the port and surrounding area for ninety-nine years; the lease included Germany's holding mining and railroad rights. Driven by imperialist rivalry, the rest of the nations followed suit. Russia occupied Port Arthur on the tip of the Liaodong peninsula in December 1897 and signed a twenty-five-year lease in March 1898. France leased Guangzhou Bay for ninety-nine years in April 1898. Great Britain leased Hong Kong's "New Territories" in June 1898 for ninety-nine years and negotiated from April to July to lease Weihaiwei for as long as the Russians held Port Arthur across the Bo Hai (see map 2). The seizure of treaty ports had thus escalated to the European control of considerable territory with substantial economic rights. In this scramble for concessions—the "carving up of the Chinese melon," as it is often denoted—imperialism had thus reached a more virulent level that boded great danger for the integrity of China. Alarm about the incipient demise of the Chinese nation spread among elites all over China. In this context, Kang had some ready ears for hearing out his reform package.

The other crucial context for the 1898 drama was the political reality of the continuing power of the empress dowager, who, for as long as her nephew sat on the throne, pulled strings from behind the scenes. Taken as a whole, the political, economic, military, and educational reforms called for in the wave of reform edicts would have drastically restructured the Chinese polity; they thus threatened the whole status quo—specifically, the world of the empress dowager and her supporters. On September 21, the empress dowager staged a coup d'état, embarked on her third regency, and put the emperor under house arrest. Kang was able to escape to Hong Kong, Liang to Japan; but six young reformers were executed. Five days after the coup, all the reform edicts were revoked.

The reform effort was put down rather easily, a fact that is often used to suggest that in China at this time change could not likely come from the top, as it had in Japan's Meiji Restoration. The Chinese political leaders seemed unable to transform the system in order to deal with the crises; perhaps they even failed to conceive of the peril the state was in. And yet the reform movement was not devoid of historical import. It did, as one historian suggests, "usher in a new phase of Chinese culture—the era of ideologies." The ideas of Kang and Liang, taking Western thought seriously and demoting Confucianism from a way of life to an ideology, "raised the curtain on the cultural crises of the twentieth century."[46] Gentry elites began to band together in associations, discussing issues and starting to solve problems in new contexts. Newspapers proliferated, sprouting up "like bamboo shoots after a spring rain," to use the stock Chinese phrase; perhaps their most outstanding feature was the nationalism that marked their pages. The discourse they began, it has been said, was really the beginning of modern Chinese public opinion. Educational reform was placed at the center of the public agenda, and it would come to fruition in the next decade. Finally, it has been suggested that the reform era led to the birth of the modern intelligentsia, differentiated from the old scholar-gentry by their being free-floating intellectuals not tied to localities and by their lack of a symbiotic relationship with and even alienation from the government. Further, the new intelligentsia, unlike the old scholar elites, struggled with problems of cultural identity, caught between the old and the new, East and West.

## The Boxer Catastrophe

The decline of the traditional state was punctuated at century's end by an outrageous and tragic constellation of events surrounding an uprising in north China. Rising out of a culture of poverty in Shandong Province, the rebellion was led by so-called Boxers, a word derived from the martial rituals in which they participated (see map 3). Composed of peasants, most of them young men, the roving Boxer bands also included women's groups. In 1898 and 1899, they attacked Christian converts and missionaries, in part because of the special privileges that converts enjoyed and in part because of antiforeign feeling. Western nations, alarmed at the attacks on missionaries, killings, and property losses, demanded that the imperial court act to suppress the uprising. Since the Boxers had adopted a slogan in support of the Qing ("Revive the Qing; destroy the foreigner"), the empress dowager had second thoughts about such suppression. Wall posters displayed in villages and towns expressed the Boxer goal:

When at last all the Foreign Devils
Are expelled to the very last man,
The Great Qing, united, together,
Will bring peace to this our land.[47]

The empress dowager responded with the Confucian line, "Heaven sees as the people sees; Heaven hears as the people hear," alluding to the idea of the Qing's Mandate of Heaven; she added: "China is weak; the only thing we can depend upon is the hearts of the people."[48] With Western pressure on the court rising, the empress dowager incredibly put her support behind the rag-tag Boxers. The political and policy bankruptcy of the Qing was clear.

Western nations determined that they would have to act to save missionaries and stop the bloodshed. But when on June 10, 1900, a British relief force marched from Tianjin, it was beaten back by Boxers and eventually by Qing imperial troops. On June 20, the German minister en route to a meeting with the Zongli Yamen was shot and killed. The next day, in a scene that rivals the theater of the absurd, the empress dowager declared war on the eight foreign powers. Having been repeatedly defeated by one country at a time, the Qing had now decided to take on eight. During the summer, Boxers besieged the legation quarters in Beijing that had become a haven to which missionaries and converts had fled—an act that gave rise in the Western press to the phrase the yellow peril. An eight-nation force of about twenty thousand men arrived in Beijing on August 14 to lift the siege; most Boxers simply disappeared into the north China countryside. The empress dowager, with the Guangxu emperor in tow, fled the city for Xi'an, eight hundred miles to the southwest, where they would remain until January 1902.

Over the next six months, Western troops joined missionaries in making forays into surrounding cities and towns, looting Chinese property. By late 1900, forty-five thousand foreign troops were in north China. The signing of the **Boxer Protocol** in September 1901 brought the nadir of the Qing court in its relations with the West (see document 4, appendix 2). The West was out for revenge: not only, as one would expect, did they call for the execution and punishment of officials who had participated in the war, but they suspended the civil service examinations for five years in forty-five cities. They ordered the destruction of more than two dozen forts and the occupation of a dozen railroad posts to allow Western troops ready access to Beijing. They expanded the legation quarters and ordered its permanent fortification. But the most disastrous for the Chinese was an indemnity, so large that many historians have come to use the same adjective to describe it: it was "staggering" in its immensity.[49] Payment for damage to foreign property and lives was to be 450 million taels (about \$333 million in 1901), a sum staggering since the complete annual Qing income was only about 250 million taels. The indemnity was to be paid in gold, with interest rates that by the date of the amortization of the debt (the end of 1940) would total about one billion taels. For a government that could not move forcefully into the modern world in part because of paucity of funds, the indemnity was an overwhelming burden. The heights of Qing glory and wealth under the Qianlong emperor had been little more than a century before, yet the state now entered the twentieth century in defeat, poverty, and humiliation.

## NOTES

1. See the discussions in Susan Naquin and Evelyn S. Rawski, *Chinese Society in the Eighteenth Century* (New Haven: Yale University Press, 1987), esp. chapters 1, 2, 4, and 6.
2. Quoted in Frederic Wakeman Jr., "High Ch'ing: 1683–1839," in James B. Crowley, ed., *Modern East Asia: Essays in Interpretation* (New York: Harcourt, Brace, Javonovich, 1970), p. 5.
3. Jonathan Spence, *The Search for Modern China* (New York: Norton, 1990), p. 94. These figures come from Ho Ping-ti, *Studies on the Population of China, 1368–1953* (Cambridge: Harvard University Press, 1959), p. 281.
4. Naquin and Rawski, p. 223.
5. Quoted in Harold Isaacs, *Scratches on Our Minds* (New York: John Day, 1958), p. 95.
6. Ibid., p. 94.
7. Spence, *Search*, p. 90.
8. See Susan Mann, *Precious Records* (Stanford: Stanford University Press, 1997).
9. Naquin and Rawski, p. 219.
10. Philip A. Kuhn, *Soulstealers: The Chinese Sorcery Scare of 1768* (Cambridge: Harvard University Press, 1990), p. 39.
11. Ibid., pp. 229–30.
12. In 1834, for example, the worth of these contributions and presents totaled more than 456,000 taels. Their willingness to pay such a sum points to the lucrative nature of the monopoly and their ability to profit from it. See Chang Hsin-pao, *Commissioner Lin and the Opium War* (Cambridge: Harvard University Press, 1964), p. 14.
13. *Canton* is the old postal romanization for the city of Guangzhou. The city was never called Canton by the Chinese.
14. Naquin and Rawski, p. 103.
15. For different interpretations of the Macartney Mission, see James Hevia,

*Cherishing Men from Afar: Qing Guest Ritual and the Macartney Embassy of 1793* (Durham: Duke University Press, 1995) and a critique of that postmodern approach in Joseph Esherick, "Cherishing Sources from Afar," *Modern China* 24, no. 2 (1998), 135–61.

16. Quoted in Peter Ward Fay, *The Opium War, 1840–1842* (Chapel Hill: University of North Carolina Press, 1975), p. 9.

17. Jonathan Spence, "Opium Smoking in Ch'ing China," in Frederic Wakeman Jr. and Carolyn Grant, eds., *Conflict and Control in Late Imperial China* (Berkeley, University of California Press, 1975), p. 151. A chest usually contained 133 pounds avoirdupois.

18. Ibid., p. 154.

19. James Polachek, *The Inner Opium War* (Cambridge: Harvard University Press, 1992), p. 79.

20. The phrase is Immanuel C. Y. Hsu's in *The Rise of Modern China* (New York: Oxford University Press, 1970), p. 228.

21. For his part in starting the war through his coercive policies, Lin Zexu was exiled to Xinjiang in far western China.

22. Spence, "Opium Smoking," p. 151. He notes that by 1900 the imports had leveled off at about fifty thousand chests per year.

23. The amount of reparations varies according to source. Spence, *Search*, says that they totaled 250,000 taels (p. 205). Hsu puts the sum at 400,000 (p. 363). Paul Cohen in *China and Christianity* (Cambridge: Harvard University Press, 1963) notes that a total of 280,000 taels of reparations were paid (250,000 to France and 30,000 to Russia), with additional sums of 212,000 taels to France and Great Britain to pay for property losses (p. 246).

24. Spence, *Search*, p. 168.

25. Spence, *God's Chinese Son* (New York: Norton, 1996), p. 54.

26. G. William Skinner, "Regional Urbanization in Nineteenth-Century China," in Skinner, ed., *The City in Late Imperial China* (Stanford: Stanford University Press, 1977), p. 229.

27. Thomas W. Kingsmill, "Retrospect of Events in China and Japan During the Year 1865," *Journal of the North China Branch of the Royal Asiatic Society* 2 (1865), 143.

28. Elizabeth J. Perry, *Rebels and Revolutionaries in North China, 1845–1945* (Stanford: Stanford University Press, 1980), p. 97.

29. Frederick Wakeman Jr., *The Fall of Imperial China* (New York: Free Press, 1975), p. 170.

30. Ibid., p. 165.

31. See the discussion in Mary Backus Rankin, *Elite Activism and Political Transformation in China* (Stanford: Stanford University Press, 1986), pp. 107–12.

32. Benjamin A. Elman, *From Philosophy to Philology* (Cambridge: Harvard University Press, 1984), p. 26.

33. For a brief biography of Feng and the suggestion that he likely coined the term, see

Ssu-yu Teng and John K. Fairbank, eds., *China's Response to the West: A Documentary Survey, 1839–1923* (Cambridge: Harvard University Press, 1953), p. 50.

34. John K. Fairbank, Edwin O. Reischauer, and Albert M. Craig, *East Asia: The Modern Transformation* (Boston: Houghton Mifflin, 1965). p. 320.

35. Teng and Fairbank, *China's Response*, p. 53.

36. The phrase comes from the British ambassador in Japan at the time. See John K. Fairbank and Kwang-ching Liu, eds., *The Cambridge History of China*, vol. 11, *Late Ch'ing, 1800–1911*, part 2 (Cambridge: Cambridge University Press, 1980), p. 88.

37. Quoted in Lloyd E. Eastman, *Throne and Mandarins* (Cambridge: Harvard University Press, 1967), p. 38.

38. Ibid., p. 33.

39. Quoted in Hilary Conroy, *The Japanese Seizure of Korea, 1868–1910* (Philadelphia: University of Pennsylvania Press, 1960), p. 66.

40. Immanuel C. Y. Hsu, "Late Ch'ing [Qing] Foreign Relations, 1866–1905," in Fairbank and Liu, *Cambridge History of China*, vol. 11, part 2, p. 109.

41. Hao Chang, "Intellectual Change and the Reform Movement, 1890–98," in Fairbank and Liu, *Cambridge History of China*, vol. 11, part 2, pp. 287–88.

42. Ibid., p. 288.

43. Ibid., p. 290.

44. This discussion of Liang Qichao's thought is based on Hao Chang, *Liang Ch'i-ch'ao and Intellectual Transition in China, 1890–1907* (Cambridge: Harvard University Press, 1971), pp. 73–120.

45. Quoted in Hao Chang, "Intellectual Change," p. 308.

46. Ibid., p. 329.

47. Joseph Esherick, *The Origins of the Boxer Uprising* (Berkeley: University of California Press, 1987), p. 300.

48. Fairbank, Reischauer, and Craig, *East Asia*, pp. 397 and 400.

49. See as examples ibid., p. 403; Spence, *Search*, p. 235; and Wakeman, *Fall of Imperial China*, p. 221.

# CHAPTER TWO

# Building State and Nation Amid Cultural Revolution, 1901–28

## THE "REVOLUTIONARY" MANCHUS

### Changing Historical Contexts

The last decade of the Manchus ended with a bang of activity, not a whimper. The activity varied from reformist to quite radical, even revolutionary. The year and a half that the empress dowager spent in Xi'an must have given her time to ponder China's predicament. Already in January 1901, she issued a statement about adopting the strong points from foreign countries in order to make up for China's weaknesses. During the course of the reforms up to the 1911 revolution, the first stirrings of a new China began to be felt—from modern-style economic developments to outbursts of nationalism and the appearance of new social forces. Certainly, if the Manchu reform effort was stimulated by China's plight vis-à-vis the outside world, it was also prompted by internal developments and change.

From the start, it should be seen that the stirrings of a new China were spatially uneven. Core areas of greater urbanization and degree of economic development, often along the coasts or important river systems, evidenced the greater degree of modern changes; peripheral backwaters showed the least. The resulting gap obviously tended to create different experiences and "worldviews" among the denizens of the respective zones of development. Cities were the sites of greatest change. They were being paved, lighted, and policed. They were the homes for wide-ranging reformist voluntary associations to deal with social wrongs and vices like opium smoking, foot binding, and gambling. Newspapers were being produced in great number, and more and more magazines appeared, focusing on current developments. One historian in discussing the welding of Chinese society together has estimated that the numbers of letters, newspapers, and magazines sent and received in 1910 were twenty-five times that in 1901.[1] Such an increase most certainly comes primarily from the core zones.

One of the hallmarks of these years in the core zones was various expressions of nationalism. Public meetings and demonstrations about British threats to Tibet, Russian influence in Mongolia and Manchuria, and French pressure in southwest China dotted the political landscape. Nationalism as resistance to foreign powers perhaps reached its high point in the 1905–7 boycott against the United States for its immigration restrictions and mistreatment of Chinese attending the 1904 World's Fair in St. Louis. Nationalism was also expressed against Western intrusion into Chinese internal affairs. An increasing number of bitter incidents in treaty ports exploded out of the Westerners' "right" of extraterritoriality. Though some provinces had eliminated the cultivation of opium, the British claimed that until the drug was extirpated from the country at large it could still import it; there was talk in some Chinese circles of another opium war. A dramatic movement of "rights recovery" developed to win back control of foreign-built and foreign-controlled railroads, with subscriptions from all social classes in core zones and from overseas Chinese.

Participating in these public displays of nationalism were not only the old leaders of society, the scholar-gentry and the gentry-merchants (the latter a new amalgam that had appeared in the sources in the last years of the nineteenth century), but new social groups who for the first time were finding public voices. Youth emerged as a new force, specifically the students who went abroad to Japan, Southeast Asia, the United States, and Europe. Those who studied in Japan and Southeast Asia became enamored of Western liberal and radical ideas and returned to China ready to remake the world. Those who studied in Europe and the United States tended to study more technical subjects; while they might not have reentered the Chinese scene with the political commitment that others evidenced, they were still affected by life in more modernized states. Another traditionally subordinated social group, women, also stepped onto the public stage as never before. They participated in nationalistic demonstrations, were members of Sun Yat-sen's revolutionary organization, advocated feminist ideas, and talked about the equality of all human beings. In the core zones, the practice of foot binding began to decrease, with newspapers reporting on the suicides of women whose mothers-in-law forbade them to unbind their feet. With the formation of new armies, imbued with patriotism, as we will see, soldiers, another traditionally downtrodden group, emerged as a force. Finally, overseas Chinese played an increasing role in Chinese developments. The Chinese diaspora had always been marked by the continuing focus of those abroad on their homeland, especially by the desire to be buried in their ancestral native place. The interests of overseas Chinese were both economic and political; the organizations of both reformists and revolutionaries in this decade sought monetary and moral support from overseas communities in Southeast Asia, the United States, and Europe.

## The Most Revolutionary Act of the Twentieth Century

For the empress dowager, reform became necessary as a tactic to build Chinese strength in order to fend off the West and to maintain the dynasty's leadership. In its reformist efforts, the government turned first to education, at the heart of any change that Confucian China might try to undertake. Traditionally, the function of education had been to train future officials, inculcating them with Confucian values. Whether Kang's and Liang's reformist ideas of popular education were making their mark or whether the empress dowager was influenced from elsewhere, she now championed the establishment of a national school system, structured on a hierarchy of schools at each territorial level of government administration: county, prefecture, province, and capital. It would parallel and feed into traditional examinations, in that sense becoming another route to traditional degrees. The thinking was that within perhaps a decade the new school system could supplant the examination system; until then, the examinations were to be somewhat modernized.[2] This dual approach did not work. There was no incentive for men to try the new route to examination success. Private tutoring for examination preparation was cheaper and a more "known" quantity than untried schools with prescribed curricula. Further, there were no provisions for financing the new schools or for finding teachers and textbooks. Instead of the examination shriveling up and disappearing, it was the new government schools that floundered.

The year 1905 was crucial in what became the Qing reform effort. That year Japan defeated Russia in a war notable for being the first victory of an Asian country over a European country. Japan's great success, in contrast to China's pitiful performance both on the world stage and in its entrance into the modern world, was a spur to greater Qing reformist activity. Another forceful impetus was the organization of anti-Qing revolutionary groups in Japan. China had sent students to Japan beginning in the late 1890s; in 1899, there were two hundred; in 1903, one thousand; and by 1906, there were thirteen thousand. Students had formed associations, many of them based upon common provincial origin, that were developing an anti-Qing bias. Seeing rapidly modernizing Japan, now a growing world power, these students naturally asked what was wrong with China; the answer more and more frequently became "the Manchus." As if to underscore the growing anti-Qing fervor, in 1905, Sun Yat-sen's **Revolutionary Alliance**, aimed at overthrowing the dynasty, was formed in Tokyo (see document 5, appendix 2). In short, by 1905, forces were afoot that propelled the Qing to more radical reform.

In August 1905, leading provincial officials urged the abolition of the civil service examination system; the empress dowager concurred and ordered its abolition. It was the most revolutionary act of the twentieth century, for the examination had been at the heart of traditional culture. It had been the chief conveyor of orthodox state and social ideology. It had created the political elites who filled all levels of the imperial bureaucracy and gave shape to the state and the key social elites, the scholar-gentry, who provided essential leadership at local levels of the polity. Now, with the abolition of the examination, there was in essence no way to promulgate an official ideology. Indeed, the reality was that there was no longer an official ideology of state. What now would be the source of political and social elites? Who would now give shape to the state and provide leadership at different levels? Indeed, once the civil service examination was gone, there was no way to stop or even slow the tides of change.

From 1906, then, education had to sink or swim with the new government school system. The problems of insufficient school buildings, inadequate funding, paucity of able teachers, paucity of textbooks—all these remained. The system tended to remain weak at its base: local elites could achieve greater prestige establishing a high school than an elementary school, so some locales had no elementary schools. Despite the problems, the education system was quickly revolutionized. A mixed Sino-Western curriculum displaced classical studies; daily school attendance in classrooms with students as peers replaced private study for an exam with one's tutor. Perhaps because of the great traditional stress placed upon education, elites took it upon themselves to open and teach in schools. The school system in any particular locality, however, was hostage to the degree of local economic development and to interested elites. Studies have shown that core-zone counties tended to have relatively well-developed school systems, whereas poorer, peripheral counties had few schools and students; nevertheless, sometimes conservative traditional outlooks even in wealthier locales retarded school construction and development.[3] Estimates of the numbers of males who attended schools remained remarkably consistent in the fifty-plus years from 1880 to the 1930s. According to Maritime Customs estimates in 1880, almost half of all males received some education in schools (then mostly so-called charitable schools); surveys done by American John Lossing Buck in the 1930s revealed that 45 percent of all males over the age of seven had experienced some schooling and that 30 percent of all men were thought to be literate.[4]

## Military Reform: Making Good Men Soldiers

A famous Chinese proverb puts it: "Good iron is not beaten into nails; good men are not made into soldiers." Chinese civilization had through the centuries emphasized the virtues of civilian rule and civil values. The empire could be won from horseback, it was said, but it had to be ruled with the writing brush. Though there was an imperial military examination that theoretically paralleled the civil service examination, it had little prestige, becoming, by late imperial times, primarily contests of strength and physical prowess. A man of ability and ambition did not route his future into the military. One of the momentous changes, however, wrought by China's nineteenth- and twentieth-century history was the revaluation of the military amid an increasing militarization of Chinese politics and society.

The opening years of the century found several types of military organizations: the weak and useless banner and Green Standard forces; the regional armies formed during the Taiping, now mainly vested interests of their leaders; and two "new armies," established by key officials in the wake of challenges from Japan. Long-time official Yuan Shikai was appointed to form the most significant of these, the Beiyang Army, in 1895. Using German instructors, he began to train men near Tianjin. Recruited from several provinces and paid well, these men became personally connected to Yuan through his leadership. It is a mark of the changing roles of military men in the early twentieth century that after 1912 ten of Yuan's Beiyang officers would become military provincial governors, and five would become presidents or premiers of China. In July 1901, the Manchus transferred to Yuan's control the other "new army," making him the key army builder in the country and the head of the New Army until his transfer to Beijing in 1907. Undertaking a wide range of institutional military reforms, the Manchus stationed New Army divisions at crucial locations across the country; but central direction of the army remained fragmented, and there was inadequate funding.

Many able men began to choose military careers after the abolition of the civil service examination system. The army seemed to present a new ladder that they could climb to social prestige and considerable power. Peripheral regions (but not the most peripheral) tended to produce, proportionally, the highest share of young men attending new military academies, like that at

Baoding near Beijing.[5] These were regions that traditionally did not produce many civil service degree holders. Thus in these areas there was likely a conscious awareness of the new possibilities. The new academies began to produce cadets who were inculcated with patriotic ideas, who brought together modern military expertise with a sense of acting for the good of the country. These academies came to use Japanese instructors instead of the more expensive Germans. Increasing numbers of graduates began to journey for further study at Japanese military academies, including future leader **Chiang Kai-shek**. There, like students in other schools, they began to talk about the nature of China's problems. By the time they returned to China to be assigned to their posts, many of them had become imbued with the anti-Manchu and revolutionary ideas of Sun Yat-sen and others.

## Constitutional Reform

The Chinese did not read the victory of Japan over Russia in 1905 simply as a triumph of Asia over Europe, but—certainly more significantly for its own path of political modernization—as a victory of a constitutional power over an authoritarian country. In 1906, the court sent missions abroad to study constitutional systems in Europe, the United States, and Japan. The clear choice was the Japanese model—retaining the monarchy, which itself bestowed the constitution—for the court sensed that this model would actually strengthen the throne's power. In August 1908, the empress dowager announced the adoption of constitutional principles and a nine-year calendar of tutelage during which constitutional forms would be established. For example, provisional provincial assemblies would be set up in 1909, with a provisional national assembly, in 1910; each year the polity would take a new step toward the full realization of a constitutional system in 1917.

Had she lived, the empress dowager might have been able to lead China into that new system, but she died in November 1908. The Guangxu emperor, under house arrest since the 1898 coup, died the day before she did; since he was at the time only thirty-seven and reportedly healthy, most historians believe that she had him killed. Regents ruled for the new, three-year-old **Xuantong emperor**. While they did not undo the constitutional schedule, many of their actions regarding the process were not politically astute; in 1911, for example, they named a cabinet that was predominantly Manchu, riling up Chinese already suspicious about the regency's policies. When the provisional provincial assembles met in 1909, they were active in calling for the speeding up of the constitutional schedule. When the provisional national assembly met in 1910, it pushed the court into agreeing to have the whole system, including a full-fledged national assembly, in place by 1913. The assemblies were indeed revolutionary organs on the provincial and national scene. The Qing traditionally had opposed elite associations and any sort of political meetings, but now they had sanctioned institutions that within a few months had shown they were becoming masters of the court.

Analysis of the last decade of the Qing suggests that the court reformed itself out of existence. Every reform that it effected hastened its own end. The abolition of the civil service examination opened the floodgates, leaving major ideological, political, and social questions without answers. Educational reforms in the sending of students abroad put the students together with their peers as never before to ask questions about the legitimacy of Manchu rule at a humiliating time in Chinese history. Military reform produced a new kind of soldier, trained in military academies with a healthy measure of patriotic propagandizing. In any stress upon nationalism, the alien "Manchus" were the most obvious "foreign" target. Administrative reform brought the reconceptualization of government institutions and raised questions about ends. Finally, constitutionalization opened the political door to the citizens, giving the people forums in which to debate, legislate, maneuver, and demand. In these arenas, it is not an exaggeration to call the Manchus' actions "revolutionary."

## The 1911 Revolution

The last act of the decade-long revolutionary drama was the revolution itself and the endgame abdication of the Manchus on February 12, 1912. The revolution on the larger national stage began almost accidentally in the city of Wuchang in the central Yangzi, when, on October 10, exploding gunpowder gave away potential rebels before they had planned to act. Acting then in desperation, they succeeded largely because the local garrison army had been depleted by the sending of army units upriver to deal with railroad unrest in Sichuan. The timing was terrible because there were no established leaders in the area who could take charge. The revolution's ideological father was Sun Yat-sen, yet when the revolution broke out, Sun was in the United States seeking funding from overseas Chinese; he did not make it back to China until December 25.

In the meantime, fighting raged between the Qing military and revolutionary forces. Yuan Shikai, the founder of the New Army, emerged as the key power broker in the struggle. A powerful traditional degree holder and dynastic official, Yuan had had no experience with republicanism, but a political deal committed the presidency of the new republic to him if he engineered the Manchu abdication. Most historians believe that the revolutionaries agreed to this in order to stop the fighting as quickly as possible so as to forestall the possibility that foreign powers in their treaty ports and concession areas might take advantage of the unrest to increase various kinds of imperialistic pressures and demands. The revolutionaries would come to rue the turn to Yuan.

In localities, the shape and the meaning of the revolution varied according to particular space. In most areas, the revolutionary acts were coups d'état, with local elites or military units seizing control. In some areas, reformist scholar-gentry and other elites who had been involved in reforms (for example, the recovery of railroad rights) simply stepped in to man temporary military governments. New Army men were often in the forefront of revolutionary action. In some areas, revolutionary organizations and secret societies were pivotal. In yet others, more peripheral than core, political and social chaos was the (dis)order of the day. People in many areas hung white flags in memory of the Ming, the last Chinese dynasty, and declared what was happening to be "restoration," the return of rule from Manchu to Chinese.

But the fuller meaning was indeed revolutionary. While the abolition of the civil service examination had destroyed the recruitment structure for political and social elites, the abolition of the monarchy demolished the whole political structure. In place for more than two thousand years, the Son of Heaven and the empire were gone, along with all the traditional political principles, laws, customs, and morality. In its place was an untried republic, as yet only a name without substance. As China entered the spring of 1912, it was beginning the process of building a new state and nation in a completely uncharted, unmarked future.

## MILITARIZATION AND POLITICAL OPTIONS

### The Republic: Problems

A new regime's initial years are often marked by political and military instability, by institutional fits and starts, by more life-and-death questions than answers. A decade before China became a republic, several powerful ideological and political forces still held the traditional Chinese state and society together: Confucianism; the state monarchy and bureaucracy; and the common classical language. With the abolition of the civil service examination, the demolition of the imperial system, and (within the next decade) the acceptance of a written vernacular, social and political fragmentation came to be a critical issue. Increasingly rapid modern changes worsened this fragmentation, not only within communities but especially *between* communities (core/periphery, urban/rural, eastern seaboard/hinterland) as they experienced change at varying rates. As the quest for China's modern identity grew more acute, new social groups (military, youth, women, and, increasingly, urban laborers) emerged, underscoring the pluralistic nature of republican society and culture. Sun Yat-sen's depiction of China as a "sheet of loose sand" seemed an apt description for the situation in which the country found itself.

There were no "how-to" manuals that could answer the difficult basic questions raised by the collapse of traditional civilization. What is the meaning of republicanism? What is its ethos and how is that ethos transferred to nonpolitical arenas? Who are the elites? What constitutes the legitimacy of elites or of a regime? How is this legitimacy to be established? Yet the broader twentieth-century Chinese revolution was born amid this political, social, and cultural incoherence, ignorance, and turmoil. It was a tortuous, often tragic quest for social approaches, patterns, and groupings that might provide the proper materials to build a public linked by common goals and interests. Like any search and experimentation, this revolution was uneven—developing in many different contexts, with many different actors, patterns, and dynamics.

## The Presidency of Yuan Shikai

From almost the beginning of his presidency, Yuan Shikai's moves betrayed a man who believed that the modern Chinese state and nation must be built from the center, with control exercised by a strong head of state and with short shrift given to popular sovereignty in the form of political parties and representative assemblies. Sun Yat-sen's Revolutionary Alliance, a revolutionary organization, was transmogrified into a political party—the Guomindang, or Nationalist Party—in the beginning days of the republic. Other parties were also formed at the time to vie in National Assembly elections held in December 1912, when there were also elections for provincial and county assemblies. The managing leader of the Guomindang was a young Hunanese, **Song Jiaoren**, who hoped to emerge as prime minister if the Guomindang gained the majority seats in the assembly. While these elections were marked by some corruption, they were remarkable for the relative smoothness with which they functioned; with the exception of elections in Taiwan in the 1990s, they were China's high point of electoral democracy in the twentieth century. The Guomindang won approximately 43 percent of the vote, a plurality among the multiple parties; they had taken 269 of 596 assembly seats.

In March 1913, as he was leaving Shanghai for Beijing to form the new government, Song Jiaoren was assassinated at the train station; Yuan was implicated in the killing. That tragedy was followed by Yuan's negotiations of a loan from a foreign consortium without even a nod to the national assembly's involvement. By the summer, open revolt had begun against Yuan's regime. This so-called "second revolution" ended in military defeat for the revolutionaries and the flight of Sun and others to Japan.

After forcing the National Assembly to ratify his election as president for a five-year term, Yuan outlawed the Guomindang in November, evicting its members from the assembly. Then in February 1914, he abolished all the assemblies—national, provincial, and county. It was clear that from Yuan's perspective, an assembly-studded political landscape was too risky and messy; he could not wield effective central control if he were challenged continually by political parties and assemblies.

Yuan's rule from 1914 until his death from uremia in June 1916 was marked by the tragicomedy of his efforts to reinstitute the monarchy and take the throne on New Year's Day 1916 as "Grand Constitutional Emperor." To Yuan, his move toward the throne may have been the logical extension of the abolition of political parties and representative assemblies: what better way to rebuild the centralized state and in the process deal with messy new forces than to do so in the mold of the monarchy, with its traditions and ethos? But it was a mistake. Even though the monarchy had been gone barely three years when Yuan began to make his first moves, reactions in 1916 showed that Chinese political culture had already cast it into the dustbin of history. Rebellion grew up out of provinces in southwest China, causing Yuan to backpedal to the presidency; his death in the midst of rebellion was undoubtedly a merciful and timely ending. In domestic policies, Yuan appears much the self-strengthener, adopting economic and education policies that would build Chinese wealth and development, but doing so with a reinstitution of tradition in the form of Confucianism as a state religion.

The outbreak of World War I presented China with the possibility of becoming a battleground for European powers that had spheres of influence on Chinese soil. To forestall that eventuality, China declared its neutrality. That action did not stop Japan from invading the German leasehold in Shandong Province in response to a request from its ally Britain to seize German properties in China. Then in January 1915, as European powers were preoccupied with the war, Japan acted to strengthen its hand in China, presenting Yuan's government with the **Twenty-one Demands**. This was a list demanding mostly economic rights and privileges in north and central China; but some demands struck more deeply into Chinese sovereignty, such as the stationing of Japanese police and economic advisers in the north. Yuan finally acceded to most of the demands, excepting the group stipulating advisers. The day of accession, May 7, was commemorated in subsequent years as National Humiliation Day.

## Descent Into Warlordism

So long as Yuan Shikai was alive, he was able to control the generals who had been trained under his command in the New Army early in the century; he had been their patron, and they, his students. With his death, the destructive genie of military competition was let loose to wreak havoc over the land; the goal was to seize Beijing and the government institutions and to be recognized as president of the republic. This struggle among the warlords, as they came to be called, produced one of the most disastrous and chaotic periods in twentieth-century China. While it technically ended in 1928, when the country was once again nominally unified, residual warlordism remained a problem into the 1940s.

Before the warlord situation became most serious in the early and mid-1920s, there was one last attempt to reinstall the monarchy. In early July 1917, a conservative military general, Zhang Xun, placed the last Qing emperor, then eleven years old, into power in the Forbidden City. But the "reign" lasted less than two weeks, as opposing generals took Beijing and ended the restoration. Never again would anyone attempt to restore the monarchy, though the chaos and destruction of the period as late as 1922 led people at least in one locality to opine "that the emergence of the rightful Son of Heaven would solve local and national problems."[6] The aborted 1917 restoration episode did reveal that the governmental institutions in the capital—the bureaucracy and the National Assembly, which had been reestablished after Yuan's death—were no longer the main players on the political stage. Those roles increasingly belonged to the military. Zhang, using military forces, had restored the emperor; opposing military forces had ousted him (and Zhang as well). Indeed, within six years, from late 1911 to the summer of 1917, struggles between military forces had three times determined the identity of the Chinese government.

In the 1920s, the governmental institutions became pawns in the struggle for military control of the capital, and by extension the country. The concerns of civilian officials focused more and more on maintaining their political power, and especially maintaining their own positions; in such a context, corruption tended to become a crucial dynamic, and often the deciding factor, in elections and policies. From mid-1916 until spring 1926, there were six different presidents of China and twenty-five cabinets. The high hopes of a productively functioning republic, with its ethos carrying the voice of the people into the halls of government, lay in shambles.

It was in fact the ethos of the military that began to infuse Chinese life. In these years, militarization began to emerge as a major dynamic of the century. While all warlords were military men and held territory of varying size, the name *warlord* covers many military types, and the different types differed in their goals. Some warlords perhaps actually had the potential to unite the Chinese nation and become heads of state. Men like central China's **Wu Peifu**, trained in both Confucianism and the military, or north China's **Feng Yuxiang**, who talked much about social reform, come to mind. These and others vied for the top. Other warlords had lesser goals, some regional, others local. Some warlords were simply thuggish. One of the more notorious was Zhang Zongchang, the "Dog-Meat General" in Shandong, whose troops were infamous for hanging strings of human heads on telegraph poles to elicit respect for their power.

Contenders for national power often formed coalitions in order to have greater numbers of troops and increased resources. Such coalitions were inherently unstable, for most often they were formed pragmatically for the realization of short-term or intermediate goals; they were not usually undergirded by close personal connections, and certainly not by ideological considerations. The essential considerations were mercenary and power-driven. Thus, coalitions would collapse if members of the group were lured away for a better deal from a rival militarist; as one militarist reportedly prognosticated, "We shall undoubtedly win. It is simply a matter of waiting for treason."[7]

The Beiyang militarists were separated into two main groups, the Anfu and the Zhili cliques. The first major war broke out between them in 1920. When the warlord of Manchuria, **Zhang Zuolin**, sided with the Zhili clique, it quickly defeated the Anfu clique. This victory, however, simply set up the next war—that between the victorious Zhili forces and the Fengtian forces of Zhang Zuolin, waged in 1922. Although the Zhili forces defeated Zhang's Fengtian troops, they had insufficient power to oust him from his Manchurian base. The third major clash, again between Zhili and Fengtian forces, was fought in 1924; it ended quickly when Zhili general Feng Yuxiang went over to Zhang's forces and the Zhili troops were defeated. But as might have been expected, by 1925 Feng and Zhang were at each other's throats in north China, a struggle that ended the next year with Zhang Zuolin in charge of Beijing. One of the tragedies of these struggles is that they were made bloodier and more destructive because various Western nations supplied arms and ammunition to the warlords they thought the best bets to seize state power. Obviously, if a pet warlord became president, the patron's position to reap benefits would be much enhanced. Examples of such foreign support were the British underwriting of central China's Wu Peifu, the Japanese support of Manchuria's Zhang Zuolin, and the Russian aid to Feng Yuxiang.

The warlord scourge led not only to loss of life, rape, widespread economic dislocation, and destruction of crops, cropland, agricultural infrastructure, and property; there were other catastrophes: warlord armies needed weapons and supplies—and that demanded money. Two sources of money that emerged as crucial to the warlord campaigns were opium and taxes. In the late Qing, the cultivation of opium had been nearly eradicated in most areas. Its ability to garner huge profits, however, made it attractive to warlords, and they forced the planting of opium instead of food crops. In some places this was accomplished by placing the land tax so high on land suitable for growing opium that opium was the only feasible thing to plant. Extraordinarily high taxes were placed on almost every conceivable item—from consumer goods to licenses, and from goods in transit to lifetime situations (for example, getting married, owning a pig, going to a brothel). Land taxes were collected far in advance—for perhaps more than ten years. With taxes reaching confiscatory levels and the taxpayers having no recourse, the economy of affected communities was wrecked; the people's livelihood was, as it were, left for dead. Further, like typhoons spawning tornadoes, warlord wars gave rise to widescale banditry. In many cases, what warlords did not succeed in destroying or taking, the bandits did.

Historians have seen the warlords, arising from a context of growing nationalism, to be the very antithesis of nationalism. Though some warlords aspired to unite the nation, the effect of their activity was radically to fragment a state whose identity had not really developed beyond that of the shadow of a collapsed civilization. Reliance on foreign arms and aid undercut the identity of a new nation standing on its own and was retrogressive in light of the late-Qing rights recovery. The very nature of warlordism produced a demoralized and devastated populace, enervating patriotism that might have inspired commitment to build a new China.

Finally, warlords and their activities clashed with the new forces of Chinese society, producing more bloodshed and tragedy. A case in point was the massacre of students near the Gate of Heavenly Peace on March 18, 1926. In the 1925–26 war between Feng and Zhang, Feng's forces had mined the sea approaches to Tianjin to prevent Zhang from landing there. The Japanese, who were Zhang's main patrons and saw the Tianjin area as their sphere of influence, protested the mining for its impact on their trade; they ordered the mines removed. Students in Beijing protested the Japanese ultimatum and interference in Chinese domestic affairs; government troops dispersed them. But on March 18, more students came out to demonstrate; when they tried to march to the office of the head of state, police opened fire and killed forty-seven students. The warlord wars had precipitated a crisis that, because of foreign interests in China, had brought about Japanese intrusion into Chinese affairs.

As tragic as was the loss of student lives on the Beijing streets, their numbers paled relative to the thousands of Chinese who had already died in the warlord struggles.[8] Lu Xun, China's most important twentieth-century writer, making specific reference to the March 18 tragedy, summed up the despair, cynicism, and sense of futility wrought by the age of the warlords:

> Time flows eternally on: the streets are peaceful again, for a few lives count for nothing in China. . . . As for any deeper significance, I think there is very little; for this was only an unarmed demonstration. The history of mankind's battle forward through bloodshed is like the formation of coal, where a great deal of wood is needed to produce a small amount of coal.[9]

## SOCIAL AND CULTURAL REVOLUTION

### *The Problem*

In one of Lu Xun's most famous stories, "A Madman's Diary," an official, suffering a fearful paranoia that everyone wants to kill and eat him, discovers an old history book: "My history has no chronology and scrawled over each page are the words: 'Virtue and Morality.' Since I could not sleep anyway, I read intently half the night, until I began to see words between the lines, the whole book being filled with the two words—'Eat people.' "[10] This scathing indictment of traditional Chinese society—that it mouths the proper Confucian pieties even as it destroys human lives—stands in a sense as a watchword for the cultural revolution that swept Chinese macroregional cores in the 1910s and 1920s. While Confucianism as an ideology had officially ended with the abolition of the civil service examination in 1905, it retained its stranglehold on the social and ethical aspects of Chinese society. In family life, the ancient Confucian social bonds emphasizing the importance of age and the male gender retained their sway, elevating the status and power of parents over children, of men over women. Children were betrothed by matchmakers in marriages to benefit families, not individuals. If one's fiancé died before marriage or if one's husband died early, the unmarried or widowed woman must remain forever chaste, choosing death rather than becoming once again intimately involved. Young women were forbidden by mothers-in-law to unbind their feet or to attend school. The power of "Confucius and sons" was literally that of life and death.

With the collapse of old verities and institutions and with the rise of new social and political alternatives, there should be little surprise that slogans like "Down with Confucius and sons" began to fill new newspapers and journals and to echo in street demonstrations. Sometimes the language of the slogan was acted out in the taking of life itself. A young woman in the distant interior of Gansu threw herself down a well rather than deal with a mother-in-law who forbade her to unbind her feet. In Hunan, a Miss Zhao, betrothed to a man she despised, slit her throat as she was being carried in her bridal chair. Sons disregarded parental wishes and even orders regarding life decisions. Suicide rates tell the tragic story: among Chinese women, suicide rates were highest among those in their late teens and twenties; in the early twentieth century, such suicides occurred at a rate more than double that of Japan, and ten times that of Sweden.

## The New Culture Movement

One extraordinarily influential vehicle for the expression of contempt for the old and hope for a new social and cultural world was the journal *New Youth*, whose publication began in 1915. Edited by a returned student from France, **Chen Duxiu**, the journal called on the young to struggle "to exert [their] intellect, discard resolutely the old and the rotten, regard them as enemies," and to be independent, progressive, dynamic, cosmopolitan, and scientific (see document 6, appendix 2).[11] With a circulation of up to sixteen thousand copies, the journal was read by students in all parts of China. Not only did it offer a forum for students to discuss issues, but from 1917 on it was written in the vernacular.

To that point, the language of printed materials, whether books, newspapers, or journals, had been classical or literary Chinese. The syntax of the classical style was difficult: it valued concision, often omitting subjects and objects; it was marked by characters that served as particles giving the sentence a tone or a particular turn; and it used no punctuation. Traditional scholars had apparently believed that anyone intelligent enough to read the classical language should be intelligent enough to know where to punctuate it. But because of the concision, the particles, and the lack of punctuation, it was not only difficult but open to all sorts of ambiguity. In addition, it had two other strikes against it: it was a great obstacle to increased literacy among the Chinese masses, and the development of a modern Chinese nation-state required a more literate public—reform of language thus was crucial. And the construction of a new political and social culture simply *required* a new language; it was impossible to build a new culture on a language intimately connected to and expressive of the old culture of "eating people." In Lu Xun's tale of the madman, the opening segment, which details the madman's "recovery" and his return to a bureaucratic "people-eating" position, is written in classical Chinese, whereas the diary itself, which the reader comes to see is not that of a madman but of one enlightened, is written in the vernacular.

Another strong proponent of the vernacular, or *baihua*, was **Hu Shi**, who had completed his doctorate at Columbia University, studying with philosopher John Dewey. Chen and Hu became colleagues at Beijing University, which, like Chen's *New Youth*, emerged as central in what came to be known as the New Culture Movement. Established in the Manchu reform effort of the early twentieth century, Beijing University did not have a reputation as a serious institution of study or research; rather, an education there was seen as a ticket to a governmental bureaucratic position. Appointed university chancellor in 1916, **Cai Yuanpei** was determined to change the reputation and the reality. If a new language was to form the basis for a new culture that was to be forged by the young, then Beijing University should be the laboratory where the shaping of that culture should be centered. Cai thus gathered scholars of every intellectual and political stripe at the university to discuss possibilities for the new China, to debate ideas about the form and shape of China's modern state, and to argue and contend in an atmosphere of unfettered academic freedom. The excitement among faculty and students involved in trying to devise a blueprint for modern China must have been almost palpable.

Although the phrase came to be associated with a policy of Mao Zedong in the 1950s, the New Culture Movement, extending into the mid-1920s, was a period when "a hundred schools of thought" contended. In essence, the movement was an intellectual revolution. In classroom and debating hall, in study societies and literary organizations, in a vast outpouring of several hundred new newspapers and journals, men and women, old and young, met and contended, their ideas set forward to battle opposing thoughts, to complement similar schemes, to challenge the status quo as well as propose remedies for the future. Anarchists, socialists, Christians, atheists, Buddhists, Marxists, pacifists, pragmatists, scientists, metaphysicists . . . the list could go on; all debated the potential viability and validity of new values. The key word was *new*, the adjective modifying various nouns to produce the names of many magazines: *Youth, Tide, Life, Literature and Art, Society, Epoch, Tides of Zhejiang*. The sense of having entered a new historical epoch in which people must act in new ways was pervasive among those involved in the debates. The emphasis on individualism was greater in this period than in any in modern China's history. The absence of a powerful state structure and the search for a new social, political, and ideological orthodoxy also created a liberating context for the young. But most important was the casting off of the ideological shackles of patriarchy and family authority, a liberation that permitted the championing of individual wills and efforts to realize individual goals.

The milieu of intellectual quest was stimulated during these years by lecture tours of foreigners of various intellectual persuasions. Hu Shi's teacher John Dewey spent 1919 and 1920 living and lecturing in China, spreading his message of pragmatism. In 1921 and 1922, philosopher Bertrand Russell lectured widely not only on his intellectual interest of mathematical logic but also on pacifism, a subject that in the violent warlord period must have struck many chords. Margaret Sanger, feminist and birth-control advocate, lectured in China in 1922, her ideas harmonizing with the period's emphasis on women's liberation. The visit of Nobel laureate Rabindranath Tagore, of India, in 1924 touched off a heated debate over Tagore's message extolling Asian cultures and warning about the importation of too much Western civilization. Such foreign lectures served as validation for some of the new ideas emerging in the intellectual debates, even as they prodded and stimulated more thought and involved more and more people in the debates.

Tagore and his supporters aside, there were widespread calls for two "men" whose backgrounds were clearly in the West and whose names became watchwords at the time and for much of the twentieth century: Mr. De and Mr. Sai. Mr. De(mocracy) became the rallying cry of those who bemoaned the shambles of the Chinese state, destroyed and undercut by warlords and venal politicians and bureaucrats. Though the memory of the brief burst of democracy in 1912 and 1913 was fading, the promise of democracy seemed strengthened by the victory of the "democratic" Allied powers in World War I and by the

Bolshevik revolution in Russia. Mr. Sai (Mr. Science) was in the vanguard of the modern world; whatever was "scientific" seemed progressive. Science was seen as an instrument of enlightenment. To follow the scientific path seemed to promise the best for the future of the nation and the individual. Though a few intellectuals bemoaned the use to which science had been put by the West, seeing in the destructiveness of the war the bankruptcy of Western values, the vast majority of Chinese saw science as a panacea for the country's ills.

## The May Fourth Movement

The New Culture Movement is part of what is generally known as the **May Fourth Movement**, an amorphous range of activities that can be dated from the founding of *New Youth* in 1915 to 1923 or 1924 and that, taken together, can be considered a cultural revolution. The movement takes its name from a demonstration, primarily of students, in Beijing on May 4, 1919, a nationalistically charged incident that substantially changed the direction and import of the whole cultural revolution effort. After Japan had seized German-held Shandong, the island-nation spent the war years concluding secret agreements with Allied powers confirming its right to maintain control of the province. Not surprisingly then, world leaders at the postwar Versailles Conference decided to allow Japan to continue to hold Shandong Province. In reaction, on May 4 about three thousand students from thirteen area colleges marched from Tian'anmen Square to the foreign-legation quarters to protest this decision. Marked by sporadic violence and numbers of arrests, the demonstration was the first salvo in what became a nationwide protest movement.

In the capital, the demonstration led to the establishment of a citywide student union, bringing together students from middle schools and high schools with those from colleges and universities; women students were specifically included. This student union served as prototype for similar organizations in Shanghai, Wuhan, Tianjin, and other cities, and ultimately for a Student Union of the Republic of China, established in June. Students served as the yeast, as it were, in a rising nationalistic ferment. At Shanghai especially, patriotic sentiment spread among businessmen, merchants, and laborers, culminating in a general strike beginning on June 5. Its goal: to try to force the Chinese delegation at Versailles to refuse to sign the peace treaty. Its trump card was that Shanghai was the economic heart of the Republic of China and that a long general strike could bring an already weak economy to its knees. The extent of the rising tide of nationalism can be seen in that even notorious underworld organizations, the Green and Red gangs, ordered their members not to disrupt the strike. The announcement on July 2 that the delegation at Versailles had refused to sign the treaty meant that the efforts of the student unions and the general strike among a wide array of the populace had led to a political victory.

Such a positive result from the perspective of patriotic Chinese had crucial ramifications for the direction of the May Fourth Movement. Two main camps began to emerge in what would become a struggle for the heart of the movement. There were those who began to point to the spring and summer of 1919 as what could be accomplished through direct political action: politically inspired organizations and a general strike had forced the government to act as the students and strikers had wanted. In order to change China, why not continue this kind of political action? How, they argued, can we build a modern Chinese culture while people who hold political power retain the power to jail and even shoot down those who are in the vanguard of modern change? First, they asserted, we must change the political system to one more conducive to other modern changes. Direct, even violent, political action must become the central focus of activity. A leading proponent of this view was Chen Duxiu, the *New Youth* editor and dean of the School of Letters at Beijing University.

The other camp contended that any meaningful political change must be preceded by, and therefore must be built upon, cultural change. By the nature of things, according to proponents of this view, cultural change cannot be engineered rapidly by tools like violence; it is a slow effort based more on evolutionary rather than revolutionary dynamics. One of the most important advocates of this path was Hu Shi, whose own predilections and education under Dewey must surely have inspired this solution. Academic study and reform were the keys. "There is no liberation *in toto* or reconstruction *in toto*. Liberation means liberation from this or that institution, from this or that belief, for this or that individual; it is liberation bit by bit, drop by drop."[12] For this reason, Hu attacked what he called *isms*, overarching systemic blueprints that offered a way out of China's predicament; specific problems, he argued, called for specific solutions, not for all-embracing creeds or systems.

There were difficulties in this approach for many Chinese. Certainly, for a civilization in crisis, this "bit by bit, drop by drop" solution was not in the least intellectually satisfying. But more important, this approach would take many years, perhaps decades, even a century or more; even then, it would bring no guarantee that it could remake China before the country might disintegrate and fall completely into Western hands. As one of the May Fourth intellectuals, Shen Dingyi, put it, "Under the present circumstances, part of the Chinese people and their land has become fish and pork on the cutting board. . . . [P]owers . . . hold their knives [in readiness]. . . . We should take over the knife, kick away the cutting board, and refuse to be fish and pork."[13] For many Chinese intellectuals and students, so recently focused on individual liberation, the emerging priority came to be the fate of the nation, the logic being that without national liberation individual liberation would be ultimately meaningless.

Thus, from 1919 on, and picking up steam into the early 1920s, the direction of the May Fourth Movement changed. For this reason, at least one Chinese historian has called the movement "an abortive revolution because its intellectual goal of enlightenment remained unrealized" when the "revolutionary imperative of national salvation had eclipsed the demands for enlightenment."[14] It is also significant that, as in traditional times, during the New Culture Movement intellectuals were in charge; they were, as one Chinese historian has put it, "the subject in relation to the object they wanted to enlighten—the people."[15] Never again in the twentieth century would that be the case, just as never again would individual liberation become a social or political goal. Once the Nationalists and Communists were ensconced in power, intellectuals would no longer be in the historical vanguard; they would become instead a distrusted group subject to all sorts of suppression and mistreatment.

The *isms* that received increasing attention for their possibilities in dealing with China's problems were Marxism, and after the success of the Bolsheviks in 1917, Leninism. A year after the Russian Revolution, *New Youth* commemorated the anniversary, and six months later (May 1919) the journal devoted a complete issue to articles on Marxism. Intellectuals and journalists formed small study groups in Shanghai and Beijing to discuss socialism and Marxism. **Mao Zedong**, a student at Beijing University, returned to his home in Hunan Province to form such a study group. The Shanghai Marxist Study Society was the first cell in what would become the Chinese Communist Party. Agents from the Communist International (Comintern) made their first linkage to Shanghai and Beijing intellectuals, who were more and more committed to Marxism in 1920. The party was formally organized in July 1921.

At the opening of the twenty-first century, when Communism in most areas of the world has collapsed after a miserable record throughout the twentieth century, it is difficult to comprehend the appeals of Marxism-Leninism to the Chinese of the early 1920s. On a most basic level, the "nothing succeeds like success" rule provides one answer: this ideology had been successful in overthrowing autocratic rule in Russia with the Leninist party model providing the vehicle to victory. A second appeal of Marxism was that it was "scientific." Marx's idea of historical materialism explained the past and the chief dynamic of historical development—that history moves through stages on the basis of the class struggle over the means of production. The theory offered a vision of revolutionary progress as one moved to the Communist utopia. The most important appeal of Marxism-Leninism was that it appeared to offer a sweeping solution to China's myriad problems. "It provided a self-consistent, universalistic, and 'scientific' view of the world's history which enabled one to reject the imperialist West in the name of Western 'scientific thought' and explain China's humiliating backwardness as due to her bondage to 'capitalist imperialism.' "[16] Leninism further offered the revolutionary vehicle, a tightly organized and controlled party, and an individual revolutionary ideal shaped by patriotism and self-sacrifice.

Historians have generally ranked the May Fourth Movement alongside the abolition of the civil service examination and the toppling of the monarchy and imperial regime as one of the most significant revolutionary milestones in the course of China's twentieth-century revolution. The first two milestones cast off the old and necessitated the as-yet-unknown new; this third milestone, while also casting off the old, began for the first time an earnest search for the new. Certainly it is an important demarcation in the intellectual and cultural history of China. It has been called China's Renaissance, perhaps in part because of the beginning use of the vernacular; it was in the Renaissance that writing in the Western vernaculars first came into practice. It has also been called the Chinese Enlightenment, a term recalling the important role of science and experimentation and the casting out of tradition. It may be called a cultural revolution, bringing to mind the Cultural Revolution of the 1960s and 1970s, in which the old and traditional were discarded, even trashed.

Because of its discarding of traditional Chinese culture, it has drawn strong reactions from various political forces whose self-definition has had almost necessarily to take a stand on the meaning of the traditional culture for a modern Chinese nation-state. For the Nationalist regime of Chiang Kai-shek and his successors, it seemed too radical a movement, destroying much good that lay in Chinese tradition and linked too closely with the rise of Chinese Communism. The Nationalists viewed the movement with considerable distrust and suspicion. The Communists, whose party grew out of the intellectual ferment and issues of the movement, while looking kindly on the May Fourth period have looked askance at the first phase, which emphasized the role of intellectuals in enlightening society so as to realize individual aspirations. Condemning emphasis on the individual as "bourgeois," the Communists throughout their history have struck out at both those who maintained such a mentality and intellectuals in general, holding that the group, by nature, seemed tainted with the toxin of individualism. Thus, the reaction of both major political parties has been tinged with negativism about this crucial modern movement.

## NATIONALISM AND ITS PROPONENTS

In the 1980s and 1990s, nationalism became a hot topic in the world. World trouble spots like the Balkans and the Middle East raised questions about the meaning of nationalism and its relationship to ethnicity. Scholars opened new inquiries into the meaning and dynamics of nationalism and its relationship to class and to gender. For Chinese early in the twentieth century, nationalism was a new concept. In imperial times, China had seen itself as the "central country," with that centrality situated clearly in its culture. But the nineteenth-century nightmare of foreign invasion and military defeat had decentered China in its own self-conception to the far periphery of nations. By the early twentieth century, Chinese political, social, economic, and intellectual leaders had been forced to see China as one of many nations and as one of the most impotent. Their understanding of the nation was relative to their experience of other nations, and because of the continuing imperialist pressure, their view was mostly unidimensional: weakness was the transcendent attribute of the Chinese nation. That weakness came to be drummed into the populace through such annual public commemorations as National Humiliation Day, the anniversary of China's 1915 acceptance of the Twenty-one Demands. The question of the early twentieth century thus became how to build national power as quickly as possible so as to forestall not only continuing national humiliations but even dismemberment.

### The Development of the Political Parties

A strong government was the sine qua non. Establishing such a government meant developing political and military forces that could defeat the warlords and their supporters and then deal with the imperialists. Sun Yat-sen was the best-known nationalist spokesman. He had fled to Japan after the brief "second revolution" against Yuan Shikai in 1913. In the next few years, Sun came to see that establishing the strong government of a full-fledged republic would require a muscular party and some effective military apparatus. In Japan, he had experimented with setting up a more tightly organized party with party members swearing personal loyalty to him, but this demand alienated so many people who were with him in Japan that Sun dropped the idea. When he returned to China in 1916, he spent most of his time in Guangzhou, reorganizing his parliamentary-style Guomindang still as an open party and trying to link himself to the area's warlord; such forces, Sun surmised, might be used for his purposes. But the party reorganization had little import, and various attempted military arrangements did not work. During these years, Sun was clearly spinning his wheels.

When Communists held their first party congress, in Shanghai in July 1921, only twelve delegates attended. They established the Communist Party, based on Marxist study cells that had met for several years and that had been advised by Comintern agents Gregory Voitinsky in 1920 and Hendricus Sneevliet in 1921; with such a small group of committed Communists, Comintern revolutionary expertise was crucial. Chen Duxiu was selected the party's secretary-general. Later that year, Sneevliet met with Sun Yat-sen to discuss China's situation and its relationship to the Soviet Union. With Moscow's approval, Sneevliet began to urge that the Communists also join Sun's Guomindang, a policy the young Communist Party did not initially support. It was a question that divided the Comintern just as it divided Chinese Communists: given the very small number of Communists and the reality that they had insufficient power to accomplish much, should Communists adopt the short-term tactic of joining bourgeois parties for national ends in a **united front** against common enemies? Lenin said yes: a temporary united front made tactical sense; once the common enemies were defeated, the united front would end and the erstwhile allies would then become enemies. Others in the Comintern (the Indian M. N. Roy and, later, Trotsky) argued that national ends should play no role as people around the world joined in class struggle against the forces of feudalism and capitalism.

Lenin won this bout in the Comintern, and, after his death, Stalin championed the same position. The sway of the Comintern over the infant Chinese party was strong. Though most Chinese Communists favored an outright alliance between the parties, after the second party congress, in mid-1922, the party agreed to accept a "bloc within" system, whereby individual Communist Party members could also join the Guomindang. This was ratified at the party's third congress, in summer 1923. Comintern agents' talks with Sun about some sort of united front had made clear he favored the "bloc within" because he ultimately did not want two major parties vying with each other.

In late January 1923, Sun's talks with a Soviet diplomat produced a joint statement noting that the Soviet system could not be introduced into China, but that Russia would support China's national independence and reunification.

The thrust of the support was tutorial: Russia would provide advice and training for Sun Yat-sen to restructure his party and to form a party army. In autumn 1923, the Comintern dispatched **Mikhail Borodin** to help reorganize the Guomindang. A Russian Jew, Borodin had lived in the United States from 1905 to 1917, had returned to Russia at the time of the revolution, and had since served as Comintern agent in Mexico and several European countries. In China, Borodin amassed substantial power quickly. Under his leadership, the Guomindang (GMD) was restructured along Leninist party lines according to the concept of **democratic centralism**, a structure that presents a façade of democratic-style discussion but that in substance, once the center has made a decision, is really centralized autocracy. Further, because of surveillance operatives at every level and in every arena of party activity, such a party is extraordinarily difficult to subvert. By early 1924, then, China's two parties were both Leninist-style organs.

The GMD's ideology was more homegrown. In 1923 and 1924, Sun had set down his own thinking about the direction and goals of the party and state; he had spoken of many of these ideas since the days of the Revolutionary Alliance. Known as the **Three Principles of the People**, they championed nationalism, democracy, and socialism (vaguely described as "people's livelihood"); the clearest of these and the one with the greatest immediate appeal was nationalism (see document 7, appendix 2). As befitted one who shaped a party and its ideas, Sun was also named party leader for life.

For any seizure of power, a capable military force was a prerequisite, even more so when the nation was ruled by congeries of warlords and when society had become increasingly used to political decisions made by force of arms. Under Borodin's leadership, a military academy was established on the island of **Whampoa**, downstream from Guangzhou. Named commandant was Chiang Kai-shek (Mandarin pronunciation, *Jiang Jieshi*), "a somewhat irregular member of Sun's entourage," who in mid-1923 had served as chief of staff of Sun's so-called Field Headquarters.[17] Chiang was also head of a delegation that spent autumn 1923 in Moscow studying military affairs. The Whampoa academy's course of study was six months; almost five hundred cadets formed the first class, beginning in June 1924. Sun's Three Principles of the People was the ideological core of their training. Faculty and administrative staff were balanced between Communists and Nationalists, with the former being part of the bloc within. Despite the conspicuous presence of Communists and

Comintern advisers (there were about a thousand Russian military advisers in China by early 1925), the cadets became fiercely loyal to Chiang and came to play a role as his most supportive faction.

## The Turning Point—1925

The realities of Chinese political culture tend to produce political parties that are composed of factions based on personal connections or of coalitions of factions and personal networks. The glue of connections that hold personal networks together is the strongest political binding agent. Factions or coalitions of factions held together by ideology, approach, or goals are much less cohesive, in both the long term and the short term. Sun Yat-sen, the most prominent national figure in China, headed a Guomindang with many factions and networks. All owed personal loyalty and support to him, but among the factions and networks there was considerable competition—and substantial disagreement about policy and ideology. On the political right were those who believed that the Russians had too much power in shaping the Chinese revolution, that Borodin had become the key player in decision making, and that the bloc within was a bad policy. On the political left were those whose political positions were similar to those of the Communists, offering some support for social and economic as well as political revolution, though they may have had doubts about the extent of power of the Soviet advisers. In the center were those like Chiang Kai-shek who were making their own way, supporters of Sun and his working with the Soviets, but capable of going to the right or left, depending on contingencies. The continual presence and important role of the Communists within the party kept the issue alive and usually, but not always, just below the surface of day-to-day activities.

Then Sun Yat-sen died. On a trip to Beijing in early 1925 to discuss the national situation with Zhang Zuolin, the warlord currently controlling the capital, he became ill. Surgery showed incurable liver cancer; he died on March 12. Transformed overnight into a national hero, Sun became a symbol of patriotism and unfinished revolution. But a symbol, for all its power, cannot hold parties together. The rumblings of discontent that had occasionally risen to the surface now became open. The situation was worsened by what has become known as the **May Thirtieth Movement**. At a Japanese-owned textile mill in Shanghai, a Chinese worker was killed by a Japanese guard. On May 30, thousands of demonstrators amassed before the police station to demand the release of several students who had been jailed after an earlier demonstration. With little warning, a British inspector gave orders to fire on the crowd, killing eleven and wounding at least twenty. These killings were compounded by more murder. In June, British troops in Guangzhou opened fire on demonstrators, killing fifty-two and wounding more than a hundred more. These shootings galvanized the Chinese people; demonstrations of rage and revolutionary fervor swept the country.

The contingencies of Sun's death and the May Thirtieth Movement put great pressure on the parties; the high feeling of the demonstrations suggested that the revolution itself was near and that revolutionary goals (which might remain vague if the revolution were not in sight) now had to be sharpened. But such honing of goals necessarily drove greater wedges between the factions and networks than already existed. The remainder of the year saw an increasingly malevolent polarization. In August, **Liao Zhongkai**, a close protégé of Sun linked to the Guomindang left wing, was assassinated, with party members from the right wing implicated in the killing. From November 1925 into January 1926, a group from the right met in the **Western Hills** section of Beijing before Sun's coffin, demanding that Borodin be dismissed and that the relationship with the Communist Party be dropped. But at the second Guomindang congress in January, 60 percent of the 278 delegates were leftists or Communists, 23 percent might be termed centrists, and only 16 percent were rightists. As a result, and indicative of the polarization, in March the rightists held their own party congress in Shanghai, charting their own direction for the future.

Meantime, Commandant Chiang at Whampoa was becoming more suspicious of the aims of the Communists. On March 20, when a gunboat commanded by a Communist officer mysteriously neared Whampoa island, Chiang, reportedly fearful that a coup against him was under way, undertook his own coup against Communists in the area. Although Borodin was not in Guangzhou, Chiang arrested more than thirty Russian advisers and declared martial law. As a result of these actions, Borodin later agreed to a substantial decrease of Communist power and prerogative in the party, allegedly because of pressures from Stalin, who evidently did not perceive the growing dangers to the Communist effort. With any immediate political threat under control, Chiang continued plans for the military campaign to unite the country. The episode had revealed Chiang's active suspicion about Communist intentions.

In July 1926, leading his National Revolutionary Army (NRA), Chiang began the **Northern Expedition**, a two-pronged campaign to reach the Yangzi River and secure south and south central China for the Guomindang. The armies on the western route, moving up through Hunan Province, most quickly reached their goal. They were already fighting in the Yangzi area in late August, and they took the key tri-city metropolis of Wuhan on October 10. Units on this western route then turned to Jiangxi Province, capturing it by November 8. Despite some serious problems—summer floods, cholera, and transport difficulties—the success of the western route NRA was remarkably rapid. There are a number of explanations. Historians have pointed to the nature of the army itself: trained solidly for two years and imbued with national feeling, this new military force was strictly forbidden to prey upon the population by looting and raping, the usual modus operandi of warlord armies. Russian advisers played key roles. The general strategy is credited to Russian general Blyukher; each corps and even some divisions had Russian advisers. There were locale-specific reasons for the success. Rivalries among four warlords in Hunan Province allowed the NRA to speed up their conquest; further, success bred success, as the early military victories in this area brought able troops from Guizhou warlords into the Nationalist cause.

But perhaps the most important reason for the relatively easy military victory of the western route army was the political work that both preceded and accompanied the campaign. The movement for farmers' associations had grown rapidly in the year following the May Thirtieth Incident. Graduates of the Guomindang's Farmers Movement Training Institute, always chaired by a Communist member of the Guomindang, had actively begun to organize farmers' associations, in 1925 mostly in Guangdong Province, but beginning in early 1926 in Hunan as well. Mao Zedong, active in the mass mobilization in Hunan, his home province, reported that from January to June 1926 the organizational activity was underground work, but it became open with the arrival of the NRA (see document 9, appendix 2).[18] This activity in addition to the army's good treatment of the people and their property helped to win over the local population to the Nationalist cause. Farmers' association members served as scouts, guides, and porters for the NRA; people along the campaign route offered food and water to the troops; farmers assisted by harassing the enemy's rear.

Coinciding with and following the successful campaign, there was a frenzy of mass mobilization of farmers and laborers. Whereas before the Northern Expedition in Hunan, Hubei, and Jiangxi, the membership in farmers' associations numbered fewer than 50,000, Communist leaders claimed by the end of 1926 that there were 1.5 million organized farmers in ninety-one counties of Hunan and Hubei alone. Most certainly an exaggeration, this figure nevertheless points to a gargantuan increase in farmers now politically mobilized. The organizers toned down the rhetoric of class struggle, stressing instead lowering rents and taxes, reducing food prices, and opening grain-storage facilities at times of shortages. But this agenda naturally incurred the hostility of landlords, who took retaliatory and often violent actions against tenants, responses that elicited violent reactions in an escalating struggle between the classes. Violent outbursts also accompanied the spread of labor mobilization. In the wake of the military victory, dozens of unions were formed by mostly Communist organizers; by spring 1927, an estimated 400,000 workers were in unions, 90,000 of them in industry. Agitation for higher wages and better working conditions led to a wave of strikes in November 1926. Joining the farmers' associations and unions in assertive public demonstrations were others, notably women and students, who took to the streets to denounce imperialism and to parade for the realization of a new Chinese nation.

Such mass activity raised the question of where the revolution was headed: should it remain primarily political in its call for ousting warlords and imperialists? or should it take on social and economic goals as well? Increasingly, in fall 1926 those two ideological stances became associated with particular places. Wuhan, where Borodin and members of the Guomindang Left had traveled, became the center of the mass mobilization. The city of Nanchang in Jiangxi Province, which Chiang made his military capital while leading the eastern route campaign, also became the capital of sorts of the Guomindang Right, now more and more headed by Chiang himself. Relations between Borodin and Chiang became bitterly hostile in late 1926; in March 1927, Borodin and the Guomindang Left named **Wang Jingwei** as Guomindang leader in direct challenge to Chiang. In response, Chiang struck out at Communists and leftists in Jiangxi. Disagreements over military strategy only exacerbated what had become an unbridgeable rift.

At the end of March, Chiang took Shanghai. Like the "softening up" of the Hunan route by precampaign organizing, the work of leftists in organizing laborers and the leadership of their unions made Chiang's task of seizing the metropolis easier. By late 1926, there were hundreds of thousands of organized workers in the city, then controlled by warlord Sun Chuanfang. In late February, as the NRA took the city of Hangzhou, to Shanghai's southwest, workers under Communist and leftist leadership staged a general strike to undercut the warlord Sun's power. Though it was broken by Sun, the six-day strike politically mobilized workers and showed the strength of Communist power. Then on March 21, another general strike was called, involving more than 600,000 workers. Heavy fighting erupted as workers cut electrical and telephone lines and occupied railway and police stations. The action paved the way for the entrance of Chiang and the NRA.

Chiang, already suspicious of the actions of leftists in Wuhan, was faced with a tense situation of leftist and labor power. After discussions with city business elites and the underworld **Green Gang**, with whom he had had ties since the 1910s, he moved to attack those who had made it easier for him to seize the city. On April 12, Green Gang members and forces loyal to Chiang attacked all union headquarters; protests in the aftermath of these attacks led to NRA soldiers opening fire on civilians. In this purge, hundreds were killed in the bloody attacks and thousands fled the city in panic. This was the beginning of what from the leftist side is called the White Terror, which spread over the country and continued well into 1928. It was an effort to destroy the power of the Left, and especially the Communists, who had attained so much power because of "bloc within" party membership. As one historian put it, "Chiang had shown his true colors: he had emerged as a representative of the 'national bourgeoisie' and [then he] defied the Guomindang [and those in Wuhan] by forming his own government in Nanjing (on April 18, 1927)."[19]

Both the Communists and the Guomindang Left in Wuhan had choices to make in the disarray brought by the purge. There were stillborn efforts to begin a rural revolution, but the political uncertainty precluded any effective action. Stalin continued to call for the Communists to work with the Left and to strike out at those allied with Chiang. Given the political realities of the purge, the secretary-general of the Chinese Communist Party (CCP) cynically said that these orders were "like taking a bath in a toilet."[20] The Left began to doubt the intentions of the Communists, especially after one agent showed left-wing leaders one of Stalin's telegrams. Their inauguration of discussions with Chiang spelled doom for the Communist effort. In late June, Russian advisers and some of Borodin's staff began to leave. The split between the CCP and the GMD Left came in mid-July; Borodin himself, after four years of substantial power on the Chinese scene, left at the end of July. The last months of 1927 saw sporadic Communist efforts to rise up and establish CCP-led regimes, but they were all short-lived and ineffective. Mao's efforts in the so-call **Autumn Harvest Uprisings** petered out when he could get only about two thousand "troops" to attack the city of Changsha. An effort to take Nanchang in Jiangxi Province was put down by a general involved in the initial uprising. The "Canton commune," founded by Communists and workers in that southern city, lasted only two days and ended in a bloodbath.

By August 1928, Chiang had reached Beijing, and at least on the map he had unified China for the first time since the death of Yuan Shikai had given birth to the warlords. The Nationalist Revolution grew out of the uneasy united-front collaboration of the two Leninist-style parties, the Chinese

Communist Party and the Guomindang. Now, in the success of the Northern Expedition, the CCP was vanquished, seemingly dead after a short life of six years. Stalin's policy of trying to call the shots from Moscow had been a tragic mistake. Yet in many ways the important role of Russian aid and advisers was a harbinger of other foreign aid that would benefit China later, from the United States in the 1940s and the Soviet Union in the 1950s. The Communist Party would rise again, but its leaders would be of a different sort than the May Fourth intellectuals who in the main had formed and given life to the party in this, its first incarnation. Finally, the Nationalist Revolution had been the springboard for the rise to power of Chiang Kai-shek. He was now faced with the immense tasks of reconstruction following years of war and of structuring a new viable Chinese state.

## NOTES

1. Mary Clabaugh Wright, "Introduction: The Rising Tide of Change," in Mary Clabaugh Wright, ed., *China in Revolution: The First Phase, 1900–1913* (New Haven: Yale University Press, 1968), p. 30.

2. For example, the old "eight-legged" style in writing examination essays was abolished in August 1901.

3. R. Keith Schoppa, *Chinese Elites and Political Change* (Cambridge: Harvard University Press, 1982), pp. 121–22.

4. Evelyn S. Rawski, *Education and Popular Literacy in Ch'ing China* (Ann Arbor: University of Michigan Press, 1979), p. 18.

5. Schoppa, *Chinese Elites*, pp. 123–24.

6. Ibid., p. 95. The opinion came from elites in Fenghua County in Zhejiang Province.

7. Cited in James Sheridan, *Chinese Warlord* (Stanford: Stanford University Press, 1966), p. 21.

8. It is difficult to estimate military casualties. One historian has suggested that until the battles in the mid-1920s, several hundred were killed per battle, but that in the mid- and late 1920s, each battle likely claimed several thousand lives. There were large numbers of troops in the field: in early 1928, the Guomindang military totaled about seven hundred thousand troops; their warlord opponents had about four hundred thousand. The number of civilian casualties is unknown. See Ch'i Hsi-sheng, *Warlord Politics in China, 1916–1928* (Stanford: Stanford University Press, 1976), pp. 138–41.

9. Cited in Jonathan Spence, *The Gate of Heavenly Peace* (New York: Viking, 1981), p. 197.

10. Lu Hsun, "A Madman's Diary," in *Selected Stories of Lu Hsun* (Beijing: Foreign Languages Press, 1972), p. 10.

11. Cited in Chow Tse-tsung, *The May Fourth Movement* (Stanford: Stanford University Press, 1967), p. 46.

12. Cited in John K. Fairbank, Edwin O. Reischauer, and Albert M. Craig, *East Asia: The Modern Transformation* (Boston: Houghton Mifflin, 1965), p. 669.

13. R. Keith Schoppa, *Blood Road: The Mystery of Shen Dingyi in Revolutionary China* (Berkeley: University of California Press, 1995), p. 65.

14. Leo Ou-fan Lee, "Modernity and Its Discontents: The Cultural Agenda of the May Fourth Movement," in Kenneth Lieberthal et al., eds., *Perspectives on Modern China, Four Anniversaries* (Armonk, N.Y.: M. E. Sharpe, 1991), p. 173.

15. Ibid., p. 174.

16. Fairbank, Reischauer, and Craig, *East Asia*, p. 670.

17. These descriptions come from C. Martin Wilbur and Julie Lien-ying How, *Missionaries of Revolution* (Cambridge: Harvard University Press, 1989), p. 87.

18. Mao Zedong, "Report on an Investigation of the Peasant Movement in Hunan," in *Selected Readings*, pp. 24–25.

19. Jonathan Spence, *The Search for Modern China*, (New York: Norton, 1990), p. 354.

20. Quoted in C. Martin Wilbur, *The Nationalist Revolution in China, 1923–1928* (Cambridge: Harvard University Press, 1983), p. 131.

# CHAPTER THREE

# Social Revolution: Alternatives for State and Nation, 1928–60

## STRUGGLES TO RECONSTRUCT CHINESE SOCIETY

### The Nature of Guomindang Control: The Republic of China, 1928–37

In the decade before Japan's 1937 invasion, both the Guomindang and a reborn Communist Party experimented with various approaches, old and new, in their efforts to establish a modern Chinese nation-state, or at least to begin that process. Having risen on the powerful wave of nationalism, Chiang Kai-shek had the opportunity to assert Chinese nationalism vis-à-vis the seemingly omnipresent imperialist powers. In this regard, by 1933 China had recovered its tariff autonomy and gained control of the Maritime Customs service; through negotiations, it was able to reduce the number of foreign concessions from thirty-three to thirteen. Because it promulgated new law codes (a Western-imposed requirement), it was able to negotiate the issue of extraterritoriality for the first time.

Chiang's power lay in three positions that he held. As president of the government, he was head of state with power to set domestic policy and to deal with foreign powers. As chairman of the party, he controlled the organ that, in line with the thought of Sun Yat-sen, was to serve as tutor for the people until their eventual realization of republicanism (see document 8, appendix 2). The length of this period of party tutelage was not spelled out. As commander-in-chief of the party army, he held military power as his most important resource. On paper, Chiang looked supreme. But the reality was otherwise. There were challenges to all three of his positions. While the Northern Expedition had technically united the country and ended the warlord scourge, "residual warlordism" remained a problem, a political and military challenge: twice in this decade, Chiang's armies launched campaigns against warlord-led armies. A revived Communist movement in southeast China emerged also as a political and military threat that led to five military campaigns. And most significant of all was the growing threat of Japan, continuously an issue from 1931 on.

And there were other problems. Chiang's political "base," the party, was not unified; it was split among factions vying for control and power. To complicate matters, the relationship between the party and the state apparatus was muddied; the two institutions were often controlled by opposing factions that frequently worked at cross-purposes. In the party, disgruntled cadres aligned themselves with residual warlords and continued to make trouble. Such political battles twice turned into military challenges from Wang Jingwei and his partisans. Chiang did not, in fact, have firm control in his party until 1938, after China was already embroiled in war with Japan. In short, Chiang had huge strikes against his being able to rule and reconstruct China effectively.

Chiang emerged as the heir to the long line of self-strengtheners stretching from nineteenth-century leaders like Li Hongzhang and Zhang Zhidong through Yuan Shikai in the early republic. Central control and decision making were key in modernizing the state. Chiang turned to communications, transportation, and industrial plants for most of his reconstructionist focus— all crucial infrastructure for defense and significant for further modernization. Not much was accomplished in the industrial arena. Blueprints for a massive four-year program to industrialize the Yangzi valley with the state's construction of communications and all kinds of industries yellowed with age because of insufficient funds. Plans to build four new steel mills produced only one small plant. By 1937, China, with its population of four hundred to five hundred million, had less industrial production than the eight million people of Belgium. Even with the attention focused on construction of highways, railroads, and telegraphs, shockingly little was accomplished. By 1937, China had the same mileage of modern highways as Spain, one third of the telegraph lines to be found in France, and less railroad mileage than the state of Illinois.

Why was so little accomplished? The political and military challenges were, of course, significant, but there were other serious challenges. Economic and fiscal difficulties were debilitating. The global context was bad enough: the worldwide depression created a terribly inopportune time for economic development and expansion. More serious for China's economic reconstruction was its insufficient and poorly structured tax base. Traditionally, the crucial tax for the Chinese government was the land tax. After many years of war, with its disruption of local economies and the upheaval of population, in many areas land ownership was unclear. A census had to be conducted before taxes could be collected, but a census was both time-consuming and expensive. Chiang and the government decided to write off the land tax: if provinces wanted to collect it, they could do so. The national government thus became dependent on tariffs and excise taxes. But both taxes were counterproductive. Tariffs handicapped trade and industry, the modern sector that the government wanted to develop; 50 percent of the government's revenue came from customs duties (as opposed to 1 percent in the United States at that time). Excise taxes on items like flour, kerosene, and tobacco were regressive, affecting most severely those least able to pay. With such a tax base, it is hardly surprising that more reconstruction was not accomplished.

Some have said that the decision not to collect the land tax for the national government was also an indication that Chiang was unwilling to tackle the problem of reining in local elites. Culture and history made the relationship of the center to the localities a major challenge. With cultural emphasis on family, personal networks, native place, and local gods, the natural focus of Chinese civilization was the local. Historical developments complicated the state's dealing with local society. Because of a weakened central regime during the late Qing and the politically and socially fragmented republic, local elites in institutions like self-government bodies and professional associations had played increasingly important political roles in their communities, undirected and undeterred by the center (when it even existed). In the view of the central government, however, considerable local autonomy was not conducive to rapid nation building and might further exacerbate sociopolitical fragmentation. Thus, Nanjing was determined to penetrate more deeply into society than had the late-imperial state, setting up a system of townships, wards, villages, and urban neighborhoods, all undergirded by the traditional *baojia* system of group mutual surveillance. Despite numerous tinkerings with local-level administration, this regime's vision of nation building remained top-down.

Another approach that provided the possibility for bottom-up social transformation was the experimental use of the locality as a potential model for the nation. Models of rural reconstruction, which were holistic attempts to modernize an area, were initially begun by private citizens. The two best-known efforts at rural reconstruction focused on education as the key to remaking China. In James Yen's Mass Education Association in Ding County (Hebei Province), market towns and villages set up "people's schools" to offer some practical education, with an emphasis on public ethics. The Nanjing regime gave considerable latitude to **Liang Shuming's**

Shandong Rural Reconstruction Institute to administer several counties (more than seventy were under the direction of the institute). The Nanjing government also became involved in setting up two experimental counties as models of bureaucratic reform. In the end, these efforts of modeling for the nation were stillborn. The war with Japan ended any further experimentation.

The Guomindang government's record in the arena of culture was not stellar. To counter the obvious appeal of Marxism to some in Chinese society, the national regime needed some sort of ideological appeal to give direction and coherence to its programs. Its choice was rather surprising: after abolishing official Confucian rites in 1928 (giving as the reason, Confucianism's superstition), the government resurrected Confucius in 1934, reestablishing those same rites, now under the management of the government itself. This action points to the profoundly conservative nature of the regime, for this was a return to the ideology and culture of the period before the May Fourth cultural revolution. It is hard to imagine how Chiang and his advisers could have thought that such action would have much appeal among those elements of the population they hoped to attract most. The recanonization of Confucius was part of a larger effort called the **New Life Movement**, which aimed to revive traditional virtues and to cultivate personal cleanliness and civic virtue. The regime's almost reactionary character is also indicated by its banning of the "little teacher" movement, a program to try to motivate school students to teach illiterate neighbors how to read.

Despite the government's attitude toward culture, the world of literature, influenced deeply by May Fourth thought, flourished during these years. Lu Xun continued to write, serving as patron to young writers and as spokesman for the **League of Left-Wing Writers**. **Ding Ling** emerged as the foremost woman writer of the late 1920s, publishing "Miss Sophie's Diary" in 1927, a story of the frustrations of a young woman obsessed by erotic feelings. Ding helped edit the League's journal. Her career would be punctuated by periods of political repression under the Guomindang and later the Communists. Important novelists at work in these years included leftist writer **Mao Dun**, who carried out the didactic Communist ideal that all literature should depict the proper relationships between classes and help to further the revolutionary cause. His most famous novel, *Midnight* (1933), describes the world of Shanghai capitalism, especially "the ferocity of the compradore-financial capitalists, the dissipated, decadent life of the bourgeoisie, the restless ennui of the young men and women of the urban petty bourgeoisie."[1] Popular also in the Nanjing decade was **Ba Jin**, whose *Family* (1933) became the best-known of his novels; it reflects the struggles in one family over issues of arranged marriage, young love, and the revolution. Yet another important novelist in the period was **Lao She**; his greatest novel, *Rickshaw* (1937), was a bleak view of the life of a Beijing ricksha puller.

## The Communist Movement

In the aftermath of the 1927–28 Guomindang purge, the Communist Party began its long march from decimation to new life. Driven underground in the cities and to mountainous areas in the southeast, it had nothing to lose by trying new strategies to build its power. While the party headquarters remained underground in Shanghai, and its leadership, still beholden to Stalin and the orthodox Marxist line, championed organizing the urban proletariat, the most important activity occurred in the countryside. During the purge, Mao Zedong retreated to Jinggangshan on the border between Hunan and Jiangxi, where in early 1928 he and **Zhu De** established the first "rural base area." In some ways, the base areas that were developed during the 1930s and 1940s across China were analogous to the Guomindang's experimental model efforts, providing local arenas for experimental policies. Mao called them "the buttocks of the revolution," places where party and army could rest and where human and material resources for revolutionary activity could be obtained.[2]

The party also established its own army under Zhu De, who had had military experience in the Guomindang army. Composed mostly of illiterate peasants and workers, the Red Army gave priority to political training, a policy that necessitated parallel organizations to direct political work and command the military. In late 1928, Guomindang military pressure forced evacuation of the Jinggangshan base and led to the Red Army's seizure of Ruijin, in Jiangxi. There on the Jiangxi-Fujian border, Mao began to organize and expand his control, establishing the Chinese Soviet Republic (the **Jiangxi Soviet**, or Central Soviet) in November 1931. At its largest, the soviet included twenty-one counties. The Party Center, from Shanghai, merged with the Central Soviet in January 1933.

During the Jiangxi period, the Communist leadership experimented with the process of land revolution and the implementation of class struggle, a strategy for which it was necessary to define class categories (see document 10, appendix 2). Mao, basing his categories on a scheme developed by Soviet Communists, divided the peasants into three groups: rich, middle, and poor. In such categorizations, social relativity was the reality, for the identity of a particular stratum was relative to others. Class ranking could thus vary according to the arena and the categorizers; it was always subject to reevaluation. As a case in point, from June 1933 to October 1934 the soviet launched a land-investigation campaign to reclassify peasants; a major issue was the demarcation between the rich peasant and the rich-middle peasant. Working with a new definition, investigators in one county changed the classification of 48 percent of the households that had earlier been categorized as landlord or rich-peasant to middle- or poor-peasant.[3] The obvious fluidity of class rankings—and land reform itself, with the utilization of class struggle, plus the eruption of violence—frightened and alienated too many people. At a time when the movement needed the support of larger numbers, it was turning too many of the most powerful people in the communities into enemies. For that reason, the land-reform experiment was discontinued, and Mao put into effect the Guomindang land law, which placed a rent ceiling for tenants of 37.5 percent of the harvest. Mao addressed gender as well as class issues in the Central Soviet, not for purposes of gender equality but to mobilize women for the national revolution. A new marriage law was announced in December 1931, outlawing arranged marriage, forbidding marriage through purchase and sale, and making divorce easy.

The standard party (Maoist) version of these years keeps Mao at center stage. Recent studies have depicted the Communist movement as much more diverse and polycentric than previously thought. Although the Jiangxi Soviet was the CCP center of power and governance, it was not the only base area that existed in the early 1930s, and its policies were not necessarily carried out in other bases. The Eyuwan (Hubei-Henan-Anhui) Soviet, led by **Zhang Guotao**, emphasized female emancipation more than the one in Jiangxi; and Zhang relied on the Red Army to carry out mass mobilization rather than engage the masses through land reform. The Xiang'exi (west Hubei and Hunan) base controlled by He Long developed more quickly and was active in more social and political arenas than the Jiangxi base. Establishing more highly developed mass associations, the base leadership promoted campaigns for land reclamation and against the evils of opium, gambling, and superstition.[4]

## The Long March

Fearful of the expansion of Communist power, Chiang launched two campaigns against the Jiangxi base, in December 1930 and May–June 1931, utilizing former warlord troops to wear down the Red Army. In both cases, the

Communists lured Guomindang armies into the base area. Overextended and without proper defensive preparations, the Guomindang forces were denied intelligence by the base's mobilized masses who then destroyed bridges to prevent them from retreating and attacked them from behind. In the third campaign, in July–October 1931, Guomindang forces penetrated deeply into the base area, but the Japanese war in Manchuria forced Chiang to retreat. The fourth campaign, in early 1933, failed, too. The fifth, and finally successful, campaign was launched in October 1933, with Guomindang forces moving slowly, building networks of roads to facilitate supply, constructing blockhouses, and undertaking political mobilization work with the masses along the campaign routes, gradually tightening the noose around the soviet. Though the Communists tried to beat back the attack using various tactics, an August meeting of CCP leaders and Comintern agent **Otto Braun** began to plan the evacuation.

In mid-October, about eighty-six thousand (including thirty-five women) broke out of the base to the southwest and began a 370-day forced march of about six thousand miles (see map 4). This was the fabled **Long March**—in the words of Edgar Snow, "an Odyssey unequaled in modern times."[5] The marchers faced bombing attacks from Nationalist forces and harassment from Tibetan troops. They marched over snow-covered mountain ranges, suffering from altitude sickness and frostbite. In marshlands, bogs swallowed people alive; the marchers had to sleep standing up lest they sink into the saturated ground. Hunger, exhaustion, and illness were their continual companions. It is perhaps not surprising that only about eight thousand survived to reach Yan'an, in Shaanxi Province. Along the way, at a momentous January 1935 meeting in **Zunyi**, in Guizhou Province, Mao Zedong emerged as leader of the party, defeating the so-called **"returned Bolsheviks,"** loyal to the Stalinist line. These Bolsheviks had taken leadership of the Jiangxi Soviet away from Mao on their arrival from Shanghai, but now they were blamed for its military defeat. Mao's earlier success in the establishment of the soviet put him in a position to take up the leadership when the returnees faltered. It was clearly Mao and his leadership who profited most from the development and perpetuation of the Long March legend.

In the annals of party history, the Long March is treated as a victory; indeed, until the late 1990s, the political leadership of the Communist Party and the government of the People's Republic was dominated by veterans of the Long March. It must be emphasized that it was necessitated by a great defeat, perhaps even proportionally greater than the defeat of 1927. Listen to Mao, writing in late 1936:

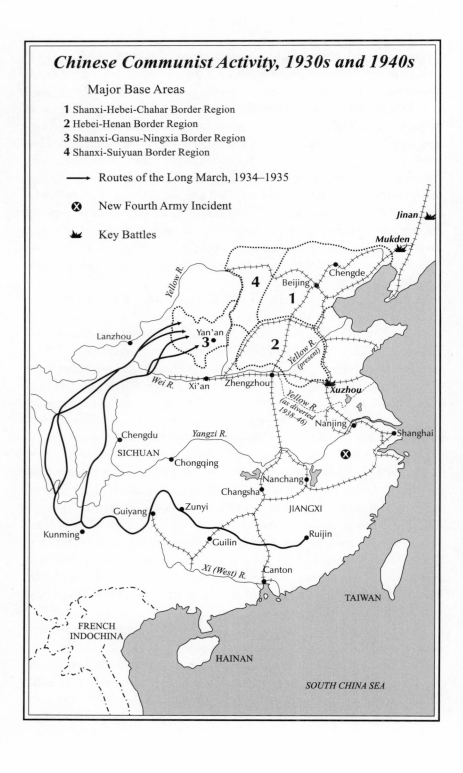

# Chinese Communist Activity, 1930s and 1940s

## Major Base Areas

**1** Shanxi-Hebei-Chahar Border Region
**2** Hebei-Henan Border Region
**3** Shaanxi-Gansu-Ningxia Border Region
**4** Shanxi-Suiyuan Border Region

⟶ Routes of the Long March, 1934–1935

⊗ New Fourth Army Incident

✷ Key Battles

Jinan

Mukden

Chengde

Beijing

Yellow R.

Lanzhou

Yan'an

3

4

1

2

Yellow R. (present)

Wei R.  Xi'an  Zhengzhou

Xuzhou

Yellow R. (as diverted 1938–46)

Nanjing

Shanghai

Chengdu

Yangzi R.

SICHUAN

Chongqing

⊗

Changsha

Nanchang

Guiyang  Zunyi

JIANGXI

Kunming

Guilin

Ruijin

Xi (West) R.  Canton

TAIWAN

FRENCH
INDOCHINA

HAINAN

SOUTH CHINA SEA

Except for the Shaanxi-Gansu border area, all revolutionary bases were lost, the Red Army was reduced from 300,000 to a few tens of thousands, the membership of the Chinese Communist Party was reduced from 300,000 to a few tens of thousands, and the Party organizations in Guomindang areas were almost entirely wiped out. In short, we received an extremely great historical punishment.[6]

Identifying the Long March as a victory surely comes in part from the fact of survival (if only of less than 10 percent)—survival of such brutal forces, natural and human. The march is an inspiring story of the defiance of and triumph over superhuman odds, of dedication and sacrifice. Most important, it produced among the survivors a sense of mission: while others had died, they had lived; and to make certain that their comrades had not died in vain, it was essential to commit their all to the revolution to assure victory. For Mao, the experience certainly strengthened his "already deeply ingrained voluntaristic faith that men with the proper will, spirit, and revolutionary consciousness could conquer all material obstacles and mold historical reality."[7] And it filled him with a sense of destiny, that he was the one to lead China out of its miserable past into a bright future.

When the Jiangxi base was evacuated, about forty-two thousand troops were left to harass and tie down Chiang's troops and to maintain a foothold and networks of support in the area. Over the next three years, they continued guerrilla activity—in what has been called the Three-Year War—in almost twenty bases mostly along the borders of eight provinces. Reportedly, the privations of living in primitive conditions in rugged mountains effected a bonding, if not as intense as for the Long March veterans, certainly equally long-lasting. Rather than attempting to mobilize local populations through mass organization, in these localities the most effective strategy was the manipulation of individuals. Thus, they sought to build power by subverting and taking control of *baojia* units and utilizing kinship ties. Since the social realities of each locale were different, the appropriate approach demanded flexibility, awareness of and sensitivity to local situations, and a willingness to learn from the locals. As one historian put it, these guerrillas sought to gain power, "living on society's margins, stretching out tendrils into it, learning its ways, and studying its social arrangements not to change it but to strike deals with it." It was a marked contrast to the bureaucratic-centralist style of the Jiangxi Soviet (and later methods at Yan'an); ultimately, as the 1940s' revolution showed, it was a more successful revolutionary strategy.[8]

## THE RAVAGES OF INVASION AND CIVIL WAR

### *Japanese Aggression, 1931–37*

Japan's interest in establishing itself on the Asian mainland went back at least as far as the 1870s. Its seizure of Korea from 1895 to 1910, the Twenty-One Demands in 1915, its eagerness to seize and hold previously German-held Shandong Province, its involvement in the Allied Siberian expedition (1918–23), and its patronage of Manchurian warlord Zhang Zuolin—all these pointed to the depth of Japan's desire for colonies, or at least land that could be treated in a colonial manner. After World War I, having already annexed Korea, Japan focused on Manchuria, a region rich in natural resources and with extensive fertile arable land. During the Qing dynasty, the reigning Manchus had kept Manchuria off-limits to Chinese immigration, desiring to maintain it as the Manchu homeland. Consequently, in the early twentieth century, it was relatively sparsely populated. Japan thus saw in Manchuria an answer to some of its problems: a base to provide raw materials for its industry, space for population movement, an abundance of arable land, and a base for further actions on the mainland. Following the Russo-Japanese War in 1904–5, Japan obtained control over the 650-mile-long South Manchurian railroad that ran from Harbin in central Manchuria to Port Arthur on the tip of the Liaodong peninsula. This holding was crucial to Japan's establishing itself in the area. After 1912, Japan encouraged Koreans, now Japanese subjects, to emigrate to Manchuria as a way of making Japan's presence more secure. By 1930, Manchuria was home to one million Japanese subjects, mainly Korean; foreign investment there was 75 percent Japanese, and of Japan's total trade with China, 40 percent was with Manchuria.

From 1912, Japan had relied on Zhang Zuolin to work with them to protect their interests. Since in the 1920s he became involved in the major warlord wars over control of Beijing, Japan's relationship to Zhang as direct patron had great potential benefit if he emerged as the Chinese head of state. But then several serious factors broke the business-as-usual situation. In the mid-1920s, forces charged out of south China carrying the banner of Chinese nationalism aimed at warlords (like Zhang Zuolin) and imperialists (like Japan). This expansion of a strong nationalism came at about the same time as difficulties began to shake the Japanese economy and as the Japanese began to question the effectiveness and wisdom of civilian party rule. Waiting in the wings was the Japanese military, which had seen its budgets slashed and size reduced under party control. As Chiang Kai-shek's Northern Expedition moved north to Beijing in 1928, his actions seemed more and more threatening to Japan's position on the mainland. Increasingly wary of what their man in Manchuria, Zhang, might do, the Japanese killed him, blowing up his train on his return from a Beijing meeting with Chiang in June 1928.

Manchuria was, of course, Chinese territory, and once Chiang established the national government in Nanjing, it set about trying to establish a greater Chinese presence there. It set up competing railroads that, using techniques like rebates and rate wars, began to eat into Japanese railroad profits. The years from 1928 to 1931 saw increasing tensions over seemingly small things—railroad "wars" and violent outbreaks between Korean settlers and Chinese over property boundaries and irrigation rights. But from the perspective of the Japanese military in the field that witnessed these things, they were magnified into a growing threat to Japan's very position. Thus, officers of field grade in Manchuria, without the agreement or even knowledge of Tokyo, acted to make Japan's position secure by scheming to take over Manchuria. On September 18, 1931, they blew up a very small section of track on the South Manchurian Railroad, blamed it on the Chinese, and used it as a pretext to begin a military campaign. Despite Tokyo's declaring that the action would be halted, the campaign continued. By early 1932, the Japanese conquest of Manchuria was a reality. In the fall, the Japanese recognized it as the independent state of Manchukuo, under the leadership of the last Qing emperor, Puyi; but the state was hardly independent, and Puyi was nothing more than a puppet. A League of Nations commission reported in autumn 1932 that Japan was guilty of military aggression in Manchuria; thumbing its nose at the world, Japan walked out of the League the next spring.

The Guomindang military's resistance against Japan in the Manchurian fighting was notoriously weak; military command in some cases ordered men about to go into battle to lay down their arms and simply surrender. The scandal for patriotic Chinese was that Chiang had established his government under the flag of nationalism, but his military decisions seemed craven and almost treasonous. Such a seemingly antinationalistic tack calls for an explanation. It should be remembered that when the so-called **Manchurian Incident** occurred, Chiang's military was in the throes of its third extermination campaign against the Jiangxi Soviet. The war in Manchuria indeed led to his ending the third campaign. Chiang believed that his army was not strong enough to take on both Japan and the Chinese Communists. In the early and mid-1930s, Chiang was depending on German military advisers to help him strengthen his armies. His response as

Japanese aggression in north China continued unabated was that the Communists must be dealt with before the Japanese: the Japanese he likened to a skin disease, while the Communists were a disease of the heart. One naturally tried to deal with a more serious heart problem before turning to a skin disease—unless, of course (as we might say in hindsight), the skin disease was melanoma, a not unlikely diagnosis given Japan's malevolent actions.

Unlike Chiang and the military, the Chinese people reacted strongly against Japan. In autumn 1931, during the Manchurian campaign, the Chinese boycotted Japanese products, cutting sale of Japanese products in China by two thirds. Likely with much pressure from the Japanese capitalists, the military declared the boycott an act of aggression and sent seventy thousand Japanese troops to Shanghai. In this undeclared war that raged around Shanghai for six weeks (January–March 1932), the Chinese army offered a forceful resistance; the fighting ended when both countries agreed to an armistice. The years from 1933 to 1937 saw the patterns repeated again and again: Japanese aggression, Chiang's appeasement, mass Chinese reaction, Chiang's brutal suppression of the demonstrating population. A list of Japan's conquests and demands in the years after the establishment of Manchukuo reads like a catalog of north Chinese property and obligations:

1. March 1933: The Inner Mongolian province of Rehe (Jehol); the province is the size of Virginia, Maryland, and West Virginia.
2. May 1933: Tangku Truce created demilitarized zone between the Great Wall and Peiping (the name by which Beijing was known from 1928 to 1949), the size of the state of Connecticut. Chinese troops must be out; Japanese troops in the area because of the Boxer Protocol could remain.
3. August 1933: Eastern part of Inner Mongolian province of Chahar, slightly larger that the state of Connecticut.
4. April 1934: Amo Doctrine: Japan would have control of all aid and development programs regarding China's financial agreements with Western nations.
5. June 1935: He-Umezu Agreement: Chinese had to remove all government organs and troops from the province of Hebei.
6. June 1935: Qin-Doihara Agreement: Chinese could not interfere with any Japanese work in Inner Mongolia.

7. September 1935: Japan demanded that the five northern provinces of China be made independent with the removal of all Chinese governments.
8. December 1935: Establishment of the Hebei-Chahar Council meant the loss of eastern Hebei Province (with the cities of Peiping and Tianjin).

Only the seventh demand was not acceded to by Chiang.

During these four years, Chiang had continuously fought the Communists: his troops fought the fourth and fifth extermination campaigns against the Jiangxi Soviet; they fought the Long March; then once they reached Yan'an, Chiang used his best troops to blockade and quarantine the Communists. The increasingly shrill cry from the masses (and one echoed by the Communists) was "why should Chinese be fighting Chinese?" at a time when the Japanese were eating them alive. The Communists were calling for a united front against Japan, the common enemy. In December 1936, in one of modern China's strangest stories, Chiang was kidnapped in Xi'an by **Zhang Xueliang**, the GMD general in command of the Communist blockade, and held for two weeks until he agreed to join in a united front with the Communists to fight the Japanese. Once agreed to, the united front did not have long to wait before being put in action. On July 7, 1937, an incident on the **Marco Polo Bridge** outside of Peiping led to shooting between Chinese and Japanese troops. For Chiang to do otherwise than fight at this point would have been politically untenable; for the Japanese military to turn back at that point was unthinkable. China and Japan were at war.

## The Sino-Japanese War, 1937–45

The Japanese military assumed the war would be short, and the beginning seemed almost a corroboration of that assumption. The attack on the Lower Yangzi region began in mid-August; and although Chinese resistance was initially intense, the Japanese troops took city after city. Chiang's government fled upstream, along with dismantled factories and university and school laboratories and libraries camouflaged on barges. First stop for the government was Wuhan, in late 1937, and then it retreated further to Chongqing, in Sichuan Province, in October 1938. A basin surrounded by high mountains, Sichuan provided a natural defensive base; its cloudy, foggy weather in autumn and winter also provided cover from Japanese bombers. By October

1938, the first phase of the war had ended and much of eastern China, containing the major industrial cities and much of the best cropland, had fallen. But the Japanese were becoming "bogged down, mired in the abdomen of China from which it could not extricate itself."[9]

The Japanese campaigns in this war were filled with atrocities—all doubtless intended to terrorize the population into submission. Best known was the **Rape of Nanjing**, in December 1937 and January 1938. At Chiang's capital, Japanese officers gave their men carte blanche to do whatever they wanted to the unfortunate Chinese civilians who could not flee or did not choose to become refugees. Countless women and young girls were raped and mutilated; babies and children were tossed in the air to be caught on bayonets; people were buried alive or roasted; old men and women were tied up and thrown into icy streams to drown. It is estimated that in the bloodbath, two hundred thousand to three hundred thousand were killed. The reason for such treatment of a civilian population is not known; perhaps the population of the capital was singled out for symbolic reasons or perhaps the Japanese were frustrated by the Chinese resistance and the specter of a long war. But Nanjing is only the best-known in a catalog of horrors inflicted by the Japanese.

In some cases, Japanese brutality was motivated by revenge. In the north, the Communists' main army, the **Eighth Route Army**, began a general campaign against Japanese forces from August to December 1940. Called the Hundred Regiments Campaign, it was the Eighth Route Army's most extensive offensive of the war; after a promising beginning, it went down to defeat. The Japanese responded with a brutal search-and-destroy backlash lasting three years (1941–44). Known as the "Three All" campaign ("kill all, burn all, loot all"), it was directed against both Communists and civilians. Most small towns and villages in the path of the Japanese troops suffered terribly. Sometimes the Japanese atrocities were simply a part of their military repertoire. In east-central Zhejiang Province, the Japanese waged biological warfare. They dropped material infected with bubonic plague on three cities, starting epidemics. Poison gas was used against at least one other city. Less well known than the infamous activities of Unit 731, which conducted bacterial warfare research on people in Manchuria, these seem to be strategies that the Japanese were very willing to use.[10]

As if Japanese brutality were not sufficient, the actions of Guomindang national and provincial regimes, especially in the adoption of scorched-earth policies, contributed substantially to the suffering of the Chinese people and laid waste the Chinese countryside. In June 1938, in an effort to stop the

Japanese advance in northern China, Chiang Kai-shek blasted open the dikes of the Yellow River, purposely flooding an immense area. The people in the region were not notified in advance, so that perhaps as many as several hundred thousand died; property losses were staggering. The action barely slowed down the Japanese troops. In other areas, there was widespread destruction of recently built highways and bridges; it was not enough simply to blow up bridges on railroad lines to stop the trains: in some areas, all the track was ripped out as well.

Because of Japanese military power, collaboration in areas they occupied was common. Within the first months of war, the Japanese established two collaborationist regimes, one in Peiping (the Provisional Government of China) and the other in Nanjing (the Reform Government); they were generally staffed by men who had once been students in Japan or had other Japanese connections. In March 1940, long-time Guomindang leader Wang Jingwei defected to the Japanese and became leader of an alternative Guomindang regime in Nanjing; his rationalization was that it was the only way to save China. Collaborationist regimes were found in counties and cities throughout the occupied areas; they were made up of men with a variety of motives—from those who wanted to protect their native places to those who wanted to profit from the political situation.

From the fall of 1938 until the bombing of Pearl Harbor in December 1941, the war was one mostly of attrition, with the Japanese holding onto the east coast and the Chinese using scorched-earth and guerrilla policies. The attack on Pearl Harbor changed the war in many ways. The United States became an ally of China, the Sino-Japanese War becoming a part of the Pacific War. From the Japanese perspective, the new war made victory in China even less likely. Having bogged down essentially since a year into the war, the Japanese now had to send troops that had been in China into the Pacific, thus stretching their manpower much more thinly. The U.S. goal was to strengthen Chiang's position sufficiently that he could win back eastern China, which could then be used as an airbase from which to attack the Japanese islands. This aim required substantial military aid, a huge logistical problem. In the opening days of the war, Chiang had brought supplies in from Hong Kong, but that route was blocked by Japan's seizure of Guangzhou in October 1938. The rail route from Haiphong in Vietnam to Kunming in Yunnan Province worked until France fell in 1940 and the Vichy collaborationists shut it off. Then shortly after the United States entered the war, the Japanese, in early 1942, cut off the last land alternative, the 715-mile Burma Road. The United States was reduced to the extremely costly strategy of airlifting supplies from India to Kunming over the Hump—mountainous northern Burma. The tonnage that the United States could airlift into China equaled the Burma Road's 1941 tonnage only in 1944. Such a relative pittance could never build Chiang's strength sufficiently.

General **Joseph Stilwell**, named Chiang's chief of staff, believed the only way to solve the problem was to reconquer northern Burma and reopen the Burma Road, a strategy that Chiang thought ridiculous. He was more taken with the idea of the use of airpower as the strategy to take back eastern China. Stilwell and Chiang bitterly disliked each other, and their relationship was one more reason for progress of any sort being difficult. Roosevelt eventually recalled Stilwell in October 1944. By that time, the strategy of using eastern China to attack Japan had long been displaced by the two-route "island hopping" campaign in the Pacific. By July 1944, five months before Stilwell's dismissal, the Pacific campaign had taken Saipan, from which the Japanese home islands could be bombed.

With Japan in the main defeated by late 1944 and early 1945, attention in China and on the part of the United States began to shift to the postwar reality of a Chinese political world tensely polarized between Chiang's Guomindang and Mao's Communists. The united front between them had not worked effectively. Though nominally under Guomindang control, the main Red Army, the Eighth Route Army, in the north was able to maneuver for its own goals. Though it lost tens of thousands of men in bitter fighting with the Japanese, it was able to use the warfare to expand its own power in north China. The war years were also important for the Communists in shaping their party strategy and in developing approaches that they would use after their seizure of power in 1949. The party became more focused on its identity, coherence—even purity. In part, this stemmed from the wartime immigration that poured into Yan'an: an estimated hundred thousand immigrants, with likely up to 50 percent of them students, teachers, journalists, and intellectuals, from 1937 to 1940. Attracted by Communist idealism, many joined the party; membership recorded as forty thousand in 1937 skyrocketed to some eight hundred thousand by 1940.[11] Faced with the issue of quality control of the membership—the threatened diminution of party cohesion and direction—the party set a firm party "line" and used it to sift out dissenters. Centralization allowed more administrative control over the enormous variation in party-controlled regions, but its downside, a growing civil and military bureaucracy, increasing routinization, and an emphasis on hierarchy soon appeared. In early 1941, the party tried to slow the rush to bureaucracy by instituting a "to the villages" (*xia xiang*) program—one that would remain a staple in its repertoire of state policies. Higher-level cadres were sent to the countryside to learn from peasants and to help decentralize various party and government functions. Later, intellectuals were sent down to break the barriers between city-reared elites and peasants; in this way, the *xia xiang* policy was a strategy to encourage greater social cohesion—even as it illustrated Mao's distrust of and distaste for intellectuals and bureaucrats. A dilemma that had plagued the Guomindang regime—determining what would be the most appropriate relationship between center and locality, between statism and local initiative—remained one of the party's most intractable problems.

An extraordinarily important strategy to attain party cohesion was the rectification campaign, the first of many in the history of the Communist Party and its political regime. By late 1940 and early 1941, the situation at Yan'an had become tense and troubled. Military developments provided the greatest threat and seem to have heightened the lack of party coherence. The Nationalists had four hundred thousand soldiers blockading the Shaan-Gan-Ning base area to its south and east. Then in the **New Fourth Army Incident** in central China (January 1941), Nationalist forces ambushed part of that army and killed more than three thousand men, ending, if not in name, any effective functioning of the anti-Japanese united front. Amid such crises, in February 1942 Mao launched the **rectification movement** to bring cadres and intellectuals to a uniformity of spirit to focus on the party's mission and to indoctrinate thousands of young people coming from coastal cities. Cadres were to participate in small group sessions studying selected documents, undertake self-criticisms, be criticized in mass meetings, and confess their errors. In the end, they were often ostracized and sent to the countryside to do menial work. In part, this was a function of the perceived health and promise of the revolutionary movement (in which the party, it was thought, could afford to dismiss and destroy party members in the name of doctrinal purity); it was also in part the radical logic of those certain they possessed the Truth.

For intellectuals, the other target of rectification, Mao expanded his thoughts on the functions of art and literature in a socialist society in May 1942 (see document 11, appendix 2). Art and literature were "powerful weapons for uniting and educating the people . . . as well as [helping] the people wage the struggle against the enemy with one heart and one mind."[12] Mao's points in this speech, and party decisions in spring 1942, presaged the future relationship of state and intellectuals and artists. Art and literature serve the "people"—workers, peasants, soldiers, not the petty bourgeoisie, students, or intellectuals—and, above all, serve the revolutionary cause. When author Ding Ling criticized the party for its sexism, she was sent to the countryside. Writer Wang Shiwei pointed out the inequalities between the lifestyles of the ruling Yan'an elite and those of the nonelites and called for lifestyle commonality for both groups. For this, party cadres attacked him, put him on "quasi-trial," and executed him in 1947.

Yet, the motive force of the revolution during the resistance war was party-directed mass mobilization and associations. Class struggle—the most important strategy of mass mobilization—appeared both in base areas and in guerrilla zones, not in the form of radical land reform (from which the party had retreated after Jiangxi), but in reducing rents, taxes, and interest. Work teams were dispatched to villages to mobilize against landlords, officials, and the "usurious" bourgeoisie. Since much of the north had few landlords and thus few problems with tenancy and rent, the key resentment among the masses there was onerous taxes. In some bases of north China, mobilization efforts were well under way by 1939–40; in others, they did not begin until 1943–44. In central China bases, reforms began only in 1941. Big landlords, more a problem in central and south China, were not generally demonized until 1943. Another technique that made class struggle tangible was the struggle meeting, the "most intense, condensed form of peasant mobilization."[13] These meetings were launched in the north against local despots by 1942 but were infrequent in central China until autumn 1943. Encouraged and facilitated by party cadres who chose the targets, struggle meetings often turned violent, as latent peasant anger erupted against village bosses and landlords. These staged events were pivotal in shaking up mass apathy and passivity and disrupting erstwhile solidarity among targets and community. There were additional strategies of mass mobilization, many of them base-specific.[14]

Mass associations were also key to the Communist revolutionary successes. Cadre work teams helped organize peasant associations primarily as bodies for economic assistance. Peasant associations helped lead efforts to reduce rent, interest, and taxes, made decisions about struggle meetings, and often were in charge of the militia. Because peasant associations in the villages carried out Communist economic policies, they directly challenged the village elites. It is no exaggeration to argue that the "rise of the peasant associations fundamentally changed rural power relations."[15] The second wave of mass organizing focused on women and workers.

The secret of Communist revolutionary success varied from place to place, from time to time, and from tactic to tactic. Communist mobilizers had to understand the locale — the natural environment, the social, economic, and political structures, and particular needs and grievances — then build coalitions with local leaders, mobilize local masses, and carry out pragmatic policies. These efforts were not always, or even often, successful; leftist excesses and rightist treachery were common; many times, contingencies rather than strategies gave the Communists their success. In Henan's Rivereast base, for example, the balance of power between the Communists and their enemies changed to the benefit of the Communists only when the Japanese withdrew their troops from the area after the beginning of the war in the Pacific in late 1941.

## The Civil War

When the Japanese announced their surrender on August 15, 1945, U.S. planes ferried half a million Guomindang soldiers into the former occupied areas to try to accept the surrender of Japanese troops before Communist troops could reach them. Since the CCP had expanded across north China throughout the war, they had a huge advantage in that region. By war's end, the CCP had nineteen base areas in the north, with an estimated population of about 90 million; announced party membership totaled 1.2 million. The race to accept the Japanese surrender was indicative of the subsequent years when the struggle to take the reins of state played itself out in a bloody civil war. The United States mediated in the dispute, and there were times when it seemed as though some sort of coalitional agreement might be reached. Mao had flown to Chongqing in August 1945 for talks with Chiang; although they toasted each other on the Double Ten anniversary — the date marking the revolution that toppled the Manchus — and issued a communiqué that recognized the importance of peaceful reconstruction, the mutual distrust and suspicion that existed between the parties seemed insurmountable. In December 1945, U.S. General **George Marshall** began a thirteen-month mediation effort. It was to no avail. Even with Marshall actively trying to bring a peace agreement, sporadic fighting continued throughout his tenure in China. He left in January 1947, blaming both parties for their intransigence. China turned quickly to widespread civil war, one of the largest wars of modern times.

In the beginning, the Guomindang had the advantage in numbers of men and amount of war materiel. The GMD forces numbered about three million men, with an estimated six thousand artillery pieces; this compared with about one million Communist troops, with about six hundred artillery pieces. Guomindang forces won the initial battles in 1946. In early 1947, however, Communist forces in Manchuria went on the offensive. Chiang insisted on committing half a million of his best men to that campaign; the cities in which they were based quickly became islands in a Communist sea. To prevent their being completely isolated and forced to surrender, Chiang instituted airlifts to Manchurian cities. It was a devastating economic blunder: Chiang used the whole military budget for the last half of 1948 in supplying only one city (Harbin) for only two months and four days. By mid-1948, the Communists had pulled roughly equal to the Guomindang in numbers of well-armed troops, and ahead in numbers of artillery pieces. In the end, the Manchurian campaign that ended in a smashing Communist victory in November 1948 cost Chiang 470,000 of his best troops and countless weapons and pieces of equipment. In the words of General David Barr, the head of the American Army Advisory Group, it "spelled the beginning of the end" for the Guomindang war effort.[16]

The battle for central China broke out just as the Manchurian campaign was ending (see map 4). Each battle now saw huge numbers of Guomindang defections, with more and more materiel falling into Communist hands. Centering on the railway center of Xuzhou, the battle of Huai-Hai began in October 1948 with the prompt defection of two Guomindang divisions. Chiang's army still had superiority in equipment and was supported by an air force. But the Communist military leaders were clearly superior strategists to the former Whampoa commandant. Chiang, who was partial to the officers who had graduated from his academy, refused to accept the advice of superior strategists (former warlords) to retreat to a more favorable position along the Huai River; he chose instead to stand at Xuzhou, where his forces were exposed on three sides. The Communist troops simply smashed these Guomindang troops. Chiang lost almost half a million men and most of his mechanized troops. He had also lost all of China north of the Yangzi. By early 1949, although fighting continued throughout the year, Chiang and his Guomindang national army had been defeated. In December, the Guomindang government fled to Taiwan.

The question of whether the Communists won the civil war or the Guomindang lost it has frequently been raised. On balance, it seems that the Communists were the superior strategists and that Chiang must be found wanting in the arena of strategizing. In the civil war as in the Sino-Japanese

War, the secret of Communist success was understanding the particular local situation and acting pragmatically. In the larger military struggle, commanders of the People's Liberation Army "appl[ied] a strategy that elevated flexibility in the field to the highest art of defensive warfare."[17] The military struggle was, on its face, the deciding factor; there were, however, underlying problems that were more significant. Military decision making was thought to be Chiang's strong suit, but it is obvious that his record is filled with blunders: his troop commitment to the Manchurian campaign, his decision to airlift supplies to maintain control of the cities, his primary trust in officers who were personally connected to him in the Whampoa clique, his weak strategy at Xuzhou, a battle that he insisted on directing personally, even though he was two hundred miles from the fighting.

But even more significant were his political and economic blunders. Repeatedly there had been calls for political liberalization, reforms that might open up the political realm to non-Communist groups, who could then share power to some degree with the Guomindang. The **Democratic League**, composed mainly of Western-style liberals, was the so-called Third Force that Chiang might have utilized to build a stronger political base, but he never did. Instead of attempting cooperation, he turned to his Guomindang secret police, who arrested and assassinated key figures in the League.

It was, in the end, Chiang's inability to deal with wrenching economic problems that likely did him in. Rampant, uncontrolled inflation gutted the economy. It began during the war, when the government was spending far more than its revenue. The government's solution was to print more money. Growing inflation was fueled by shortages of consumer goods, business restrictions, corruption, speculation, and hoarding. The exchange rate for Chinese dollars vis-à-vis U.S. dollars stood at 7,000 to 1 in January 1947, at 18,000 to 1 at the end of February 1947, and 45,000 to 1 in August 1947. Prices in July 1948 were three million times higher than they had been in July 1937. And it even deteriorated further. In the county of Xiaoshan, in Zhejiang Province, on the eve of the Communist takeover in April 1949, a picul of rice (about 133 pounds) cost more than 8 billion Chinese dollars, 785,400,000 times more than in 1937. At this rate, each *grain* of rice cost about 2,500 Chinese dollars.[18] With such a rate of inflation, Chiang lost not only the city-dwellers—businessmen, salaried classes, intellectuals, workers—but those in the countryside as well. The collapse was total. On October 1, 1949, Mao Zedong declared the formal establishment of the People's Republic of China (see map 5).

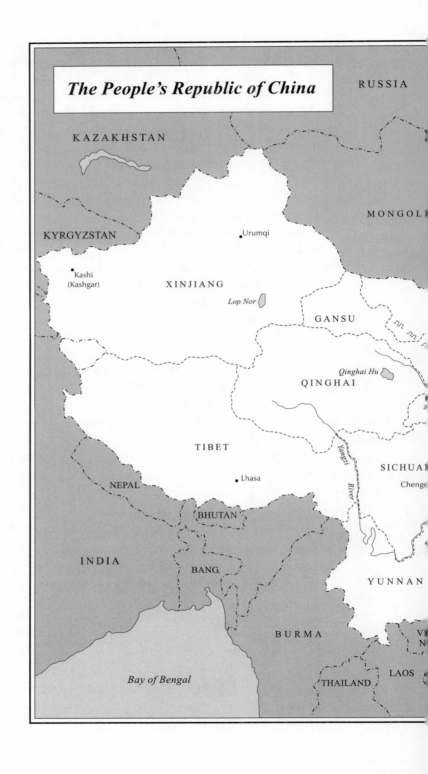

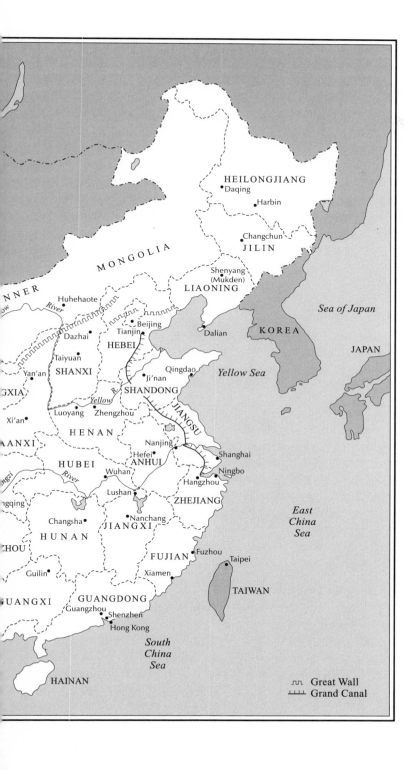

## THE YEARS THAT WERE FAT

The first years of the People's Republic, when Mao talked about the New Democracy that was being established, are generally seen as being the most successful period of Communist rule under Mao's control (see document 12, appendix 2). The debilitating inflationary cycle was broken; reconstruction after years of war and turmoil began; the Communists were able to inaugurate their programs; the People's Liberation Army was able to fight the U.S. army to a stand-off in Korea. If they were not years that were exactly fat, then for many Chinese they were years when the "starvation" of foreign control, national weakness, and domestic turmoil began to fade into the past.

One of the most significant changes wrought by the revolution and, in large part, by Mao himself was a change in "mentality" or "worldview." Traditional Chinese social thought had emphasized that a major force in all lives was fate. One was fated to be born male or female, rich or poor; to be betrothed to this or that individual; to live in this place or that; to be subject to this earthquake or that flood. And one must accept that fate. It was a world where forces of nature, society, and the realities of birth dominated humans. Mao's revolutionary romanticism and strong populist faith advanced the position that humans did not have to be cowed before fate, that with willpower and determination they could transcend their fates. Part of a poem titled "Swimming," which he wrote in 1956, puts it:

Standing at a ford, the Master once said:
"Thus life flows into the past!"

Breeze shakes the masts
While Tortoise and Snake Hills are motionless.
A grand project is being conceived—
A bridge will fly across
And turn a barrier into a path.
To the west, new cliffs will arise;
Mount Wu's clouds and rains will be kept from the countryside.
Calm lakes will spring up in the gorges.
Were the goddess still alive
She would be amazed by the changes on this earth.[19]

Through large-scale construction projects and by the forceful and positive changes brought by the Communist regime in its first eight years, Mao had brought this new view of humans and their capabilities into play in the Chinese social, political, and natural worlds.

## Land Reform

Land reform—the heart of the Chinese revolution—had already begun in the late 1940s, before the Communist military victory. According to **Liu Shaoqi**, the objectives of land reform were "to free the rural productive forces from the shackles of the landlords' feudal land-ownership system, so as to develop agricultural production and open the way for new China's industrialization."[20] The process entailed destruction of the old system and construction of a new system of collective rural production. Given the ecological and social variety of the Chinese countryside, the introduction of land reform across China was problematic. In the north, where in the 1930s only about 10 to 15 percent of farmers rented their land, landlordism was not a major problem; the peasant usually tilled the land that he owned. In the south and southwest, in contrast, where tenancy rates reached up to 56 percent in Sichuan, the exploitation of tenants by absentee landlords was common. In addition, the social and political culture varied sharply from area to area: in the south, lineage groups dominated villages and communities, while in the north secret organizations like the Elder Brothers' Society and the Red Spears frequently exercised control. There were also major differences within regions: in the Shaan-Gan-Ning base area, the Yan'an subregion was "sparsely populated, bandit-ridden badlands"; in stark contrast, the subregion directly to its north had dense population, high tenant rates, intensive farming, and thriving commerce.[21]

People's attitudes and expectations toward land reform were also partly shaped by the huge range of regional wartime experiences. The generally peaceful Shaan-Gan-Ning base, for example, did not experience the almost continuous, often brutal warfare with which much of the north had to contend. The Japanese controlled parts of central and southern China for varying lengths of time, some areas not at all. Manchuria had undergone a long period of Japanese colonial rule. The southwest had been the Guomindang base, subject to Japanese bombing but not ground warfare. The party had seized much of the north in the midst of war, but in east, central, south, and southwest China the Communist armies took huge chunks of territory with relatively little military action. In the north, then, the party sponsored land reform mostly before and during the civil war, while in the south reform took place after the establishment of the new national government. In sum, the party's approach to land reform had to vary according to the time and the place that it occurred.

In north China, it was often characterized by a violent settling of old scores with local elites. In late 1945, violence lashed out at elites and even at middle and poor peasants who had collaborated with the Japanese. A party directive in May 1946 gave license to leagues of poor peasants and peasant associations to expropriate and redistribute land and property; the directive specifically ordered cadres to let locals deal with the problems themselves, a policy that actually encouraged extremism among the masses. The party linked land reform with military mobilization of the populace against attacks by Guomindang forces, which in early 1946 had unleashed an unexpectedly strong military offensive. In response, county men formed militia units; local paramilitary units transported ammunition and supplies; women's associations became involved in intelligence activities; youth associations worked in rear areas; cultural teams did propaganda work; and peasant associations oversaw army recruiting. The party continually emphasized the connections among land reform, recruitment, and military mobilization. Because the violent excesses of the land-reform effort began to alienate far too many at a time when the civil war still raged, from 1948 to 1950 the party stepped in to encourage more moderation in an effort to diminish the killing of landlords and rich peasants, expropriation of land from middle peasants, and attacking of commercial and industrial enterprises.

After the party came to power in 1949 and promulgated the agrarian reform law (June 1950), massive land reform began in all areas. The Communist regime faced huge challenges; there had been no advance work in most areas and there was little, if any, structural readiness for great social change. Class sentiments were not developed. In many areas of the south and east, tenancy was linked to lineage and to village membership. Given the all-important kin and native-place networks, it was difficult for villagers to understand what "feudal" class structures were, or what exploitation meant. The mobilizational pattern used in the north was imitated elsewhere: target local tyrants, introduce the struggle meeting, and inaugurate a rent-reduction campaign. Work teams played a much larger role in land reform after 1949 than in the north in the 1940s. Despite their involvement, violent outbursts erupted, and an estimated one to two million landlords were executed. Although revolutionary change was uneven, an estimated 88 percent of households in the countryside had completed the "land to the tiller" movement by summer 1952.

Some six years after it had begun, land reform had revolutionized ways of thinking. Ding Ling, whose feminism had created trouble at Yan'an, redeemed herself with the party in her positive account of land reform, *The Sun Shines Over the Sanggan River* (1948), accorded a 1951 Stalin prize in literature, the highest national honor officially awarded by the USSR from 1939 to 1953. The social and political horizons of countless poor and middle peasants "had been broadened by the class-oriented perspective of the CCP."[22] Land reform had created new functional associations that tended to displace old kinship, religious, and voluntary associations. The common experiences of class struggle fostered a stronger social cohesion among those struggling against landlords and village tyrants and also produced a new demarcation of "us" from "them." While in the old society, for any local community "them" was most likely the outsider, the person from a different native place, now the "other," the "enemy," was in the community itself, where his status as class alien could be resurrected at will.

## Other Aspects of Revolution

Land reform benefited one group in Chinese society that had not been able to hold land before: as a result of the Marriage Law of 1950, single women, divorcees, and widows could own land in their names. Going beyond that of the Jiangxi period, the Marriage Law abolished the traditional family system "based on arbitrary and compulsory arrangements and the superiority of man over woman." The new system was based "on equal rights for both sexes, and on the protection of the lawful interests of women and children."[23] Women, as well as men, could initiate divorce proceedings. Infanticide was prohibited (see document 13, appendix 2).

As in land reform, the urban phase of the revolution targeted and attacked class enemies. In 1951–52, the party went into battle against what it called non-Communist bourgeois values. Targeted in the **Three-Anti Campaign** were party cadres, government bureaucrats, and factory managers; the goal was to eliminate waste, corruption, and bureaucratic mismanagement. Targets of the **Five-Anti Campaign** were the national bourgeoisie—industrialists and big businessmen—for their vices including bribery and tax evasion. Since none of these mostly urban groups had yet been subject to constraints, the campaigns seemed brutally intense to many. Like the land-reform campaigns, they created a sense of an enemy presence and a distrust that fractured old relationships and created new commonalities and identities.

Like the Guomindang regime in the late 1920s and early 1930s, the Communist regime sought to sink its roots deeply into the Chinese political landscape. The Communist government formalized the work, education, and residence unit (*danwei*) to enforce surveillance, control, political conformity, and ideological correctness at the lowest level of the polity. As an arm of the state, the danwei was most effective. Members of the danwei oversaw essential aspects of daily life, such as administering housing and medical care facilities, dispersing ration coupons, managing birth-control programs, and mediating marriage disputes. From the 1950s into the 1980s, they had directed mobilization of the populace in political campaigns, and they had managed surveillance and control. But if the danwei illustrates the commitment to statism, the burgeoning mass organizations, based on shared interests or sometimes specific objectives, provided the balancing social framework to enlarge the masses' horizons; they joined together the whole country, across provincial and regional lines. In 1953, for example, trade union membership had climbed to twelve million; there were nine million in the New Democratic Youth League (the pre-1957 name of the Communist Youth League); and no fewer than seventy-six million women joined the Women's Federation. They were especially significant forces in the parade of mass campaigns that marched across the landscape of the People's Republic, providing another framework for implementing the party's directives and a venue for mass mobilization.

## The Korean War

In foreign affairs, Mao had decided to "lean to one side"—that of the Soviet Union. He had traveled to Moscow in early 1950 to sign a Valentine's Day accord with Stalin, though Stalin's treatment of Mao was worse than rude. From the perspective of the United States at the time, such an accord meant simply that the perceived Communist threat was monolithic. With the invasion of the Republic of Korea by the Democratic Republic of Korea in June 1950, the cold war became hot. The United States and other nations acting under the flag of the United Nations came onto the Korean peninsula at a time when the defeat of South Korea seemed imminent. The Inchon landing in September 1950 saved the day, turning a North Korean rout into a panicky retreat. United Nations forces then invaded the North, in the process turning the goal of "containing" Communist North Korea into "liberating" that state.

President Truman, fearing that China might use U.S. concentration on the Korean war as cover for an attempted seizure of Taiwan, had sent the U.S.

Seventh Fleet into the Taiwan Straits in the opening days of the war to pre-clude such an eventuality. China saw the U.S. as the world's foremost impe-rialist nation, once more intervening in the Chinese civil war. By the fall of 1950, that imperialist was now leading the charge up the Korean peninsula toward Chinese territory. Even before the Inchon landing, China had warned that it would intervene if UN forces invaded North Korea. UN Commander Douglas MacArthur had made increasingly belligerent state-ments about the artificiality of the border between China and North Korea, about bombing sites in China, and about "unleashing" Chiang Kai-shek against the mainland. It was certainly an inopportune time for Chinese mil-itary action, the government's having established its power less than a year before; but it was clearly threatened by UN actions. In late fall, Chinese troops in large numbers entered the war, totaling 700,000 very quickly. It was a brutally costly war. An armistice was not reached until mid-1953, and many Chinese were killed in the last year of the war by withering UN firepower. Altogether, 2.3 million Chinese fought in the war, and there were from 360,000 to 500,000 casualties.[24]

At home, the Chinese government rallied the masses to the war's support; for example, communities contributed money for the construction of planes and other war materiel. The party whipped up hatred for the United States through the campaign of "**Resist America, Aid Korea**" and by targeting "counterrevolutionaries." Especially at risk were former Guomindang mem-bers or Guomindang military who were now suspected of sabotage. Executions of suspects were rife. In Guangdong Province alone in the period from October 1950 to August 1951, more than twenty-eight thousand people were executed.

## The Hundred Flowers Movement and Its Aftermath

By 1952, through such techniques as stringent control of government spend-ing and paying wages on the basis of "commodity-basket" values, China had tamed the cruelly rampant inflation that had gutted the economy in the late 1940s. By 1953, it was ready to announce its first Five-Year Plan, to be built on the Soviet model of state-controlled economic development. These were years when thousands of Soviet engineers and technical advisers were sta-tioned in China to teach Soviet methods; the focus was on heavy industry. The Chinese followed their Soviet patrons to the letter, and the plan was remarkably successful: most of the goals set forth were substantially exceeded. As examples, the actual production in physical output of coal by 1957 had reached 115 percent of the plan's goal, almost 130 percent of the goal for steel, 220 percent for units of machine tools, and 188 percent for truck units.

In the midst of this considerable economic success, the party under Mao's leadership kept the country's intellectuals demoralized and mostly cowed into silence. The Yan'an heritage—party control over thought, art, and litera-ture—held sway. In the early years of the People's Republic, whenever there was forthright criticism of the party or its policy, as in the 1955 case of author **Hu Feng**, the critic opened himself to vicious attacks; Hu's criticism unleashed a nationwide campaign against him. Despite such a possibility, many intellectuals were obviously dissatisfied with their second-class citizen-ship and with an increasingly bureaucratized party-state. A new literary voice, **Wang Meng**, in autumn 1956 published a short novel, *The Young Man Who Has Just Arrived at the Organization Department*, which pointed to the unre-sponsive and arbitrary nature of party leaders.

Most historians believe that by 1956, Mao, despite his distrust and dislike of intellectuals, had come to see that China could not progress as fast as it might if it ignored its intellectuals or kept them permanently intimidated. He and others apparently thought that, though there might be more critics like Wang Meng, their criticism would deal with processes and personal dis-gruntlements and not with the party or its policies. Although there was con-siderable disarray in the party over the policy, Mao was able to get the Hundred Flowers movement going in April 1957. Calling for the blooming of a hundred flowers and the contending of a hundred schools of thought, Mao and the party leaders asked for comments on the state of affairs. The goal was to achieve a greater unity for the challenges ahead. For five weeks in May and June, the flowers bloomed, intellectuals apparently convinced that the Yan'an restrictiveness had been lifted. Criticisms of basic party poli-cy and of the party itself were brutally frank: "[N]ot since the spread of the May Fourth movement . . . had there been such a concerted and political outcry."[25] Moreover, the criticism spread quickly to other groups, including farmers and urban workers.

Within a month, the party moved to quash the movement it had started: an antirightist campaign was announced. It was a bitter harvest for intellectuals and artists. The execution of the campaign was itself an object lesson in party arbitrariness: a statement by the party center that there might be up to 10 per-cent of the leaders who were "rightist" in any area was taken to mean that local party branches had to find 10 percent who must be tagged as "rightist." Within the next few months, more than three hundred thousand intellectuals lost careers and titles, were jailed, or were sent to labor camps or to do heavy labor in the countryside. Some committed suicide. Most were not rehabilitated until 1979, many of those posthumously. Clearly, the years were not yet fat for many Chinese. Mao's China had brought hope to many; it had taken the first bold economic steps in the remaking of China; it had stood up to the United States; and yet none could know that by 1957 its significant accomplishments were already in the past and that the years ahead would bring Chinese life to its most desperate pass yet.

## COMMUNIZATION AND MILITARIZATION

### Collectivization

The expansion of agricultural production was essential to serve as a base for China's industrialization. Policy makers saw collectivization as key because it facilitated state extraction of resources, agricultural mechanization, and greater efficiencies. The creation of **mutual aid teams**, formalized versions of traditional practices of peasant cooperation in sharing labor and farm animals and tools, was the first step. In a typical team, the number of cooperating households was generally ten or fewer, and in many areas they were members of the same kinship group. By the end of 1952, an estimated 40 percent of all peasant households were team members, and the figure reached 92 percent in 1956.

Approximately three to five teams (thirty to fifty households) were joined to comprise the lower-level **agricultural producers' cooperative** (APC), the next stage of collectivization. This semisocialist unit was characterized by "central management but private ownership": members contributed land, draft animals, and equipment as capital shares to the cooperative and received payment, after wages were deducted, for their contributions. The pace of the establishment of lower-level APCs varied. They were organized in some areas in 1951, but areas in southeast China did not establish their first APCs until 1954 and 1955. By that time, local resistance had begun to rise against the movement, especially where mutual aid teams had not been developed and cadres had moved directly from private ownership to the lower-level APC.

Even though it seems obvious that for collectivization to become solidly rooted in the local socioeconomic terrain it would take substantial time, the party-state repeatedly revealed a "great leap" mentality. In this framework, with Mao leading the way, the leadership decided to push full steam ahead to upper-level APCs, at the very time when only 15 percent of peasant house-holds were members of lower-level APCs. Frenetic organizing in the last months of 1955 led to the spectacular rise of membership in lower-level APCs to more than 80 percent of peasant households in January 1956. A remarkably ironic and tragic aspect of these revolutionary developments is that the party leadership abandoned the strategy of pragmatically developing cohesive socioeconomic units that had brought them political and military victory. As a result, they destroyed what they had tried to build.

Higher-level APCs were more revolutionary than their lower-level prede-cessors. Much larger, they comprised two hundred to three hundred house-holds; private ownership was ended, with land owned by the collective; and there were no payments for contributions of land and other assets. By the end of 1956, almost 88 percent of peasant households had become members in higher-level APCs. Many peasants considered the establishment of the high-er APC, or collective, as "a turning point in their relationship to both the party-state and the rural cadres." Peasants sensed a loss of control over their lives; marketing restraints, quotas, and rations increasingly confined their actions, and cadres as state agents became daily more central.

## The Great Leap Forward

Attempting to turn the "great leap" mentality into a reality, in 1958 the party speeded up the collectivist movement by launching the **Great Leap Forward**, a visionary campaign to both communize and militarize Chinese society. A Politburo resolution in August 1958 called the people's communes "the basic social units of Communist society"; it called for "actively us[ing] the form of people's communes to explore the practical . . . transition to communism."[26] The commune, on average made up of about 5,500 households, became the locality's main governmental unit and socioeconomic organization in charge of agricultural production, industry, commerce, health, social services, and education. Private plots and private ownership of livestock were ended. Most of the earnings were paid on a per capita basis, and hence differences between incomes on communes were greatly reduced.

Two commune structures perhaps best epitomized the Great Leap—the backyard steel furnace and the commune mess hall. Rooted in Mao's ideal-istic populism was the sense that if the masses had a participatory stake in production, their energies would be marshaled and production would increase dramatically. Industry had generally not been located in the coun-tryside. Mao believed that communes should develop local industries through which people could contribute their productive capacities. Steelmaking was one such area. For the cause, people contributed iron tools and implements, window frames, pots and pans—all to go into the making of pig iron. What was produced cracked easily and was thus completely useless; it filled train cars that sat in train yards around the country. Useful iron products, in many cases necessary for daily tasks, had been turned into something without value.

Perhaps no change made a greater difference than commune mess halls. From the perspective of agricultural production, mess halls "meant that each commune member had three extra hours for work or study, labor productivity had been raised by about 30 percent, and six million units of female labor power had been released from domestic chores."[27] Gone was a traditional centerpiece of farm life—the daily coming together of family for shared meals; in its place was eating in mammoth rooms with large numbers of people, most of them strangers. Though the policy was not directed against the family, it probably subtly eroded the closeness of the kin unit. Commune nurseries and kindergartens meant that grandparents no longer needed to watch their grandchildren; instead, they could spend their time with other elderly people at "happiness homes." Parents who chose to send their children to boarding primary schools and even boarding kindergartens lost considerable contact and control at an early age. The state thus impinged far more deeply on people's lives than ever before, penetrating into family life and beginning to replace traditional practices with governmental services.

These revolutionary changes improved the status of women. Communization freed them from daily cooking responsibilities and child care so that they could work on the land. From one perspective, this helped to equalize the status of men and women. For the first time, rural women achieved their own economic identity; an estimated 90 percent performed farm labor in 1958–59. But this policy was not for purposes of gender equity. It came, like the Yan'an period's emphasis on the "national woman," for purposes of the party-state.[28] In essence, the party was redefining women primarily as workers who labored with men outside the home; it was saying that the *proper* woman served the state, not simply the family.

The militarization of Chinese society that had been gradually increasing since the first years of the century culminated with the people's communes, which were organized into military units and renamed brigades (sometimes, companies) and subdivided into production teams, or platoons. The use of military terminology points to the degree of regimentation the party-state was imposing on the masses, as well as the militarization of labor. The rhetoric of the time was also permeated by the military ethos. In speaking of competing with other communes for production, cadres in one Guangdong commune declared: "In order to promote the leap forward, we shall compete with other districts in the entire county. Our soldiers and horses are strong, our generals brave and numerous. . . . We dare to be challenged. Clad in our armor and ready in our formations, we await the battle cry."[29]

The establishment of the commune militia continued the trend. Every able-bodied citizen between the ages of fifteen and fifty was in the ordinary militia, and those aged sixteen to thirty were in the "hard-core" militia. By January 1959, 220 million men and women had become militia members. Although even most hard-core militia members never fired a gun, they were "psychologically mobilized" by the training of two to three hours per day. Leaders insisted that militia members adhere to "rising, eating, sleeping, setting out to work, and returning from work" at the same times: "This greatly strengthened the collectivization of life and organizational discipline, and nurtured the fighting style in production and work." The use of military terminology was to induce peasants to work even harder. They became "fighters" on the "agricultural front"; the countryside became the "battlefield"; and nature itself became an "enemy" to be overcome.[30]

By the end of 1958, it was clear that the Great Leap had fallen very far short—in fact, flat on its face. The fiasco with steelmaking and its ripple effect on the economy at large was compounded by a worsening agricultural tragedy. Though the harvest was dismal, grain production estimates had been extremely overinflated. The state's levy of grain, based upon the estimates of the harvest, took most of what was produced, leaving little for the masses. People in the countryside were beginning to go hungry. At a party central committee meeting in December, Mao lost the presidency of the PRC to Liu Shaoqi, at least in part because of the encroaching disaster.

In July 1959, at a conference of leaders at **Lushan** in Jiangxi Province, Mao clashed over the Great Leap with Defense Minister **Peng Dehuai**. Peng charged that the Leap was not working, that the huge grain harvest figures were not credible, and that he was concerned about the direction of policies. Mao went for the jugular, attacking Peng for his "right opportunist" remarks and accusing him of complaining to Khrushchev about Great Leap policies on a trip to Warsaw Pact countries in June. The USSR's leader had then offered critical comments about the policies. If these circumstances continued, Mao bitterly declared, he might go to the mountains to form another Red Army to attack the party. At the month-long meeting, Peng was dismissed, and

**Lin Biao**, a strong supporter of Mao, was named new defense minister. One scholar has pointed to the Lushan conference as marking the beginning of the unraveling of the "political consensus" of the leadership group that had formed at Yan'an.[31]

## The Flight and the Famine

In the middle of the growing economic crisis, in the summer of 1960, Khrushchev suddenly called back to the Soviet Union all the scientists, engineers, and industrial advisers that had been working in several hundred Chinese enterprises. What in part led to the decision was the Soviet leader's pique at Mao for abandoning the Soviet model in the Great Leap, and his desire to teach China the importance of the Soviet connection. The pull-out also followed generally worsening relations between the erstwhile Communist allies. In a June meeting in Bucharest, for example, the Sino-Soviet split erupted in the open with Khrushchev and **Peng Zhen**, the Chinese delegate, attacking each other in scathing denunciations. In mid-July, the Soviet advisers in China received their orders to leave.

The short-term effects on China were severe, especially in light of the economic crisis and the institutional turmoil into which the Great Leap had thrown party and state. "The abruptness of the withdrawal meant that construction stopped at the sites of scores of new plants and factories. . . . Spare parts were no longer available . . . and electric power stations . . . were closed down. Planning on new undertakings was abandoned."[32]

The crisis of declining grain harvests was exacerbated in 1960 by natural disasters. Typhoons caused devastating flooding in parts of south China and in Manchuria; drought was so severe along the Yellow River that its water level was decreased by two thirds; insect pests affected vast areas. More than 60 percent of farmed land was affected, resulting in paltry harvests. Grain output had been at 200 million tons in 1958; it dropped to 170 million tons in 1959 and to 144 million in 1960—a 28 percent decline from two years earlier. The depth of the tragedy is revealed by the fact that per capita food production would not again reach its pre-1957 level until the early 1970s.

Such statistics can only suggest the nightmare of these years for the masses. An estimated thirty million people starved to death in one of the world's largest famines (1960–62), worsened by nature but stemming from human policies. People were not allowed to become refugees and move to other areas in search of food. Most did not know the extent of the famine, only what was happening in their areas. Starving people ate rice husks, corncobs, weeds, grass, tree bark, even earth itself in an effort to stay alive. Malnutrition was rampant. Indeed, as a Chinese economist noted, "the Great Leap exacted a "high price in blood."[33] The years that were fat had ended in starvation and death.

## NOTES

1. The quotation is from the book jacket to Mao Dun, *Spring Silkworms and Other Stories* (Beijing: Foreign Languages Press, 1979).

2. Lyman Van Slyke, "The Chinese Communist Movement During the Sino-Japanese War, 1937–1945," in John K. Fairbank and Albert Feuerwerker, eds., *The Cambridge History of China*, vol. 13, *Republican China, 1912–1949*, part 2 (Cambridge: Cambridge University Press, 1986), p. 631.

3. Jerome Ch'en, "The Communist Movement, 1927–1937," in Fairbank and Feuerwerker, *Cambridge History of China*, vol. 13, part 2, p. 195.

4. See, for example, Gregor Benton, *Mountain Fires: The Red Army's Three-Year War in South China, 1934–1938* (Berkeley: University of California Press, 1992) and Odoric Y. K. Wou, *Mobilizing the Masses: Building Revolution in Henan* (Stanford: Stanford University Press, 1994).

5. Edgar Snow, *Red Star Over China* (New York: Random House, 1938), p. 177.

6. Mao Zedong, "Strategic Problems of China's Revolutionary War," in *Selected Works of Mao Tse-tung*, vol. 1 (London: Lawrence Wishart, 1954), p. 193, cited in Maurice Meisner, "Yenan Communism and the Rise of the Chinese People's Republic," in James B. Crowley, ed., *Modern East Asia: Essays in Interpretation* (New York: Harcourt, Brace, Jovanovich, 1970), p. 274.

7. Meisner, "Yenan Communism," p. 271.

8. This information on the three-year war comes from Gregor Benton, "Under Arms and Umbrellas: Perspectives on Chinese Communism in Defeat," in Tony Saich and Hans van de Ven, eds., *New Perspectives on the Chinese Communist Revolution* (Armonk, N.Y.: M. E. Sharpe, 1995), pp. 124–26. See also Benton's *Mountain Fires*.

9. Immanuel C.Y. Hsu, *The Rise of Modern China* (New York: Oxford University Press, 1970), p. 686.

10. For the activities of Unit 731, see Sheldon H. Harris, *Factories of Death: Japanese Biological Warfare, 1932–1945, and the American Cover-Up* (London: Routledge, 1994).

11. John Wilson Lewis, *Leadership in Communist China* (Ithaca: Cornell University Press, 1963), p. 110, cited in Van Slyke, "The Chinese Communist Movement," p. 620.

12. Tony Saich, *The Rise to Power of the Chinese Communist Party: Documents and Analysis* (Armonk, N.Y.: M. E. Sharpe, 1996), p. 1123.

13. The phrase is Ch'en Yung-fa's in *Making Revolution: The Communist Movement in Eastern and Central China, 1937–1945* (Berkeley: University of California Press, 1986), p. 220.

14. The examples from Henan are in Odoric Wou's magisterial study *Mobilizing the Masses.*

15. Ch'en Yung-fa, *Making Revolution*, p. 221.

16. Hsu, *Rise of Modern China*, p. 730.

17. Suzanne Pepper, "The KMT-CCP Conflict, 1945–1949," in Fairbank and Feuerwerker, *Cambridge History of China*, vol. 13, part 2, p. 781.

18. R. Keith Schoppa, *Xiang Lake: Nine Centuries of Chinese Life* (New Haven: Yale University Press, 1989), p. 225.

19. Cited in Jerome Chen, *Mao and the Chinese Revolution* (London: Oxford University Press, 1965), p. 346.

20. Quoted in Edwin E. Moise, *Land Reform in China and North Vietnam* (Chapel Hill: University of North Carolina Press, 1983), p. 106.

21. Pauline Keating, "The Yan'an Way of Co-operativization," *China Quarterly* 104 (December 1994): 1029–31.

22. The phrase comes from Frederick C. Teiwes, "Establishment and Consolidation of the New Regime," in Roderick MacFarquhar and John K. Fairbank, eds., *The Cambridge History of China*, vol. 14, *The People's Republic*, part 1 (Cambridge: Cambridge University Press, 1987), p. 87.

23. "The Marriage Law of the People's Republic of China, May 1, 1950," reprinted in J. Mason Gentzler, *Changing China* (New York: Pantheon, 1977), p. 268.

24. The following numbers will show the extent of the Chinese commitment: China used 66 percent of its entire field army (the equivalent of twenty-five field corps), 62 percent of its artillery (seventy divisions), 70 percent of its air force (twelve divisions), all three of its tank divisions, ten railway-engineering divisions, and two public-security divisions. See James I. Matray, *Historical Dictionary of the Korean War* (New York: Greenwood Press, 1991), p. 92.

25. Jonathan Spence, *The Search for Modern China* (New York: Norton, 1990), p. 571.

26. Quoted in Allen S. Whiting, "The Sino-Soviet Split," in MacFarquhar and Fairbank, *Cambridge History of China*, vol. 14, part 1, p. 500.

27. Issue of October 25, 1958, cited in Roderick MacFarquhar, *The Origins of the Cultural Revolution, Vol. 2: The Great Leap Forward, 1958–1960* (New York: Columbia University Press, 1983), p. 103. This was the situation specifically in Henan Province.

28. See the discussions in Christina K. Gilmartin et al., eds., *Engendering China* (Cambridge: Harvard University Press, 1994). Especially helpful are Gao Xiaoxian, "China's Modernization and Changes in the Social Status of Rural Women" and Lisa Rofel, "Liberation, Nostalgia, and a Yearning for Modernity." The term *national woman* is Tani Barlow's.

29. Helen Siu, *Agents and Victims in South China: Accomplices in Rural Revolution* (New Haven: Yale University Press, 1989), p. 176.

30. Quoted in MacFarquhar, *Origins*, pp. 101–2.

31. Kenneth Leiberthal, "The Great Leap Forward and the Split in the Yan'an Leadership, 1958–1965" in Roderick MacFarquhar, ed., *The Politics of China, 1949–1989* (Cambridge: Cambridge University Press, 1993), p. 111.

32. "The Sino-Soviet Split—The Withdrawal of the Specialists," *International Journal* (Toronto) 26, no. 3 (1971): 559, cited in Maurice Meisner, *Mao's China and After* (New York: Free Press, 1986), p. 249.

33. The economist was Sun Yefang. Cited in Thomas P. Bernstein, "Stalinism, Famine, and Chinese Peasants," *Theory and Society* 13, no. 3 (1984), p. 343.

# Economic Disasters and Miracles: 1960 to the Present—Whither State and Nation?

## CULTURAL AND ECONOMIC CATASTROPHE

### The Two Lines

The cataclysm of the Great Leap Forward created a schism in the party leadership. Not only had Mao ousted Peng Dehuai at Lushan, but his whole approach came to be seen negatively by the president of the PRC, Liu Shaoqi, and the CCP secretary-general, **Deng Xiaoping**. As the state began to recover from the disasters of the late 1950s, a dispute between the Maoist line, with its fundamentalist approach, and the Liu-Deng line, with its pragmatic approach, began to fester.[1] Though Mao clearly saw that the Great Leap had failed, he was not particularly concerned: he still had faith in his Communist goals and in motivating people through moral incentives. People would give their all for the goals of revolution and building a strong China simply because of the essentiality of those goals. Mao was hostile to established, bureaucratized party cadres and to "experts" of any variety. It was much better to be ideologically correct than to have the correct factual knowledge; better, in other words, to be Red than expert. The masses in any case had more innate abilities and common sense than the intelligentsia. Mao was ready to rely on them and on a more ad hoc, guerrillalike style in governing. Perpetual revolution through perpetual class struggle was a necessity because class enemies of the people would rear their ugly heads to challenge the people.

In contrast, the Liu-Deng line believed that the failure of the Great Leap was a disaster that must not be repeated. The party-state could most motivate the masses by offering material incentives. People who worked harder than others, who produced more than others, should be rewarded with bonuses or higher wages. These incentives would be more meaningful for people than moral encouragement, suasion, and propaganda. Mao railed that such policies smacked of "revisionism," a revising of Marxism through capitalist tactics—a practice he associated with Khrushchev. In the "Red or expert?"

debate, Liu and Deng came down squarely with expertise. Getting the job done was the main criterion for what was the right or wrong method of doing it. One of Deng's most famous statements addressed the issue: "It doesn't matter if the cat is white or black, so long as it catches rats."[2] More pragmatic than Mao, the Liu-Deng line valued the stability and knowledge of bureaucratic approaches and technocratic abilities. It also valued political stability in order to make the gains necessary for building a modern socialist nation.

In the late 1950s, Mao had shown increasing tendencies to practice party administration in guerrilla fashion, depending on small, informal meetings for major decision making. In the aftermath of the Great Leap, Mao's comrades restored collective decision making in an effort to restrain him, relying on larger, more formal, central work conferences to which experts were invited. Both Liu and Deng spoke of serious shortcomings in the party leadership. Mao as party chairman still had a commanding presence in the party and thus still had the power to intervene directly in any situation.

In 1962, Mao began a **Socialist Education Campaign** to focus on problems among local cadres and to restress the value of class struggle. The campaign almost immediately became grist for the struggle between the two lines. The campaign work was to be undertaken by large work teams, whereas Mao would have chosen to use the masses more directly. When Liu and Deng rewrote directives for the work teams, deemphasizing class struggle, Mao saw his program for rectification become a tool for revisionists to reassert party control in the countryside. Mao became convinced that the Chinese revolution was in danger. Seeing himself and the revolution as one and the same, he felt compelled to destroy the party that he had spent his life building but that now, in his estimation, had gone so wrong.

## The Cultural Revolution: The Red Guard Phase, 1966–69

On August 5, 1966, Mao wrote a big-character poster in Beijing—BOMBARD THE HEADQUARTERS—thus launching a ten-year experiment in madness that destroyed untold numbers of lives and careers and led to tremendous property losses (see documents 14 and 15, appendix 2). It was, in the words of one analyst, "one of the most extraordinary events of this century."[3] It was in part a personal power struggle—Mao had reportedly felt so out of power that he had to rebuild his own power base in Shanghai and fight his way back. It was also a struggle over the direction of the revolution: would it be pragmatic reform undertaken gradually by bureaucrats and technocrats? or revolutionary change brought by young Red Guards in a never-ending cacophony of class struggle? It was, in addition, Mao's quest for revolutionary immortality and purity.

Although rebellious student groups had begun to form in May at schools around the country, they were monitored by party work teams until late July, when Mao ordered the withdrawal of the work teams. In August, under their own authority, they reorganized themselves as **Red Guards**; within a short period of time, Red Guard groups were organized at most colleges and middle schools. Shouting slogans like "It is justified to rebel," a million young people assembled on August 18 in Tian'anmen Square to see Mao at sunrise on top of the Gate of Heavenly Peace: he would be their "great helmsman," their Supreme Commander. Mao enjoined them to destroy the four "olds"— old ideas, habits, customs, culture. They were to lead the rebellion against party and state leadership. Announcing that his successor would be Lin Biao, Mao made no secret of the fact that the two leaders under the Cultural Revolution gun were Liu Shaoqi and Deng Xiaoping.

The last months of 1966 were chaotic. Red Guard units fanned out over China, seeking out and destroying anything representative of the feudal past and the bourgeois present. Homes were ransacked; museums and libraries were pillaged; books and newspapers, the notes and writings of intellectuals, religious statues and art, recordings of Western music were trashed. But this "revolutionary action" went well beyond *things*. People became the targets very quickly, especially intellectuals. Red Guard youths tortured and beat them. The humiliation and degradation they suffered drove many to suicide. The best-known such victim was Lao She, author of *Rickshaw, Cat Country*, and a number of important plays. Middle-school Red Guards again and again ordered him to struggle meetings; they ransacked his house and burned his books. Authorities found his body in a lake in late August, a victim of suicide by drowning. Some twelve million Red Guards journeyed to Beijing on their own "Long March" to see their Red Sun; the last immense rally in the square came near the end of November. As the fall progressed, more frequently than not Red Guard units engaged in violent fighting with rival groups of Red Guards and groups of farmers and workers who resented the youths inserting themselves forcibly into local situations they knew nothing about.

One of the Red Guard slogans was "destruction before construction." In Mao's mind, the construction necessary was rebuilding the party, or at least the local and national power structures. But what model to use? On the basis of the successful ousting of existing authorities in Shanxi and Heilongjiang Provinces, the revolutionary committee emerged as the favored new power structure. Composed of revolutionary masses (Red Guards and the workers' Revolutionary Rebels), party cadres, and the People's Liberation Army (PLA), the revolutionary committee became the new structure promoted by Mao and his colleagues. The appearance of the army in the local and provincial leadership structures was important. Since party structures were weak, if functioning at all, and since factionalism, often violent, made any constructive action impossible, the army emerged as key power broker and important player in both political and economic matters. Mao became increasingly dependent on the army for maintaining some degree of stability. The most dangerous situations developed where revolutionary masses formed factional ties with military commanders. In July 1967, in Wuhan, the key regional military officer and his troops briefly mutinied against Beijing, backing down only after the government sent superior force.

By late summer 1967, China was on the verge of anarchy. Rebels took over the Foreign Ministry offices in Beijing for two weeks, installing "proletarian internationalism." Their tenure in foreign affairs ended in the seizure and burning of the British diplomatic compound in Beijing. Battles were erupting all over the country between revolutionary rebel groups who were seizing weapons from military bases and the PLA; they were bloody and destructive. The reality was outright civil war. In early September, Mao ordered the PLA to restore order. It was not quickly accomplished. In the spring and summer of 1968, a new wave of violence erupted between competing rebel groups, allegedly encouraged by Mao's wife, **Jiang Qing**, who had emerged as the cultural dictator of the revolution. The renewed internecine conflict finally burned itself out at Qinghua University in Beijing, a denouement hastened by Mao's visit and scolding of the student radicals.

This violent phase of the Cultural Revolution ended with the meeting of the Ninth Party Congress in April 1969. Waged to destroy the party as it had developed, the revolution ended by reasserting party control. But there was a change in party structure—the rising power of the military. In many ways, the twentieth-century trend of the militarization of Chinese politics and society is seen in the new face of the party. Of the new party central committee, composed of 279 members and alternates, 45 percent was from the PLA, 28 percent from the revolutionary party cadres, and 27 percent from the revolutionary masses. With the conclusion of this violent phase, there was a substantial migration of people from cities to the countryside. More than four million students from high schools and universities (many of them former Red Guards) were sent to the countryside to live with farmers and undergo a period of reeducation, an experience that left many without college opportunities and that helped to create a "lost generation" of disillusioned, cynical, and even antisocial adults. Many party cadres and bureaucrats, too, were shipped away to the greater poverty and inconvenience of farm life; they were sent for so-called productive labor and political study—more realistically, this was hard labor and indoctrination—at so-called May Seventh Cadre Schools. Up to three million bureaucrats and party cadres spent time in the countryside. The length of time spent in the countryside for members of both groups was undetermined.

Any post-mortem of this phase of the Cultural Revolution must assess both the short-term and long-term results. An estimated half million Chinese were killed during this phase. The harassment, persecution, and torture of intellectuals and writers was widespread. The indictment against the Gang of Four (the extreme leftists in control during much of the Cultural Revolution) at their trial in 1980–81 specified that "2,600 people in literary and art circles, 142,000 cadres and teachers in units under the Ministry of Education, 53,000 scientists and technicians in research institutes, and 500 professors and associate professors in medical colleges and institutes" were persecuted and that "an unspecified number" of them died.[4] Mistreatment of party cadres and government officials was rife. The purge rate of provincial and regional officials was 70 to 80 percent; about three million people were purged and only rehabilitated in the late 1970s. Others suffered beatings, torture, death. The best-known was Liu Shaoqi. A former president of the government and a leader in the Communist Party since 1923, he was denounced as a "renegade, traitor, and scab hiding in the Party, a lackey of imperialism, modern revisionism, and the Guomindang reactionaries."[5] Liu was placed under house arrest; he was tortured and beaten by Red Guards; and he was left to die, ill, untreated, and isolated in a prison in 1969.

Among the Cultural Revolution's long-term consequences was a weakening of the body politic; these years produced fragmented leadership by shattering the party and setting in its place weak institutions. The struggle between the two lines had not been decisive. Mao and the radicals had had to pull back and in the second phase of the Cultural Revolution (1969–76) had to bring back Deng Xiaoping into leadership circles. It has been suggested that another consequence of this experience was an enduring factionalism that grew out of the struggles of the Cultural Revolution. Finally, there was the "lost generation"—those who had lost faith in the moralistic rhetoric of Mao and above all in the validity of the Communist political system; it is not surprising that they would be open to the expansive materialism that would mark the 1980s and 1990s.

## The Cultural Revolution: Factionalism and Fragmentation, 1969–76

If the first phase of the Cultural Revolution stimulated the rise of a kind of malignant factionalism, the second phase was marked by faction-induced fits and starts. At least four factions toyed with taking the leadership of the Cultural Revolution in their own particular ideological direction: Lin Biao (ultraleftist military); Mao and the Gang of Four (ultraleftist); Zhou Enlai (centrist); Deng Xiaoping (pragmatist). Beneath the surface, a common concern to all was the question of Mao's successor.

Lin Biao, a hero of the Manchurian campaign in the civil war, had been named defense minister after the ouster of Peng Dehuai in 1959. He had been one of Mao's strongest supporters during the first phase of the Cultural Revolution and had been instrumental in building up the cult of Mao. With the success of the military at the Ninth Party Congress (1969), his star seemed to be rising even higher. Although he had been linked with Mao's wife, the radical Jiang Qing, and the Gang of Four of which she was a part during the Cultural Revolution, his main power base had become the military. Now he was at odds with Mao. The original source of tension between Lin and Mao, who in 1966 had named him his successor, is not clear. Lin may well have thought that Mao's pulling back from the radicalism of the Cultural Revolution was forfeiting any gains that had been made in the movement. There were ill feelings also over matters of foreign policy. Fighting with the Soviet Union had erupted on an island in the Ussuri River in March 1969, and in August there was a serious outbreak of fighting in Xinjiang; word had also gotten out from Eastern Europe that the Soviet Union was bandying about talk "about a 'surgical strike' against Chinese nuclear weapons installations."[6] This context gave rise to a possible rapprochement with the United States, as a way of attaining greater national security in light of the tensions with the Soviet Union. Ideologically, such a rapprochement was insupportable in Lin's opinion; he reportedly opposed such a policy. In terms of personal ambition, Lin wanted the post of the presidency of the government to be written into the constitution and pressed Mao to reassume that post. Mao resisted these demands, irritated at Lin's persistence. Mao perceived that Lin wanted the post himself and that he was manipulating the political situation to his own ends.

Mao and Lin were on a collision course. Mao attacked those closest to Lin, almost goading him to act. Lin complied, beginning to plan a coup for early 1971. The objective of Plot 571 was to arrest two men in the Gang of Four and precipitate a crisis that Lin could use the military to handle. In the end, perhaps because of late-summer comparisons Mao made between Lin and ousted leaders Liu Shaoqi and Peng Dehuai, the plot was changed: they would try to assassinate Mao by blowing up his train. The plot did not evolve as devised, and Mao escaped. On September 13, when Lin and his entourage attempted to flee, apparently to the Soviet Union, their plane crashed in Mongolia, killing all on board. Questions about Mao's judgment of his comrades-in-arms arise from Lin's attempted assassination (questions already raised by Mao's treatment of Liu Shaoqi). Even more, the in-house machinations and treachery in this episode raise questions about the supposed salutary impacts of the Cultural Revolution on political culture.

The years after Lin's demise saw increasing manipulation of the political scene by the Gang of Four to try to establish their position as Mao's successor. Their sense of urgency was greater because of Premier Zhou Enlai's cancer and Mao's own failing health; he was ill with Parkinson's disease. A rather mysterious political campaign, the **Anti-Lin [Biao], Anti-Confucius campaign**, in early 1974 coupled the radical Lin and the reactionary Confucius; it was apparently aimed at Zhou Enlai. More important, when Zhou was permanently moved to the hospital in mid-1974, Mao had to choose someone to do Zhou's job, managing the daily business of the country. Mao's surprise choice—an outrage to the Gang of Four—was Deng Xiaoping, the number-two target during the Cultural Revolution. The choice is explained through Mao's still considerable fears of the military and the role that it could play in politics. Mao wanted an old comrade that key generals could trust—one who could take over the Military Affairs Commission and maneuver the officers out of close involvement in politics.

Policy documents produced under his direction during Deng's year in power indicate the direction he would take China during the 1980s and 1990s, and why the Gang of Four would oppose him. In his comments on a document dealing with industry, among other things, Deng called for the introduction of foreign technology, putting "quality first," and restoring material incentives. Jiang Qing, the main spokesperson for the Gang of Four, repeatedly sparred with Deng. Jiang had apparently become estranged from Mao, having moved away from the government compound of Zhongnanhai; however, the source of their alienation is unclear.

The year 1976 was traumatic for the Chinese nation. In January, Zhou Enlai died. Mao replaced him with a dark horse, **Hua Guofeng**, not with Deng Xiaoping, whose policies and views Mao did not want permanently in place. In mid-March, people in small groups began to leave wreaths for the memory of Zhou Enlai at the Heroes Monument in Tian'anmen Square; the numbers of people doing so daily escalated until, on April 4—the Qing Ming festival day, when Chinese traditionally tend the graves of their family dead— approximately two million visited the square with wreaths. Some eulogies simply praised Zhou; others attacked the Gang of Four. The Gang, believing that the masses in remembering Zhou were really saying that Deng should be his rightful successor, collaborated with other officials to declare what was happening a "counter-revolutionary incident." The next day, when people returned in large numbers, police had removed all the wreaths. Violence broke out and police vehicles were burned. Eventually, stick-wielding public security forces and Beijing garrison troops appeared, beating people still at the square.

There were more shocks to come. In early July, Zhu De, the founder of the Red Army during the days of the Jiangxi Soviet, died. Later in the same month (July 28) a devastating earthquake leveled the city of Tangshan, near Tianjin, killing at least a quarter of a million people; some estimates went as high as two thirds of a million, but no matter which figure is true, the magnitude of the disaster was overwhelming. Traditionally such disasters were seen as the natural world's reflection of similar traumas in the world of humans. Then on September 9, Mao died. The moment had come that all the maneuvering in the last years of the Cultural Revolution had been geared to. The members of the Gang of Four, who were not as prepared for eventualities as their opponents, were arrested on October 6. A Chinese scholar put it tersely: "When Jiang Qing was arrested at her residence, her servant spat on her. The Cultural Revolution was over."[7]

There was yet a coda to the story of the Cultural Revolution, the trial of the Gang of Four (November 1980 to January 1981) and the resolution on party history adopted in the summer of 1981. Among other charges, the Gang was accused of persecuting party and state leaders—persecuting 729,511 party cadres and citizens and killing 34,800 of them. All four were found guilty; all but Jiang Qing confessed. Jiang and one other were sentenced to death with extended reprieves; the others were given prison terms. It was a political trial. The four could be blamed and the slate wiped clean; but no one asked how millions of Chinese could be so led astray into such disastrous policies by a handful of plotters. Jiang herself committed suicide in prison in 1991.

The "Resolution on Certain Questions in the History of Our Party Since the Founding of the PRC" noted that Mao's contributions far transcended his mistakes. But it criticized Mao severely for extending the scope of the 1957 Anti-Rightist Campaign, for his leftist errors in the Great Leap Forward, for undercutting Leninist principles through his sponsoring a personality cult and his "personal arbitrariness," and for his "erroneous left theses" that gave rise to the Cultural Revolution. In the end, it said that "chief responsibility for the grave left error of the Cultural Revolution, an error comprehensive in magnitude and protracted in duration, does indeed lie with Comrade Mao Zedong."[8] Perhaps it was economic expert Chen Yun who best captured Mao's historical role: "Had Chairman Mao died in 1956, there would have been no doubt that he was a great leader of the Chinese people. . . . Had he died in 1966, his meritorious achievements would have been somewhat tarnished, but his overall record was still very good. Since he actually died in 1976, there is nothing we can do about it."[9]

## REFORM AND REPRESSION

### *Openings*

By mid-1977, Deng Xiaoping had been reappointed to his old governmental positions. Although he was subordinate to Hua Guofeng, he was primed to move toward control of the polity. In 1977 and 1978, policies bore the imprint of both men, with Hua continuing to rely basically on Mao's way and Deng championing projects that necessitated high scientific and technological abilities (for example, work on an ICBM warhead–delivery system, nuclear tests, a seabed cable to Japan, and construction of the first oil tanker larger than fifty thousand tons). The projects were indicative of what emerged as Deng's program of the **Four Modernizations**, a term actually first used by Hua; it referred to the areas of agriculture, industry, national defense, and science and technology. The program depended on policy changes that promoted a decade of "opening" in politics, economics, and culture in both international and domestic arenas.

Events in the four months from December 1978 to March 1979 were harbingers of the domestic and foreign policies that the Chinese government would use for the remainder of the century. First, taken chronologically, in mid-December, the announcement came from Washington and Beijing that the United States and China would normalize relations on January 1, 1979. China was opening to the larger international community, turning away from the Maoist focus on self-reliance. Deng's visit to the United States in January 1979 gave expression to that new policy. Second, at the Third Plenum of the Eleventh Central Committee in late December, policy considerations involving the Four Modernizations were clarified:

Carrying out the Four Modernizations requires great growth in the productive forces . . . diverse changes in those aspects of the relations of production
. . . not in harmony with the growth of productive forces, and . . . changes
in all methods of management, actions, and thinking that stand in the way
of such growth.[10]

Economic reform was, in other words, necessary to achieve the desired ends.
The second policy trend was apparent in the winter 1979 crackdown on citizens who were putting posters on **Democracy Wall**, a Beijing city wall, offering commentary and criticisms about public policies; it had earlier been permitted by Deng himself. The arrests, especially of **Wei Jingsheng**, whose
poster had called for a **Fifth Modernization**, democracy, pointed to the political repression that would accompany the economic progressivism of the
regimes of Deng and **Jiang Zemin** (see document 16, appendix 2).

The opening of China to the outside world is perhaps best epitomized by
its U.S. relations. Fears of the Soviet Union had caused China's willingness to
entertain a closer relationship to the United States. Negotiations by both
countries led to President Richard Nixon's visit to China in February 1972.
The **Shanghai Communiqué** noted the differences in the two nations' policies and outlooks, with the United States not challenging the position (held
by both Taiwan and China) that "there is but one China and that Taiwan is a
part of China."[11] The two countries agreed that trade and cultural and scientific exchanges should be increased and that they should work to establish full
diplomatic relations. Announcement of Nixon's trip in part had led to China's
admission to the United Nations in October 1971. The number of countries
that established diplomatic relations with China rose from 57 in 1970 to 119 in
1979—China's greatest number of international ties since the 1949 establishment of the regime. By May 1989, that number had risen to 137 nations.

The December 1978 plenum signaled the growing significance of economic rationales for expanding both the international opening and the
domestic opening. Such an emphasis meant the expansion of foreign trade
and, something new, of foreign investment. Beginning with a handful of
loans, credits, and **joint ventures**, the opening eventually led to full foreign
ownership and operation in some cases. In 1979, four **special economic zones**
on the southeast coast were opened to offer special concessions to foreign
investors. Fourteen more were added in 1986; in that year, Hainan Island, in
the South China Sea, was also so designated. Joint ventures in these and other
cities have especially helped to create a flourishing private sector. China
replaced Taiwan in the World Bank and the International Monetary Fund. In

the 1980s, an increasingly large influx of foreign travelers stimulated the rapid growth of the tourist industry, even as ever greater numbers of Chinese were traveling abroad. The numbers of students going overseas to study grew rapidly. From 1979 to 1989, there were more than sixty thousand regular students studying abroad, and the total number of student visas from 1983 to 1988 reached 150,000. In 1987–88, there were six thousand foreign students and thirty-six thousand foreign experts and staff in China. The goals of these exchanges were obviously access to foreign items that could assist in realizing the Four Modernizations. In assessing how the whole issue of international opening relates to another theme of the 1980s and 1990s—that of repressing politically suspect ideas—policy makers have recognized that an opened window may let in some mosquitoes and flies, but that they can be quickly swatted down.

## Economic Reforms

Reform of the economy utilizing capitalist techniques (or in Chinese governmental euphemism, "socialism with Chinese characteristics") has been the most important shaping feature of Chinese life since Deng's reforms began. In the beginning, reforms focused on the farms. With the abolition of the people's communes in 1983, a quarter century after their establishment, family farming again emerged as the model. Farmers did not gain the right to own their land; instead, they got access to the land through a fifty-year lease from the collective, during which time they could buy, sell, and inherit the property. This new policy initiative—in addition to the **"responsibility system,"** which let farmers keep profits after remitting taxes to the state (see below)—served as incentive for the rapid expansion of family farming. The new system also prompted farmers to shift resources into cash crops that would bring greater return. These changes produced a remarkable rise in agricultural production and in farmers' living standards. Accounts of newly rich farmers purchasing all the modern conveniences and luxuries, even their own airplanes, became commonplace. By the late 1990s, homes of farmers on the southern shore of Hangzhou Bay, near the city of Hangzhou, looked inside and out like those in many U.S. suburbs: they were attractive, modern, two-story homes with garages, satellite dishes, and every modern convenience.

In urban centers, private and collective business and industrial enterprises quickly began to compete with and challenge state-sector business and industry. The state tried to stimulate entrepreneurial types to establish private and collective enterprises apart from the state sector. The old model in which the state received all business and industry profits was superseded by an industri-al "responsibility system" (paralleling the one for farmers) in which an enter-prise retained half the profits after the deduction of production costs and after it had remitted a 55 percent tax on revenues to the state. Price controls on small consumer items were removed, with prices determined by the market. In the mid-1980s, the state initiated efforts to begin privatizing in the state sec-tor. The growing private sector, especially in the 1990s, energized urban economies. The resulting new enterprises provided job opportunities to large numbers of rural migrants.

The pace of national development in the late 1980s and the 1990s was noth-ing short of breathtaking. Journalist Nicholas Kristof looked at the history of the rate of development—specifically, at the length of time it took various countries to double their per capita gross domestic product after the start of serious industrial modernization. It took England fifty-eight years from the late eighteenth century; it took the United States forty-seven years from 1839; it took Japan thirty-four years starting in 1885. China, in startling contrast, has been doubling its per capita GDP every ten years.[12] Kristof is probably on tar-get with his contention that "the explosion of wealth in China may prove to be the most important trend in the world during this age."[13] Indeed, one of the hallmarks of the reform period was the exaltation of material incentives over ideology. Another Deng dictum (almost as famous as the one about a cat catching rats) carried the day: "To get rich is glorious." On a 1992 trip to the special economic zone of Shenzhen, after some uncertainties in the years after the Beijing bloodshed in 1989, he had underscored that slogan, calling for ever faster economic development (see document 19, appendix 2).

## Political Repression

If there was greater economic (and social) freedom in the 1980s and 1990s, there was little in the political realm. The closing of Democracy Wall in 1979 at the beginning of the economic reforms was symbolically indicative of the repressive political policies that accompanied the reforms in the regimes of both Deng Xiaoping and his successor Jiang Zemin. In 1981 came a campaign against **bourgeois liberalization**, with many arrests, perhaps most notably of three Guangzhou men collectively known as Li Yizhe; in 1974 they had writ-ten a lengthy defense of the rule of law and a criticism of the party. In 1983, conservatives in the party pushed another campaign against "spiritual pollu-tion," which they saw as a result of the economic reforms. In the early 1980s, literary dissent was also attacked by the party.

More serious difficulties erupted in late 1986. In the midst of some flagging of the economic reforms, debate had begun in the summer, even among party leaders, over the advisability of some greater political reforms (see document 17, appendix 2). Astrophysicist **Fang Lizhi**, one of China's leading scientists, began to call for basic political change. Yet in the fall, when laws regulating local candidates for the National People's Congress were announced by Beijing, they were even more restrictive than previous ones. In December, student demonstrations against these restrictions began in the city of Hefei, Anhui Province, home of Fang Lizhi. The demonstrations spread to sixteen other cities. Students called for greater freedom, an end to party nepotism, and better university dormitories and cafeterias. The government crackdown was rapid. The party's general-secretary, **Hu Yaobang**, one of Deng Xiaoping's chosen successors, who had called for conciliation, took the fall, resigning from his post in January 1987. There were arrests of students and the firing of Fang Lizhi and other academic officers.

The late 1986–early 1987 demonstrations were the precursor for the so-called Democracy Movement in the spring of 1989. Using the sudden death of their erstwhile supporter Hu Yaobang on April 15 as pretext, students took to the streets of Beijing, and eventually to streets in cities all over the country. They called for the same reforms that had been their cry more than two years earlier, a general call for "democracy." Party leaders immediately used combative language to denounce the demonstrations. Student leaders, however, seemed filled with a sense of destiny, organizing huge demonstrations to commemorate the seventieth anniversary of the May Fourth Incident (see document 18, appendix 2). Some flagging of student commitment in the anniversary demonstration's aftermath was revived by a hunger strike, staged at Tian'anmen Square, the destination of the demonstration marches. The hunger strike brought support from Beijing society at large. By mid-May, demonstrators were being supported and joined by workers, teachers, police, doctors, nurses, and journalists. Student occupation of the square was a huge embarrassment to the Chinese government when Mikhail Gorbachev arrived on May 15 to normalize relations between China and the Soviet Union. Shortly after his departure, party hardliners defeated any chance that **Zhao Ziyang**, the party chairman, would remain in power; like Hu Yaobang, Zhao was one of Deng's chosen successors and a potential student supporter.

Martial law was declared on May 20; units of the PLA were to clear the streets of demonstrators. But the people of Beijing took to the streets to block the advancing soldiers and to dissuade them from taking action against the demonstrators. For two weeks the stalemate continued. On May 30, the demonstrators unveiled a styrofoam and plaster statue, the Goddess of Democracy, ironically the last major effort of the movement. In the early morning hours of June 4, the crackdown occurred. Many citizens died along the western reaches of the Avenue of Eternal Peace that ran along the north side of the square; in the square itself there were few, if any, casualties. The government's rationale for the crackdown was fear of anarchy and "counter-revolution": the formation of independent workers' unions, the large numbers of citizens from many walks of life who had become involved in supporting the movement, the actions of the people of Beijing in immobilizing the PLA, and the rhetoric of the students convinced conservatives in the leadership, epitomized most clearly by Premier **Li Peng**, that the movement had to be stopped. From the perspective of the demonstrators, the *People's* Liberation Army had been mobilized for the first time against the people. Around the world there was shock, dismay, and condemnation that the government had not been willing to seek a compromise and had resorted instead to brute force; threatened retaliation, however, did not generally materialize. With the arrests of many leaders of the movement, the government once again enforced at least outward conformity to its rule. In the end, after trials in early 1991, eighteen dissidents were sentenced to prison, for from two to thirteen years. Fang Lizhi and his wife, who took refuge in the U.S. embassy following the episode, were allowed to leave the country in June 1990.

In regard to the issues of political dissent, the decade of the 1990s saw a continuing on-again/off-again policy, with periodic roundups of dissidents and periodic releases of dissidents from prison. In part this seemed to reflect the government's effort to respond to foreign criticism about its human rights policy so as to avoid various kinds of penalties that foreign nations might apply; on the other hand, the erratic policy reflected the continuing distrust and fear among the leadership about the potential for political trouble if a more liberal policy were adopted. Thus, for example, one of the 1989 student leaders, **Wang Dan**, was sentenced to four years in prison in 1991, but was released in 1993. Later he was reimprisoned, then was allowed to leave China in 1998. Similarly, the most famous dissident, Wei Jingsheng, imprisoned since the Democracy Wall episode of 1979, was freed, reimprisoned in 1995, and in 1997 released and allowed to leave China. A remarkable debate, nationally televised, between party General-Secretary Jiang Zemin and U.S. President Bill Clinton in June 1998 that dealt with human rights issues, among others, raised hopes that the government might be beginning to change its views. But late in 1998, a series of arrests of dissidents trying to form an alternative political party once again dashed hopes that any such change was occurring.

## STATE DECENTRALIZATION AND NATIONAL POWER

The reforms of the 1980s and 1990s took 180-degree turns from the Mao years in two spheres: state power and international relations. In the first, China in the Deng years retreated from the totalitarian centralization of the first three decades of the People's Republic to a state political configuration of perhaps surprising decentralized diversity. In the second, China left the Maoist policy of the Cultural Revolution period—a kind of self-reliant isolation—for a policy of international engagement expressive of its rising national power.

### *State Decentralization: The Economy and Politics*

The economic reforms brought a shift in economic decision making to the lower levels of the Chinese polity (see document 20, appendix 2). Since the industrial and agricultural resources and facilities that would bring economic development were situated in localities across the country—not in Beijing—policy makers at the center decided that local communities must have the capability to use local resources to try to spur economic growth and stability. The deal that the center and localities cut was that localities could initiate policies different from those espoused and promoted in Beijing so long as they maintained the desired stability. Such an exchange has provided localities with a weapon—threats about possible resulting instability—to fend off unwanted central intrusion into the economy. In what must be seen as a fragmentation of authority in the political system, the last two decades of the century thus saw considerable flexibility in the contours of government. Governing bodies at the provincial, city, county, and township levels have gained immense initiative power, both political and economic, and have become forcefully powerful in the economy. They have done so at the expense of the central state bureaucracies that stretch from Beijing into those same localities. It is, however, probably inaccurate to see this development as indicative of a weakened state system, since the center relies on the localities' leadership for strengthening the regime as a whole.

Gone are the days when party cadres enforced struggle meetings and promoted egalitarianism; their focus is on working to realize and sustain economic growth. The reality is that much of the local government's budget is funded by profits from collective and private enterprises. A case in point involves one Su Zhiming, party cadre and mayor of a town near Guangzhou, who in 1993 disregarded Beijing's order to halt the import of new cars by ordering more than forty more, including a Rolls-Royce. The cash came from the profits of more than thirty local companies managed by the town government, monies that pay the incomes of town officials. Because of the prosperity, in that year officials received bonuses six times their salaries; Su's income was higher than the CCP general-secretary's.[14] The town kept the cars.

As the reform system has evolved, lower levels in the nested hierarchy of territorial administration (township, county, city, province, and thence to the center) can generally choose their goals and policies unless they run counter to those of higher levels. Problems have come to be dealt with at the lowest level, where consensus can be reached on methods of handling them; most of the decisions on day-to-day issues have been made at the low and middle levels of the system. Goals and policies are set through negotiations among local officials. Discussion, consensus building, bargaining, and deal making have become the modus operandi in the absence of set institutional mechanisms or any firm constitutional framework. During the reform period, provincial and city people's congresses have occasionally demonstrated their independence. During 1997–98, instead of officials being appointed, local elections for village and township leaders were held in some areas—another indication of the vast changes sweeping the country. On the whole, then, the actual pattern of government under the reforms varies greatly across locations, issues, administrative levels, and time.

Negotiations about the construction of the controversial Three Gorges Dam on the Yangzi River reveal the kind of deal making that is a cardinal attribute of decision making under the reforms. Proponents of the dam argued that it would provide both flood protection and electric power for central Yangzi provinces like Hubei and Hunan; indeed, severe floods in 1990 and 1998 underscored the need for the dam. On the other hand, opponents point out that more than a million people who live west of the dam site—mostly in Sichuan Province—will have their homes, cities, and cropland inundated and will be forced to resettle. Sichuan will receive no flood benefits from the dam, and will obtain little of the generated electrical power.

Deal making became necessary because none of the main political actors—the Provinces of Sichuan, Hunan, and Hubei, and the pertinent central-government ministries—had decision-making authority over the others. The Ministry of Water Resources, the chief institutional proponent of the dam, headed negotiations among parties who for various reasons were opposed. Among the deals was agreement to limit the height of the dam to 175 meters, rather than the more than 200 meters in the original design—a plan that, had it been implemented, would have flooded the city of Chongqing. The height limit will also make Chongqing the major entrepôt between

Sichuan and the provinces downstream since the reservoir behind the dam will end at the city. To help in the cost of resettling the displaced residents, Sichuan has received special investment funds from the State Planning Commission. Finally, to deal with fears of the Ministry of Transportation that the dam might harm shipping along the river, the decision was made to build the dam with an intricate system of ship lifts.

The center has not given up all its power. It appoints all provincial leaders, with city, county, and in some areas township leaders appointed by the next higher level. It maintains substantial coercive powers, controlling as it does crack units of the People's Liberation Army and civilian security agencies. Despite allowing immense local flexibility in economic matters, it retains considerable economic power as allocator of scarce resources like petroleum and electric power, as source of expertise in matters of economic development, and as controller of the money supply. Its degree of authority varies according to issue arena, population control being one where it is especially strong.

The reforms have promoted a pattern of regional growth, with southeastern coastal areas the most dynamic. In the four "special economic zones" established in 1979—Shenzhen (near Hong Kong), Zhuhai (near Macao), and Shantou and Xiamen, across the Taiwan Straits from Taiwan—the central government built plants to the specifications of investors and supplied a well-trained labor force at relatively low wages. Numerous incentives, including low tax rates, attracted investors, as did the resource advantages of the coastal regions: higher skill levels of workers, better infrastructure, and easy accessibility. The interior areas have lagged far behind in economic development, with the gap in per capita wealth increasing rapidly. Rural per capita income in the Shanghai area is three to five times higher than in interior provinces. There are marked differences within provinces as well, giving rise to localities vying with other localities for access to economic resources and opportunities. It is not surprising that the reforms have been seen as thus encouraging decentralization.[15]

People in the more rural interior have become in many cases bitterly envious of the more urban southeast coastal region. Television transports pictures of the coastal prosperity, evidence of the huge gap in living standards between the areas, thus only stimulating more resentment. Certainly, the tensions between urban and rural are not a new phenomenon in China, but they are a reminder that in the modern past, whenever choices had to be made about urban and rural initiatives, the state has usually favored the cities. In severe Yangzi flooding in the summers of 1990 and 1998, for example, the state chose

to save cities downstream by blasting open dikes and embankments and flooding farmland. Cities were saved but farmers lost everything—their homes,
crops, and farm animals.

Rural areas have not always remained quiescent. Farmers of the 1990s have
expressed their anger in occasional violent outbursts. Angry over new highway
taxes, thousands of Sichuan farmers in January 1993, for example, stormed
township government offices, torching a police car and burning homes of
township leaders. For a time, the farmers were appeased by government dec-
larations, but when the county government several months later announced
its determination to collect the new taxes, the farmers erupted in violence
again. Thousands launched a minirebellion, attacking more office buildings,
obstructing traffic, burning homes and vehicles, and seizing a policeman as
hostage. Episodes like this raised questions about future urban-rural relations
and especially relations between developed coastal and less-developed interi-
or regions that increasingly perceive themselves as impoverished have-nots
being taken advantage of by those who already have achieved a substantial
prosperity.

## On the International Stage: Greater China

In China's dealings on the world stage there are various categories of key relationships: what might be called "greater China," including Hong Kong,
Macao, Taiwan, and Tibet; East Asian neighbors, like Japan, Korea, and
Vietnam; and powers beyond, especially the United States and Russia. An
overview of these relationships reveals China's importance as an international player.

In its relationship to those entities in "greater China," China's most important purposes have been to regain control over units that have been separated
from it (Hong Kong, Macao, and Taiwan), and to retain control of Tibet,
which China sees as within its orbit.

Hong Kong was composed of three parts: the island ceded to Britain following the Opium War; the Kowloon peninsula, ceded to Britain in 1860; and
the New Territories, leased by Britain for ninety-nine years in 1898. In the
early 1980s, China made it known not only that it would not renew the leasehold over the New Territories when it ended in 1997, but that it also wanted
to negotiate the return of the other two parts of Hong Kong. Aware that it
could not militarily defend Hong Kong if the Chinese wanted to take it, the
British took part in negotiations that led to an agreement in September 1984.
Britain agreed to return Hong Kong on July 1, 1997; the Chinese agreed that

for fifty years after that date, Hong Kong would retain a capitalist economy and would become a "special administrative region" under a formula of "one country, two systems." During that fifty years, until 2047, English would remain the official language; Hong Kong residents would not pay taxes to China; and the city's economy would remain generally autonomous. China would, however, control Hong Kong's defense and foreign policy. Although there was considerable skittishness on the part of Hong Kong residents about this agreement, especially after the events of 1989 in Beijing, the transfer of Britain's former Crown colony to China went off without a hitch in July 1997. Similar negotiations with Portugal over the return of Macao occurred in 1985, with the agreement that the peninsula would be returned to China in December 1999. The eagerness of the Chinese government to have these two entities returned—the first two parts of China taken by Western imperialists— was shown by the clock erected on the east side of Tian'anmen Square that ticked off the seconds until the transfer of Macao.

The case of Taiwan has been much more difficult. Both the People's Republic and Taiwan argue, as the United States had recognized in the Shanghai Communiqué of 1972, that "there is one China and that Taiwan is a part of China." During the martial-law regime of Chiang Kai-shek (1949–75), the Taiwan position was that the Beijing regime was an illegitimate one run by "Communist bandits." Chiang's goal was to retake the mainland. His rule on Taiwan was made more difficult because those who had fled to the island at the end of the civil war in the 1940s were only about 10 percent of the population; the newcomers controlled the other 90 percent, the Taiwanese who had lived on the island before the arrival of the Guomindang. Chiang allowed the Taiwanese to participate in the island's economy, but allowed them no political power. Under the pretense that his government still was the legitimate government of China, Chiang insisted that the national assembly elected on the mainland in 1947 must continue to serve until new elections in all provinces could be held. Thus, Taiwanese could vote only for provincial positions.

During the leadership of Chiang's son, **Chiang Ching-kuo** (1978–88), there were marked changes in Taiwan's international context and within Taiwan's politics. On January 1, 1979, the United States, one of Taiwan's clos- est allies, severed diplomatic relations with Taipei as it established relations with Beijing. The mutual-defense treaty between Taiwan and the United States was also abolished. The U.S. declaration noted that "the Government of the PRC [w]as the sole legal government of China" and expected that the PRC's relationship with Taiwan "will be settled peacefully by the Chinese themselves."[16] In domestic Taiwan politics, in part as a result of the mainland Guomindang leaders' beginning to die off, Chiang Ching-kuo began to appoint native Taiwanese to key positions in the party. During the last year or so of his presidency, Taiwanese played an increasingly important role in governing.

Chiang's vice-president and successor, **Lee Teng-hui** (1988– ) was a native Taiwanese who moved quickly to democratize the country. He lifted martial law, allowed a free and open press, and permitted non-Guomindang candidates to participate in elections. He lifted all restrictions for Taiwanese to travel to the PRC; within several months, the numbers of Taiwanese traveling to the mainland reached ten thousand per month. Taiwan businessmen now participated directly in PRC economic development, being able to dispense with the Hong Kong agents that they previously had to work through. As for Taiwan's relationship to China, Lee acknowledged that there was only one China and stressed that he did not sympathize with the Taiwan independence movement, but his Taiwanese identity made the Beijing regime suspicious. Lee's policy of "flexible diplomacy"—seeking in various ways international recognition for the Taiwan government—also antagonized Beijing policy makers.

Anything that suggested a tilt toward greater independence for the Taiwan regime reverberated loudly in Beijing. In the middle of the 1990s, the main opposition to the Guomindang was the Democratic Progressive Party, which had a strong Taiwanese identification. Beijing watched elections closely and used military games off the northern Taiwan coast in March 1996 to try to intimidate Taiwan voters. These military exercises followed those of the previous summer, conducted to show Beijing's displeasure with Lee Teng-hui's requesting and receiving a visa to attend a reunion at Cornell University. PRC editorials portrayed Lee as "traitorous to the cause of Chinese nationalism and putting personal ambition above the safety and security of the Chinese citizenry."[17] This seeming overreaction points to the rocky road that appears to lie ahead for peaceful reunification. The "one country, two systems" model of the Hong Kong reunification was discussed in the mid-1990s but without any enthusiasm on the Taiwan side.

Both the PRC and the Guomindang government on Taiwan believe that Tibet is a integral part of China. First made a Chinese protectorate in the middle of the eighteenth century, Tibet fell out of the Chinese orbit with the collapse of the empire. In October 1950, China invaded the country and forced the Dalai Lama, Tibet's spiritual leader, to sign an agreement giving Beijing control in 1951. In 1959 and again in 1987, armed rebellion against Chinese control was forcefully put down; in the first rebellion, the Dalai Lama fled to India for sanctuary. After that, he traveled all over the world seeking support for the Tibetans' indigenous Buddhist culture, was received by world leaders, and was awarded the Nobel Peace Prize. Beijing's fear is that his visibility and considerable respect on the world stage might cause Tibetans to become more determined to win their independence.

## On the International Stage: East Asia

Relations with the reigning economic giant in East Asia, Japan, have been basically economic. In 1978, in conjunction with the signing of a peace treaty, the two countries signed long-term trade agreements that opened the way for Japan's assistance in China's economic development. In the early 1980s this assistance became specific with a $10 billion industrial-aid agreement. There was joint Sino-Japanese exploration for oil in the North China Sea as Japan invested heavily in the Liaodong peninsula in southern Manchuria. In part, it was this involvement in an area where Japan had been deeply involved before World War II, coupled with memories of the nightmarish war experience in the 1930s and 1940s, that gave rise to some malaise about Japan's role. Japan's seeming inability to accept full responsibility for its actions in the war exacerbated the situation. In 1985, after the Japanese prime minister visited the Shinto shrine in Tokyo where some Japanese war criminals were buried, students in Beijing took to the streets to protest the visit. Other Japanese actions, including textbook revisions downplaying and rationalizing Japan's wartime roles, have kept the political relationship between the two countries polite but less than cordial. State visits have continued. In 1991, the Japanese prime minister visited Beijing, followed in 1992 by the Heisei emperor, the first visit ever by a Japanese emperor to China. The CCP general-secretary, Jiang Zemin, visited Japan in 1998.

While China has remained a close ally of North Korea, its relationship with South Korea has also become close. Attracted by possibilities of technical assistance, given South Korea's level of economic development, China and the Seoul regime opened diplomatic relations in 1992. Trade developed quickly, and South Korea focused much of its substantial China investment in Shandong Province.

The other traditionally close tributary state, Vietnam, has been a different story. Whereas in the years before the Cultural Revolution China had offered advice and some assistance to North Vietnam in its war against the United States, in the 1970s relations turned icy. China had established close relations with the Communist Khmer Rouge in Cambodia; however, the reign of terror unleashed on the country when the Khmer Rouge took power in 1975 led in various ways to increasingly bad relations between Cambodia and Vietnam. Vietnam invaded Cambodia in late 1978, establishing a regime that it could control. China was embittered by these actions and by the enmity shown by the Vietnamese regime to ethnic Chinese. In 1978, China withdrew all its aid from Vietnam; in February 1979, it invaded Vietnam "to teach it a lesson." The campaign ended in a month, China having nothing to show for it but high casualties and evidence that the PLA was, as one writer put it, "deficient in modern warfare."[18] The military action poisoned relations between China and Vietnam for the rest of the century.

Of increasing concern after the mid-1990s was China's aggressive stance regarding the Spratly Islands in the South China Sea. It claimed that almost all of the South China Sea falls under its sovereignty and therefore that the reportedly rich oil reserves off the Spratly Islands belong to China. The difficulty here is that the islands are also claimed by Taiwan, the Philippines, Malaysia, Brunei, and Vietnam. Various small incidents and China's tough rhetoric ratcheted up tensions.

### On the International Stage: The United States and the Soviet Union/Russia

It is clear that by the 1990s the People's Republic had "some of the trappings of a global power": it was a permanent member of the United Nations Security Council, a participant in the World Bank, the International Monetary Fund, and the Asian Development Bank, and possessor of a nuclear arsenal and its means of delivery.[19] Its relations with the global powers, the United States and, before its collapse in 1991, the Soviet Union, ran from warm to chilly in the 1980s and 1990s. From the initial corporate agreements in late 1978 with Coca-Cola and Boeing, United States–based firms have greatly expanded operations in China; U.S. investments have grown and trade has rapidly increased. But the 1989 Beijing tragedy poisoned relations with the United States. It left the trading relationship throughout the 1990s in annual jeopardy as the conservative U.S. Congress debated each year whether to give the PRC most-favored-nation status (allowing them to trade at the normal tariff level enjoyed by U.S. trading partners). As memories of the crackdown on the 1989 movement continued to be the lens through which many in the United States viewed China, the U.S. government found fault with China's record on trade, technology transfers, human rights, and various strategic issues. Beijing's response to the frequent criticism was that the United States was trying to contain and isolate China; the tone of the relationship was not helped by the U.S. sale of planes to Taiwan and by the U.S. deployment of ships in the vicinity of military exercises off Taiwan in the spring of 1996.

State visits by Jiang Zemin in 1997 and President Clinton in 1998 seemed to thaw the oftentimes chilly relationship. But in 1999, that thaw turned into an icier chill than had existed since diplomatic relations were begun two decades earlier. Charges of alleged Chinese espionage at U.S. nuclear facilities and alleged Chinese efforts to buy influence through 1996 presidential campaign contributions led to intemperate, often ignorant, and frequently politically tinged anti-Chinese rhetoric in the U.S. Congress. For their part, the Chinese interpreted the May 1999 NATO bombing of the Chinese embassy in Belgrade as purposeful—a warning shot, as it were, about what the U.S. would consider doing if China tried any military actions in Taiwan or Tibet. The subsequent violent reactions by the Chinese public at the U.S. embassy in Beijing reflected the widespread sense in China that through its demeaning accusations, its keeping China out of the World Trade Organization, and its bombing of the Chinese embassy, the United States was trying to contain China and keep it from the world role it feels it deserves. As the world moved toward the twenty-first century, the future for relationships between the two powers looked far from bright.

The hostility with the Soviet Union that had led to the cutoff of Soviet assistance and aid in 1960 and to outright war in early 1969 did not begin to subside until the presidency of Mikhail Gorbachev. In 1985, tensions began to ease as trade and cultural contacts were expanded, consulates were reopened in Shanghai and St. Petersburg, and China purchased Soviet aircraft. Gorbachev's trip to Beijing in May 1989, at the time of the student demonstrations, formally ended the split that had existed between the two countries since the late 1950s. The Soviet Union's collapse in 1991 left a weakened Russia, with whom, by the mid-1990s, China was undertaking some exchanges.

## SOCIAL AND CULTURAL CHANGE

In the summer of 1988, a six-part television documentary, *River Elegy (Heshang)* brought into focus the issue of where China was headed as it neared the next century. Using vivid symbols, especially that of the Yellow River, the film was bluntly critical of the "dogmatic chauvinism inherent in classical Confucianism and revolutionary Maoism alike" and highly positive about modern Western ideas, values, and institutions.[20] In the film, the narrator intoned,

> Today . . . the Chinese sigh, yet another sigh . . . why is it that our feudal era never ends, why is it as endless as the ceaseless flow of the Yellow River? . . . history grinds on, slowly and heavily, in the river bed which has accumulated silt and sand of the ages. . . . It needs a great flood to wash it away. This great flood is already upon us. It is none other than industrialized civilization.[21]

Not surprisingly, the party's central propaganda department banned the film. It aired only once. The period since 1949 had seen first one extreme: ideology above all else; then the 1980s and 1990s saw another extreme: the glorification of money and wealth above all else. Where was China's soul?

## Growing Wealth and Its Discontents

In 1980, in Guangzhou's Nanfang Department Store, south China's leading department store, the only shelves stocked sufficiently were those with canned food, Thermos bottles, and plastic toys. For other kitchen and home products, there was often only one selection available for shoppers. In sharp contrast, by 1990 the store reportedly was abundantly stocked with a host of items, even having a whole section offering video games and videocassettes.[22] Another indication of the remarkable changes: in Guangzhou in 1980, there were 1.5 color televisions and 1.5 washing machines per hundred households, and too few refrigerators to count. Thirteen years later, in 1993, there were 99.3 color televisions, 97.3 washing machines, and 92.7 refrigerators per hundred households. Rampant consumerism has become the idol and pastime of at least the prosperous regions of the country. The shortening of the official work week in 1994 and 1995 from forty-eight to forty hours did not mean extra leisure time for many workers, but simply made possible working at another job in order to make more money. While in the 1980s the common purchases were color televisions, stereo/tape recorders, electric fans, washing machines, and refrigerators, in the 1990s the hot-ticket items included high-tech sound systems, videocassette recorders, and air conditioners. It is telling that the main thrust of television advertising has been directed to individual self-fulfillment—making one's life more pleasant and satisfying while making oneself healthy and attractive. Reportedly, "not a single advertisement uses patriotism, revolutionary spirit, or socialism to sell its product."[23]

Guangzhou polls taken in 1994 showed that of the 461 participants in the poll, close to 80 percent were pleased by the availability of goods and more than 60 percent felt positive about the overall economic impacts of the reforms. Yet more than 50 percent were unhappy about other economic issues; those named most included personal income, opportunities to make money, ability to change jobs, ability to obtain medical care, and housing conditions. They also expressed dissatisfaction with an array of social and political issues—educational conditions, the environment, crime, and traffic. Dissatisfaction about personal income and opportunities to make money were at the top of the list for individuals looking at themselves, especially in relation to others. Newspapers remarked on the prevalence of the "red-eye" disease—open jealousy among large numbers of city residents of those who, in the wake of the reforms, were more wealthy than they.[24] The tendency toward conspicuous consumption among the nouveaux riches only exacerbated discontent with their economic situation. Two of the most resentful and rankled groups were intellectuals and educators. Teachers and educational administrators, finding that waitresses in joint-venture hotels were paid at least double what they, the professionals, had been getting, began to set up their own streetside stalls or stands to market whatever they could in order to try to keep up financially.

There were various reasons for bitterness over income disparity. The ideological hackles of Communist Party members were raised because income disparity was a clear indicator of the reemergence of capitalism and its evils. Some in positions of authority feared that the increasing income disparity threatened social harmony and comity. Many who were not doing well under the new situation believed that those who were succeeding were in some way receiving unfair advantages. Such groups included those in rural areas as opposed to the cities, state-sector workers as opposed to private-sector workers, and all groups as opposed to party cadres, the latter being always accused of greed and corruption. In sum, the new reality of income disparity created a variety of social fissures that were not conducive to social harmony.

The reforms were also negatively received by those who were deeply troubled by what they perceived as the jettisoning of all values except "getting rich"—a goal that increasingly seemed to mean that the end (gaining wealth) justified any means. To many, the commodification of many aspects of social life under the watchword of "to get rich is glorious" sounded tawdry and immoral compared with the selfless, patriotic language of Maoism. It is not surprising that in the mid-1990s a "Chairman Mao craze" grew out of a nostalgic enthusiasm for Mao. It included photographs of Mao that truckers and taxi drivers hung for good luck on their rearview mirrors, and an album, *Red Sun*, composed of rock renditions of revolutionary songs, which set "an all-time record for monthly sales of a pop music album."[25] As to the question of whether the reforms had destroyed China's "soul," one party official, an erstwhile supporter of the reforms, said in 1993, "The level of morality has dropped drastically. Girls think nothing of coming from villages for a short stint as a prostitute and then going home proud of the money they take back. *Nothing* is guiding people—not Marxism, not Confucianism, not religion. At least religion put the fear of hell into one, but now people don't believe in those things."[26] Some pointed out that a higher standard of living could not replace more substantive values, but even if everyone agreed with that premise, there was no agreement on what those general social and ethical values should be.

## Collateral Social Changes

For many individuals, the reforms have meant both greater freedom of choice in life decisions and in social mobility; with that greater freedom has come, in some cases, added responsibilities. The responsibility system in both agriculture and industry has given family farmers and enterprises choices in what, how, and how much to produce and then what to do with the profits. For enterprises, this has heightened the powers of factory managers and directors. As the state decentralized economic decision making, institutions like schools and the media had to take on more fund-raising activities that inevitably raised new issues. For example, in selling advertising space and time in the print and broadcast media, respectively, the media have for the first time opened up to the likelihood of sponsors' pressure in matters of what is being covered and how. Additional individual responsibilities have also come from the decentralization that has occurred. Until the mid-1990s, workers did not have to contribute funds for medical care or for pensions, but thereafter medical insurance coverage required copayment, and payments into pension plans were common.

One of the reforms' most popular aspects was increased social mobility among both masses and elites. This greater freedom, however, brought responsibilities and sometimes added social problems. In the days before the reforms, higher education was free if a student's entrance examination scores were high enough. Upon graduation, however, individuals were assigned positions without any control over what the positions were or where they were located. In the mid-1990s, colleges and universities began charging tuition;

government financial support went only to those with the highest examination scores. But under the new system, graduates could choose whatever position they wanted to apply for. The new freedom of horizontal and vertical social mobility stimulated the opening of employment agencies that provided choices among appealing job opportunities. Individuals thus became freer in making their own decisions.

The most dramatic social mobility was evident among the masses, especially the rural masses. From 1984 to 1988, an estimated one hundred million farmers, freed from restrictions holding them on their land, migrated to towns and cities. This so-called floating population, driven by dreams of getting richer, represented a kind and degree of social mobility that many government leaders saw as potentially disruptive and dangerous. Without housing, employment, or connections, they traveled to cities, most often arriving without return tickets. They slept in railroad stations, under highway overpasses, or on the streets. "Floaters," if they found work at all, usually took low-wage jobs that other workers disdained: as hawkers, street vendors, or prostitutes. Many panhandled; beggars appeared in large numbers. In most cities, there was a substantial rise in street crime, especially petty theft. Generally, the floating population remained quiescent, but the possibility of trouble seemed just beneath the surface of city life. For these people there were no regular safety-net welfare subsidies because they had left their places of residence and, without work, were not attached to any work or residence unit. Their lack of such units (*danwei*) created a potentially serious political problem for Chinese authorities, for these units had played especially important control functions from the early days of the People's Republic. As political scientist Kenneth Leiberthal noted, "The reforms [have] thus erod[ed] the fundamental link the Maoist system created to handle the relationship between the state and society."[27]

Just as students had found that free postgraduation choice of job involved a trade-off of tuition payments, so workers, who liked the reforms in part because it gave them the opportunity to choose their jobs and their locations, also found a not-so-comfortable trade-off: the state no longer guaranteed a job. The problem of unemployment began to reach major proportions because of the population problem (see below). Of the estimated 580 million people in the workforce in the mid-1990s, 160 million resided in urban areas; the rest, about 420 million, were in the countryside. Estimates suggest that the rural work force actually needed would total something fewer than 200 million; of the remaining 200 million-plus, about 100 million found employment in rural industries. But that still left a surplus of 100 million people without employment (ergo, the floating population). But the problem was actually worse because the rural population was growing by roughly 15 million a year. The possible social and political implications of the resulting unemployment became a serious, and possibly staggering, problem. Compounding this already bleak situation was the late-1990s announcement of plans to shut down inefficient and costly state-sector enterprises, thereby substantially increasing the number of unemployed. To stave off a situation that might give rise to social unrest, the state constructed an economic safety net of unemployment insurance, a minimum wage, and social protection of workers in foreign businesses (through pensions, health insurance, and disability payments).

One of the most explosive developments stimulated by reform was widespread corruption, which often involved those at or near the top of the party hierarchy. Eliminating it was one of the main objectives of the 1989 demonstrators. Corruption played two roles vis-à-vis the reforms: corrupt individuals took advantage of the reforms to themselves gain wealth; but, ironically, corruption also facilitated the reforms. In order to solicit and keep up support for the reforms, Deng Xiaoping allowed party leaders (and their families) to benefit from new opportunities provided. Children of these men assumed positions from which they could achieve fabulous profits. Making use of personal and family connections, they manipulated lucrative stock and real-estate deals, gained insider information, attained hard-to-get licenses, and, when accused, avoided legal prosecution. Many of them became spectacularly wealthy through what in essence was an abuse of power. One of the most infamous came to light in the spring of 1995: the Beijing municipal government was caught accepting bribes for the issuance of construction permits. In an effort to show that it would no longer tolerate such behavior, the state sacked the mayor, Politburo member Chen Xitong; the vice-mayor committed suicide.

Corruption had been a problem in traditional China as well as in the late twentieth century, in part at least because of the indistinct lines between the public and private realms. As a corollary, institutional realms like government and market could also be blurred for manipulation. Whatever the cultural and institutional bases that allowed for corruption, in the late 1980s and 1990s, when government officials might earn only 300 yuan per month (whereas a waitress in a joint-venture hotel could earn 900 or 1000 yuan), they often chose to use their positions to add to their salaries. Thus Communist Party cadres and heads of work and neighborhood units—the officials who gave permission for marriage, renting an apartment, and even having a baby—frequently demanded bribes. Petty graft and bribery became common on a day-to-day basis, both within the party and government and without.

Environmental concerns were also brought into clearer focus by the changes wrought by reforms. The development of a consumer society was a culprit here. The rapidly increasing numbers of gasoline-powered vehicles intensified both noise and air pollution. City air was filled with industrial smokestack emissions, vehicle emissions, and above all by the pollution caused by the major source of cheap fuel, soft coal. Even in rural areas, as industries proliferated, the sky was obscured by the noxious pollution and yellow-brown haze of rural chemical and fertilizer factories. Another environmental issue of serious concern was land usage. Farmers began to abandon their land for what they deemed more profitable pursuits. In addition, cropland was being converted to other uses to bring more money: fish ponds, forests, grazing lands, rural enterprise sites, and even golf courses (forty reportedly were constructed in Guangdong's Pearl River region). Such land-use conversion led to a marked decline in arable land: during the last thirty years, the net loss of arable land totaled about a million acres per year, reducing China's already tiny total by close to 10 percent.[28] Though in the past three decades China has had a sufficient supply of grain to feed its masses, declining acreage of arable land coupled with the continuing huge population problem has not seemed to bode well for the future. What it meant for individual farmers and their families was also problematic; while in 1973 arable land per capita had been 1.6 mu, by 1993 it had fallen to 1.2 mu, and by 2030 it is projected to fall to .83 mu (a mu is about one sixth of an acre).

In sum, the social, economic, and cultural implications of the reform movement of the 1980s and 1990s were wide-ranging. Positive impacts were obvious: increase in standards of living, the availability of large numbers of consumer goods, and substantially greater freedom and choice in major life decisions. But the negative spin-offs loom ominously: the enlarging wealth gap between the coastal regions and the interior; the growing floating population and attendant problems of unemployment and social order; the issues of corruption, the deterioration of the environment, and the ethical-cultural question about the nature of "China's soul."

## The Population Question

The statistics revealing the declining per capita amount of land point to the difficult problem of population control. While the important issue of limiting population growth was broached in the 1950s, nothing was done to effectuate any policy in that regard until the late 1970s. Indeed, in the 1960s and early 1970s, families often produced five or six children. In the mid-1970s, the government began to disperse birth-control devices and turn up the volume on population-control propaganda. The reality was that population had to be controlled for there even to be a chance of raising living standards. In 1980, Hua Guofeng, on his way out as party chairman, called for a one-child-per-family policy, except among minority peoples. This call was followed by a new marriage law that raised the marriage age for men to twenty-two (up from twenty) and for women to twenty (from eighteen). When 1981 statistics showed that about six million one-child families had had another baby and that more than 1.5 million families with five children or more had had another baby, the government put teeth into the population-control effort. For women who had one child, it ordered compulsory insertion of an IUD; if there were more than one child, there was to be mandatory sterilization of wife or husband. Birth-control cadres had the job of carrying out sterilization quotas and, if necessary, forcing abortions, even in late term. Families who had more than one child lost various welfare and medical benefits and might be fined, or even, in the rural areas, lose their land. Such policies enforced the international image of a totalitarian state intruding into the most personal decisions, even as China was expanding its reforms in liberalizing ways.

Despite this rigorous birth-control program, China continued to see rapid population growth. In part this came from the difficulties of enforcing the program. As a gesture to farmers, who under the economic reforms stood to increase their profits with more children as fieldworkers, couples in rural areas were allowed to have more than one child. Even in urban areas, however, the one-child dictum was difficult to enforce effectively. In the early 1990s, about one third of all births were second children; close to one sixth were third children.[29] This situation was worsened by the freedom of movement brought by the reforms and the breaking away of many from the controls of their work and residence units. In the mid-1990s predictions for the future were dire. If the population growth rate in 1995 continued, China's population in 2000 would be more than 1.3 billion; by 2015 it would top 1.5 billion. The population then would have tripled that existing at the establishment of the PRC in 1949, and the total grain required to feed China's populace would be almost 50 percent more than the total 1994 harvest.[30]

Other social and cultural issues raised by the population-control policies have often been noted. The one-child-per-family policy produced problems with regard to the custom of the son's caring for aging parents; if that one child was female, she would be married off, leaving no one to fulfill that traditional role and perhaps leaving the parents in a precarious social and economic position. Reports of female infanticide surfaced in some areas. With ultrasound technology available, there was a rash of abortions of female fetuses. The government stepped in and forbade the procedure for that use. Nevertheless, statistics showed that the number of births of males was greater than what should have been the number of females (114 to 100), a statistic that points to social problems likely to be produced by a surplus of males once the marriage age is reached.

Perhaps most significant, the one-child-per-family policy, if in the main generally successful, would ultimately achieve a cultural revolution. The concept of the family was being changed. Gone certainly was the old ideal (however different was the reality) of the extended family. Not only were there no siblings, but aunts, uncles, and cousins would all disappear. Without siblings, the single child was doted on by parents, for he or she became the only way that the family line could be extended (another reason for the desire for sons). Some commentators noted that this pampering had produced a generation of so-called "little emperors," the first generation of fat children that China had ever seen.

## Troubles in Education

Even before the Cultural Revolution, China's educational system was in shambles. With his distrust of experts and his championing of populism, Mao's socialist line in education, in place before the Cultural Revolution, meant the advocacy of such policies as "in examinations, students should be allowed to whisper to each other and to hire others to take examinations for them. If your answer is right, I copy yours. Copying is good too. . . . When I cannot do what you have done, then let me copy. . . . Teachers giving lectures should allow the students to fall asleep. If the lecture is no good, it makes no sense to force others to listen."[31] The Cultural Revolution gave that system the coup de grâce. Schools closed down; students became Red Guards; teachers and administrators were humiliated, beaten, fired, even murdered. Almost all of the research institutes of the Chinese Academy of Sciences, "the pacesetters for scientific research and theory," were abolished; when schools began to reopen in the early 1970s, they had only 1950s Soviet texts to use in teaching science.[32]

Deng's reform program took education away from its connection to labor and mass movements and from its emphasis on politics rather than substance. Schools and universities got rid of school-run farms and factories and reestablished the policy of having the school day take place completely in the class-room. The six-year curriculum for primary and secondary schools and the four-year curriculum for universities were reestablished. At the beginning of Deng's reforms, the situation was quite bleak. According to the 1982 census, the most painstaking taken by China in its history, 0.87 percent of China's labor force had college degrees, 10.54 percent had a high school diploma, 26 percent had a junior high education, 34.38 percent had quit after elementary school, and 28.2 percent were illiterate; 73.69 percent of China's farmers had not had any education after primary school. Perhaps most shocking was that among Communist party cadres, only 5.85 percent had a college degree and only 21.87 percent had a high school diploma; in fact, fully 26.96 percent had attended only primary school.[33]

While the Deng years saw the beginning of more serious, substance-based education, the reforms themselves tended to have a negative impact on education. As making money became the measure for success and legitimacy, and because teachers were poorly paid, able teachers left the field by the thousands, and potential teachers chose other occupations. The value of education was diminished as most in society pursued wealth through various enterprises. In the countryside especially, the reforms became a reason for children and teenagers to drop out of school and do farm labor to help their families. In this regard, there was reportedly an increasing opposition even to primary school attendance in some areas. In addition, by the middle 1990s rising tuition and fees dissuaded many from pursuing any education. Already in 1988 more than seven million children had dropped out of schools. In that same year, the State Statistical Bureau determined that 230 million people in China—about 19 percent of the population—were illiterate.

## Intellectuals and the Arts

With Mao's death in 1976, a very slow thaw began in the state's thirty-four-year icy grip on intellectuals and the arts. Bitter memories of the suffering of the Anti-Rightist Campaign of 1957 and the Cultural Revolution, when intellectuals had been murdered and had committed suicide, led to the production in the late 1970s of mildly dissident writings that were called "scar literature." But shades of the Maoist period persisted. Although the Third Plenum of the Eleventh Party Congress in December 1978 called on intellectuals "to liberate their thoughts, to break into previously forbidden zones, and not to fear a return of repressive policies,"[34] the Democracy Wall repression began only a few months later. The first years of the 1980s saw a return to a colder climate for intellectuals and artists. Conservatives set in motion the antibourgeois liberalization campaign; in the arts, its main target was screenwriter **Bai Hua**, whose script for *Unrequited Love* was attacked for its picture of the victimization of a character during the Cultural Revolution. While Bai was the main object of attack, all unofficial publications felt party-state pressure during these years.

From mid-1985 to the end of 1986 there was another thaw, in part a result of increasing contacts with the outside world and the removal of a conservative propaganda chief. Experiencing a "period of enhanced creative expression," intellectuals debated issues like humanism, socialist alienation, and the relevance in the mid-1980s of Marxist economic theory. In addition, this period saw the development of professional associations in a number of technical and academic fields, the establishment of several progressive journals and newspapers, and the publication of large numbers of social commentaries. Involved in the latter were men like Fang Lizhi, Shanghai literary figure **Wang Ruowang**, investigative journalist **Liu Binyan**, and Communist Party theoretician Su Shaozhi. Important new works of art, literature, theater, and film were also produced.[35]

This outpouring of cultural expression was cut short by the tensions engendered in late 1986 by the student demonstrations. For most of the intellectual and art world, the new deep freeze, greatly worsened by the Beijing events in 1989, lasted into the early 1990s. Two exceptions were film and popular music. In the late 1980s, the so-called Fifth Generation of directors (filmmakers who came of age after Mao) emerged to lead a motion-picture revolution with a series of films praised and given prizes around the world. Most were banned in China for their political overtones. **Zhang Yimou** first came to prominence with *Red Sorghum* (1987), which won the Golden Bear at the 1988 Berlin Film Festival. His 1990 film *Judou* was the first Chinese film to be nominated for an Academy Award for Best Foreign Film. That was followed by another Academy Award nomination for *Raise the Red Lantern* (1992). Many of Zhang's films focused on conflicts between strong-willed women, on the one hand, and the intransigence of Chinese traditions and the forcefulness of Chinese patriarchal repression, on the other. It was little wonder that the films were first banned in China. Another important director, **Chen Kaige**, won the top award at the Cannes Film Festival for his 1993 *Farewell, My Concubine*. In music, Cui Jian was China's rock star, a long-haired "hero to urban youth in every province." Though the government tried to obstruct his visibility by canceling concerts and keeping him off television, "his raspy outbursts of alienation [became] the anthems of his generation." His audacious attacks on the system drew the ire of censors, who could not, in any case, stop distribution of a 1991 cassette in which a line of a song read, "Look—we've come to the end of the Golden Road"—"Golden Road" being slang for Communism.[36]

In the money-crazed 1990s, the literary bombshell was not one of political dissent but a popular novel focusing on the once-forbidden topic of sex. The 1993 novel *A City in Ruins* by Jia Ping-ao was a sensation, selling half a million copies within a few months of its publication. In this story of the sexual exploits of a middle-aged writer, the "author usually depicts sex graphically and in minute detail, in the fashion of hard-core porno-erotic novels."[37] Whether the popularity was or was not a sign that China's money madness would lead the art world into an anything-for-money frenzy, the judgment coauthored by two journalists seems valid: "Literature, music, and the popular press have largely wriggled free from the commissars' grip, so that these days almost anything is permitted if it does not directly challenge the party." Their further hopeful judgment, however, must wait the passage of time for corroboration: "The government, it seems, has lost control of the cultural world, the information channels, the social forces, the individual's mind. What is emerging is the embryo of a civil society."[38]

## NOTES

1. Scholars have suggested that the two-line approach is too simplistic and covers a more complex reality; for purposes here, however, drawing the line starkly highlights the most essential differences in understanding subsequent events. See Kenneth Lieberthal, "The Great Leap Forward and the Split in the Yan'an Leadership, 1958–1965," in Roderick MacFarquhar, ed., *The Politics of China, 1949–1989* (Cambridge: Cambridge University Press, 1993), p. 125.

2. Richard Baum, *Burying Mao: Chinese Politics in the Age of Deng Xiaoping* (Princeton: Princeton University Press, 1994), p. 29.

3. Harry Harding, "The Chinese State in Crisis," in MacFarquhar, *Politics of China*, p. 148.

4. Ibid., p. 242.

5. Ibid., p. 226.

6. MacFarquhar, "The Succession to Mao and the End of Maoism, 1969–1982," in MacFarquhar, *Politics of China*, p. 263.

7. Ibid., p. 310.

8. Maurice Meisner, *Mao's China and After* (New York: Free Press, 1986), pp. 463–64.

9. *Ming Bao*, January 15, 1979, p. 1. Cited in Roger Garside, *Coming Alive: China After Mao* (New York: Mentor Books, 1982), p. 190.

10. "Quarterly Documentation," *China Quarterly*, no. 77 (1979): 168.

11. "Quarterly Documentation," *China Quarterly*, no. 50 (1972): 402.

12. Nicholas D. Kristof and Sheryl Wudunn, *China Wakes* (New York: Random House, 1994), p. 316.

13. Ibid., p. 14.

14. Kenneth Lieberthal, *Governing China* (New York: Norton, 1995), pp. 300–301.

15. Ibid., p 323.

16. Quoted in Jonathan Spence, *The Search for Modern China* (New York: Norton, 1990), p. 667.

17. John Bryan Starr, "China in 1995: Mounting Problems, Waning Capacity," *Asian Survey* 36, no. 1 (1996): 23.

18. Craig Dietrich, *People's China* (New York: Oxford University Press, 1994), p. 265.

19. Lieberthal, *Governing China*, p. 332.

20. Baum, *Burying Mao*, pp. 231–32.

21. Cited in Dietrich, *People's China*, p. 277.

22. Charlotte Ikels, *The Return of the God of Wealth* (Stanford: Stanford University Press, 1996), p. 55.

23. Ibid., p. 66.

24. Lieberthal, *Governing China*, p. 308.

25. Elizabeth J. Perry, "China in 1992: An Experiment in New-Authoritarianism," *Asian Survey* 33, no. 1 (1993): 18.

26. Cited in Ikels, *Return*, p. 269.

27. Lieberthal, *Governing China*, p. 168.

28. Starr, "China in 1995," 17.

29. The data comes from Spence, *Search*, p. 736.

30. The data is cited in Starr, "China in 1995," 17.

31. Quoted in Suzanne Ogden, *China's Unresolved Issues* (Englewood Cliffs, N.J.: Prentice Hall, 1989), p. 319.

32. The phrase is Ogden's; ibid., 320.

33. Spence, *Search*, p. 690.

34. Perry Link, ed., *Stubborn Weeds* (Bloomington: Indiana University Press, 1983), p. 20.

35. Baum, *Burying Mao*, pp. 189–90.

36. Kristof and Wudunn, *China Wakes*, p. 286.

37. Jianying Zha, *China Pop* (New York: New Press, 1995), p. 133.

38. Kristoff and Wudunn, *China Wakes*, p. 279.

# PART II

# Compendium of Key Events, Terms, Institutions, and Figures

The Compendium is a dictionary of historical events, figures, and terms. It is divided into eleven sections containing some 250 separate entries. The Compendium is user-friendly: entries within each section are alphabetical and each entry is found in the index. The reader can use the Compendium for rapid identification of names and terms, a special help for those unfamiliar with Chinese names. Biographical entries also include the birth and death dates (when known) of the figures. These entries supplement the narrative; in many cases, they contain even more information than that in part 1.

In some instances, there is a possibility of overlap between categories, for example, among party leaders, military figures, and leaders of dissent, rebellion, and revolution. In such cases, I suggest the reader turn first to the index. Entries in the section on writers include the titles of major publications available in English translation.

## MAJOR EVENTS AND MOVEMENTS

**Anti-Lin (Biao), anti-Confucius campaign** (1973–74)—This mass movement rather cryptically linked and criticized the ultraleftist Lin and the ultrarightist Confucius as embodiments of feudal Chinese society. It was the last major campaign phase of the Cultural Revolution.

**Anti-Rightist Campaign** (1957)—This party-initiated movement came against alleged rightists in the Chinese Communist Party, many of whom had been emboldened to offer criticism of the party and government by the party's own call for the Hundred Flowers Movement. More than thirty thousand intellectuals lost their positions, were imprisoned, or were sent to do forced labor. Many were not rehabilitated until 1979.

**Arrow War** (1856–60)—Sometimes called the Second Opium War, this war, waged by Britain and France against China, was fought for expanded treaty and trade rights. Marked by the sacking and looting of the Qing Summer Palace, the war ended with foreign nations able to establish permanent diplomatic representatives in Beijing.

**Autumn Harvest Uprisings** (1927)—Led by Mao Zedong, these peasant attacks on a number of towns in Hunan Province were the desperate efforts of the Comintern to recover from Chiang Kai-shek's purge and to save at least a vestige of the Communist Party. All of the uprisings were put down. In their aftermath, Mao and others fled to Jinggangshan in Jiangxi Province and Mao lost his post in the Politburo.

**Bandung Conference** (1955)—Held in Bandung, Indonesia, and attended by representatives from twenty-nine Asian and African countries, this conference was the first step onto the international stage by the People's Republic of China. Its theme was peaceful coexistence. Zhou Enlai emerged as spokesman of Asian-African nationalism against the forces of Western colonialism.

**Battle of Huai-Hai** (1948–49)—A decisive battle in the Chinese civil war, this protracted struggle in east central China revealed both Communist superior military maneuvering and Nationalist military mistakes and impracticality. The results of the battle also stemmed from uncooperative distrust among Guomindang generals, inadequate Nationalist use of superior U.S. weapons, and inability to use to good effect the Nationalist monopoly in the air.

**Beijing Massacre** (1989)—This was the bloody culmination of a remarkable six weeks of demonstrations for democracy and reform by students, workers, professionals, and commoners against the party and government. Protests before the crackdown were marked by massive street marches, a hunger strike, and the erection of a statue, the Goddess of Democracy. The movement was crushed by the People's Liberation Army under orders from the alarmed government.

**Boxer Uprising** (1898–1900)—A popular uprising in north China against foreigners in general and Christian missionaries and their converts in particular. It was patronized by the empress dowager and the court, a stance that led to the military invasion of China by eight foreign nations. The uprising ended in the harsh Boxer Protocol, with its massive indemnity, arguably the nadir of the modern Chinese relationship with the West.

**Cultural Revolution**—See **Great Proletarian Cultural Revolution**.

**December Ninth Movement** (1935)—This student movement targeted Chiang Kai-shek's unwillingness to fight Japanese aggression; instead, the

Chinese Nationalists were fighting Chinese Communists. Beginning with street demonstrations in Beijing, the movement spread to major cities around the country. It helped create a political atmosphere that was favorable to a Nationalist-Communist united front against Japan.

**Democracy Wall** (1978–79) — This wall to the west of the Forbidden City was initially a government-sanctioned site for posters offering criticisms and calls for greater freedom and democracy. Wei Jingsheng, the chief dissident of his generation, emerged at this time, calling for a "fifth modernization" — democracy. In early 1979, when the party deemed the criticisms too sensitive, it began a crackdown, closing down the wall and, in a general repression, arresting and imprisoning Wei and others.

**Double Ten** (1911) — Still celebrated as National Day in Taiwan, this holiday commemorates the beginning of the revolution (October 10, 1911) that led to the abdication of the Manchus. The event began as an accident in the city of Wuchang, when revolutionaries unintentionally ignited gunpowder; the explosions forced them to act prematurely, but a number of contingencies helped them to succeed.

**February 28 Coup** (1947) — A bloody Nationalist purge of Taiwanese intellectuals and political leaders for their part in antigovernment demonstrations over maltreatment of Taiwanese by the recently arrived Nationalist forces. The arrests and executions of thousands poisoned the air between Nationalists and Taiwanese.

**Five-Anti Campaign** (1952) — This mass movement against the capitalist class (especially industrialists and businessmen) and its practices helped to end traditional industrial and business enterprises, leading to the Communist Party's goal of state economic control. Staged concurrently with the Three-Anti Campaign, this effort was aimed at eliminating tax evasion, bribery, cheating on state contracts, and theft of government property and state economic information.

**Great Leap Forward** (1958–61) — This mass campaign initiated by Mao Zedong was an effort to move China's economic development abreast of Western countries within fifteen years. Hoping to unleash mass participatory power, the leadership called for the establishment of people's communes organized in military fashion; industry was to be decentralized to the communes. The campaign so destabilized the Chinese economy that both industrial and agricultural production suffered drastically. Its cruelest impact was its contribution to causes of the worst famine in human history.

**Great Proletarian Cultural Revolution** (1966–76) — This mass campaign, fueled by Mao Zedong's effort to regain the power he lost as a result of problems caused by the Great Leap Forward, mobilized especially the young as Red Guards in a bid to destroy old traditions and customs. Its dynamics included ideological differences and personal power struggles. In 1967–68, escalating violence between Red Guard units and other "revolutionary" forces brought the nation to outright civil war. In 1969, the situation compelled Mao to order the military to rein in the out-of-control struggles. The Cultural Revolution's repercussions (it led, for example, to factional fighting in the party) continued into the 1980s.

**Hundred Days' Reform** (1898) — Spearheaded by two Chinese, Kang Youwei and Liang Qichao, this summer effort at institutional reform was supported by the Manchu Guangxu emperor. During the Hundred Days, there were wide-ranging reforms, all of which seemed to challenge the status quo of the empress dowager and her allies. The reform effort came to an end with a coup by the empress dowager — suggesting, according to some historians, that China was not yet ready for institutional change.

**Hundred Flowers Movement** (1957) — After the generally successful first years of the People's Republic, the party leadership called for intellectuals to criticize the Communist Party, encouraging the "blooming" of a hundred flowers and the "contending" of a hundred schools of thought. In less than two months, however, this attempt at some liberalization was swallowed up by the party's antirightist movement against those who had offered criticism.

**Jiangxi Soviet** (1931–34) — Formed in 1931 at a time when the Nationalists ruled most of China, this soviet was a Communist enclave in Jiangxi Province. Under the general direction of Mao Zedong, the soviet organized the first sustained class struggle–land reform movement, but the policies had to be reined in when they antagonized too many people. A marriage law was announced that called for free marriage choice, outlawed arranged marriages, and made divorce simple. The soviet also worked to strengthen the Red Army. Besieged by Nationalist forces from 1931 on, it collapsed in 1934 in the defeat leading to the Long March.

**Long March** (1934–35) — This was the legendary, six-thousand-mile trek of the Communists after the collapse of the Jiangxi Soviet. Pursued by the Nationalist military, of the roughly one hundred thousand who began the march, only eight thousand to nine thousand survived the trek through mountains, swamps, and other treacherous terrain. The march's experience and memory served as a central myth and psychological bulwark of the PRC regime, and its veterans provided leadership of the party into the late 1990s.

**Lushan Conference** (1959) — This confrontational party conference came in the midst of the disaster of the Great Leap Forward. Defense Minister Peng

Dehuai was ousted, to be supplanted by Lin Biao; Mao also lost power, succeeded as president of the PRC by Liu Shaoqi. The conference set the stage for the personal power struggle that developed into the Cultural Revolution.

**Macartney Mission** (1793)—This British mission to the Chinese court attempted to expand and extend trade and establish diplomatic relations between the two countries. Macartney was treated as a tributary emissary; when he had an audience with the emperor, he was expected to perform the ritual kowtow but instead, as a compromise, he went down on one knee. His mission was rebuffed and the Canton system continued as before.

**Manchurian Incident** (1931)—On September 18, the Japanese military, acting independently of the Tokyo Foreign Office, blew up a small section of the South Manchurian railroad track north of Mukden (Shenyang) and used it as the pretext to seize Manchuria. The aggression continued until the Japanese had taken Manchuria. In early 1932 it became Manchukuo, with the last Qing emperor serving as puppet ruler.

**Marco Polo Bridge Incident** (1937)—Japanese troop maneuvers on the night of July 7 near this railroad bridge ten miles west of Beijing led to the disappearance of a Japanese soldier. Assuming he had been captured by the Chinese, Japanese troops attacked the Chinese position. The skirmish was isolated, but neither side could afford to back down politically; it thus became the first battle of the eight-year Sino-Japanese War.

**May Fourth Movement** (1915–24)—Sometimes called the Chinese Renaissance, or Chinese Enlightenment, this cultural revolution, named for the date of a political demonstration over decisions at the post–World War I Versailles Conference, called for the destruction of traditional culture, including the traditional family system and the classical language. The movement emphasized the importance of science and democracy for China's development.

**May Thirtieth Movement** (1925)—Nationwide demonstrations and strikes erupted after the killing of unarmed Chinese students and workers in Shanghai, gunned down during a street protest on orders of a British police commander. The subsequent nationalistic outcry, which reached deeper into the countryside than ever before, served as the context for the Northern Expedition.

**Muslim Rebellion—southwest China** (1855–73)—A rebellion with complex roots: it involved Muslim disgruntlement over taxes; struggles between Chinese and Muslims over gold and silver mines; and alliances among various ethnic groupings, Muslims, and Han Chinese. Above all, it was caused by resentment of non-Han groups over the Han Chinese efforts to more fully assimilate them into the Chinese state. Difficult terrain, Qing ineptitude, and the abilities of the Muslim rebel Du Wenxiu lengthened the struggle to almost two decades.

**Muslim Rebellion—northwest China** (1862–73)—This rebellion in Gansu and Shaanxi Provinces grew out of Chinese-Muslim antagonisms. Initial poor leadership of Qing forces lengthened the rebellion. Eventually, it was bloodily suppressed by Zuo Zongtang, a famous anti-Taiping leader, two years after the rebellion's leader, Ma Hualong, had been killed.

**New Fourth Army Incident** (1941)—An attack on the Communist New Fourth Army in east central China by Guomindang forces in January led to several thousand Communist deaths. This episode increased the bad blood existing between the Communists and Nationalists. It effectively ended the second united front formed in 1937 to fight the Japanese.

**New Life Movement** (1934)—This campaign was Chiang Kai-shek's attempt to counter Communist ideology with a mix of traditional Confucian values, nationalism, and authoritarianism that some have likened to fascism. It had little appeal to many of China's young and to those whose views had been affected deeply by May Fourth thinking. It failed in its effort to create a cogent and attractive ideology.

**Nian Rebellion** (1853–68)—Affecting areas in Shandong, Henan, Anhui, and Jiangsu, this mostly guerrilla movement had strong class dynamics, with rebels seizing the property of the wealthy. Scorched-earth policies were first successful for the rebels, but later government forces led by Taiping suppressors Zeng Guofan and Li Hongzhang used the same strategy to defeat the rebels led by Zhang Loxing.

**Northern Expedition** (1926–28)—Led principally by Chiang Kai-shek, this military expedition, beginning in Guangdong Province, united China in its attack on warlords and imperialists. A two-front campaign, the march led to Wuhan in central China and Shanghai on the east coast. During the march, party polarities increased, in the end giving rise to Chiang's purge of the Communists and the end of the first united front.

**Opium War** (1839–42)—This war, on the face of it fought for the British right to smuggle opium into China, might best be seen as resulting from culture clash between China and the West. It effectively ended the Canton system and led to the establishment of the system of treaty ports wherein China lost a substantial amount of sovereignty to Western nations and Japan. It might be seen as the first assault in the barrage of more than a century of Western demands on and depredation of China.

**Rape of Nanjing** (1937)—One of World War II's worst war crimes, this assault on Chiang Kai-shek's capital occurred when Japanese officers gave their men carte blanche in their treatment of Chinese. The result was a reign of terror: arson, robbery, vast numbers of rapes, and a massacre of up to two hundred thousand Chinese civilians by Japanese troops.

**Rectification Movement** (1942) — In this campaign, the aim of Mao Zedong and the party leadership was to squelch dissent over Communist policies in Yan'an, to deal with local Communist partisans, and to solidify Mao's sinicized Marxism-Leninism as party doctrine. Reeducation was the chief method of rectification used. Individuals targeted included rival party leader Wang Ming and intellectuals like Wang Shiwei and Ding Ling.

**Resist America, Aid Korea Campaign** (1951–52) — In this party-state mass campaign, patriotic themes were used to direct anger at actions by United Nations forces (especially those of the United States) in the Korean War. The Chinese entered the war in late 1950, and many Chinese contributed heavily to the war effort. The party also used the campaign to target those declared to be enemies of the people.

**Self-strengthening Movement** (1860s–1870s) — To respond to China's deepening foreign and domestic crisis in these decades, some Chinese espoused what was called self-strengthening — the use of Western techniques to preserve the Chinese essence, or Western means to further Chinese ends. Self-strengtheners first purchased guns and ships from the West; they then began to manufacture their own ships and weapons. Later self-strengtheners established military academies, iron foundries, shipping companies, and textile mills.

**Sino-French War** (1883–85) — The first test of so-called self-strengthening, this war was fought over the status of Vietnam. China desired to maintain Vietnam's tributary status; France wanted to incorporate Vietnam into the French Empire. France defeated China handily. The most crushing defeat was at Fuzhou, where the French destroyed the shipyard and one quarter of the Chinese navy.

**Sino-Japanese War** (1894–95) — This war, ending in their defeat by Japan, was shocking to the Chinese, who traditionally scorned the Japanese as dwarf people. It was fought over the status of Korea: China wanted to maintain Korea's tributary status; Japan wanted to bring Korea into its sphere. The clash ended with the loss of Taiwan to Japan, which also gained predominant rights in Korea.

**Sino-Japanese War** (1937–45) — An estimated twenty million Chinese died in the war. The conflict resulted from Japan's aggressive territorial interests in China; it destroyed most of the modern construction of the Nanjing decade (1928–37), made China vulnerable to atrocities such as the rape of Nanjing, and exposed Chinese civilians to biological and chemical warfare. After the bombing of Pearl Harbor in 1941, the conflict merged into World War II, with China and the United States becoming allies.

**Socialist Education Campaign** (1963–64)—Spearheaded by Mao Zedong, this was an effort to reinvigorate socialist values after the disaster of the Great Leap Forward and its famine. Contrary to Mao's wishes, the Liu-Deng group was able to prevail in its strategy of having party cadres head up work teams to direct the campaign. Consequent disagreements that grew out of this campaign—rifts between Mao and Liu-Deng proponents—contributed to the origins of the larger Cultural Revolution.

**Taiping Rebellion** (1851–64)—This was the largest rebellion in world history. It involved much of south and central China and killed an estimated twenty million Chinese. Instigated by Hong Xiuquan and fueled by religious fanaticism, the rebellion's religious and political ideology was a mix of traditional Chinese utopianism, Christianity, and Buddhism. Dogged by poor strategy, it disintegrated internally and was put down by regional armies led by Chinese officials.

**Three-Anti Campaign** (1951–52)—A mass movement against bureaucratic corruption, waste, and obstructionism, this party-state campaign—a counterpart of the Five-Anti Campaign—targeted government, party, and industry officials. It increased the government's control over labor.

**Tianjin Massacre** (1870)—An explosion of public violence, this grew out of Chinese misgivings about an orphanage and its practices in a French Catholic compound at Tianjin. When a French consul lost control and shot a servant in the local magistrate's office, protesters became a mob, killing the consul and Roman Catholic priests and nuns. The incident led to more French economic demands.

**Tian'anmen Incident** (1976)—This outpouring of remembrance at Tian'anmen Square for Premier Zhou Enlai in early April—the time for the annual traditional remembrance of the dead—was seen by the Gang of Four as an attack on them and their policies. Prevailing upon Mao, they had him pronounce it counterrevolutionary, blaming Deng Xiaoping and forcibly suppressing the demonstrators by arresting hundreds and sending many to prison camps.

**Tian'anmen Massacre** (1989)—See Beijing Massacre.

**Tongzhi Restoration** (1860s and 1870s)—Named for the reign-period of the emperor, the so-called restoration was not very effective. It involved various reconstruction efforts (e.g., self-strengthening) following the midcentury rebellions and foreign attacks, but lacked sufficient fiscal resources or strong political commitment. Most of the effective reforms were carried out by local elites; hence, it must be seen as a devolution of state power.

**White Lotus Rebellion** (1796–1804)—A movement in north-central China, this was a rebellion, fueled by Buddhist millenarianism, against the Qing dynasty. It took the Qing a long time to crush it—a fact often cited as an index of the extent of Qing military weakness.

**Xi'an Incident** (1936)—A still-mysterious episode in which Chiang Kai-shek was kidnapped by his own commander, Zhang Xueliang. Chiang had used key troops to blockade the Communists at Yan'an. When Zhang stopped the blockade, Chiang flew to the area to investigate, only to be seized by Zhang. The December kidnapping eventually led to the establishment of the second Nationalist-Communist united front against the Japanese.

**Zunyi Conference** (1935)—From January 15 to 18, during the Long March, Communist Party leaders in Guizhou met for a postmortem on the Jiangxi Soviet's defeat. Mao Zedong, having lost power at the start of the march to students who had returned from study in Moscow, now won out. Bo Gu and Otto Braun were ousted, Mao's views prevailed, and he thus regained party power.

## TERMS

**baihua**—Vernacular Chinese. The vernacular came into use in Chinese writing during the May Fourth Movement.

**baojia**—A traditional system of mutual surveillance in which one thousand households, a *bao*, were divided into ten *jia* of a hundred households each. Each household was responsible for informing on the others.

**bourgeois liberalization**—A phrase used in the 1980s by the Communist Party to denote the negative side of opening to the West: the possibility that Communist control might be eroded by bourgeois principles.

**country trade**—Trade between India and China that was controlled by the British East India Company in the late eighteenth and early nineteenth centuries. Initially trafficking mainly in spices, birds' nests, and other such items, it became chiefly known for its increasing emphasis on opium.

**danwei**—A work unit or neighborhood unit in post-1949 China that functions for various political, social, economic, and surveillance ends. Danwei power was weakened by the economic reforms of the 1980s and 1990s.

**democratic centralism**—A Leninist concept in which dialogue and debate take place freely at various levels before a decision is made, but after central authorities make the decision, all must unequivocally accept and support it. The concept underlay the formation of the Leninist party; it served as the model for the establishment of both the Chinese Communist Party and the Nationalist Party.

**extraterritoriality**—Part of the treaty-port system granting privileges to foreigners. Under extraterritoriality, a foreigner accused of a crime was tried in a court controlled by the consul from his own country rather than in a Chinese court. This privilege increasingly became an irritant to the Chinese when Westerners began to claim it for their Chinese workers, protégés, and Christian converts. The West held onto this "right" until 1943.

**four modernizations**—Announced by Deng Xiaoping in 1978, these goals aimed to modernize agriculture, industry, defense, and science and technology. The modernizations were the rationale for the economic reforms of the last two decades of the twentieth century.

**fifth modernization**—The name was taken from a wall poster written by Wei Jingsheng on Democracy Wall in 1979. It attempted to add the term *democracy* to Deng's four modernizations.

**guandu shangban**—The phrase, which translates as *official-supervised, merchant-managed*, refers to the nature of nineteenth-century industrial ventures. Shaped into bureaucratic capitalism by Chiang Kai-shek's regime in the 1930s, it followed the model of the imperial salt-monopoly administration.

**jinshi**—The highest level in the Chinese civil service examination system, this degree qualified candidates for top bureaucratic posts and perhaps participation in the Hanlin Academy.

**juren**—The second-level degree in the Chinese civil service examination system. Holders of the degree qualified for all lower-level, and some higher-level, bureaucratic positions.

**joint ventures**—Undertakings, often in heavy industry or in the service sector, in which both Chinese and foreign firms have invested.

**lijin**—A tax instituted in 1853 that lasted to the dynasty's end. Levied as a commercial transit tax or a sales tax, its monies went to the provinces.

**macroregion**—A term coined by anthropologist G. William Skinner to describe a physiographic regional unit in China. Skinner sets it forth as a more appropriate unit than an administrative area (e.g., a province) for economic, social, historical, and cultural analysis.

**mass line**—The mass-line policy, developed during the Communist years at Yan'an, emphasizes giving heed to the needs and will of the masses. The party and bureaucracy were to accept input from the people, rather than depending on a top-down administrative approach.

**memorial**—In imperial times this was a statement of facts, a petition, or a remonstrance addressed by an official to the government.

**most favored nation**—In the nineteenth century, when the treaty system was unequal, this term described a country that would receive from China all the rights held by any other country. In the late twentieth century, the term was used worldwide for status accorded to trading partners in good stead with a given country.

**New Democracy**—Mao's concept in his 1940 "On the New Democracy." The words describe, among other things, a "democratic" state that is controlled by a coalition of revolutionary classes under the leadership of the proletariat and peasantry.

**qingliu**—"Virtuous" or "moral" scholars in the Qing. At various crises, groups of literati attacked government policy for not holding closely enough to a morality that they saw themselves as representing (e.g., in the Sino-French War, in the name of this morality—which they believed made China morally superior to France—they called on the government to continue the disastrous war).

**responsibility system**—In Deng Xiaoping's agricultural reforms, responsibility for farming was returned to individual farm families under contract with local production teams. The system increased incentive, allowing families to keep whatever was left after tax payments.

**returned Bolsheviks**—Students who had studied at Moscow's Sun Yat-sen University from 1926 to 1930. Hewing to the Comintern line, they opposed Mao's leadership in the 1930s and 1940s.

**scramble for concessions**—A general term for the efforts of Western and Japanese imperialists in the late 1890s to lease Chinese cities and their environs. In these concessions, various economic privileges were exercised, including control of railroads and mining.

**shengyuan**—The lowest-level degree in the Chinese civil service examination system. It brought prestige and elite status, but did not entitle holders to bureaucratic office.

**special economic zones**—Cities along the southeast coast selected in the late 1970s and 1980s to receive direct foreign investments. Under policies aimed at stimulating industrial development and enhancing foreign trade, these cities spearheaded China's drive to modernize the region.

**Three People's Principles**—The basic ideology of the Guomindang set forth by Sun Yat-sen. The principles are nationalism, democracy, and, somewhat nebulously, "people's livelihood."

**united front**—Two organizations, often working at cross-purposes, joined together to attain intermediate goals beneficial to each. Two such combinations of the Communist Party and the Nationalist Party were from

1922–27, against warlords and imperialists, and from 1937 to 1941, against Japan.

**yamen**—The government compound housing Chinese provincial and subprovincial offices and the living quarters of officials.

## INSTITUTIONS AND ORGANIZATIONS

**agricultural producers' cooperatives**—Two forms of these cooperatives existed in the land reform of the 1950s. A lower-level cooperative comprised thirty to fifty households; land was still held by the tillers. Upper-level cooperatives, developed later, comprised one hundred to three hundred households; in these, private holding of land was abolished in favor of cooperative ownership. The time of establishment of the coops varied, depending on location.

**Army of the Green Standard**—Ming forces were known by this name after the Manchu takeover. This force was similar to a national guard, in contrast to the "banner army" of the Manchus. By the turn of the nineteenth century, their effectiveness had declined, and in many cases they were a scourge, pillaging communities into which they were sent.

**banner system**—In the early seventeenth century, Manchu troops and their families were assigned membership in eight groups, differentiated by their banners—red, blue, white, and yellow, four plain and four bordered. The banners provided bureaucracy-like organization in military affairs and denoted units for population registration. The system is seen as one of the foundations of Manchu success.

**Blue Shirts**—A rigidly disciplined secret police organization that gathered intelligence and was personally loyal to Chiang Kai-shek in the 1930s and 1940s. Led by Dai Li and other former Whampoa cadets, they became known for brutal treatment of those perceived as subversive and for assassinating Chiang's opponents.

**CC Clique**—An influential, right-wing Nationalist Party faction. The clique was formed by brothers Chen Guofu and Chen Lifu, staunch loyalists of Chiang Kai-shek and nephews of Chen Qimei, close ally of Sun Yat-sen during the 1911 revolution. Organized in 1927 as the Central Club (*zhongyang julebu*), it held dominant power in a number of provincial parties and governments.

**Canton system**—A trading system between Westerners and Chinese that was modeled on the traditional tributary system. From 1760 until the end of the Opium War, the system restricted Westerners to trading only at Canton and to living only on an island in the Pearl River. Among other things, the system specified when they could come and how long they could stay and refused them permission to enter the walled city, learn Chinese, ride in sedan chairs, or communicate directly with Chinese officials.

**Central Committee**—The Communist Party's powerful executive, decision-making body. When not meeting, it delegates its powers to the Politburo, which maintains a small Standing Committee that has what amounts to supreme power. The size of the committee has varied.

**China Merchants' Steam Navigation Company**—Begun in 1872 in the self-strengthening efforts of Li Hongzhang, this was one of the earliest "modern" firms. Established to end the foreign domination of coastal shipping, it operated according to the "official-supervised, merchant-managed" principle. Much of its income came from government contracts for the transport of tax grain.

**Chinese Communist Party**—Established in 1921, the party has ruled the People's Republic of China since the nation's establishment in 1949. The party's first phase, as part of the 1920s' united front, ended in disaster, but it restructured its base on the peasantry and defeated the Nationalist Party in the civil war. Since 1949 it has sought economic modernization for China, trying various approaches that have consistently been accompanied by political repression.

**civil service examination system**—The exam system was central to the traditional Chinese polity. It produced China's political, intellectual, social, and cultural elites, educating them in the Confucian orthodoxy. The examinations were held at three levels, with those who gained a top-level degree taking the plum political-bureaucratic positions; lower-level graduates served as social elites in their localities. The rate of passing was no higher than 1 to 3 percent.

**Crescent Society**—A literary society founded in 1923, originally as a private club for students who had studied in the United States and England. Its stress was on the transcendent values of reason and culture. Trumpeting a kind of romantic idealism, it was accused of retreating from the real world to one of art and pure thought.

**Democratic League**—This "third force" in the 1940s, positioned between the Communist Party and the Nationalist Party, tended to Western liberal, democratic ways. It appealed to intellectuals. Chiang Kai-shek mistrusted the league, and Nationalist police attacked its members, driving many to join the Communists.

**Eighth Route Army**—A Communist army in northern China. One of the two most important armies during the Sino-Japanese War of 1937–45 (the other was the Fourth Route Army), it was nominally under Guomindang command. The army inculcated into its soldiers the necessity of careful and positive treatment of the local population, actively organizing mass associations and spreading the Communist message.

**Ever-Victorious Army**—A mercenary military force in the Shanghai region, the army was organized and led by foreigners (American Frederick Townsend Ward and Englishman "Chinese" Gordon). The object was to protect the area from the Taipings, but in the large scheme of things, despite the name and counter to myth, the Ever-Victorious Army had little to do with defeating the Taiping.

**Five Yuan Structure**—The main bureaucratic organizational structure of the Nationalist government from its beginning in 1928 in Nanjing. The five yuan were the Executive Yuan, a "cabinet" composed of ministries; the Legislative Yuan; the Judicial Yuan; the Examination Yuan; and the Control Yuan. The executive, the most important, managed the major ministries, the military, economic policy, and provincial and local relations.

**Fuzhou shipyard**—With the Jiangnan arsenal near Shanghai, the shipyard was one of two early, key self-strengthening industrial efforts. Established in 1866 by Zuo Zongtang, it included an arsenal and a technical school. Foreign advisers taught navigation and mechanical skills there. It was destroyed in the Sino-French War.

**Green Gang**—A secret Shanghai-based society with branches in Lower Yangzi cities; it controlled organized crime in the Republican period. Its leaders, especially Du Yuesheng, became extraordinarily wealthy and powerful, often serving as political brokers in periods of crisis. The Nationalist Party used the gang against Communists and to control labor strikes.

**Hanlin Academy**—The think tank of the Qing government in Beijing. Composed of officials with top-level civil service degrees, it advised the emperor and helped make policy. Many well-known figures served in the academy for a time.

**hong merchants**—In the Canton system, these merchants monopolized trade from the Chinese side. Operating at the behest of the government, they purchased their position in the monopoly and maintained it by gifts and contributions to the state and its officials. They were responsible for the behavior of foreign crews and for paying transit taxes.

**Imperial Maritime Customs Service**—An institution established in the 1850s during the Taiping Rebellion to collect customs revenue for the Chinese government. Capably led for many years by Irish-born Robert Hart and staffed by an international bureaucracy, it had branches in all treaty ports.

The service reportedly provided the Chinese government with monies for early modernizing projects.

**Jiangnan arsenal**—One of the two earliest key self-strengthening industrial efforts in the mid-nineteenth century, the arsenal was established at Shanghai in 1865. It produced ships, ammunition, tools, and machinery. Western scientific and engineering works were translated there.

**League of Left-Wing Writers**—Established in 1930, this organization upheld creative and aesthetic views based on socialist realism as promoted by the Soviet Union. Although Lu Xun helped found the organization, he became appalled by the iron grip that ideology came to hold on its members.

**Lifan Yuan**—Established in the late Ming, this office handled affairs with Mongols, Tibetans, Russians, and other ethnic groups to the northwest and west of China, but not states with which China had traditional tributary relationships. Those were overseen by the Board of Rites.

**mutual-aid teams**—These groupings were at first voluntary, then mandatory. They formed a transitional step in PRC land reform—after the "land to the tiller" phase before moving on to the collectivist phase in the 1950s. Teams shared resources and labor while maintaining ownership of their land. The length of time the teams existed varied from place to place, depending on completion of the "land to the tiller" phase.

**Nationalist Party** (the Guomindang)—A political party that developed from Sun Yat-sen's pre-Republican period Revolutionary Alliance. In the early republic, before being outlawed by Yuan Shikai in 1913, it functioned as an open parliamentary party. In the 1920s, it became a Leninist-style party, led by Sun until his death in 1925. The party's army united China in 1928 under Chiang Kai-shek. From 1928 to 1949 it was essentially (and sometimes only theoretically) the governing institution in China, vying almost continually with a revived Communist Party. Defeated in the civil war, the Nationalist Party and Chiang fled to Taiwan, where the party remained in total control until the late 1980s. Other parties then challenged its dominance.

**New Army**—China's first modern army. This force was organized under the leadership of Yuan Shikai in the early twentieth century. Cadets for the army trained at a military academy in Tianjin, where they were inculcated with the values of nationalism. Many later studied in Japan, where, in some cases, they developed a strong anti-Manchu animus. The army played a crucial role in the Qing defeat.

**New Fourth Army**—A Communist army in central and southeast China composed initially of men who stayed behind when their comrades left on the Long March. They were an effective force of guerrilla partisans. An attack made on the army by supposedly friendly Nationalist forces in January 1941 is seen as marking the end (actual, if not nominal) of the second united front.

**people's communes**—Organized in military-style units (e.g., brigades and platoons), these PRC communes were the central political and economic administrative units from the time of the Great Leap Forward until their abolition in the early 1980s. Mao considered them to be the last step on the collectivist road. Revolutionary in many ways, including the changes they made in family life and gender relationships, they were ultimately too big a step for the Chinese willingly to take.

**Revolutionary Alliance**—Sun Yat-sen's revolutionary organization. Founded in Tokyo, Japan, in 1905, it called for the overthrow of the Manchus and the establishment in China of a republic. The alliance was attractive to many Chinese students studying in Japan and it became the main revolutionary organ, although it was not responsible for instigation of the subsequent revolution. Many of its leaders became important figures in the party when the alliance became the Guomindang.

**Western Hills faction**—This group has a reputation as an ideologically reactionary faction of the Nationalist Party; it should, however, be seen as one that came together to fend off the growing power of the Comintern—more specifically, the power of Mikhail Borodin—in the Chinese revolution of the 1920s. Not ideologically monolithic, it was more a coalition of personal networks.

**Whampoa Military Academy**—A military school established by the Nationalist Party in 1924. The academy's superintendent was Chiang Kai-shek. Its cadets, who were crucial in the success of the Northern Expedition, formed an increasingly important base for Chiang. This was the so-called Whampoa clique. Many Whampoa graduates also played a role in Chiang's paramilitary Blue Shirts.

**Zongli Yamen**—An office established ostensibly to manage foreign affairs in the aftermath of the Arrow War (1856–60). It managed the first steps toward modernization (in the self-strengthening program) and oversaw translation of Western works dealing with international law. The office managed the sending of diplomatic missions and ambassadors abroad, although most foreign policy crises continued to be handled by officials appointed ad hoc.

## TREATIES AND INTERNATIONAL SETTLEMENTS

**Boxer Protocol** (1901)—A disastrous end to the disastrous Boxer episode. This document is often seen as marking the nadir of China's foreign affairs under the empire. Its main stipulations, signed with the eight nations that put down the Boxer Uprising, drastically curtailed Chinese sovereignty: it established a permanent foreign guard at the Legation Quarter in Beijing, mandated the destruction of key fortifications, and agreed to the stationing of foreign troops between the capital and the sea. China was also prohibited from holding its civil service examination for five years in more than forty cities. Most devastating was the indemnity that China had to pay: £67.5 million (450 million taels, or $333 million). The indemnity crippled China's already woeful economic development.

**Shanghai Communiqué** (1972) — This "joint communiqué" was issued in February 1972 at the end of U.S. President Richard Nixon's ice-breaking trip to China. It included statements on each country's role in world affairs. Most crucial here were the agreement of the two countries that "there is but one China and that Taiwan is a part of China" and the announced decision to work toward the normalization of relations between the two countries.

**Treaty of Nanjing** (1842) — The agreement between China and Great Britain that ended the Opium War. The first treaty in what became known as the unequal treaty system, it opened up four new ports at which trade could occur; in addition to the existing port of Guangzhou (Canton): Xiamen, Fuzhou, Ningbo, and Shanghai. The treaty ceded Hong Kong island to Great Britain, ended the Canton system, declared that a fixed tariff would be set (thus freezing China's ability to respond to foreign economic pressures), and ordered the payment of a $21 million indemnity.

**Treaty of Shimonoseki** (1895) — China, shocked at losing a war to Japan, ceded to Japan the islands of Taiwan and the Pescadores as well as the Liaodong peninsula in southern Manchuria. Under the treaty China also recognized Korea's independence, thus ending the long-time China-Korea tributary relationship. The treaty opened up four more ports to trade (Chongqing, Suzhou, Hangzhou, and Shashi), gave Japanese citizens the right to set up manufacturing and industry in China, and mandated the payment of an indemnity of two hundred million taels to Japan. The terms might have been harsher had not the Chinese minister Li Hongzhang been shot by a Japanese fanatic: the final details of the treaty were changed when Russia, Germany, and France intervened (the so-called Triple Intervention), demanding that Japan give back the Liaodong peninsula. Under threat of war, Japan complied.

**Treaty of Tianjin** (1858) — Concluded during the Arrow War (sometimes called the Second Opium War), this treaty in effect ended the tributary system since it established permanent residence in Beijing for foreign diplomats.

It also opened ten new treaty ports (Nanjing, Hankou, Dengzhou, Jiujiang, Jinjiang, Shantou, Danshui, Tainan, Qiongzhou, and Niuzhuang) and allowed foreign travel with valid passport throughout China and without passport for one hundred li (about thirty-three miles) around treaty ports. Permission was granted for foreign missionaries to move throughout China unhindered; transit tax *(lijin)* for foreign imports was set at 2.5 percent of the value of the goods; and two indemnities were mandated: four million taels for Great Britain, two million taels for France.

**Treaty of Wangxia** (1844)—Signed on July 3 by U.S. representative Caleb Cushing and Chinese diplomats, this was the first U.S.-Chinese treaty. It asserted the right of extraterritoriality and gave the United States most-favored-nation status. The United States also received the right to open and operate hospitals and churches in the treaty ports. The agreement called for treaty revision within twelve years.

**Twenty-one Demands** (1915)—A group of economic and political demands made by Japan on the presidential administration of Yuan Shikai. Presented in January, after Japan's successful action in ousting the Germans from Shandong Province in the first month of World War I, the demands were listed in five groups. The first four called for wide-ranging economic privileges throughout China, in Manchuria, Mongolia, Shandong, the Yangzi valley, and the southeast coast. The fifth group, which required that the Chinese hire Japanese advisers for the administration of all political, economic, and public security (police and military) issues, would have been in effect the establishment of a Japanese protectorate of China. When Yuan signed the demands on May 7 under a Japanese ultimatum, he did not agree to the fifth group. During the Republic, May 7 was commemorated as National Humiliation Day.

## · EMPERORS

**Daoguang emperor** (reigned 1821–51)—Born in 1782, the Daoguang emperor, as he grew to adulthood, became known as a man with great interest in Confucian learning. His reputation as a tentative and faltering ruler comes from the trauma of the opium crisis and the war. A biographer said his conduct of the war "displayed his weaknesses—indecision, ignorance, and miserliness" (Hummel, *Eminent Chinese of the Ch'ing Period*, p. 575). Another biography notes that he ruled in "a period of turmoil and uncertainty when demographic crisis was eating away at the vitals of imperial government at the local level" (Jane Kate Leonard, *Controlling from Afar*, p. 3). In his handling of the Grand Canal Crisis (1824–26), he appears grounded in practicality, flexible in problem solving, and with considerable vision and conscientiousness. He was a man aware of his weaknesses: his will stipulated that no tablet praising his accomplishments be set up at his tomb.

**Guangxu emperor** (reigned 1875–1908)—Born in 1871, the Guangxu emperor labored his entire reign to escape the control of his aunt the empress dowager, Cixi. Coming to power at age three, the emperor saw his rule taken by Cixi, as regent, until 1889. Even after her retirement that year, she continued making decisions and appointments over which he had no veto power. In 1898, he broke from her and supported the institutional reform program of Kang Youwei; after a hundred days, she instigated a coup against him, in effect putting him under house arrest. He died a day before her death in 1908, perhaps murdered on her orders. Reportedly he was intelligent and studious; his tragic life came from his inability to break free of Cixi's control.

**Jiaqing emperor** (reigned 1796–1820)—Born in 1760, the Jiaqing emperor saw a reign filled with wide-ranging crises: the aftermath of the corruption of the courtier He Shen and his cronies; the White Lotus and Miao rebellions; the 1813 rebellions that reached Beijing; active pirates on the southeast coast; and floods along the Yellow River seventeen times in the twenty-four years he ruled. Though conscientious and frugal, he was not adept at handling the myriad problems that beset the empire.

**Qianlong emperor** (reigned 1736–96)—Born in 1711, the Qianlong emperor ruled China during its zenith of power and wealth. Military conquests in east-central Asia, surpluses in the national treasury, and a rapidly expanding population were the strengths of his reign. But the positive aspects were balanced by expanding corruption in the later years of his rule, the literary inquisition of the 1760s and 1770s, a population that overburdened resources (the downside of population expansion), and a weakness in dealing with social unrest. In an act of filial respect—not wishing to reign longer than his grandfather—he formally abdicated in 1796; in essence, however, he continued to rule until his death in 1799.

**Tongzhi emperor** (reigned 1862–75)—Born in 1856, the Tongzhi emperor, although nominally emperor for thirteen years, actually reigned for less than two years (Feb. 1873–Jan. 1875). He ascended the throne at age six on the death of his father. His mother, the empress dowager, Cixi, served as regent from late 1861 until 1873; she maintained considerable power even after he took over the throne in his teens, interfering in his public and personal life. His name was associated with the rather feeble reconstruction efforts following the midcentury rebellions and wars, but he was ineffectual because of his personal characteristics and his smothering mother.

**Xianfeng emperor** (reigned 1851–61)—Born in 1831, the Xianfeng emperor ruled at a time of almost countrywide rebellion and foreign invasion. Though at a more normal time his abilities might have led to a decently successful reign, he was unable to deal with the overwhelming crises, leaving more and more decision making to his officials. After the British and French attack in 1860, he fled to Rehe, never returning to the capital.

**Xuantong emperor** (reigned 1908–12)—Born in 1906, the Xuantong emperor abdicated at age six. His father and foster mother were regents for his reign, which ended the Qing dynasty. He was allowed to live in the Forbidden City until 1924. For twelve days in 1917, he was restored to the throne following a short-lived coup engineered by a general. In 1932 he became emperor of the Japanese puppet regime in Manchukuo. He died in 1967, a gardener in Beijing.

## QING DYNASTY GOVERNMENT LEADERS

**Cixi** (1835–1908)—The empress dowager ruled China directly for thirty-seven years and indirectly for eleven, from 1860 to 1908. Throughout this time, Western threats became increasingly ubiquitous and domestic problems festered. Producing the only heir to the Xianfeng emperor, Cixi emerged as de facto regent for her minor son in 1861, serving until 1873. She gained increasing power in making policy and appointed key officials. On the death of her son the Tongzhi emperor, she became regent in 1874, choosing as emperor her nephew, thereby outraging those whose proper Confucian views held that succession must be passed to the next generation. In 1889, the Guangxu emperor took power. However, after Cixi's coup against the reformers led by Kang Youwei in 1898, she placed the emperor under house arrest; she ruled until her death. During her last seven years, she undertook a number of remarkable educational, military, administrative, and constitutional reforms. It is hard to know how much of her reputation for corruption, conspiracies, and authoritarian control came from her gender in this patriarchal state and how much existed in reality. In the course of her career she moved across the political spectrum in her approach to policy from conservative, even reactionary, to progressive in the last years of her life.

**Guo Songtao** (1818–91)—A *jinshi* degree holder of 1847, Guo served in many bureaucratic posts before his appointment as ambassador to England in

1876, including grain intendant, salt controller, acting governor, and judicial commissioner. He was the first Chinese ambassador to be assigned to a Western country. His positive reports of modernization in the West, especially of the importance of railroads, the telegraph, and various technologies, gained him the suspicion and opprobrium of conservative officials. When he returned, he went into self-imposed exile; he continued, however, to advocate such changes.

**Hart, Robert** (1835–1911) — British-born, Hart worked in the British consulates in Canton and Ningbo before he became inspector-general of the Chinese Imperial Maritime Customs. Hart saw himself as working for the Chinese state and he operated the customs efficiently, and generally in the state's interests. The money he forwarded to the Beijing government was instrumental in funding projects like the Beijing Interpreters' School as it was transformed into a college. He oversaw all aspects of customs procedures and a staff (by 1875) of more than four hundred foreigners. They maintained accurate trade statistics and information on local conditions throughout the country.

**He Shen** (1750–99) — Courtier and official, he was the confidante of the Qianlong emperor from 1775 until the emperor's death in 1799. He amassed immense power and wealth due to the emperor's patronage. He served as president of the Board of Revenue; lieutenant general of a Manchu banner (the Bordered Blue); one of the directors-general of the compilation project of the imperial library; president of the Board of Civil Office; and grand secretary. He held as many as twenty posts concurrently and held many titles of nobility. He was in charge of the Macartney embassy in 1793. He was married to the emperor's youngest daughter in 1790. He's name has become synonymous with unfettered corruption. After the Qianlong emperor's death, he was arrested and his wealth confiscated; he was permitted to commit suicide.

**Li Hongzhang** (1823–1901) — A *jinshi* degree holder from 1847, Li was the most powerful official in the last half of the nineteenth century, involved in many of the major events and developments of the times. With Zeng Guofan, his patron and friend, he played a crucial role in leading provincial armies to end the Taiping Rebellion and to crush the Nian rebellion. His most important official post was as governor-general of Zhili from 1872 to his death. He dealt with every important international matter of the time, including negotiating with Japan over Korea and France over Vietnam, serving as plenipotentiary to end the Sino-Japanese War, and negotiating with Russia on the route of the Trans-Siberian Railroad. For many years he headed one of the navy fleets. He played crucial roles in self-strengthening and industrialization. He helped set up and owned a large amount of stock of the China Merchants' Steam Navigation Company, did initial work in promoting the construction of railroads, and sponsored the first telegraph lines. Li proposed the establishment of technical schools to carry out more effective modernization. He had great power and wealth, and his probity was sometimes in question.

**Lin Zexu** (1785–1850)—A *jinshi* degree holder of 1811, Lin served in the prestigious Hanlin Academy. Known as Lin the Blue Sky because of his incorruptibility, he served in numerous official positions: civil service examiner, financial and judicial commissioner, intendant, director-general of conservancy, and governor-general. His most famous assignment was, however, as imperial commissioner to deal with the opium problem in Guangdong Province in the late 1830s. His placing of British merchants under house arrest for six weeks and his destruction of opium stocks became for the British a cause for what is today known as the Opium War. Though he was exiled as a result, he reemerged quickly as an important official in various posts, especially in west and southwest China.

**Liu Kunyi** (1830–1902)—Beginning his career in helping to suppress the Taiping and bandit groups, Liu was rewarded with promotion to governor of Jiangsu Province. He served lengthy tenures in several governor-generalships from the 1860s into the 1890s. He is perhaps best known for his strong stand against Boxer activity in central China and against the involvement of south and central China in the Qing dynasty-declared Boxer War. Near the end of his life, he and Zhang Zhidong submitted joint memorials encouraging major reforms in the administrative, educational, and military arenas. He was, in the words of a biographer, "honest, far-sighted, and dependable when faced with difficult situations."

**Prince Gong** (1833–98)—The sixth son of the Daoguang emperor, the prince negotiated the 1858 Treaty of Tianjin and the subsequent 1860 Convention of Peking with the British and French. He also negotiated the treaty with Russia that ceded territory east of the Ussuri River. He founded the Zongli Yamen and headed it for twenty-seven years (1861–84 and 1894–98). This office oversaw the establishment of the Interpreters' College. During the 1870s and 1880s, his power diminished in the face of the jealousy and surging personal power of Cixi, the empress dowager. The crisis with Japan in 1894 brought him back into power briefly. His conduct of foreign affairs was known for conciliation.

**Qishan** (d. 1854)—He served in high provincial positions (governor and governor-general) from 1819 to 1841 and from 1847 to 1851. Appointed in 1841 to take the place of Lin Zexu in dealing with the British, he was unsuccessful in ending the Opium War, and for this he was banished briefly. Returning to officialdom, he was banished again in the early 1850s for brutal treatment of ethnic groups in northwest China.

**Qiying** (d. 1858) — Serving in high positions (president and vice-president) of various central government boards in the 1820s and 1830s, he negotiated the Treaty of Nanjing that ended the Opium War, as well as subsequent treaties with Western powers. He was ordered to commit suicide for his actions in negotiation with the British during the Arrow War in 1858.

**Sheng Xuanhuai** (1844–1916) — Failing three times to pass the *juren* degree, Sheng won fame another way. He entered the service of Li Hongzhang as his chief deputy for economic affairs. From 1873, when he served as assistant manager of the China Merchants' Steam Navigation Company, until his death, he was closely tied to that company. Serving in various capacities, he developed the important concept of company organization called "official supervision, merchant management." He was one of the most important industrial entrepreneurs in the last years of the Qing. He headed, among other enterprises, the imperial telegraph administration, the first successful modern cotton mill in China, the Hanyang Ironworks, and the imperial railway administration. Sheng organized the first modern-style bank in China (1897). He founded two Western-style colleges, Beiyang College in Tianjin (1895) and Nanyang College in Shanghai (1896). He served as head of the Board of Posts and Communications in the last years of the Qing.

**Tan Sitong** (1865–98) — Son of a *jinshi* degree holder who served as governor of Hubei Province, Tan marched to a different drummer. In 1895, he sought out Liang Qichao and became interested in the reform activity and ideology of Kang Youwei. A brilliant intellectual, he edited the first newspaper in Hunan and led a significant study society, the Reform Association of South China, thus becoming a leader of the reform movement. He is also known for his "A Study of Benevolence," written in 1896–1898, detailing his synthesis of Confucianism, Buddhism, Christianity, and Western science to develop a more congenial way of life. Appointed on September 5, 1898, as a secretary to the Grand Council to facilitate reform measures in the Hundred Days, he was executed twenty-three days later in the aftermath of the empress dowager's coup.

**Weng Tonghe** (1830–1904) — Tutor to the Guangxu emperor, Weng served as his guardian, adviser, and almost as father. He served in high posts: president of the Board of Revenue, president of the Censorate, president of the Board of Punishments, president of the Board of Works, grand councilor, member of the Zongli Yamen, and associate grand secretary. However, he is best known for introducing Kang Youwei and the ideas of reform to the emperor. These actions led to his forced retirement through conservative pressure at the beginning of the Hundred Days. Late in 1898, because of his recommendation of Kang Youwei, he was deprived of all his ranks and kept under house arrest.

**Wenxiang** (1818–76)—A *jinshi* degree holder, he played important roles in foreign policy-related efforts, often serving as assistant to Prince Gong. These included the founding of the Zongli Yamen and the Tongwenguan ("China's first national institution of Westernized education"), and various episodes like the Ryukyu Island dispute with Japan and the dispatch of the Burlingame mission in the late 1860s. He had a reputation for incorruptibility, conscientiousness, capability, and straightforwardness.

**Yuan Shikai** (1859–1916)—Failing twice to pass the *juren* examination, Yuan purchased an administrative title and received a post at a military headquarters through his father's connections. Through his record and ties to Li Hongzhang, he became resident-general in Korea from 1885 to 1894 and founder of the New Army (later called the Beiyang Army) in the first years of the twentieth century. He succeeded Li Hongzhang as governor-general of Zhili Province in 1901. Ousted from his positions by Manchu regents in 1908, he emerged from the revolution of 1911 as the first president of the Republic of China. His vision focused on a centralized regime that could give coherent direction to the new China. He tended to authoritarianism: he abolished political parties and the self-government bodies that had been formed in the late Qing–early Republic. In the end, he was infatuated with the old model of the imperial state; he died in the middle of a rebellion begun against him after he tried to reestablish the monarchy. On his death, former Beiyang subordinates plunged China into the period of warlordism.

**Zeng Guofan** (1811–72)—A model of the Confucian official, Zeng was the most significant Chinese civil servant of the mid-nineteenth century. A *jinshi* degree holder (1838) and member of the Hanlin Academy, he served with distinction in various capacities. He is best known for his formation of a Hunan army to defend against the Taiping Rebellion and for his role in the suppression of the Nian rebels. He became a grand secretary in 1867. Appointed governor-general of Zhili Province in 1868, he was called on to handle the aftermath of the Tianjin Massacre (1870). Known for foresight, incorruptibility, and great perseverance, he was an excellent judge of men: many of the more than eighty men who served on his personal staff later became famous in their own right.

**Zhang Zhidong** (1837–1909)—A *jinshi* degree holder (1863), Zhang spent the years 1867 to 1877 in civil service examination posts. Greatly concerned with issues of scholarship, he became tutor in the Imperial Academy in 1879. Beginning in 1884, he served in various governor-generalships. He became arguably the foremost spokesman for self-strengthening. After the Sino-French War, he established arsenals, the first modern mint, and the Guangya Academy. Interested in railway building and industrial development, he was also involved in the Hanyeping Ironworks, cotton mills, and silk factories. He established the nucleus of a modern military force, hiring German instructors. His "Exhortation to Study" (1898) proposed a program of gradual modernization based upon education, revitalized Confucianism, and Western technology. After the Boxer episode, he presented proposals for modern reforms.

**Zuo Zongtang** (1812–85)—A *juren* degree holder (1832), Zuo early in his career experimented with agricultural methods, living a quiet life. From the age of forty, however, until his death he was continuously devoted to military activity. As military leaders and statesmen, Zuo, Zeng Guofan, and Li Hongzhang made up the triumvirate of civil officials that dealt with the mid-nineteenth-century rebellions. Zuo campaigned against the Taiping rebels; he was involved in the suppression of the Nian rebels; and he was instrumental in the bloody suppression of the Muslim rebellion of the northwest. At the end of the latter, he tried to reconstruct some of what the rebellion had destroyed. In 1884, he was put in charge of the country's military affairs at the time of the crisis with France over Vietnam.

## LEADERS OF DISSENT, REBELLION, OR REVOLUTION

**Borodin, Mikhail** (1884–1948)—Emigrating to the United States early in the twentieth century, Borodin studied at Valparaiso University; he then established his own Chicago school for émigrés. Returning to Russia after the Bolshevik Revolution, he became an important Comintern agent in Mexico, Spain, England, and the United States. Sent to China in 1923, he reorganized the Guomindang, using the Leninist model of "democratic centralism." He served as general Soviet adviser during the turbulent years of the Northern Expedition. He had great power on the Chinese scene, incurring the wrath of conservative Guomindang cadres. He was expelled from China in Chiang Kai-shek's purge. He died in a Siberian labor camp.

**Braun, Otto** (1900–74)—Comintern agent and military adviser to the Chinese Communist Party from 1932 to 1939, he was involved in the decision to evacuate the Jiangxi Soviet in October 1934. At the Zunyi Conference, Mao bested him and the "returned Bolsheviks" that he supported.

**Chai Ling** (b. 1967)—A leader of the 1989 demonstrations in Beijing calling for reforms and "democracy," Chai emerged as one of the most radical of the commanders at Tian'anmen Square. She called explicitly for bloodshed that might "awaken" the masses of Chinese. Other leaders have alleged that she was jealous of the power she accrued, and uncompromising in terms of strategy. She fled to France in the aftermath of the episode.

**Ch'en Ch'i-mei** (Chen Qimei) (1876–1916)—An anti-Manchu revolutionary, Chen was a strong ally of Sun Yat-sen in the 1911 revolution. Jealous of his own power, he was involved in the assassination of Tao Chengzhang, a leader of an opposing revolutionary organization. In 1913 and—after a year of exile in Japan—in 1915–16, Chen was a strong opponent of Yuan Shikai, using Shanghai as his base. During that period he became a strong patron of Chiang Kai-shek. He was assassinated by Yuan Shikai's agents. His nephews Ch'en Guo-fu and Ch'en Li-fu remained important allies of Chiang Kai-shek during his rule in the 1930s and 1940s. In his home province, Ch'en Ch'i-mei became a symbol during the Nanjing decade of the connection of Chiang's regime to the revolutionaries of the 1911 period.

**Feng Yunshan** (1822–52)—A distant relative of Hong Xiuquan, he was one of Hong's first converts to Taiping Christianity and one of its most active early proselytizers. He organized the God-Worshippers' Society. Known as the South King, he was killed on the Taiping campaign in Hunan Province.

**Hong Rengan** (1822–64)—A cousin of Hong Xiuquan and one of Hong's first converts to Taiping Christianity, he became Hong's chief of staff. He was called the Shield King. Unlike other Taiping leaders, he became interested in self-strengthening, especially via Western elements such as steamships, trains, life insurance, and modern banks.

**Hong Xiuquan** (1813–64)—The leader of the largest rebellion in history, the Taiping, Hong was ethnically Hakka. A failed examination candidate, in a severe illness he had a vision in which he conceived of himself as the "younger brother of Jesus" given a charge by God to "exterminate the demons." Hong later determined that the demons were the Manchus, and the movement that he and his cohorts organized, the God-Worshippers, became the base of a movement that turned into an anti-Manchu crusade. Hong wrote the Taiping scriptures and set down ideology and policies for the movement. Initially militarily successful, the rebellion bogged down when the leaders settled in Nanjing; it disintegrated when the religious fanaticism turned in on itself and Hong's "kings" began to slaughter each other and when regional armies commanded by Chinese officials destroyed his kingdom. Hong died in his palace, wearing imperial yellow.

**Huang Xing** (1874–1916)—A holder of the lowest of the three civil service degrees, Huang studied in Japan and imbibed the heady brew of anti-Manchu thought. In 1903–4, he founded the Society for the Revival of China (the Huaxinghui), which in 1905 merged with Sun Yat-sen's Revolutionary Alliance. Like Sun and Kang Youwei, he spent from 1905 to 1911 planning revolts in the hope that they might grow to full-scale revolution. The uprising he led in Guangzhou in April 1911, although defeated, became an important historical milestone celebrated by later Republican revolutionaries. During the fighting in late 1911 he led revolutionary forces, and in 1913 was a leader of the military campaign against Yuan Shikai. He broke with Sun over Sun's efforts to tighten party control in Japan through the establishment of a new party, the Gemingdang. Huang was in the United States from 1914 until 1916.

**Li Xiucheng** (d. 1864)—A farm worker who rose to become one of the most successful of the Taiping military leaders, Li was named the Loyal King in 1859. He was interested in and open to the West. He was caught and executed on the collapse of the Taiping movement in 1864.

**Peng Pai** (1896–1929)—Born into a landlord family, Peng studied in Japan from 1918 to 1921, graduating from Waseda University, where he became enamored of socialism. Joining the Communist Party in late 1921, he organized farmers in Guangdong from 1922 on. In 1927, he formed the Hailufeng Soviet, confiscating land amid violent struggles of tenants against landlords. Surrounded by hostile Guomindang forces, the soviet was crushed by Nationalist government troops in 1928. Peng escaped, only to be turned in by a fellow Communist in 1929. He was executed.

**Qiu Jin** (1875–1907)—Revolutionary and feminist, Qiu Jin left her husband and children and studied in Japan, posing for photographs in men's clothing and with dagger unsheathed. She returned to her native Shaoxing in 1907 to head a school, but mainly to become involved in anti-Manchu revolutionary activities. She was executed for her part in a plot to assassinate the governor of Anhui Province and start a rebellion.

**Red Guards**—Mao's chief agents in the Great Proletarian Cultural Revolution. The Red Guards, made up mainly of young adults and youths, wanted to experience their own version of the Long March by going to see the Red Sun in Beijing. Mao wanted them to participate in a revolution to destroy "old" culture and the party. As radicalism became more doctrinaire, Red Guard units fragmented, with various groups claiming to be more Red than others. The movement exploded in violence and the PLA had to rein it in.

**Shen Dingyi** (1883–1928)—Landlord, provincial politician, May Fourth journalist, and member of the Guomindang and the Communist Party, this controversial figure sponsored the first rent-resistance movement of the 1920s. Shen served as patron for future Communist activists, undertook rural-education projects, and sponsored a rural-reconstruction effort in his home county. He was assassinated in 1928, probably the victim of Guomindang fears and distrust.

**Shi Dakai** (d. 1863)—Born into a wealthy farm family but of Hakka ethnic background, Shi became an important general of the Taiping. Styled the Collateral King, he was one of the rebellion's best-educated officers. He was an excellent and popular military leader, known for using wily stratagems. Shi surrendered to government forces and was executed in summer 1863.

**Sneevliet, Hendricus** (alias Maring) (c. 1887–1942)—A Dutch Communist who had been active in Communist organizational work in Indonesia in 1917–18, Sneevliet was sent to China by the Comintern in 1921. He represented the Comintern at the organizational meeting of the Chinese Communist Party and performed an important role as broker among the CCP, the Guomindang, and Soviet interests. He left China in 1923. He was executed by Nazi police after his capture in the Dutch struggle against Germany.

**Wang Dan** (b. 1970)—One of the foremost leaders of the 1989 democracy movement, Wang was arrested and imprisoned until 1993. He was rearrested in May 1995 and sentenced to eleven years in prison for attempting to subvert the state. His appeal of this sentence was denied in late 1996, but he was freed in April 1998 and allowed to fly to the United States for medical treatment.

**Wei Changhui** (d. 1856)—This leader of the Taiping Rebellion, the descendant of a wealthy family, was known as the North King. When the Taiping leadership was disintegrating, Hong had Wei kill Hong's chief competitor, Yang Xiuqing. In a bloodbath, Wei killed about twenty thousand of Yang's supporters as well. Hong eventually had Wei killed to deal with the problem thus created.

**Wei Jingsheng** (b. 1950)—The best-known dissident in the last twenty years of the century, Wei first came to prominence with his call for a "fifth modernization" at the time of the Democracy Wall episode (1978–79). He was arrested and sentenced to fifteen years of hard labor. Rearrested in 1995 and again sentenced to another long term, he was released for medical treatment in the United States in 1997. His letters from prison and other writings, *The Courage to Stand Alone*, were published that same year.

**Wu'er Kaixi**—A prominent leader of the 1989 democracy movement, Wu'er fled China after the government crackdown; he became a spokesman for dissidents who had left the country. In the early 1990s, rumors of corruption and misuse of funds contributed for the democratic cause swirled around the émigré group.

**Yang Xiuqing** (d. 1856)—In the Taiping Rebellion hierarchy, Yang was known as the East King. When he spoke, it was as the voice of God the Father, thus one-upping the founder Hong Xiuquan, the Heavenly King. The two came increasingly into conflict and Hong commissioned Wei Changhui, the North King, to kill Yang.

**Zou Rong** (1885–1905)—An anti-Manchu writer whose main work *The Revolutionary Army* put forth his ideas about overthrowing the Manchus and establishing a republic. In 1903, the Qing government issued warrants for Zou's arrest; Zou turned himself in, was tried, and sentenced to two years in prison. He died one month before his scheduled release.

## NATIONALIST PARTY
## (GUOMINDANG/KUOMINTANG) LEADERS

(Wade-Giles romanization is used for names of leaders whose dates reach into the Nationalists' Taiwan period.)

**Ch'en Ch'eng** (Chen Cheng) (1897–1965)—A graduate of the Baoding Military Academy, Ch'en, a native of Zhejiang Province, became closely linked to Chiang Kai-shek while teaching at the Whampoa Military Academy. He became one of Chiang's most important generals and, during the Nanjing decade, was second in command to Chiang in both party and government. He served as governor of Taiwan at the time of the Nationalist exodus from the mainland. Elected vice-president of the Republic of China in 1954 and reelected in 1960, he also was president of the Executive Yuan from 1950 to 1954 and again from 1958 to 1963.

**Ch'en Kuo-fu** (Chen Guofu) (1892–1951)—A native of Zhejiang, Ch'en was nephew of Ch'en Ch'i-mei (Chen Qimei), the 1911 revolutionary and close ally of both Sun Yat-sen and Chiang Kai-shek. He and his brother Ch'en Li-fu headed the right-wing CC clique, one of the strongest in the Kuomintang. From 1925 to 1945, he had great influence on the course of government. He chaired the party's organization department from 1926 to 1932 and again in 1944. He held various positions in national and provincial governments, including acting head of the Control Yuan (1928–32), governor of Jiangsu Province (1933–37), and chair of the government personnel office (1939–45). His health declined rapidly in the mid-1940s and his participation in public affairs ceased.

**Ch'en Li-fu** (Chen Lifu) (b. 1900) — Brother of Ch'en Guo-fu and nephew of Ch'en Ch'i-mei, Ch'en received an M.S. degree in mining engineering from the University of Pittsburgh in 1925 and retained a strong focus in his career on science and technology as the route by which China could be modernized. He chaired the party's investigation division from 1928 into the late 1930s. He served in a number of other posts, including secretary-general of the party's headquarters (1929–31), chair of the organization department (1932–36, 1938–39, 1944–48), minister of education (1938–44), and vice-president of the Legislative Yuan (1948–50). He moved to the United States in 1950.

**Chiang Ching-kuo** (Jiang Jingguo) (1909–88) — The oldest son of Chiang Kai-shek, Chiang was educated in the Soviet Union, where he spent twelve years. He married a Russian woman. He returned to China in 1937 and served his father's government in various positions. After the flight to Taiwan, his influence in the government increased steadily as he served in various posts in the defense ministry. He succeeded his father as president and Kuomintang chair in 1978. During the last years of his presidency, he began to open up the political process, appointing more Taiwanese to important posts.

**Chiang Kai-shek** (Jiang Jieshi) (1888–1975) — A native of Zhejiang Province, Chiang studied at military schools in China and Japan. Following military action in the 1911 revolution, he became closely associated with Ch'en Ch'i-mei. After Ch'en's assassination in May 1916, Chiang remained in Shanghai. He was sent by Sun Yat-sen in 1923 to the Soviet Union for talks. Named commandant of the Nationalist Party's new military academy at Whampoa, he began to build substantial power and to side increasingly with the party's right wing. He commanded the Northern Expedition (1926–28) and became president of the Republic of China, chair of the party, and commander-in-chief of the army in 1928. Challenged in the 1930s in party and government by residual warlords, Communists, and the Japanese, he finally agreed to join the Communists in a united front against the Japanese in late 1936. During the 1937–45 war, his government was based in Chongqing. When civil war raged from 1947 to 1949, Chiang's was a losing cause: having failed to deal with an array of desperate domestic problems, he lost the civil war to the Communists. He fled to Taiwan, where he retained his posts until his death, modernizing the island but all the while enforcing martial law and excluding Taiwanese from his government.

**Tai Chi-t'ao** (Dai Jitao) (1891–1949) — A graduate of Japan University, Tai at age twenty-one became Sun Yat-sen's personal secretary, a position he retained until Sun's death in 1925. During the May Fourth period, he was a journalist. After Sun's death, his right-wing thinking became open. He attended the meeting of the Western Hills faction in 1925–26 and became one of the strongest anti-Communist commentators on Sun's Three People's Principles. He served on the Guomindang's Central Executive Committee and chaired the Examination Yuan from 1928 to 1948. In poor health, he committed suicide.

**Dai Li** (1895–1946)—A native of Zhejiang, Dai was a graduate of Whampoa Military Academy and became close to Chiang Kai-shek. Very effective as intelligence officer on Chiang's staff in the late 1920s, over time he became the chief intelligence officer in the government. A reputation for effective espionage, brutality in suppressing dissent, and expertise in planning and executing guerrilla actions against the Japanese made him legendary. He was elected to the party's Central Executive Committee in 1945. Dai was killed in a plane crash.

**Ho Ying-ch'in** (He Yingqin) (1890–1987)—A graduate of a Japanese military academy, Ho was one of Chiang Kai-shek's most dependable officers. His important positions included chief of staff (1938–44), minister of war (1930–44), commander-in-chief of the Chinese army (1944–46), chief Chinese representative on the United Nations Military Advisory Commission (1946–48), and chairman in Taiwan of the Strategy Advisory committee in the 1950s.

**Hu Hanmin** (Hu Hanmin) (1879–1936)—A revolutionary leader in the last decade of Manchu control, Hu was also a close ally of Sun Yat-sen. At the First National Kuomintang Congress in 1924, he was elected the top-ranking member of the Central Executive Committee. His political leanings were to the right; some of his associates were implicated in the assassination of Liao Zhongkai in 1925. President of the Legislative Yuan from 1928 to 1931, he fell out of favor with Chiang Kai-shek and in the latter year was placed under house arrest. He was rehabilitated and reelected to the Central Executive Committee in 1935, but died before taking up the post.

**K'ung Hsiang-hsi** (Kong Xiangxi) (H. H. K'ung) (1881–1967)—An undergraduate at Oberlin, K'ung received an M.A. in economics from Yale in 1907. He married Soong Ai-ling, Sun Yat-sen's secretary in Japan during Sun's exile. K'ung became minister of industry and commerce for the new Guomindang government in 1928 and minister of finance from 1933 to 1944. He retired from public life in 1945 and died in the United States.

**Lee Teng-hui** (b. 1923)—Chiang Ching-kuo's vice-president and successor, Lee was a native Taiwanese who moved quickly to democratize the country. He lifted martial law, allowed a free and open press, and permitted non-Kuomintang candidates to participate in elections. He lifted all restrictions for Taiwanese to travel to the PRC. His policy of "flexible diplomacy"—seeking in various ways international recognition for the Taiwan government—antagonized Beijing policy makers.

**Liao Zhongkai** (1878–1925)—Born in San Francisco, Liao attended Waseda and Chuo universities. He became involved with Sun Yat-sen and the Revolutionary Alliance. In the 1920s, in talks in Japan with Comintern representative Adolf Joffe, he facilitated the united front between the Communists and the Guomindang and the "bloc within" arrangement for party membership. He was assassinated five months after Sun's death, when he held various party posts and was in the provincial government in Guangdong.

**Song Jiaoren** (1882–1913)—An early member of Huang Xing's revolutionary Society for the Revival of China, Song went as a student to Japan, eventually studying at Waseda University. He became a member of the Revolutionary Alliance. After the 1911 revolution and Guomindang victories in the elections for National Assembly in early 1913, he was expected to become premier but was assassinated in Shanghai by agents of President Yuan Shikai.

**Sung Tzu-wen** (Song Ziwen) (T. V. Soong) (1894–1971)—A 1915 graduate of Harvard University, Sung was a key figure in the establishment of Republican China's financial system. A brother-in-law of Chiang Kai-shek, he served in many capacities for the Guomindang government: governor of the Central Bank of China, minister of finance, president and vice-president of the Executive Yuan, and minister of foreign affairs. Described occasionally as China's J. P. Morgan, Sung also began a number of profitable corporations under the auspices of the China Development Finance Corporation. He retired to the United States.

**Sun Yat-sen** (Sun Yixian) (1866–1925)—Founder of the Nationalist Party, Sun was trained as a medical doctor in Hong Kong. In his twenties he became involved with anti-Manchu activities. An aborted revolt in 1895 was the start of his revolutionary career. In 1905, he organized the Revolutionary Alliance, the first revolutionary organization to not only set forth anti-Manchuism but also promise a republic and action to enhance the people's livelihood. On an around-the-world fund-raising trip when the 1911 revolution broke out, he concurred with others that Yuan Shikai should become president of the new republic. Then Yuan's authoritarianism brought the 1913 rebellion; Sun was exiled to Japan. Sun's agreement in the early 1920s to accept Comintern help in the reorganization of the Guomindang and the establishment of a party army gave new life to the revolutionary movement. His death from cancer at a moment when his goals seemed near attainment helped to transform him into a symbol of patriotism—the father of his country. His Three People's Principles became the central ideology of the Nationalist Party.

**Wang Jingwei** (1883–1944)—Graduating from Tokyo Law College in 1906, Wang joined the Revolutionary Alliance and became closely associated with Sun Yat-sen. In 1910 and 1911, he was imprisoned after his attempts to assassinate the Manchu prince regent. Wang joined Sun in efforts in the late 1910s to establish an oppositional regime. He was elected to the Nationalist Party's Central Executive Committee in 1924. Associated with the more liberal wing of the party, following Sun's death and the Northern Expedition he emerged as one of Chiang's opponents. In 1940, he collaborated with the Japanese in establishing a government at Nanjing, reportedly believing that such an approach was the only method of preserving the national interests of China. He died before war's end.

## COMMUNIST PARTY (GONGCHANDANG) LEADERS

**Bo Gu** (Qin Bangxian) (1907–46)—From 1926 to 1930, Bo studied at Sun Yat-sen University in Moscow, becoming one of the so-called "Twenty-eight Bolsheviks" who returned to China to oppose first the leadership of Li Lisan and then of Mao Zedong. He served as secretary-general of the Communist Party from 1932 to 1935; he was relieved of that post at the Zunyi Conference during the Long March. From 1936 to 1946, he was a liaison officer in talks between the Communists and Nationalists. He became head of the New China News Agency from 1941 to 1945 and editor of the *Liberation Daily* (*Jiefang ribao*), the official Communist newspaper. Elected to the Central Executive Committee in 1945, he was killed in a plane crash, returning from Chongqing to Yan'an.

**Chen Duxiu** (1879–1942)—A *shengyuan* degree holder (1895), Chen spent two periods of study in Japan and one in France. In 1915, he founded and edited the most celebrated periodical in modern Chinese history, *New Youth* (*Qingnian zazhi*), which championed the development of a new culture. He served as dean of the College of Letters at Beijing University from 1917 to 1919, influencing many students and intellectuals in the cultural revolution known as the May Fourth Movement. He helped found the Chinese Communist Party and was unanimously elected secretary-general of the party, a post he held until 1927. With the collapse of the united front in that year, Chen was replaced by Qu Qiubai. Though he briefly remained an important voice in the party, he was formally expelled in 1930 for opposing the Comintern line.

He organized and led a Trotskyite opposition group to the CCP from 1930 to 1932, when he was arrested by the Guomindang government and charged with "endangering the republic." Tried and sentenced to fifteen years in prison, he was paroled in 1937. He died lonely and largely forgotten.

Chen Yi (1901–72)—One of the most outstanding field commanders in the 1930s and 1940s, Chen studied and worked in France from 1919 to 1921 and studied at Sino-French University in Beijing from 1923 to 1925. He became instructor of political science at Whampoa Military Academy, working under Zhou Enlai. He participated in the Northern Expedition and the Autumn Harvest Uprising, and after that debacle joined Mao in the Jiangxi Soviet. In late 1930, at Mao's order, Chen liquidated an opposition movement at Futian, in Jiangxi. The violent purge became known as the Futian Incident. He did not participate in the Long March, staying behind to rebuild forces in the southeast: those forces became the New Fourth Army. From 1941 to 1946, he was the army's acting commander; he later became commander. In 1949, his army designated as the Third Field Army took the Shanghai region. For almost a decade, he was Shanghai mayor. He was appointed minister of foreign affairs in 1958, a post he held into the Cultural Revolution period, during which he was attacked for opposing Mao's mass campaign.

Chen Yun (1905–95)—Chen worked as a typesetter at the Commercial Press in Shanghai, joining the Communist Party in 1924 and becoming a labor organizer. After participating on the Long March until May 1935, he went to Moscow, returning to Yan'an in 1938, when he became director of the Central Committee's organization department. He moved into economic policy-making positions in the 1940s and after 1949 became the government's most important economic planner. He played a key role in helping the economy revive following the Great Leap Forward. Attacked during the Cultural Revolution, he emerged in the 1980s as an opponent of swift economic change and its alleged bourgeois contamination. In 1989, he was a staunch opponent of the democracy movement and of party chairman Zhao Ziyang.

Deng Xiaoping (1904–97)—Deng, in Paris from 1920 to 1925, joined the French branch of the Chinese Communist Party. He spent several months in Moscow. In 1930, after Communist organizing work in Guangxi Province, he joined Mao in the Jiangxi Soviet. After the Long March, Deng served in various places as political commissar. He was first elected to the Central Committee in 1945. After holding key regional and national posts in the 1950s, at the Eighth Party Congress (1956) he was chosen secretary-general of the Central Committee, thus ranking fourth among party leaders. As the struggle on economic and social policy between Mao and the pragmatists intensified, he became increasingly associated with Liu Shaoqi. He was attacked during the Cultural Revolution but reemerged in 1978. Taking the premiership from Hua Guofeng in 1980, in the last twenty years of the century he launched economic reforms that changed the face of China. He played the pivotal role in the decision to use military force to suppress the demonstrators and crush the democracy movement of 1989.

**Gao Gang** (1905–54)—In 1926, Gao entered the Zhongshan Military Academy in Shaanxi, where two of his teachers were Deng Xiaoping and Liu Zhidan. He joined the Communist Party that year. He was involved in military and propaganda work in north China in the mid-1930s. He held important posts under Mao at Yan'an. After World War II, he was instrumental in planning the economic recovery of Manchuria. In the early 1950s, he was reportedly considered one of the ten most important men in the Communist Party, becoming chair of the State Planning Committee in 1952. Accused of being involved in an antiparty alliance in 1954-55, however, Gao was stripped of all his posts and expelled from the party. He committed suicide.

**Hu Yaobang** (1915–89)—A veteran of the Long March, Hu became a protégé of Deng Xiaoping, working under him during the Sino-Japanese War. He headed the Communist Youth League for fourteen years. Attacked in the Cultural Revolution, he reemerged with Deng in the 1970s. He served as head of the Chinese Academy of Social Sciences. In 1981, he became secretary-general of the party, sharing Deng's stance on the wisdom of major economic reforms. One of two of Deng's anointed successors, he was nevertheless ousted from his post in early 1987 after he reportedly supported student demonstrations late in 1986. His sudden death in April 1989 was the event around which students massively expanded their earlier demonstrations, and that led to the bloody crackdown on the streets of Beijing.

**Hua Guofeng** (b. 1921)—During the Sino-Japanese War, Hua joined Communist guerrillas in the struggle against Japan. He worked his way up from a position as a low-level cadre in Hunan Province to head the new Hunan provincial committee following the Ninth Party Congress in 1969. He had earlier come to Mao's attention because of his support of the Great Leap Forward. He became premier following the death of Zhou Enlai in January 1976 and party chairman after Mao's death later that year. In October 1976, he ordered the arrest of the Gang of Four. He was ousted from power by Deng Xiaoping in 1980.

**Jiang Qing** (1914–91)—An actress with the stage name of Lan Ping, Jiang became the third wife of Mao Zedong. She became involved with Mao in the mid-1930s at Yan'an, to which she had traveled as part of the Shanghai film community. She did not emerge as politically significant until the Cultural Revolution, when she became a self-appointed "cultural tsarina," prescribing theater repertoires and artistic standards. During this time she became a leading figure in the Gang of Four, the ultraradical group that, despite the chaos the Cultural Revolution had engendered, wanted to continue it. She was arrested after Mao's death and tried with the Gang in 1980–81. She was sentenced to death, but was given a series of reprieves. Jiang committed suicide in prison.

**Jiang Zemin** (b. 1926) — Educated in the Soviet Union as an electrical engineer, Jiang was mayor of Shanghai from 1985 to 1989. With a reputation as an urbane leader who spoke several languages and had been able to attract foreign investments, he also likely had ties to conservative premier Li Peng. He was elected to the Politburo at the Thirteenth Party Congress (1987). In June 1989, in the wake of the crackdown in Beijing, Jiang was named secretary-general of the party. In 1991, he was named head of the Military Affairs Commission and also the president of the People's Republic.

**Kang Sheng** (1898–1975) — After studying under Qu Qiubai at Shanghai University, Kang joined the Communist Youth League and the party in the early 1920s. Trained by the Soviet secret service in the 1930s, he became an important leader of the Yan'an rectification movement. In the 1950s, Kang, a leader in security and intelligence work in general, was one of Mao's chief advisers on matters of ideology, especially as they related to the Soviet Union. Hailing from the same hometown as Jiang Qing, Mao's wife, he had a close relationship with her. Like Jiang Qing, Kang was concerned about revolutionary ideological purity, especially as it related to literature and the arts; the two thus formed a natural alliance. Kang became a key player in stimulating the Cultural Revolution. He was named to the standing committee of the Politburo at the Ninth Party Congress in 1969 and the Tenth Party Congress in 1973.

**Li Dazhao** (1889–1927) — Li studied at Waseda University in Japan from 1913 to 1916. He became head librarian and professor of history, economics, and political science at Beijing University in 1918. An important May Fourth leader and frequent contributor to *New Youth*, Li formed close personal relationships with students and played an important role in stimulating interest in Marxism. A founding member of the CCP, he was elected to its central committee at the Second Party Congress (1922). He facilitated the establishment of the united front and served as the main director of the party's propaganda and organizational work in north China. Orders for his arrest were issued after the March 18, 1926 Tian'anmen incident that he had helped organize. In April 1927, he was seized in a raid on the Soviet embassy, where he had taken refuge. Li was hanged on April 28.

**Li Lisan** (1900–1967)—In France on a work-study program from 1919 to 1922, Li joined the French branch of the Chinese Communist Party. He became a leading labor organizer, working especially with miners and railroad workers. He played a major role directing strikes in the May Thirtieth Movement. In the aftermath of Chiang Kai-shek's purge, he rose swiftly in party ranks, by 1928 becoming de facto, if not de jure, party head; he dominated party policy making. He authored the "Li Lisan line," which called for the urban proletariat to direct military uprisings—a policy he hoped would revitalize the party. When the line was tried at Changsha in summer 1930, the uprising was quickly put down. Li was ousted and sent into a fifteen-year exile in the Soviet Union. On his return to China, he was reinstated as a member of the Central Committee. Li was vice-chairman of the All-China Federation of Labor from 1948 to 1953 and labor minister in the government from 1949 to 1954.

**Li Peng** (b. 1928)—When his father died at Guomindang hands in 1930, Li was protected, like several other orphans, by Zhou Enlai and his wife. He studied electrical engineering in Moscow, returning to China in 1955 for a career in the electrical industry. Supported by Chen Yun, he became minister of power in 1979. He rose rapidly in the party hierarchy, becoming deputy prime minister, a member of the Central Committee, and by 1985 a member of the Politburo. At the Thirteenth Party Congress (1987), he became a member of the Standing Committee of the Politburo, and in 1988 became premier, a post he held until 1998. The major hardline conservative in the 1989 crackdown, Li announced martial law shortly before the June 4 tragedy.

**Li Xiannian** (1907–92)—Reared in a working-class family, Li early on worked as a carpenter. He joined the Communist Party in 1927, forming his own guerrilla band. He became an important leader of anti-Japanese guerrilla forces in central China. In the early PRC, he worked to consolidate government control in the south central region and Hubei. Made minister of finance in 1954, he was elected to the Central Committee in 1956 and served as president of the PRC from 1983 to 1988.

**Lin Biao** (1907–71)—A graduate of the fourth class at Whampoa Military Academy, Lin participated in the Northern Expedition and joined the Communist Party in 1927. He became head of the Red Army Academy, training guerrilla commanders in the Jiangxi Soviet. He participated in the Long March, and at Yan'an again headed the army academy, under its new name, the Anti-Japanese Military and Political University. He won substantial victories against the Japanese and served as liaison between Yan'an and Chongqing. Lin was elected to the Central Committee in 1945. The hero of the Manchurian campaign during the civil war, he was made a marshal of the PRC in 1955. He replaced Peng Dehuai as defense minister in 1959, and became the second ranking member of the party in 1966. Lin is given credit for helping to change the PLA into a conventional modern army, but he also helped fuel the madness of the Cultural Revolution. He was perhaps most responsible for the rising cult of Mao, compiling the famous "little red book" of Mao quotations. Though named Mao's successor, Lin reportedly plotted a coup against him. The coup failed. Lin died in a plane crash in Mongolia, ostensibly trying to escape to the Soviet Union.

**Liu Shaoqi** (1898–1969) — Liu was chosen by the Comintern to study in Moscow in 1921–22. On his return, he worked with Li Lisan in organizing miners, steel workers, and railroad workers. In the Jiangxi Soviet he continued organizing rural workers for labor in arsenals and workshops. Participating in the beginning of the Long March, he left to continue political work in various regions. At Yan'an he wrote his most important political report, *How to Be a Good Communist*. A biography has called him, "the Chinese Communist party's foremost expert on the theory and practice of organization and party structure." He held important posts in the first decade of the PRC, culminating with appointment to the PRC presidency (1959). Long considered Mao's likely successor, increasingly he was linked to the pragmatists in the party in opposition to the Maoists. Liu thus became the main target during the Cultural Revolution. He and his wife were humiliated and tortured. He was purged from the party and left to die, alone and untreated for pneumonia. He was rehabilitated by the party in February 1980.

**Liu Zhidan** (1903–36) — Described by Edgar Snow as a "modern Robin Hood," Liu was an important Communist guerrilla leader in northern Shaanxi Province. By early 1935, he and several other leaders had carved out the Shaanxi-Gansu Soviet and organized Red Army units; their area was the final destination of the Long March. Subsequent years saw the newcomer marchers having to work out policies and programs with these local native partisans. In a 1936 campaign against Nationalist forces, Liu was mortally wounded.

**Mao Zedong** (1893–1976) — Born into a peasant family in Hunan, Mao was graduated from the Hunan First Normal School in 1918. He spent late 1918 and early 1919 at Beijing University, auditing courses and working under Li Dazhao in the library. A founding member of the Communist Party, he joined the Nationalist Party under the "bloc within" system. In the mid-1920s, Mao organized peasant associations. After the purge of 1927–28, he rose rapidly in the party, with Zhu De and others establishing the Jiangxi Soviet (1931–34), where he first experimented with land reform and class struggle. Defeated by Chiang's fifth extermination campaign, Mao led the Long March to Yan'an. Along the way, at the Zunyi Conference in January 1935, he regained predominant power in the party, having briefly lost it to the so-called returned Bolsheviks. In Yan'an, Mao spent time setting forth his ideology, in effect sinicizing Marxism-Leninism, and experimenting with various approaches (including the mass line and reeducation) that would become hallmarks of the PRC. With victory in the civil war, Mao established the People's Republic of China on October 1, 1949. He oversaw eight years of successful reconstruction and the launching of the new regime. His zealous revolutionary romanticism and jealous desire for personal power soon began his (and China's) descent into tragedy and terror, starting with the Anti-Rightist Movement in 1957 and the increasing horrors of the Great Leap Forward and the Cultural Revolution. Until his death in 1976, he remained the supreme leader and policy maker for party and state.

**Peng Dehuai** (1898–1974)—One of the most important Communist generals, Peng joined the Communist Party in 1928 at a time when he already commanded guerrilla forces. He accompanied Mao on the Long March, commanding the First Front Army. Elected to the party's Central Committee in 1945, during the civil war Peng continued to command the First Front Army and maintained control until 1954. He became commander of Chinese forces during the Korean War, signing the armistice at Panmunjom in 1953. In 1954 he became minister of defense, and in 1956 he was reelected to the Central Committee and the Politburo. During the Great Leap Forward, Peng was ousted as defense minister at the August 1959 Lushan Conference. His criticism of the Great Leap Forward and his supposedly having discussed it with arch-enemy Khrushchev led Mao to dismiss him. He died imprisoned, his guards refusing him reading and writing material, even sunlight.

**Peng Zhen** (1902–97)—After joining the Communist Party in the mid-1920s, Peng worked at organizing railroad workers and miners. He served many times in his career as a subordinate to Liu Shaoqi, with whom he had close connections. At Yan'an in 1942, Peng became director of the Central Party School and played a pivotal role in the rectification campaign of 1942–43. He was elected to the Central Committee in 1945. He served as mayor of Beijing and in other significant party and government posts from 1949 to 1966, when he was ousted during the opening days of the Cultural

Revolution. Rehabilitated, he returned to the Politburo in 1979. He took a hardline conservative attitude, opposing the pace of Deng's economic reforms. When he retired in 1988, he was chair of the Standing Committee of the National People's Congress.

**Qu Qiubai** (1899–1935)—Early in his career, Qu was an avid scholar of Russian and of Buddhism. He was in the Soviet Union from 1920 until 1923, serving as Moscow correspondent for the *Morning Post* and writing accounts of his impressions, later published in book form. On his return, he was elected to the Communist Party Central Committee at the Third Congress (1923). In 1924, he was one of the first Communists to be elected to the Guomindang Central Committee (as an alternate member). In summer 1927, Qu was elected to replace Chen Duxiu as party secretary-general, but the bloody defeat of the Canton commune in December led to his denunciation for "left opportunism" and to his summons to the Soviet Union, where he stayed until 1930. From 1931 to 1933 he was an important figure in the League of Left-Wing Writers, producing critical writings on literature and culture and translations of Russian and other Western works. In 1934, he went to the Jiangxi Soviet and was appointed to be the people's commissar of education and director of the art bureau of the soviet government. When the marchers left on the Long March, Qu stayed behind to be in charge of propaganda. He was caught by Nationalist forces while attempting to return to Shanghai and was imprisoned and executed.

**Rao Shushi** (b. 1901)—Rao attended Shanghai University, joining the Communist Party in 1925. He worked in labor organizing in Shanghai in 1927. Political commissar of the New Fourth Army after 1942, he was elected to the party's Central Committee in 1945. After the Communist victory, he was appointed to significant posts in east China. In 1953, he was a member of the State Planning Committee and became director of the party's central organization department. In the first major purge after the establishment of the regime (1954–55), he lost all his posts when he and Gao Gang were charged with forming an "anti-party alliance." Nothing is known of him after this purge.

**Wang Ming** (Chen Shaoyu) (1907–74)—The leader of the so-called Twenty-eight Bolsheviks (the returnees from the Soviet Union), Wang served as main translator for Comintern representative Pavel Mif, arriving in the summer of 1930. Wang had studied Russian in the USSR from late 1925 until 1930. Pavel and the Twenty-eight Bolsheviks first challenged the current leadership of Li Lisan. Wang served for a year as party secretary-general, then returned to the Soviet Union as Chinese representative to the Comintern (1932–37). He had a different ideological stance, which led Mao to attack him:

Wang was one of the main reasons Mao launched his rectification campaign in 1942–43. Wang did not play an important role in postwar China.

**Ye Jianying** (1897–1986) — A 1919 graduate of Yunnan Military Academy, Ye went to Whampoa Military Academy in 1924 as deputy director of the class-room instruction department. In the Northern Expedition, he was chief of staff of the First Army. He joined the CCP in the fall of 1927, and his regiment pro-vided military support for the brief Canton commune. He studied Marxism-Leninism and military affairs in the Soviet Union from 1928 to 1931, returning to the Jiangxi Soviet to serve in top military posts. As chief of staff of the Third Red Army Group, he was with the advance contingent on the Long March. In the united front, the two main Communist armies, the Eighth Route Army and the New Fourth Army, were brought into the Nationalist military as the Eighteenth Army Group; Ye served as chief of staff for the commander-in-chief Zhu De. After the war, these two remained in the same positions for the PLA. Elected to the Central Committee in 1945, Ye became the dominant Communist leader in south China from 1949 to mid-1954. He opposed the Cultural Revolution and served as power broker following Mao's death.

**Zhang Guotao** (1897–1979) — A graduate of Beijing University, Zhang par-ticipated in the May Fourth demonstration and had close ties to both Chen Duxiu and Li Dazhao. Li taught him Marxism, and Zhang helped Li form the first Communist cell in north China. He attended the First Congress of the CCP (1921) and was elected head of the organization department. He worked in labor organizing, chairing the China Trade Union Secretariat and organizing the famous strike of the Beijing-Hankou railroad workers that war-lord Wu Peifu crushed bloodily. He was active in the anti-imperialist agitation of the May Thirtieth Movement. While Mao moved to Jiangxi after the purge of 1927–28, Zhang was sent to the border areas of Hubei, Henan, and Anhui to the Eyuwan Soviet, a Communist base that had to be abandoned in the face of one of Chiang's armies. Zhang and others retreated west to Sichuan to try to expand Communist influence there. When the Long March rendezvoused with Zhang's forces, Zhang and Mao clashed sharply over strategy (where to move) and control of military forces. Zhang took armies west to Sikang, while Mao moved on to Yan'an. In 1938, Zhang defected to the Nationalists and never again played a major political role. When the PRC was established he went to Hong Kong, later moving to Canada.

**Zhao Ziyang** (b. 1919) — Born into a Henan landlord family, Zhao joined the CCP during the early days of the Sino-Japanese War. After the establish-ment of the PRC, he worked in directing land reform in Guangdong Province, where he rose to become the province's second-ranked party official. Sent to Inner Mongolia during the Cultural Revolution, he returned to Guangdong in 1971, serving as first secretary of the provincial party; he was also elected to the Central Committee. Transferred to Sichuan in 1975, he undertook economic reforms and by 1977 had the economy making substantial progress. In 1979, Zhao became a member of the Politburo. A strong supporter of Deng's economic reforms, he became premier in the early 1980s and party secretary-general in 1987. When he supported, or at least was open about, the democracy demonstrations in 1989, he was removed from his party posts and placed under house arrest.

**Zhou Enlai** (1899–1976)—One of the best loved and most admired men among the leadership of the PRC. Zhou studied at several universities in Japan from 1917 to 1919, returning to China to participate in May Fourth activities. He went to France in 1920 with the work-study program; there he became a Marxist, attending the founding of the European branch of the Chinese Communist Party. He returned to China in 1924 and served as secretary to the Guangdong provincial committee and as deputy director of the political science department at Whampoa Military Academy. Zhou organized labor unions in Shanghai as advance work for the Northern Expedition; arrested by Nationalist forces, he was released. He was elected to the Central Committee in 1927. After a brief time in the Soviet Union, he went to the Jiangxi Soviet in 1931, serving in various political and military functions. When Mao regained power at the Zunyi Conference on the Long March, Zhou became his deputy on the military directorate. Zhou played a role in the release of Chiang Kai-shek after his kidnapping in December 1936. During the war, he was principal Communist liaison officer to the Nationalists. In the postwar talks initiated by General George Marshall, Zhou was the chief Communist negotiator. At Liberation, Zhou became premier, a post that made him "principal administrator" of the bureaucracy implementing reconstruction and modernization. In addition, he was foreign minister, thus having major responsibility for China's foreign policy and emerging as China's chief spokesman to the world about China's policies. He represented China at the Geneva Conference (1954) and the Bandung Conference (1955). Although the title of foreign minister went to Chen Yi in 1958, Zhou continued to play important diplomatic roles. In the Cultural Revolution, he tried to protect certain people in the government but never went so far as to upset Mao and the Gang of Four. His death from cancer in early 1976 was followed by the April Tian'anmen incident, when a mass outpouring of affection in memory of Zhou was suppressed by the Gang of Four.

**Zhu De** (1886–1976)—Beginning his career as a military and police offi-

cer in Sichuan Province, in late 1922 Zhu went to Germany and studied spo-
radically at two universities. That same year, he joined the German branch
of the CCP and spent most of his time propagandizing Marxist thought and
participating in student demonstrations—activities for which he was
expelled from Germany in 1926. He was involved in the Communists' ill-
fated attempt to seize Nanchang in August 1927. He and Mao joined in the
establishment of the Jiangxi Soviet, where Zhu became commander-in-chief
of the Red Army. Popular with the troops and establishing good working relationships with his officers, Zhu saw his reputation grow. When war with
Japan broke out, he served as commander-in-chief of the Eighth Route Army.
In June 1945, Zhu was elected the second-ranking member of the party on
the Central Committee, the Politburo, and the Secretariat. His posts after the
establishment of the PRC included permanent membership of the
Politburo, vice-chairmanship of the government, and chairmanship of the
standing committee of the National People's Congress. He reportedly sided
with the Liu-Deng pragmatic policies and supported Peng Dehuai at the
Lushan Conference.

   **Zhu Rongji** (b. 1929)—Zhu was graduated from the Electric Motor
Engineering Department of Qinghua University in 1951, two years after join-
ing the CCP. From 1952 to 1975 he worked for the State Planning
Commission as deputy division chief. Attacked during the Anti-Rightist
Campaign in 1957, he was rehabilitated in 1978. He did a three-year stint
(1975–78) at the Ministry of Petroleum Industry and had important posts at the
State Economic Commission from 1979 to 1983. In 1987, he became deputy
party secretary for the Shanghai party bureau, and he served as mayor of
Shanghai from 1988 to 1990. Zhu became known as a no-nonsense economic
administrator who had substantial contacts with foreign businessmen. He was
elected to the Standing Committee of the Politburo in 1992; the next year he
was named deputy prime minister, director of the Bank of China, and chair of
the economic and trade office. He became premier in 1998.

## MILITARY FIGURES

   **Bai Chongxi** (1893–1966)—After graduating from Baoding Military
Academy in 1916, Bai returned to his home province of Guangxi. With fellow
provincials Li Zongren and Huang Shaohong, he formed over a number of
years of warlord battles what became known as the Guangxi clique. In 1926,
Chiang Kai-shek agreed to incorporate their forces into the Nationalist army.

In 1927, Bai, as field commander of the Eastern Route Army of the Northern Expedition, took Hangzhou and Shanghai; on April 12, he unleashed the terror on Shanghai workers and leftists that inaugurated the more than yearlong purge of Communists and leftists. In the 1930s, the relationship between the clique and Chiang and his government was turbulent. Chiang never brought them into his confidence or trusted them, although historians have claimed they were far more capable than many men Chiang depended upon. From 1946 to 1948, Bai served as minister of defense. He fled to Taiwan, where he was a member of the Kuomintang Central Committee and served as vice-director of the president's strategic advisory commission.

**Duan Qirui** (1865–1936) — Duan was graduated at the top of the first class at the Beiyang Military Academy in 1887. Selected to study military science in Berlin, Duan spent 1889–90 in Germany. In the late 1890s and early 1900s, he became one of Yuan Shikai's chief military aides. He served in key posts in the early Republic, including minister of war (1912–14), premier through most of the period from April 1916 to October 1918, and provisional president from November 1924 to April 1926. In the warlord turmoil that followed Yuan Shikai's death, Duan was a chief player in the coalitional wars as head of the so-called Anhui clique.

**Feng Yuxiang** (1882–1948) — Known as the "Christian general" (he was said to baptize his troops with fire hoses), Feng was one of the most able of the warlords. His base of power was in north China, from the Province of Shaanxi east and north to the capital. In areas that he controlled he undertook social reforms and was active in public reconstruction and renewal projects. He often looked to the Soviet Union for supplies. He was a key player in the warlord wars that ravaged north China. He supported the Northern Expedition, but in 1929 and 1930 militarily challenged Chiang Kai-shek's power. In the 1930 fighting, Feng's army was soundly defeated; he played no further important political role.

**Li Zongren** (b. 1890) — Fellow provincials Bai Chongxi and Huang Shaohong joined Li to comprise the so-called Guangxi clique, a potent military triumvirate who controlled an able warlord army. Their army was incorporated with the Nationalist army in the Northern Expedition, but in the 1930s the relations between the clique and Chiang Kai-shek ran the gamut from cold war to hot war. Li became the Nationalist government's vice-president in 1948, and acting president in 1949 when Chiang, as window dressing, resigned briefly. Li retired in the United States in December 1949; he went to live in the PRC in 1965.

**Marshall, George** (1880–1959) — U.S. general and secretary of defense.

After World War II, Marshall undertook a much publicized mission to try to bring the Communists and Nationalists together. He spent from December 1945 to January 1947 trying to heal the breach between the two. A January 1946 cease-fire was engineered and plans for a coalition government drawn up. But by mid-1946, the cease-fire collapsed, first in Manchuria and then more generally. Neither side was willing to make the necessary compromises. Marshall left, blaming both sides for intransigence.

**Senggelinqin** (d. 1865)—A Mongol prince, Senggelinqin first became known for his success in annihilating the Taiping northern expedition in 1855, thus eliminating any possibility that the Taiping might try a more general invasion in the north. He and his troops saw action again in the Arrow War against Britain and France in 1859 and 1860; this time defeated, with triumphant foreign forces destroying the imperial summer palace, he was deprived of title and rank. Called on again to deal with the threat of the Nian rebellion, Senggelinqin won many battles but was killed in an ambush in Shandong Province.

**Stilwell, Joseph** (1883–1946)—A U.S. Army general, Stilwell was appointed as commander-in-chief of U.S. forces in the China-Burma-India theater following Pearl Harbor. Despite the fact that Stilwell had studied Chinese in China and thus had good command of the language and an understanding of Chinese culture, he despised Chiang Kai-shek. Since part of Stilwell's role was to serve as liaison between Washington and Chiang, the two were thrust together far too much for either to stand. The personal enmity exacerbated disagreement over wartime strategy. In the end, Roosevelt recalled Stilwell in 1944.

**Ward, Frederick Townsend** (1831–62)—From Salem, Massachusetts, this soldier of fortune organized the so-called Ever-Victorious Army to defend Shanghai and foreign interests against the Taiping. This mercenary force led by foreign officers clearly indicated that the West was siding with the Qing in its struggle with the Taiping. It did not play any notable role in the general suppression of the rebellion. Ward died in battle.

**Wu Peifu** (1874–1939)—A *shengyuan* degree holder of 1896, Wu was graduated from the Baoding Military Academy in 1903. In the warlord wars that raked many areas of China from 1916 to 1928, Wu was a major player, the leader of the so-called Zhili clique. Dominant in north China after wide-scale war in 1922, he lost control of Beijing in 1924; he continued to hold major power in central China until he was ousted in the Northern Expedition. The British looked favorably upon Wu and were willing to offer supplies and assistance, hopeful that he would be able to unite China and ultimately repay them the favor. Wu is also remembered for his bloody suppression of a 1924 railroad strike that had shut down the Beijing-Hankou Railroad: thirty-five workers were killed and many more were injured. Interestingly, there was also a possible British connection to Wu's decision to act so forcefully: the British controlled the mines for which the railroads provided service.

**Yan Xishan** (1883–1960) — Graduating from a Japanese military academy in 1909, Yan passed the *juren* examination the same year. From 1912 to 1949, he controlled all or at least part of his native province of Shaanxi. As a warlord, he was continuously involved in shifting coalitions in the large campaigns in northern China. He allied himself with Feng Yuxiang in 1930 against Chiang Kai-shek but came up the loser. In the 1910s and the 1930s he undertook substantial economic and social reforms in Shaanxi that earned it the sobriquet "model province." In the mid-1930s, he was pulled within the Guomindang sphere when Chiang named him vice-president of the Military Affairs Commission. He was commander-in-chief of the Second War area during the resistance war against Japan. From June 1949 to March 1950, he served as both defense minister and president of the Executive Yuan in the Guomindang regime.

**Zhang Xueliang** (b. 1898) — The son of warlord Zhang Zuolin, Zhang was graduated from the Fengtian Military Academy in 1919. On his father's assassination in June 1928, he inherited control of Manchuria and became known as the Young Marshal. The loss of Manchuria to Japan sullied Zhang's reputation, but in 1935 he was assigned as deputy commander-in-chief in operations to blockade the Communists in their northwest Shaanxi base. Meetings with Zhou Enlai in mid-1936 led Zhang to see the necessity of a Communist-Nationalist united front against the Japanese. In late fall 1936, Zhang stopped the anti-Communist blockade. When Chiang flew to Xi'an to investigate, Zhang kidnapped him and held him for two weeks until he agreed to form the united front. Chiang flew back to Nanjing, holding Zhang under arrest. Since that day Zhang has remained under house arrest.

**Zhang Zuolin** (1875–1928) — Born into a peasant family and without an education, Zhang began his military career fighting in the Sino-Japanese War (1894–95). He consolidated his control over Manchuria in the aftermath of Yuan Shikai's death in 1916. A major warlord (he is known as the Old Marshal — see Zhang Xueliang, above), he participated in the shifting warlord coalitions that produced the massive civil wars in north China during the early and mid-1920s. Zhang continually had to deal with the threats of the Soviet Union and Japan, both of which were interested in establishing themselves in Manchuria. The Japanese were especially concerned about what the rise of Chinese nationalism, as seen in the May Thirtieth Movement and the Northern Expedition, might mean for their Manchurian interests; not certain about being able to trust Zhang in the changing political context, they blew up his train as he was returning from a meeting with Chiang Kai-shek in Beijing. The Old Marshal was succeeded by his son Zhang Xueliang.

## INTELLECTUALS, WRITERS, AND ARTISTS

**Ba Jin** (b. 1904)—Born Li Feigan in Sichuan, Ba Jin was graduated from the Southeastern University middle school in 1925. He studied in France from 1927 to 1929. From 1929 to 1946, he was prodigiously prolific, publishing twenty novels and more than seventy short stories. His most famous novel, *Family* (1931), is a melodramatic tale of three brothers, each struggling to find his way amid the May Fourth period's cultural revolution. Ba Jin's novels of this period (e.g., *Trilogy of Love*, 1931–35) had great appeal for youthful readers because they dealt with new life choices that had to be made in the context of a changing China. Critics rate *Cold Nights* and *Ward Four*, both published in 1946, among his best works. The first details the devastating impacts of war on human hopes and goals. The second, which deals with a hospital unit for the poor where the patients are treated callously, is thought to depict a microcosm of the state of China after the war. After the establishment of the PRC, even though Ba did not join the Communist Party, he held many positions of importance. He was vice-chair of the Union of Chinese Writers, a member of the presidium of the All-China Federation of Literary and Art Circles, and a deputy to the National People's Congress. He wrote little after 1953. Criticized for comments he made during the Hundred Flowers Movement, he was brutally persecuted during the Cultural Revolution. Rehabilitated, he became in the 1980s one of the most respected of the elder generation, being elected chair of the Writers' Association in 1985.

**Bai Hua** (b. 1930)—Born in Henan as Chen Youhua, Bai, a noted poet, in 1981 became a cause célèbre for his story and later screenplay *Unrequited Love* (*Kulian*). It was attacked for its depiction of the victimization of a character during the Cultural Revolution; in the end, the body of the protagonist is found lying on the bare earth in the shape of a question mark. Made into a film, it was banned by Deng Xiaoping and Hu Yaobang. Bai became the leading "negative example" in a nationwide campaign attacking "bourgeois liberalization." By day, Bai worked in the cultural institutes of the Wuhan Military Region, and the military was most irate because the film script implied that the foundation of Maoist China was more feudal superstition than socialist ideals, and that national interests had not been served by the Communist Party in the years of the Cultural Revolution. The affair underscored the basic relationship in the Chinese state between politics and culture.

**Bei Dao** (b. 1949) — Born Zhao Zhenkai in Beijing, Bei is an author of fiction and poetry and was coeditor of the underground literary journal *Today*, published in 1978–80 and again beginning in the late 1980s. Because of the Cultural Revolution, his formal education ended in his first year of senior high school; he was a Red Guard in the Cultural Revolution. In 1969, because he was the eldest son and provided the support for the family, he was assigned to a construction company near Beijing rather than being sent to the countryside. He began writing both fiction and poetry in the 1970s. His novel *Waves* was, according to scholars Bonnie McDougall and Kam Louie, "a pioneer in reintroducing subjectivity, multiple narrative, and interior monologue into contemporary Chinese fiction." An account of five characters' perceptions of certain episodes, the novel is a sharp representation of the corruption and social disarray of the 1970s. His poetry, as in "The Answer," is defiant against the absurdities of the party-state, but he is also well known for poetry about love and friendship. Authorities criticized his poetry as "obscure"; in some quarters, therefore, he is known as the leader of the "obscure" poetry school. In the mid-1980s, he became a member of the Beijing Writers' Association and published his collected poems in the official press. His writings were translated into many languages. By the mid-1990s, he had moved to the United States.

**Cai Yuanpei** (1868–1940) — A *jinshi* degree holder (1890) and a member of the exclusive Hanlin Academy, Cai from 1898 to 1901 served as principal of the Sino-Western School in his native city of Shaoxing, Zhejiang. In 1904, he helped found and became the leader of the Restoration Society, an anti-Manchu revolutionary society. Cai studied in Germany from 1907 to 1911. When he returned, he was named minister of education in the new Republican government. He returned to Europe from 1913 to 1915, helping to sponsor a work-study program in France. In 1916, Cai was named chancellor of Beijing University, a post he held until 1926. That tenure encompassed the May Fourth Movement, a time of searching for the direction and the nature of modern China. Cai made the university a laboratory for that search, bringing in teachers of all political, social, economic, religious, and philosophical views, so that figuratively a hundred schools of thought could contend. Academic freedom was the hallmark of the day. He made frequent trips abroad during these years, receiving honorary degrees from the University of

Paris and New York University. During the Northern Expedition, he linked himself to Chiang Kai-shek and was named to the Central Supervisory Committee of the Guomindang, became a member of the State Council, and served briefly as president of the Control Yuan. In 1928, Cai founded and served as first president of Academia Sinica, the most important advanced study and research institution in China. When Yang Quan, Academia Sinica's secretary-general and an important figure in the China League for Civil Rights, was assassinated in 1933 after criticizing the government, Cai resigned all positions; he left public life in 1935. He died in anonymity in Hong Kong.

**Cao Yu** (1910–96)—China's leading twentieth-century playwright, from 1926 to 1930 Cao attended Nankai Secondary School, where he acted in many plays, the school having one of the most active drama societies in China. He graduated from Qinghua University in 1934, majoring in Western languages and literature. During his last year as an undergraduate, he wrote *Thunderstorm*, described by a critic as "the most famous dramatic work of the pre-war period and possibly the most performed play in the modern Chinese theatre." He taught at the Tianjin Normal College for Women and at Fudan University. He did not join the Communist Party until 1957. Not afraid of criticizing the excesses of the Great Leap Forward, he was targeted during the Cultural Revolution. Rehabilitated in the late 1970s, he was celebrated as a star and made a number of trips abroad. He supported the government crackdown in 1989. Other major plays include *Sunrise* (1935—winner of the Da Gong Bao prize); *Wilderness* (1936); *Peking Man* (1940); *Family* (1941); and *Bright Skies* (1956).

**Chen Kaige** (b. 1952)—Son of Chen Huaiai, a filmmaker from an earlier generation of Chinese socialist realism, Chen was graduated from the Beijing Film Institute in 1982. He is one of the so-called fifth generation of filmmakers, a school that emphasizes the visual and aural qualities of film rather than dramatic and literary elements and that has strong political commitments. His major films include *Yellow Earth* (1986), *Life on a String* (1991), *Farewell, My Concubine* (1993), *Temptress Moon* (1996), and *The Emperor and the Assassin* (1998). He has won top festival prizes at Cannes (for *Farewell, My Concubine*), Berlin, and Tokyo; *The Emperor and the Assassin* won a prize for technique at the 1999 Cannes Film Festival.

**Ding Ling** (1904–86)—Born Jiang Bingzhi in Hunan Province, Ding was the first writer to show women liberating themselves in Chinese society. Active in the May Fourth Movement, she studied at several schools in Shanghai and Beijing. Her most famous work, "Miss Sophie's Diary," was published in 1928. Joining the Communist Party in 1932, she was arrested by

Guomindang agents in 1933 and held in detention for three years. In 1936 she traveled to Yan'an. Her writings from this time on shifted from an emphasis on feminism to furthering the Communist cause; nevertheless, she did not lose sight of gender issues. She expressed disappointment at the treatment of women in the base areas; for that she became a target of the Yan'an Forum in 1942. Her last novel, *The Sun Shines Over the Sanggan River*, a study of land reform in north China, won the Stalin Prize for Literature in 1951. In the early PRC, she was editor-in-chief of key literary journals, posing a threat to Zhou Yang and his faction. For this she was criticized, and in the Anti-Rightist Campaign she was exiled to a desolate region in north China. From that time until the end of the Cultural Revolution, she was in either jail or labor camps. Returning to Beijing in 1979, she became vice-chair of the Writers' Association. In the 1983 campaign against spiritual pollution, she sided with the hardline conservatives, attacking younger writers. She became increasingly unpopular with other writers; at the Writers' Congress in 1985, she was not reelected to the executive board. In reaction, she founded a new literary magazine, *China*, and encouraged controversial contributions, which led to its being shut down. She died shortly afterward.

**Fang Lizhi** (b. 1936)—A dissident scholar given sanctuary in the United States. Fang went to study astrophysics at Beijing University in 1952; within five years, at age twenty-one, he became a victim of the Anti-Rightist Campaign, cast out of the party. He was rehabilitated in the first years of Deng's rule and named vice-president of the University of Science and Technology in Hefei, Anhui. In that post, he spoke openly of the need to create a more open society that tolerated differences. In December 1986, when the party was insisting that elections for congresses be limited to party slates, there were protests in Hefei; the protests spread around the country, and hardline conservatives suppressed the students, ousted party chair Hu Yaobang, and struck out at Fang and others whom they saw as encouraging the students. Fang was ousted from the CCP and lost both his teaching position and his research post. In January 1989, he inaugurated a wave of petitions to Deng Xiaoping calling for the release of political prisoners. In the aftermath of the 1989 crackdown in Beijing, Fang and his wife were given sanctuary in the U.S. embassy and left the country for the United States in 1990.

**Fei Xiaotong** (b. 1910)—China's most famous sociologist, Fei was an undergraduate at Yanjing University and did his master's work at Qinghua University. He received a British Boxer Indemnity Fund scholarship and studied anthropology with Bruno Malinowski at the London School of Economics. His most important work uncovered and analyzed social patterns in rural society. His 1939 publication of *Peasant Life in China* made him the leading intellectual among Chinese non-Marxist social scientists. During World War II, Fei went to Yunnan, where by 1941 he headed the sociology department and became field director of the Yanjing-Yunnan Station for Sociological Research. His 1947 book *From the Soil* has become the classic theoretical work about the distinctive structure and values in Chinese society. From the Anti-Rightist Campaign in 1957 until the end of the Cultural Revolution, Fei was disgraced, removed from his positions, and compelled to give up his academic work. Rehabilitated in 1979, he became first head of the Chinese Society of Sociology.

**Feng Guifen** (1809–74)—After attaining his *jinshi* degree in 1849, Feng assumed a position in the Hanlin Academy. Serving as a civil service examiner, his early career was disrupted by mourning periods for his parents. During the Taiping, he directed the Jingye Academy in Shanghai and the Ziyang and Chengyi Academies in Suzhou; he also served as an important adviser to both Zeng Guofan and Li Hongzhang in their suppression of the Taiping, and he helped raise militia units to defend Suzhou from the Taipings. He is best known for his competence as a student and practitioner of statecraft. His essays, analyzing the public problems of the time, reveal a man with progressive spirit who had knowledge of foreign affairs and of Western science, plus an awareness of the pressing need for domestic reform and competent, uncorrupted government.

**Feng Zikai** (1898–1975)—A graphic artist, cartoonist, and essayist, Feng studied with famed painter and calligrapher Li Shutong. With another of Li's students, he opened the Shanghai Private Arts University in 1920. He went to Japan to study oil painting in 1921, returning the following year to teach and increasingly to draw sketches and cartoons. He used simple line brush drawings to portray people and to criticize Chinese society from the 1920s to the 1940s. He taught at Zhejiang University and the Chongqing Academy of Art. Named president of the Shanghai Art Academy in 1960, in 1962 he became vice-chair of the Joint Federation of Literature and Arts World in Shanghai.

**Fu Baoshi** (1904–65)—Landscape painter Fu studied at the Tokyo School of Fine Arts from 1933 to 1935. In 1934, he held a one-man show in the Matsuzakaya Department Store in the Ginza. Returning from Japan to China, he spent most of his career at the National Central University. In his painting he focused on landscapes, figures, and figures in landscapes. One of the striking features of many of his paintings was the monumentality of scale. According to critic Michael Sullivan, "even his small album leaves a breadth of vision, an air of mystery, a poetic intensity, not matched by any other modern Chinese artist."

**Guo Moruo** (1892–1978) — Though Guo went to Japan to study medicine, his interest was literature. He said that from his early teen years, "his pastimes included reading, revolution, masturbation, and flirtation with male prostitutes, opera performers, and fellow schoolboys." He read widely in Western and Asian literature. He was a founder of the Creation Society, a literary society that published several periodicals to popularize "art for art's sake." In 1924, he was converted to Marxism-Leninism. In 1926, he became dean of the College of Arts at Sun Yat-sen University in Guangzhou and revivified the Creation Society. He participated in the Northern Expedition and the Nanchang uprising, joining the Communist Party in 1927. He spent 1928 to 1937 in Japan, focusing on paleography and ancient Chinese history. Early in the Sino-Japanese War, Guo published five historical plays. In July 1949, he became chair of the All-China Federation of Writers and Artists. He held various posts in the government as well as the presidency of the Chinese Academy of Sciences. He generally supported all the governmental twists and turns in the 1950s and 1960s.

**Hu Feng** (b. 1903) — Although a Marxist, Hu apparently never joined the Communist Party. He came to prominence in Shanghai's left-wing literary circles with his patronage of Lu Xun, as a professional editor and writer, and as a member of the League of Left-Wing Writers. His career was marked by continual struggle with orthodox Communist critics like Zhou Yang, who argued that politics and ideology were paramount literary concerns. Hu had more traditional analytical views, contending that politics and ideology were secondary. Given Mao's position on the preeminence of politics and ideology in art, he was on the constant defensive. Despite attacks by Zhou Yang in 1951, Hu gave a report to the Central Executive Committee in 1954 that set forth his position rejecting the idea that politics and ideology should have a stranglehold on literature. As a result, he was the target of a 1955 campaign led by Zhou Yang that tried to paint him as a counterrevolutionary. He was arrested and imprisoned.

**Hu Shi** (1891–1962) — Hu received his undergraduate degree from Cornell University, graduating Phi Beta Kappa; he received his Ph.D. in 1917 from Columbia University, a student of John Dewey. That same year, he became professor of philosophy at Beijing University. He became a leader in the effort to replace the system of writing Chinese in its classical form with the vernacular. When the New Culture movement split over political issues, Hu championed the idea that educational and cultural reform must precede political change; he also argued the pragmatist's position that change must come incrementally in evolutionary fashion, not with the sweeping changes of some *ism*.

In 1931, he became dean of the College of Arts at Beijing University; he held that post until 1937. He prided himself on being a "no party, no faction" intellectual, steering clear of involvement in either party. He served as Chinese ambassador to the United States from 1938 to 1942, remaining in the United States until 1946 and returning two years later. In 1958, he assumed the presidency of Academia Sinica in Taiwan, where he died four years later of a heart attack.

**Huang Binhong** (1864–1955)—A landscape painter, Huang failed to attain a civil service degree. In 1907, he became an editor at the Shenzhou Guoguang She publishing house, which produced volumes of reproductions of major works of painting and calligraphy. Huang wrote and edited works on traditional painting and was a member of organizations championing the traditional style. From 1937 to 1948, he served as professor at the Beijing National Academy of Art, and from 1948 to his death he was professor at the Hangzhou Academy. His favorite source of landscape images was Huangshan in Anhui Province. His "dense textures and nervous brushstroke" helped revive the so-called Anhui School, which had been almost destroyed by the Taiping Rebellion.

**Kang Youwei** (1858–1927)—By the time he attained his *jinshi* degree in 1895, Kang had already made a huge impact on the intellectual world of the late nineteenth century. In 1891, he had shaken up that world with the publication of *The Forged Classics of the Wang Mang Period*, in which he attacked the authenticity of the classic texts that were considered the Confucian canon. This attack threw into question the reluctance to depart from their prescriptions in moving toward change. In 1897, his *Confucius as a Reformer* further argued that Confucius himself had argued for institutional change. In 1898, he got the ear of the young Guangxu emperor through the auspices of the imperial tutor. From June into September 1898, he was able to have the emperor issue many decrees installing institutional reforms, including modernizing the military and the postal system, abolishing sinecure posts, and establishing a national school system. The hoped-for changes were killed by the empress dowager's coup, after which Kang had to flee the country. In Canada in 1899, he founded the Society to Protect the Emperor, an organization that in subsequent years would vie with Sun Yat-sen's revolutionary organizations for the money and support of overseas Chinese. Though his social ideas were remarkably radical, he remained a monarchist for the rest of his life, even trying to get warlords in the 1920s to revive the Qing.

**Lao She** (1899–1966)—Lao graduated from Beijing Normal School in 1918, taught at a secondary school, and in 1924 taught at the University of London's

School of Oriental Studies. He returned to China in 1929 and taught at Qilu University in Jinan. Lao, ethnically Manchu, from 1936 on concentrated on his writing. His strongest novels are social and political critiques of the China of his day. In *Cat Country* (1932) he describes the land of that name (which in fact is China) as "dirty, crowded, and ridden with inequality." *Camel Xiangzi* (1936) is a trenchant critique of the life of the Beijing lower classes. In 1937, he was chosen unanimously to lead the Chinese National Federation of Anti-Japanese Writers and Artists. He lectured in the United States in 1946, staying on until 1949. He returned to Beijing to hold important cultural posts in the new regime. An unfinished novel, *Beneath the Red Banner* (written 1961–62 but not published until 1979) has been found by critics to be the "most interesting" of his later works. He was beaten by Red Guards early in the Cultural Revolution; extremely depressed, he committed suicide.

**Liang Qichao** (1873–1929) — Paramount intellectual of the first twenty years of the twentieth century, Liang was also Kang Youwei's most important pupil. Involved with Kang in the various reform activities of the mid- to late 1890s, Liang had to flee to Japan following the Hundred Days of 1898. Liang read deeply into Western writings on politics and society and traveled extensively raising money for Kang's Society to Protect the Emperor. His periodical *Renovation of the People*, begun in 1902, developed a readership within four years of more than fourteen thousand, some in China and some abroad. Liang bitterly opposed Sun's Revolutionary Alliance and the ideas it set forth in its paper *The People's News*. After 1912, Liang, seen by many as one of the intellectual leaders of the time, broke with Kang and joined a political party. He served in several capacities in the administration of Yuan Shikai, in the process infuriating many who saw Yuan as a villain. After Yuan's death, Liang spent some time in politics, but gave it up as futile. In 1919–20 he visited Europe, becoming convinced by the World War I experience that Western civilization was morally sterile. He taught Chinese history at Nankai University in Tianjin until shortly before his death.

**Liang Shuming** (1893–1988) — Attracting the attention of Cai Yuanpei with an essay on Buddhism, Liang was invited to teach at Beijing University in 1917. In his *The Cultures of East and West and Their Philosophies*, he attempted to show "that Chinese culture was relevant to the modern world" and that, in the midst of the May Fourth rejection of traditional culture, Chinese traditional culture was still relevant. He left the university in 1924. From 1927 to 1937, he worked in rural reconstruction projects: from 1927 to 1931 in Guangdong and Guangxi, and from 1931 to 1937 as head of the Shandong Rural Reconstruction Institute, which controlled two counties as a reconstruction project. Reacting strongly against Marxist class analysis, he emphasized education and harmonious class relations as the key to positive rural change. He became active in various Third Force organizations, plotting a middle course between the Communists and Nationalists. He was secretary-general of the China Democratic League from 1945 to 1946. Though he continued to live in the PRC, he was never reconciled to its rule, in the mid-1950s being a frequent target of the party.

**Lin Fengmian** (1900–91)—A painter, Lin went to France in the work-study program set up by Cai Yuanpei. He studied at the Ecole Superieure des Beaux Arts in Dijon. He responded to the contemporary trends in Western painting, especially modeling his work on Matisse. In a postimpressionist style, he produced paintings of birds, flowers, landscapes, and figures. He was professor at the Beijing Academy of Art in 1926; he founded the Hangzhou Academy of Art in 1927. In the early PRC and during the Cultural Revolution, he was criticized for his style by party hardliners who saw it as not proletarian—not politically correct. Lin settled in Hong Kong in 1977. He is seen as the creator of "an influential modern style": many major modern artists were his students in Hangzhou.

**Liu Binyan** (b. 1925)—Born in Manchuria, Liu joined the Communist Party in 1944, shortly after graduating from high school. He became an investigative journalist in Beijing in 1951. Reports he wrote in 1956 attracted so much interest that he was admitted to the Writers' Association. Attacked during the Anti-Rightist Campaign, he was thrown out of the party; until he was rehabilitated in the late 1970s, his work could not be published. He became a correspondent for the *People's Daily* in 1977, focusing on investigating high-profile cases. In 1987, in the campaign against bourgeois liberalization, he again lost his party membership. In 1988, Liu went to Harvard University with a Nieman fellowship. He remained in the United States.

**Liu Haisu** (1896–1994)—A painter whose medium was oil, Liu painted landscapes, figures, and still life. In 1912, he founded his own art school, which later developed into the Shanghai Academy of Art. In 1914, he introduced the nude model into Chinese art schools. He studied in Japan (1918–19) and Europe (1931–35). In 1939, when he went to Southeast Asia with his collection of works to raise money for the Chinese Red Cross, he was captured by the Japanese (in Java). By 1946, he had reestablished the Shanghai Academy of Art. In 1958, he became a professor in the Nanjing Academy of Art. During the Cultural Revolution he was placed under house arrest. In 1983, he became director of the Nanjing Academy of Art and a professor in the Shanghai Academy of Art.

**Lu Xun** (1881–1936) — Born Zhou Shuren in Shaoxing, Lu is the most important Chinese writer of the twentieth century. In Japan from 1902 to 1909, he switched his career goals from medicine to literature. After teaching in secondary schools and a brief stint in the Ministry of Education under Yuan Shikai, Lu began his career in vernacular fiction with "The Diary of a Madman" in 1918. This was followed by "Kong Yiji" and "Medicine" (1919) and, perhaps his most powerful work, "The True Story of Ah Q" (1921). By that time his reputation was secure. His fiction output was limited to about thirty short stories, but he also wrote poetry and short, satiric — often sardonic — essays (*zawen*). All his work castigated traditional Chinese culture as well as the contemporary Chinese scene; he found modern China's problems to stem from Chinese faults rather than the depredations of imperialist nations. Lu never joined the Communist Party, though he had close relations with individual Communists and was active in the formation of the League of Left-Wing Writers. His outright hostility to the Guomindang made him after 1930 a "marked man"; in fact, after 1933 he was not able to publish anything under his name. Mao Zedong, in his essay "On the New Democracy," called Lu "the supreme commander in China's cultural revolution."

**Mao Dun** (1896–1981) — Born Shen Yanbing, Mao studied for two years in Beijing before taking a job at Shanghai's Commercial Press. He became increasingly active in Communist activity — working, for example, in 1926 in the Shanghai Propaganda Bureau of the CCP. His first novel, which dealt with the violent aftermath of the Northern Expedition, a trilogy titled *Eclipse*, was, according to a critic, "the first sustained effort in modern literature to give a coherent picture of a significant historical period in twentieth-century China." His masterpiece, *Midnight* (1933), depicts Shanghai's industrial and commercial scene in crisis because of the forces of international capitalism. One of his best-known short stories, "Spring Silkworms," also looks at the impact of capitalism on farm life. Though he continued to write, his contributions to creative literature ended in the 1940s. In 1949, he was named minister of culture for the PRC government. Though he was targeted briefly during the Cultural Revolution, he subsequently held numerous positions in the literature and art worlds.

**Shen Congwen** (1902–88) — From the Miao ethnic minority, Shen became a soldier from age sixteen to twenty-one, during which time he experienced episodes of horror and heroism that became the source for many of his stories. He wrote fiction, plays, essays, and poetry. During his career, he wrote more than two hundred short stories and ten novels, the quality of which was uneven. Shen joined the Crescent Society. In his career he taught at various universities, including Beijing, Wuhan, Qingdao, and, during the war, South-West United University in Yunnan. His novella *The Border Town* (1934) probes the theme of "innocence in the sexual awakening of a young woman" in an undeveloped area along the Hunan-Sichuan border. He stopped writing after 1949. While his "nostalgic pastoralism" was attacked during the Cultural Revolution, his work came to be much more popular in the changed conditions of the 1980s.

**Wang Meng** (b. 1934) — The son of a professor of philosophy in Beijing, Wang joined the Communist Party in 1948. One story made him famous and also proved his downfall. In 1956, *The Young Man Who Has Just Arrived at the Organization Department* was published in *People's Literature*. It depicted the incompetence and laziness of the Communist bureaucracy. For this he was pilloried in the Anti-Rightist Campaign and sent for five years to a rural area for hard labor. Released in 1961, he was, however, in 1963 forcibly sent to Xinjiang Province, where he stayed until 1979. *The Scenery Here*, published in 1978, won an award and increased his stature. In 1985, he was elected to the Central Committee; he was minister of culture from 1986 to 1989. In the 1980s, despite his being in official positions, he published some experimental and controversial literature (e.g., *The Man with Movable Parts*, 1987). He resigned from the government in the wake of the Beijing crackdown of 1989.

**Wang Ruoshi** (b. 1926) — With a philosophy degree from Beijing University, Wang went to work for the *People's Daily* in the early 1950s. A CCP member, Wang reportedly owed his promotion at the newspaper to Deng Tuo, one of the first victims of the Cultural Revolution. In 1979, he criticized the Mao personality cult as "modern superstition" and talked about the necessity of humanism and the reality of "socialist alienation." For these kinds of statements, Wang was removed from his post as deputy editor of the newspaper in October 1983 as part of the campaign against spiritual pollution.

**Wang Ruowang** (b. 1918) — Wang, who became a well-known dissident and gadfly author, joined the Communist Youth League and the League of Left-Wing Writers in Shanghai in 1933. Arrested by the Guomindang for satirizing Chiang Kai-shek, he was imprisoned for three years. In 1937 he went to Yan'an, where he became a CCP member but also edited a wall newspaper critical of the party; the party stopped the display and sent Wang to Shandong. During the Hundred Flowers Movement, Wang published numerous essays (*zawen*) highly critical of the party. Purged in the Anti-Rightist Campaign, he did not resurface until 1979. His writings in the early 1980s were mostly essays, but two works of fiction, a short story "The Sad Canal" and a novella *Hunger Trilogy*, focus on the arbitrariness and cruelty of government policy. In 1987, he was thrown out of the CCP in the movement against bourgeois liberalization.

**Wei Yuan** (1794–1856) — As a *juren* degree holder, Wei accepted an appointment to work on a compilation of essays by Qing scholars on social, economic, and political problems. This experience spurred an interest in current events that shaped Wei's life. He received the *jinshi* degree in 1844 and became a magistrate in 1849. He served as adviser to Governor Tao Zhu of Jiangsu Province. Wei produced much valuable scholarship, in classics as well as history (a history of the Yuan dynasty and a military history of the Qing up to the Daoguang period), and — his most important work — geography (a geography of foreign countries).

**Wen Yiduo** (1899–1946) — Born into the gentry, Wen entered Qinghua University in 1912. He first wrote classic-style poetry, but in the May Fourth period began writing in the vernacular. In the United States from 1922 to 1925, he studied at the Chicago Art Institute and Colorado College. Ambivalent about the West, he admired its literature but believed that the West simply preyed upon China. This ambivalence was reflected in his collection *Dead Water* (1928). In 1926, he joined the Crescent Society and became editor of *Poetry*. After the Northern Expedition, he was named a professor of English and American literature at Nanjing University. He went to Kunming with the exodus to the southwest to teach at South-West United University. Feeling a need for political commitment, he joined the Democratic League in 1946 and criticized the Nationalist Party. He was subsequently assassinated by the party's secret police.

**Wu Han** (1909–69) — Wu had Hu Shi as an early patron. He majored in history at Qinghua University and became an authority on the Ming dynasty. During the Sino-Japanese War, he joined the Democratic League in Kunming. In the 1950s Wu was named head of the history department of Qinghua University and in 1952 was also appointed deputy mayor of Beijing. Asked by superiors to use his historical expertise to write on Hai Rui, a Ming dynasty official whom Mao had mentioned in March 1959 as a "model" for contemporary bureaucrats, Wu composed an essay and a Peking opera based on the story of this official who dared to speak his mind. The latter became the launching point for the Cultural Revolution, for Mao and others thought Wu meant to analogize Hai to Peng Dehuai, who had been dismissed by Mao at the Lushan Conference. Wu became one of the first targets of the campaign; he spent the last three years of his life in prison.

**Yan Fu** (1854–1921) — Yan attended the School of Navigation of the Fuzhou Shipyard, where he studied English. Graduating in 1871, he was involved in naval affairs for a few years. The Qing government sent him to England for two years of study from 1877 to 1879, where Yan became obsessed with discovering the secret of Western strength and wealth. Frustrated with his naval position on his return and by his four failures to pass the *juren* degree, he began writing essays attacking those isolationist Chinese who shunned basic change from the West. He then set out to translate and comment on key Western works, seeing himself as an intellectual publicist. His excellent translations brought to Chinese audiences the works of Charles Darwin, Herbert Spencer, Adam Smith, and John Stuart Mill; his work made a permanent imprint on the intellectual history of early twentieth-century China. He indicated that his criteria for translation were "fidelity to the original, intelligibility of expression, and elegance of style."

**Zhang Ailing** (Eileen Chang) (1921–95)—Zhang attended the University of Hong Kong, gaining early recognition for her short stories of cosmopolitan Shanghai. Her most famous early novella was *The Golden Cangue* (1943). Famous for her psychological portrayal of human relationships, she left China after the establishment of the PRC, settling in the United States. She published three novels under her English name, including the anti-Communist *The Rice-Sprout Song* (1955) and *Naked Earth* (1956), a depiction of Chinese prisoners in the Korean War. Though she made little impact on the PRC, she was very influential in Taiwan.

**Zhang Binglin** (1868–1936)—With wide-ranging intellectual interests, Zhang became more politically focused with the defeat of China by Japan in 1895. He became involved in reform activities with Kang Youwei and Liang Qichao in the late 1890s. However, Zhang's anti-Manchuism flowed more into the revolutionary stream of Sun Yat-sen than with the monarchism of Kang. In 1903, Zhang became a supporter of the anti-Manchu Shanghai newspaper *Subao* and wrote the preface to Zou Rong's *The Revolutionary Army*. After being imprisoned for three years because of this involvement, he went to Tokyo to become editor of the *People's News*, the mouthpiece of Sun's Revolutionary Alliance. After 1912, he helped form a political party and served the Yuan regime briefly. When he failed to bring about any coordinated opposition to the corrupt Beijing government in the late 1910s, he retired from public political life in 1918. He spent the rest of his life in classical scholarship, being most famous for his work in philology and textual studies.

**Zhang Daquan** (1899–1983)—Zhang studied textile weaving and dyeing in Japan from 1916 to 1919, briefly becoming a Buddhist novice on his return. During the 1920s and 1930s, he painted and focused on becoming a connoisseur and dealer. He spent 1941 to 1943 at the Dunhuang caves, copying

Buddhist wall paintings. After the war, Zhang lived in Brazil and the United States, returning to Taiwan in 1977. Critic Michael Sullivan says that his reputation rests on "his encyclopedic knowledge of the tradition, on his phenomenal technical skill, on his capacity for work, and . . . on his power to produce paintings that were often huge in scale and conception and bold in their handling of ink and color."

**Zhang Yimou** (b. 1950) — Born in Shaanxi, Zhang had the stigma of his father having been a major in the Guomindang army; the Cultural Revolution stopped his education in secondary school. During that campaign, he worked on a farm and for seven years as laborer at a spinning mill. He took up painting and still photography. In 1979, he was first rejected at the Beijing Film Institute as being too old to enroll, but he was accepted on an appeal by the minister of culture. He was graduated in 1982. His major films include *Red Sorghum* (1987), for which he won a Golden Bear at Berlin; *Judou* (1990) and *Raise the Red Lantern* (1991), both of which received Academy Award nominations; *Story of Qiu Ju* (1992); *To Live* (1994); *Shanghai Triad* (1995); and *Keep Cool* (1997).

**Zhou Yang** (b. 1908) — The literary theorist Zhou began his career as secretary-general of the League of Left-Wing Writers from 1931 to 1936. He rapidly made enemies of Lu Xun and Hu Feng. He argued that literature was primarily a political tool and weapon. In 1937, he went to Yan'an where he became president of Yan'an University and dean of the Lu Xun Arts Institute. From 1945 to 1949, he had leadership posts at North China Union University and the North China Associated Universities. His views remained anti-intellectual and anti-West. He strongly attacked author Wang Shiwei in 1942–43. His pursuit of and attacks on Hu Feng in the early to mid-1950s seemed to become almost a personal vendetta. He himself was attacked at the opening of the Cultural Revolution for his support of Wu Han's play *Hai Rui Dismissed from Office*. He was rehabilitated in the late 1970s and, in an about-face, argued in the 1980s that "humanism" was the proper philosophy for literature.

# PART III

# Resource Guide

The Resource Guide directs the reader to the most important English-language sources on modern Chinese history. There are three sections. The first includes annotated bibliographies of sixty-one general works and more than 430 of the most authoritative sources. The second section provides data on thirteen documentary and twenty feature films that can enhance understanding of modern Chinese history. The third section annotates important electronic resources to further explore China and its past, listing sites that are primarily launching pads for further search.

## ANNOTATED BIBLIOGRAPHY OF SELECTED WORKS

### *General Works*

BIBLIOGRAPHIES

*Bibliography of Asian Studies*. Published by the Association for Asian Studies. Annual, beginning in 1956. A comprehensive bibliography of books, articles, and government documents.

Hayford, Charles W., comp. *China, New Edition*. World Bibliographical Series, vol. 35. Oxford: Clio Press, 1997. A comprehensive volume, copiously and judiciously annotated. It has useful cross-references. Three indices, of authors, titles, and subjects, make it especially user-friendly.

Skinner, G. William, comp. *Modern Chinese Society: An Annotated Bibliography*. Stanford: Stanford University Press, 1973. In 3 vols. Provides useful notes on published secondary sources in all disciplines on topics from the Qing dynasty to the Communist period. Vol. 1 covers sources in English, vol. 2, sources in Chinese, and vol. 3, sources in Japanese.

Zurndorfer, Harriet T. *China Bibliography: A Research Guide to Reference Works*

*About China Past and Present.* Leiden: E. J. Brill, 1995. More than a bibliography, this helpful collection covers the full range of reference works and offers instruction on how to search out information on many topics.

## SURVEY HISTORIES AND SYNTHESES

Dietrich, Craig. *People's China: A Brief History.* New York: Oxford University Press, 1994. A mostly political overview of China since 1949. Written for undergraduates and general readers, it effectively intersperses thumbnail biographical sketches of key figures at appropriate places in the text.

Eastman, Lloyd E. *Family, Field, and Ancestors: Constancy and Change in China's Social and Economic History, 1550–1949.* New York: Oxford University Press, 1988. This synthesis covers major social and economic themes in Chinese life; it is a good introduction to essential topics for understanding Chinese developments.

Ebrey, Patricia, ed. *Chinese Civilization and Society.* New York: Free Press, 1993 (rev. ed.). This sourcebook of texts and documents brings life to China's traditional and modern social, cultural, and intellectual history. The editor provides useful introductions.

Fairbank, John K. *Late Ch'ing China, 1800–1911.* Cambridge: Cambridge University Press, 1978. Part 1 (Cambridge History of China, vol. 10) is a thoroughgoing series of essays on major developments in the nineteenth century. Most chapters cover up to roughly 1875. Part 2 (Cambridge History of China, vol. 11) focuses on material from the 1870s to the collapse of the Qing.

——. *Republican China, 1912–1949.* Cambridge: Cambridge University Press, 1978. In two parts (Cambridge History of China, vols. 12 and 13), this series of essays covers major developments, trends, and dynamics in the twentieth century, 1912 to 1949.

——. *The United States and China.* Cambridge: Harvard University Press, 1981. Though now out of date, this survey by the dean of China scholars in the United States still offers insights.

Fairbank, John K. and Merle Goldman, eds. *China: A New History.* Cambridge: Harvard University Press, 1998. Somewhat unusual for a textbook, this magisterial volume includes specific references to the interpretations of major historians.

Grieder, Jerome. *Intellectuals and the State in Modern China: A Narrative History.* New York: Free Press, 1981. A survey of key political thinkers up to 1949, showing their relations to and their thinking about the state. Especially strong on the New Culture period of the 1920s.

Hsu, Immanuel C. Y. *The Rise of Modern China.* New York: Oxford University Press, 1995. A standard textbook with particular strength in political and diplomatic topics.

Jansen, Marius. *Japan and China: From War to Peace, 1894–1972.* Chicago: Rand McNally, 1975. A textual survey of Chinese and Japanese relations, marked by a richly nuanced analysis of cultural relations that underlay diplomatic ties.

Leiberthal, Kenneth, Joyce Kallgren, Roderick MacFarquhar, and Frederic Wakeman Jr., eds. *Perspectives on Modern China: Four Anniversaries*. Armonk, N.Y.: M. E. Sharpe, 1991. These insightful essays focus on themes suggested by anniversaries of the beginning of the Opium War (1839), the May Fourth incident (1919), the establishment of the People's Republic (1949), and the Beijing Spring (1989).

MacFarquhar, Roderick and John K. Fairbank. *The People's Republic*. Cambridge: Cambridge University Press. Part 1, *The Emergence of Revolutionary China, 1949–1965* (Cambridge History of China, vol. 14 [1987]) is a collection of essays detailing the political, economic, and social developments and trends up to the Cultural Revolution. Part 2, *Revolutions Within the Chinese Revolution, 1966–1982* (Cambridge History of China, vol. 15 [1991]), a continuation of part 1, includes coverage of literature and developments on Taiwan from 1949 until 1982.

Meisner, Maurice. *Mao's China and After: A History of the People's Republic*. New York: Free Press, 1999 (3rd ed.). A standard treatment, especially strong on politics and ideology. This edition carries the analysis through the end of the Deng years.

Naquin, Susan and Evelyn S. Rawski. *Chinese Society in the Eighteenth Century*. New Haven: Yale University Press, 1987. An important survey of the nature of eighteenth-century politics, society, and culture; a strength is its use of macroregions to illustrate the vast differences to be found in China.

Rawski, Thomas and Lillian Li, eds. *Chinese History in Economic Perspective*. Berkeley: University of California Press, 1992. Ten essays that provide an overview of important economic themes.

Ropp, Paul, ed. *The Heritage of China: Contemporary Perspectives on Chinese Civilization*. Berkeley: University of California Press, 1990. Thirteen essays focusing on an impressive gamut of cultural and historical themes.

Schaller, Michael. *The United States and China in the Twentieth Century*. New York: Oxford University Press, 1990. A standard text for undergraduates.

Smith, Richard J. *China's Cultural Heritage: The Qing Dynasty, 1644–1912*. Boulder, Colo.: Westview Press, 1994. This interesting volume discusses a wide range of cultural topics that bring the nature of the Qing dynasty to life.

Spence, Jonathan. *The Search for Modern China*. New York: Norton, 1999 (2nd ed.). Extremely detailed, this long textbook has elegantly written narrative and rich illustrations.

——. *The Gate of Heavenly Peace: The Chinese and Their Revolution, 1895–1980*. New York: Viking, 1981. Using the examples of several key intellectuals and writers, this volume depicts the often tragic effects of revolutionary change on people's lives.

Teng, Ssu-yu and John K. Fairbank. *China's Response to the West: A Documentary Survey, 1939–1923*. Cambridge: Harvard University Press, 1954. The documents reviewed reveal the range of Chinese responses to Western challenges.

Thompson, Laurence G. *Chinese Religion: An Introduction*. Belmont, Calif.: Wadsworth, 1988. A standard textbook overview.

Wakeman, Frederic, Jr. *The Fall of Imperial China*. New York: Free Press, 1975. The strength of this text is its analysis of Qing society and of the social impacts of political change.

## DICTIONARIES AND ENCYCLOPEDIAS

Boorman, Howard L., ed. *Biographical Dictionary of Republican China*. New York: Columbia University Press, 1970. In 4 vols. These sometimes lengthy biographies of key political, military, and economic leaders, and intellectuals and artists provide a rich introduction to the Republican period (1912 to 1949).

Brandon, James R., ed. *The Cambridge Guide to Asian Theatre*. Cambridge: Cambridge University Press, 1993. Country-specific chapters (China, Taiwan, Hong Kong) look at the development of theater and opera.

Hook, Brian, ed. *The Cambridge Encyclopedia of China*. Cambridge: Cambridge University Press, 1991. A basic reference work running to several hundred topical articles.

Hucker, Charles. *A Dictionary of Official Titles in Imperial China*. Stanford: Stanford University Press, 1985. Source for all official Qing period titles, with brief descriptions of their functions. Also covers other dynasties.

Hummel, Arthur, ed. *Eminent Chinese of the Ch'ing Period (1644–1911)*. Washington, D.C.: U.S. Government Printing Office, 1943, 1944. In 2 vols. An essential reference work providing brief biographies of more than eight hundred Chinese, Manchu, and Mongol leaders who died before 1912.

Klein, Donald W. and Anne B. Clark, eds. *Biographic Dictionary of Chinese Communism, 1921–1965*. Cambridge: Harvard University Press, 1971. In 2 vols. Brief biographies of key leaders (governmental and nongovernmental) up to the beginning of the Cultural Revolution. These sketches are good vehicles for entry into Communist history.

Lamb, Malcolm. *Directory of Officials and Organizations in China: A Quarter Century Guide*. Armonk, N.Y.: M. E. Sharpe, 1994. Gives personnel and organizational changes from October 1968 until June 1993 of more than ten thousand officials in more than 790 governmental and nongovernmental organizations.

Leung, Edwin Pak-wai, ed. *Historical Dictionary of Revolutionary China, 1893–1976*. New York: Westport, 1992. Brief but significant articles surveying events, organizations, and men and women, both Chinese and foreign.

## ATLASES

*Atlas of the People's Republic of China*. Beijing: Foreign Languages Press, 1989. The standard official atlas.

Blunden, Carolyn and Mark Elvin. *Cultural Atlas of China*. New York: Facts on File, 1983. This attractive and interesting introduction to the Chinese past includes hundreds of maps, pictures, and charts on a rich array of topics.

Hsieh Chiao-min and Jean Chine Hsieh. *China: A Provincial Atlas*. New York:

Macmillan, 1995. A useful and user-friendly atlas. Part 1 (general maps) details such topics as population density and transport; part 2 has provincial landform maps.

Institute of Geography, Chinese Academy of Sciences and State Planning Committee, State Information Center, Institute of Statistics, State Statistical Bureau, comp. and ed. *The National Economic Atlas of China.* Hong Kong: Oxford University Press, 1994. Contains more than 250 maps that detail the economic development of the country; the material dates to 1990.

Times Newspapers. *The Times Atlas of China.* London: Times Newspapers, 1974. Standard atlas.

## JOURNALS

*Asian Survey: A Monthly Review of Contemporary Asian Affairs.* Berkeley: University of California Press, 1961– . Monthly. This important journal especially covers contemporary political affairs. Each beginning-of-the-year issue surveys the crucial events of the preceding year.

*Asian Theatre Journal.* Honolulu: University of Hawaii Press, 1984– . Semiannual journal that includes essays on historical and contemporary theater, reviews, and translations of plays.

*Beijing Review.* Beijing: Foreign Languages Press, 1979– . Weekly. The successor to *People's China* (1950–57) and *Peking Review* (1957–79). Considered to be an official publication of the government, this journal includes descriptive and analytical articles on a wide range of topics as well as official documents.

*Bulletin of Concerned Asian Scholars.* Boulder, Colo.: Bulletin of Concerned Asian Scholars, 1968– . Quarterly. An antiestablishment publication begun during the Vietnam War, this journal continues to publish essays dissenting from "established wisdom."

*Bulletin of the School of Oriental and African Studies.* London: School of Oriental and African Studies, 1917– . Three times annually. This journal of articles and reviews contains wide-ranging topics on the premodern period.

*China Business Review.* Washington, D.C.: National Council for U.S.-China Trade, 1974– . Bimonthly. Current information and comment on business activity.

*China Information.* Leiden: Documentation and Research Center for Contemporary China, 1986– . Quarterly. On aspects of contemporary China; includes reviews. The contributors to this journal are mostly European and Australian scholars.

*China Journal.* Canberra: Australian National University, 1979– . Semiannual. Until 1995 was called the *Australian Journal of Chinese Affairs.* Articles and reviews on modern China.

*China Quarterly.* London: School of Oriental and African Studies, 1968– . Quarterly. Journal focused on the People's Republic of China, although it also contains articles on Communist history in the earlier republican period. Its "Quarterly Chronicle and Documentation" section provides excerpts from important documents.

*China Review International.* Honolulu: University of Hawaii Press, 1994– .
Semiannual. Contains lengthier book reviews than those standard in journals.
Covers books published in European and Asian languages.

*Far Eastern Economic Review.* Hong Kong: Review Publishing Company, 1946– .
Weekly. An important periodical that covers all aspects of life in all of Asia,
although its focus is economics and politics. Especially strong in China coverage.

*Journal of Asian Studies.* Ann Arbor: Association for Asian Studies, 1941– . Quarterly.
The standard and most influential U.S. academic journal focusing on all aspects of
Asian studies. Contains articles and reviews. Published until 1956 as *Far Eastern
Quarterly*.

*Late Imperial China.* Baltimore: Johns Hopkins University Press, 1975– . Semiannual.
Scholarly articles. This most important journal focusing on the Qing dynasty was
formerly published as *Ch'ing-shih wen-t'i*.

*Modern China.* Los Angeles: Sage Press, 1975– . Quarterly. Articles and occasional
review essays on aspects of Chinese history and development in the Republic and
People's Republic.

*Modern Chinese Literature.* Boulder: University of Colorado. Semiannual. Covers
modern literature from the PRC, Taiwan, and Hong Kong. Articles, reviews, and
translations.

*Twentieth-Century China.* Ann Arbor: Center for Chinese Studies. Semiannual.
Articles and occasional research notes on twentieth-century history. Formerly published as the *Chinese Republican Studies Newsletter* and *Republican China*.

## NEWSPAPERS

*Asian Wall Street Journal.* Hong Kong: Dow Jones Asia, 1976– . Daily on weekdays.
Excellent interpretive coverage of business, politics, society, and culture.

*China Daily.* Beijing: China Daily. 1981– . Daily. Published in English, this is practi-
cally an official PRC newspaper.

*China Post.* Taipei: China Post. 1952– . Daily. An independent newspaper published
in English.

*Foreign Broadcast Information Service.* Washington, D.C.: U.S. Department of
Commerce, 1941– . Daily. Compilation of translated radio broadcasts.

## Politics

### AUTHORITY AND DISSENT

Barmé, Geremie and Linda Jaivin, eds. *New Ghosts, Old Dreams: Chinese Rebel
Voices.* New York: Times Books, 1992. Anthology of literature and the arts of reactions following the crushing of the 1989 movement.

Benton, Gregor and Alan Hunter, eds. *Wild Lily, Prairie Fire: China's Road to
Democracy, Yan'an to Tian'anmen, 1942–1989.* Princeton: Princeton University

Press, 1995. Documents with notes on dissent, beginning with Wang Shiwei's 1942 essay "Wild Lily" and covering episodes through the 1989 tragedy.

Chan, Anita. *Children of Mao: Personality Development and Political Activism in the Red Guard Generation*. Seattle: University of Washington Press, 1985. Examines issues of authority and personality in the lives of fourteen political activists during the Cultural Revolution.

Dai Qing. *Wang Shiwei and "Wild Lilies": Rectification and Purges in the Chinese Communist Party, 1942–1944*. Eds. David Apter and Timothy Cheek. Armonk, N.Y.: M. E. Sharpe, 1993. Details Wang's Yan'an dissent and reactions to it as an early indication of Communist antipathy to criticism and dissent.

Goldman, Merle. *China's Intellectuals: Advise and Dissent*. Cambridge: Harvard University Press, 1981. Looks at intellectuals and politics in the years from the Great Leap Forward to the Cultural Revolution.

——. *Literary Dissent in Communist China*. Cambridge: Harvard University Press, 1967. Covers the years from 1940s Yan'an until the Great Leap Forward.

——. *Sowing the Seeds of Democracy in China: Political Reform in the Deng Xiaoping Era*. Cambridge: Harvard University Press, 1994. Studies the wide swings between political toleration and repression in the world of literature and culture.

Han Minchu and Hua Sheng, eds. *Cries for Democracy in China: Writings and Speeches from the 1989 Chinese Democracy Movement*. Princeton: Princeton University Press, 1990. Translations with commentary on a wide variety of writings ranging from flyers to tape transcriptions from 1989.

Liu Binyan. *A Higher Kind of Loyalty: A Memoir by China's Foremost Journalist*. New York: Pantheon, 1990. An autobiography of a key intellectual concerning dissent and its consequences in the People's Republic.

Nathan, Andrew. *Chinese Democracy*. Berkeley: University of California Press, 1990. An important study that looks at efforts to realize democracy from the early twentieth century to the late 1980s.

Shen Tong. *Almost a Revolution*. Boston: Houghton Mifflin, 1990. A student leader in the events of 1989, Shen gives an insider's view from the student perspective.

Yan Jiaqi. *Toward a Democratic China: The Intellectual Autobiography of Yan Jiaqi*. Honolulu: University of Hawaii Press, 1992. An important figure in Deng's 1980s regime, Yan describes his ideas on democracy and socialism.

## BIOGRAPHIES

Bergère, Marie-Claire. *Sun Yat-sen*. Trans. Janet Lloyd. Stanford: Stanford University Press, 1998. May become the standard biography of this important national figure.

Byron, John and Robert Pack. *The Claws of the Dragon: Kang Sheng—the Evil Genius Behind Mao—and His Legacy of Terror in People's China*. New York: Simon & Schuster, 1992. Sensational title notwithstanding, this book provides important evidence about this eminence grise and state-security apparatchik.

Chang Kuo-t'ao. *The Rise of the Chinese Communist Party: The Autobiography of*

*Chang Kuo-t'ao*. Lawrence: University of Kansas Press, 1972. In 2 vols. Provides detailed accounts of competition and maneuvering within the party.

Chang, Sidney and Leonard H. D. Gordon. *All Under Heaven: Sun Yat-sen and His Revolutionary Thought*. Stanford: Hoover Institution Press, 1991. Analyzing Sun's thought, the authors offer a favorable view of Sun's contributions to modern China.

Chu, Samuel C. and Kwang-ching Liu, eds. *Li Hung-chang and China's Modernization*. Armonk, N.Y.: M. E. Sharpe, 1994. A balanced judgment on Li's various roles in the late nineteenth century.

Feigon, Lee. *Chen Duxiu: Founder of the Chinese Communist Party*. Princeton: Princeton University Press, 1983. A political biography of this May Fourth activist and academic. Probes aspects of his thought.

Gillin, Donald G. *Warlord: Yen Hsi-shan in Shansi Province, 1911–1949*. Princeton: Princeton University Press, 1967. A study of this warlord who attempted modern self-strengthening reforms, all of which were dashed in the Sino-Japanese War.

Goodman, David S. G. *Deng Xiaoping and the Chinese Revolution: A Political Biography*. London: Routledge, Kegan Paul, 1994. A standard biography, covering the leader from his early career to his reforms in the 1980s and 1990s.

Jacobs, Dan. *Borodin: Stalin's Man in China*. Cambridge: Harvard University Press, 1981. Using mainly Russian sources, the author depicts the international career of this Comintern agent who wielded considerable power in China in the 1920s.

Jansen, Marius. *The Japanese and Sun Yat-sen*. Cambridge: Harvard University Press, 1954. Probes the Japanese connections that Sun developed and the nature of his Japanese support in the first decade of the century.

Li Zhisui. *The Private Life of Chairman Mao*. New York: Random House, 1994. A thoroughly critical view of the private and public life of the Great Helmsman (even to the point of describing his sex organs) by the doctor who treated him, and at the end embalmed him.

McCormack, Gavan. *Chang Tso-lin in Northeast China, 1911–1928: China, Japan, and the Manchurian Idea*. Stanford: Stanford University Press, 1977. The standard biography of the able, though opium-addicted, warlord of Manchuria.

Pong, David. *Shen Pao-chen and China's Modernization in the Nineteenth Century*. Cambridge: Cambridge University Press, 1994. This biography of a self-strengthener argues that the main reason for the lack of success of this policy lay at the imperial court.

Schiffrin, Harold Z. *Sun Yat-sen: Reluctant Revolutionary*. Boston: Little, Brown, 1980. A standard biography written for the nonspecialist.

Sheridan, James. *Chinese Warlord: The Career of Feng Yu-hsiang*. Stanford: Stanford University Press, 1966. Standard biography of this northern Christian warlord who was often allied with the Soviet Union.

Terrill, Ross. *The White-Boned Demon: A Biography of Madame Mao Zedong*. New

York: Simon & Schuster, 1992 (new ed.). Probes the background and political manipulations of this leader of the Gang of Four.

Wou, Odoric Y. K. *Militarism in Modern China: The Career of Wu Peifu*. Folkestone, England: Dawson, Australian National University Press, 1978. Standard biography of a Confucian militarist supported by the British.

## LEADERS AND INSTITUTIONS

Bachman, David. *Bureaucracy, Economy, and Leadership in China: The Institutional Origins of the Great Leap Forward*. Cambridge: Cambridge University Press, 1991. This study of the structures of policy making in the mid-1950s argues that the Great Leap originated in a bureaucratic power struggle.

Bartlett, Beatrice. *Monarchs and Ministers: The Grand Council in Mid-Ch'ing China, 1723–1820*. Berkeley: University of California Press, 1990. An analysis of the relationship between emperors and their key bureaucrats and therefore of the nature of imperial control.

Bernhardt, Kathryn, and Philip C. C. Huang, eds. *Civil Law in Qing and Republican China*. Stanford: Stanford University Press, 1994. A series of studies, this volume stresses the importance of civil law against the backdrop of changing society.

Chang Chung-li. *The Chinese Gentry: Studies on Their Role in Nineteenth Century Chinese Society*. Seattle: University of Washington Press, 1955. A numerical analysis of the gentry coupled with discussion of their makeup and the nature of their lives.

Ch'u T'ung-tsu. *Local Government in China Under the Ch'ing*. Cambridge: Harvard University Press, 1962. A comprehensive description of government at the department and county levels, focusing on structure and function.

Eastman, Lloyd. *The Abortive Revolution: China Under Nationalist Rule, 1927–1937*. Cambridge: Harvard University Press, 1974. Analyzes the social, political, economic, and military realities and dynamics that helped give rise to the Nanjing regime's military dictatorship.

Guy, R. Kent. *The Emperor's Four Treasuries: Scholars and the State in the Late Ch'ien-lung Era*. Cambridge: Harvard University Press, 1987. The author revisits the famous "literary inquisition" of this emperor, detailing the reasons for and effects of the empirewide search for books and manuscripts.

Harding, Harry. *Organizing China: The Problems of Bureaucracy, 1949–1976*. Stanford: Stanford University Press, 1981. A study of the various efforts to shape the government bureaucracy for purposes of control and reliability.

Ho Ping-ti. *The Ladder of Success in Imperial China: Aspects of Social Mobility, 1368–1911*. New York: Columbia University Press, 1962. An examination of the civil service examination and social mobility among elites; provides statistical evidence to suggest a large amount of mobility.

Levine, Marilyn. *The Found Generation: Chinese Communists in Europe During the Twenties*. Seattle: University of Washington Press, 1993. Examines the roles and experiences of young Chinese in the work-study movement and their formation of ECCO (European Chinese Communist Organizations).

Lieberthal, Kenneth. *Governing China: From Revolution Through Reform*. New York: Norton, 1995. A standard, comprehensive analysis of government and politics in China, rich in detail and insight.

MacKinnon, Stephen R. *Power and Politics in Late Imperial China: Yuan Shikai in Beijing and Tianjin, 1901–1908*. Berkeley: University of California Press, 1980. Examines the tenure of Yuan as he undertook reforms as governor-general of Zhili Province.

Rankin, Mary Backus. *Elite Activism and Political Transformation in China: Zhejiang Province, 1865–1911*. Stanford: Stanford University Press, 1986. A detailed look at the roles of local elite reformers and activists who, the author claims, opened up a public sphere, taking the lead in education, famine relief, and reforms.

Schoppa, R. Keith. *Chinese Elites and Political Change: Zhejiang Province in the Early Twentieth Century*. Cambridge: Harvard University Press, 1982. A regional systems analysis that categorizes and studies local sociopolitical elites in four development zones from the mid-1910s to 1927. A study in sociopolitical dynamics.

Schurmann, Franz. *Ideology and Organization in Communist China*. Berkeley: University of California Press, 1968. An analysis of Mao's application of ideology to organizations in various political and economic arenas.

Tien Hong-mao. *Government and Politics in Kuomintang China, 1927–1937*. Stanford: Stanford University Press, 1972. An analysis of the Nanjing regime; solid if unimaginative.

Young, Ernest P. *The Presidency of Yuan Shih-k'ai: Liberalism and Dictatorship in Early Republican China*. Ann Arbor: University of Michigan Press, 1977. Sees Yuan not so much as a betrayer of the revolution but as a man committed to centralization as a way of reform and to holding imperialism at arm's length.

## MILITARIZATION AND THE MILITARY

Joffe, Ellis. *The Chinese Army After Mao*. Cambridge: Harvard University Press, 1987. A study of the changes in military policy and strategy after 1978.

Kuhn, Philip A. *Rebellion and Its Enemies in Late Imperial China: Militarization and Social Structure, 1796–1864*. Cambridge: Harvard University Press, 1970. A pathbreaking work exploring the structure and course of local militarization and of the roles of local elites in politics and society.

Lewis, John Wilson and Xue Litai. *China Builds the Bomb*. Stanford: Stanford University Press, 1988. A study of the debate over and the development of nuclear weapons in the 1960s.

——. *China's Strategic Seapower: The Politics of Force Modernization in the Nuclear Age*. Stanford: Stanford University Press, 1994. Focuses on the policies and strategies involved in building a nuclear-powered submarine fleet and submarine-based ballistic missiles.

McCord, Edward A. *The Power of the Gun: The Emergence of Modern Chinese Warlordism*. Berkeley: University of California Press, 1993. A study of the process by which local military forces transformed themselves into political players in larger arenas.

Rawlinson, John L. *China's Struggle for Naval Development, 1839–1895*. Cambridge: Harvard University Press, 1967. Shows how the nature of the self-strengthening process led by regional figures produced the regionalization of naval forces.

## NATION, REGION, LOCALITY

Dittmer, Lowell and Samuel S. Kim, eds. *China's Quest for National Identity*. Ithaca: Cornell University Press, 1993. Written by scholars from various disciplines, these essays explore what it means to be Chinese.

Duara, Prasenjit. *Rescuing History from the Nation: Questioning Narratives of Modern China*. Chicago: University of Chicago Press, 1995. A historiographical study of histories focusing on the nation-state and twentieth-century Chinese nationalists.

Henriot, Christian. *Shanghai, 1927–1937: Municipal Power, Locality, and Modernization*. Berkeley: University of California Press, 1993. A study of governance in Shanghai; includes analysis of local, provincial, and national relationships.

Lary, Diana. *Region and Nation: The Kwangsi Clique in Chinese Politics, 1925–1937*. Cambridge: Cambridge University Press, 1974. From the viewpoint that the regional power of this warlord group was inimical to national cohesion.

Min Tu-ki. *National Polity and Local Power: The Transformation of Late Imperial China*. Trans. Choe Hei-ji; eds. Philip Kuhn and Timothy Brook. Cambridge: Harvard University Press, 1990. Essays by a prominent Korean historian. Min surveys various political topics from the late Qing period.

Oi, Jean. *State and Peasant in Contemporary China: The Political Economy of Village Government*. Berkeley: University of California Press, 1989. Focusing on state grain policy, this study explores relationships between the center and localities.

Shue, Vivienne. *The Reach of the State: Sketches of the Chinese Body Politic*. Stanford: Stanford University Press, 1988. Four essays explore center/locality and center/periphery relationships and their ramifications.

Waldron, Arthur. *From War to Nationalism: China's Turning Point, 1924–1925*. Cambridge: Cambridge University Press, 1995. In this revisionist work, the author claims that warlord wars in the mid-1920s were crucial for the rise of nationalism and revolution, more important in fact than the May Fourth Movement.

## POST-MAO POLITICS

Baum, Richard. *Burying Mao*. Princeton: Princeton University Press, 1994. The author shows Deng in the period 1975 to 1993 maneuvering among various factions in both policies of economic reform and political repression.

Bonavia, David. *Verdict in Peking: The Trial of the Gang of Four*. New York: Putnam, 1984. A description, based on trial testimony, of the Gang of Four's schemes.

Brugger, Bill and David Kelly. *Chinese Marxism in the Post-Mao Era*. Stanford: Stanford University Press, 1990. Argues that the events of 1989 occurred because the government, in its drive to economic reform, ignored ideological sources that might have lent it greater legitimacy.

Che Muqi. *More Than Meets the Eye*. Beijing: Foreign Languages Press, 1990. Written by a journalist, this account gives the official government position on 1989.

Des Forges, Roger, Luo Ning, and Wu Yen-bo, eds. *Chinese Democracy and the Crisis of 1989: Chinese and American Reflections*. Albany: State University of New York Press, 1993. Essays analyze the course of the 1989 Democracy Movement in historical perspective.

Dittmer, Lowell. *China Under Reform*. Boulder, Colo.: Westview Press, 1994. A survey of the impacts of economic reform on politics.

Fewsmith, Joseph. *Dilemmas of Reform in China: Political Conflict and Economic Debate*. Armonk, N.Y.: M. E. Sharpe, 1994. This solid analysis considers conflicts stimulated both by policy disagreements and personal power struggles.

Kau, Michael Ying-mao and Susan H. Marsh, eds. *China in the Era of Deng Xiaoping: A Decade of Reform*. Armonk, N.Y.: M. E. Sharpe, 1993. Conference essays that look at reform's impacts on politics, economics, the military, and foreign policy.

Kelliher, Daniel. *Peasant Power in China: The Era of Rural Reform, 1979–1989*. New Haven: Yale University Press, 1992. In this study, the outcomes of rural reforms stem as much from peasant initiatives and response as from policies established by the center.

Kristof, Nicholas and Sheryl WuDunn. *China Wakes: The Struggle for the Soul of a Rising Power*. New York: Times Books, 1994. An impressive book by two journalists. Interesting anecdotes and descriptions shed light on Deng's China.

Lee Hong Yung. *From Revolutionary Cadres to Party Technocrats in Socialist China*. Berkeley: University of California Press, 1991. A study of party elites from the time of the Cultural Revolution into the Deng reforms. Analyzes the elites' composition, structures, and conflicts.

Lieberthal, Kenneth and David Lampton, eds. *Bureaucracy, Politics, and Decision Making in Post-Mao China*. Berkeley: University of California Press, 1992. These excellent conference papers cover an array of political issues.

Lieberthal, Kenneth and Michel Oksenberg. *Policy Making in China: Leaders, Structures, Politics, and Processes*. Princeton: Princeton University Press, 1988. This important study uses a range of techniques, including interviews, to detail the policy-making issues named in the title.

Ogden, Suzanne, Kathleen Hartford, Lawrence Sullivan, and David Zweig, eds. *China's Search for Democracy: The Student and Mass Movement of 1989*. Armonk, N.Y.: M. E. Sharpe, 1992. A documentary history of the people's movement, including posters, flyers, songs, and radio broadcasts.

Oksenberg, Michel, Lawrence Sullivan, and Marc Lambert, eds. *Beijing Spring 1989:*

*Confrontation and Conflict: The Basic Documents.* Armonk, N.Y.: M. E. Sharpe, 1990. Presents official documents relating to the crisis of 1989.

Pei Minxin. *From Reform to Revolution: The Demise of Communism in China and the Soviet Union.* Cambridge: Harvard University Press, 1994. An important comparison of the two regimes as well as of the dynamics of political and economic liberalization.

Schell, Orville. *Mandate of Heaven: A New Generation of Entrepreneurs, Dissidents, Bohemians, and Technocrats Lays Claim to China's Future.* New York: Simon & Schuster, 1994. An interesting anecdotal description of life in China after the events in spring 1989.

Shirk, Susan. *The Political Logic of Reform.* Berkeley: University of California Press, 1993. An analysis of institutions and decision making.

Simmie, Scott and Bob Nixon. *Tiananmen Square.* Seattle: University of Washington Press, 1989. Accounts of participants in the tumultuous days of spring 1989.

Vogel, Ezra. *One Step Ahead in China: Guangdong Under Reform.* Cambridge: Harvard University Press, 1989. This study of Guangdong Province is the continuation of the author's excellent *Canton Under Communism* (1969).

Wasserstrom, Jeffrey and Elizabeth Perry, eds. *Popular Protest and Political Culture in Modern China.* Boulder, Colo.: Westview Press, 1994. Essays on a variety of social and cultural aspects of the events in 1989.

## REFORM AND RECONSTRUCTION

Cohen, Paul and John Schrecker, eds. *Reform in Nineteenth-Century China.* Cambridge: Harvard University Press, 1976. Essays, many of them quite short, examine the contexts, nature, and meaning of late nineteenth-century reform efforts.

Hayford, Charles W. *To the People: James Yen and Village China.* New York: Columbia University Press, 1990. A study of the famous 1920s–1930s Dingxian experiment in rural reconstruction.

Kwong, Luke S. K. *A Mosaic of the Hundred Days: Personalities, Politics, and Ideas of 1898.* Cambridge: Harvard University Press, 1984. Kwong's study argues that Kang Youwei and Liang Qichao were not as central to the Hundred Days of reform as other studies have suggested.

Reynolds, Douglas R. *China, 1898–1912: The Xincheng Revolution.* Cambridge: Harvard University Press, 1993. This study suggests that the Manchu reform movement was as important as, or even more important than, the 1911 revolution itself.

Wright, Mary C. *The Last Stand of Chinese Conservatism: The T'ung-chih Restoration, 1862–1874.* Stanford: Stanford University Press, 1957. This early study sees an official "restoration" or renewal of Confucian rule after the midcentury rebellions.

## REVOLUTION (1911)

Dirlik, Arif. *Anarchism in the Chinese Revolution.* Berkeley: University of California Press, 1991. Traces the origins of social radicalism to the beginning years of the century, when young Chinese were most influenced by anarchism.

Esherick, Joseph. *Reform and Revolution in China: The 1911 Revolution in Hunan and Hubei*. Berkeley: University of California Press, 1976. This analysis argues that an urban reformist elite played the crucial role in late Qing reform and the 1911 revolution.

Price, Don C. *Russia and the Roots of the Chinese Revolution, 1896–1911*. Cambridge: Harvard University Press, 1974. Russia is seen as the Chinese revolutionary model.

Rankin, Mary Backus. *Early Chinese Revolutionaries: Radical Intellectuals in Shanghai and Chekiang, 1902–1911*. Cambridge: Harvard University Press, 1971. Study stresses the secret-society backgrounds of many of the revolutionary organizations and the important revolutionary links between Shanghai and Zhejiang Province.

Rhoads, Edward J. M. *China's Republican Revolution: The Case of Kwangtung, 1895–1913*. Cambridge: Harvard University Press, 1975. A solid study, set in a province, of the revolution and its contexts.

Tsou Rong. *The Revolutionary Army: A Chinese Nationalist Tract of 1903*. Trans. John Lust. The Hague: Mouton & Co., 1968. The famous anti-Manchu essay, both an epitome and a harbinger of revolutionary anti-Manchu fervor.

Wright, Mary C., ed. *China in Revolution: The First Phase, 1900–1913*. New Haven: Yale University Press, 1968. Important early essays on the revolution; the widespread change that the editor sees in her introduction was largely an urban phenomenon.

Zarrow, Peter. *Anarchism and Chinese Political Culture*. New York: Columbia University Press, 1990. This study shows the resonance between anarchist ideas and aspects of Chinese political culture.

## REVOLUTION (NATIONALIST)

Fitzgerald, John. *Awakening China: Politics, Culture, and Class in the Nationalist Revolution*. Stanford: Stanford University Press, 1996. Stressing the politics and culture of mass "awakening," this study sees this awakening as part of the historical record itself but also as a technique for building the nation-state.

Isaacs, Harold. *The Tragedy of the Chinese Revolution*. Stanford: Stanford University Press, 1961. A classic journalistic account of the Nationalist revolution (1925–27).

McDonald, Angus, Jr. *The Urban Origins of Rural Revolution: Elites and Masses in Hunan Province, 1911–1927*. Berkeley: University of California Press, 1978. An interesting social history of an important province.

Schoppa, R. Keith. *Blood Road: The Mystery of Shen Dingyi in Revolutionary China*. Berkeley: University of California Press, 1995. Written as a murder mystery, this book suggests new ways of approaching and understanding the revolution in China, especially in the 1920s.

Wilbur, C. Martin and Julie Lien-ying How. *Missionaries of Revolution: Soviet Advisers and Nationalist China, 1920–1927*. Cambridge: Harvard University Press, 1989. An encyclopedic volume, rich in documents and material on the Nationalist revolution.

## REVOLUTION (COMMUNIST, 1921–60)

Apter, David and Tony Saich. *Revolutionary Discourse in Mao's China.* Cambridge: Harvard University Press, 1994. Using postmodern theory, the authors probe the nature of revolutionary imagery and language in Maoist China.

Belden, Jack. *China Shakes the World.* New York: Monthly Review Press, 1970. Reprint of 1949 edition. A classic journalistic report covering the Communist revolution in north China in the late 1940s.

Benton, Gregor. *Mountain Fires: The Red Army's Three Year War in South China, 1934–1938.* Berkeley: University of California Press, 1992. This is a major contribution that decenters the Mao-focused picture of the revolution. It examines the actions of Communist forces left in southeast China after the Long March.

Bianco, Lucien. *Origins of the Chinese Revolution, 1915–1949.* Stanford: Stanford University Press, 1971. An overview of the causes and development of the revolution from the May Fourth period to the end of the civil war.

Ch'en Yung-fa. *Making Revolution: The Communist Movement in Eastern and Central China, 1937–1945.* Berkeley: University of California Press, 1986. Indispensable in revealing the complexity and diversity of the Communist revolution during the Sino-Japanese War.

Compton, Boyd, trans. *Mao's China: Party Reform Documents, 1942–1944.* Seattle: University of Washington, 1952. Documents related to the important rectification campaign in Yan'an.

Dirlik, Arif. *The Origins of Chinese Communism.* New York: Oxford University Press, 1989. The author's thesis is on the importance of anarchism to Chinese radicalism and also to the origins of the Communist Party.

Galbiati, Fernando. *P'eng P'ai and the Hai-Lu-Feng Soviet.* Stanford: Stanford University Press, 1985. The best and most detailed study of this local revolutionary effort.

Hartford, Kathleen and Steven Goldstein, eds. *Single Sparks: China's Rural Revolutions.* Armonk, N.Y.: M. E. Sharpe, 1989. This important volume of strong essays is made even more significant by the historiographical essay written by the editors.

Hinton, William. *Fanshen: A Documentary of Revolution in a Chinese Village.* New York: Monthly Review Press, 1966. A classic and dramatic depiction of land reform in Long Bow village in Shaanxi Province through 1948.

Johnson, Chalmers. *Peasant Nationalism and Communist Power: The Emergence of Revolutionary China, 1937–1945.* Stanford: Stanford University Press, 1962. An important but much debated study, Johnson's work finds the secret of Communist success not in land reform and social revolution but in the nationalism stimulated by Japanese aggression.

Levine, Steven. *Anvil of Victory: The Communist Revolution in Manchuria, 1945–1948.* New York: Columbia University Press, 1987. This study sees the important Communist victory in Manchuria as basically military, rather than social, economic, or ideological.

Saich, Tony, ed. *The Rise to Power of the Chinese Communist Party: Documents and*

*Analysis, 1920–1949.* Armonk, N.Y.: M. E. Sharpe, 1994. If any book can be called essential for understanding the period, this is it. The volume has 1,430 pages; the choice of documents is first rate and the sections of commentary, read together, provide the best textbook for the period.

Saich, Tony and Hans van de Ven, eds. *New Perspectives on the Chinese Communist Revolution.* Armonk, N.Y.: M. E. Sharpe, 1995. A conference volume that stands almost in a class by itself; essay after essay is important in opening up new ways of seeing the revolution.

Schram, Stuart and Nancy J. Hodes, eds. *Mao's Road to Power: Revolutionary Writings, 1912–1949.* Armonk, N.Y.: M. E. Sharpe, 1994– . When completed, this series will form the most comprehensive collection of Mao's pre-1949 writings.

Selden, Mark. *China in Revolution: The Yenan Way Revisited.* Armonk, N.Y.: M. E. Sharpe, 1995. A revised and expanded version of Selden's earlier *The Yenan Way in Revolutionary China,* this book argues that Maoist policies devised in Yan'an in the 1940s became a blueprint for policies after the establishment of the PRC.

Siu, Helen F. *Agents and Victims: Accomplices in Rural Revolution.* New Haven: Yale University Press, 1989. Surveys the relationship between local elites and government from the early Qing into the 1980s.

Snow, Edgar. *Red Star Over China.* New York: Random House, 1937. The journalistic classic reporting on the dramatic rise of the Communists in the 1930s and on their conflicts with the Nationalists.

Van de Ven, Hans. *From Friend to Comrade: The Founding of the Chinese Communist Party, 1920–1927.* Berkeley: University of California Press, 1991. Traces the organization of the party from loose networks into a Leninist party.

Vogel, Ezra. *Canton Under Communism: Programs and Politics in a Provincial Capital, 1949–1968.* (Cambridge: Harvard University Press, 1969). An analysis of revolution through its various phases from "liberation" to the Cultural Revolution.

Wou, Odoric. *Mobilizing the Masses: Building Revolution in Henan.* Stanford: Stanford University Press, 1994. The empirical richness, analytical care, and continual awareness of the complex and diverse possibilities of revolutionary change make this essential reading.

## THE CULTURAL REVOLUTION

Bernstein, Thomas. *Up to the Mountains and Down to the Villages: The Transfer of Youth from Urban to Rural China.* New Haven: Yale University Press, 1977. A thorough treatment of the mobilization of twelve million youths in the forced migration to the countryside.

Cheng Nien. *Life and Death in Shanghai.* New York: Grove Press, 1986. A popular account of social dislocation and suffering during the Cultural Revolution.

Dittmer, Lowell. *China's Continuous Revolution: The Post-Liberation Epoch, 1949–1981.* Berkeley: University of California Press, 1987. A solid analysis that shows the interaction of leadership, ideology, and political process.

——. *Liu Shao-ch'i and the Chinese Cultural Revolution: The Politics of Mass*

*Criticism*. Berkeley: University of California Press, 1974. A standard biography of Liu, stressing political themes.

Forster, Keith. *Rebellion and Factionalism in a Chinese Province: Zhejiang, 1966–1976*. Armonk, N.Y.: M. E. Sharpe, 1990. Detailed and compelling, this is the only book-length study of the Cultural Revolution as seen in one province.

Gao Yuan. *Born Red: A Chronicle of the Cultural Revolution*. Stanford: Stanford University Press, 1987. A moving account by a Red Guard.

Hinton, William. *Hundred Day War: The Cultural Revolution at Tsinghua University*. New York: Monthly Review Press, 1972. A chilling depiction of the violence and factionalism that tore apart "China's MIT." The action escalated from cold weapons to missiles and other hot projectiles.

——. *Shenfan: The Continuing Revolution in a Chinese Village*. New York: Vintage, 1983. This continues the study of Long Bow village from 1948 through the Cultural Revolution.

Joseph, William, Christine Wong, and David Zweig, eds. *New Perspectives on the Cultural Revolution*. Cambridge: Harvard University Press, 1991. A reappraisal of the period in light of new sources.

Lee, Hong Yung. *The Politics of the Chinese Cultural Revolution: A Case Study*. Berkeley: University of California Press, 1978. A standard chronological analysis of the revolution, looking at the politics of bureaucracy, mass manipulation, and factionalism.

MacFarquhar, Roderick. *The Origins of the Cultural Revolution*. New York: Columbia University Press, 1974, 1983, 1997. In 3 vols. A magisterial work. Vol. 1 is *Contradictions Among the People, 1956–1957*; vol. 2, *The Great Leap Forward, 1958–1960*; vol. 3, *The Coming of the Cataclysm, 1961–1966*.

Thurston, Anne F. *Enemies of the People*. New York: Knopf, 1987. A vivid account of the Cultural Revolution told through the experiences of its intellectual victims.

Whyte, Lynn T., III. *Policies of Chaos: The Organizational Causes of Violence in China's Cultural Revolution*. Princeton: Princeton University Press, 1989. Finds the foundation of the Cultural Revolution in the dynamics of the *danwei*, class categorization, and continuing political campaigns.

Yue Daiyun and Carolyn Wakeman. *To the Storm: The Odyssey of a Revolutionary Chinese Woman*. Berkeley: University of California Press, 1985. This memoir of a university professor covers the years from the late 1940s into the 1980s.

## Society

GENERAL

Davis-Friedmann, Deborah. *Long Lives: Chinese Elderly and the Communist Revolution*. Cambridge: Harvard University Press, 1983. A study of problems and policies that arise in dealing with the growing number of elderly in China.

Fei Xiaotong. *From the Soil: The Foundations of Chinese Society*. Berkeley: University of California Press, 1992. The classic description of the dynamics of Chinese society and culture—the essential book for understanding Chinese society. First published in 1947.

Freedman, Maurice. *The Study of Chinese Society*. Stanford: Stanford University Press, 1979. Essays by one of the most important Western anthropologists to study the Chinese in both China and overseas communities.

Hsu, Francis L. K. *Americans and Chinese: Passages to Difference*. Honolulu: University of Hawaii Press, 1981. A comparison of daily practices and beliefs growing out of cultural and psychological differences between Chinese and Americans.

Parish, William L. and Martin King Whyte. *Urban Life in Contemporary China*. Chicago: University of Chicago Press, 1984. An analysis of social and economic life in Chinese cities.

——. *Village and Family in Contemporary China*. Chicago: University of Chicago Press, 1978. An analysis of Chinese society in Guangdong Province at the close of the Mao era.

Schoppa, R. Keith. *Xiang Lake—Nine Centuries of Chinese Life*. New Haven: Yale University Press, 1989. A study of long-term change and development in the society and ecology around a reservoir in Zhejiang Province from the early twelfth century through the early 1980s.

Skinner, G. William. *Marketing and Social Structure in Rural China*. Ann Arbor: Association for Asian Studies, 1993. A collection of pathbreaking essays that argued that the spatial-cultural horizon of a Chinese peasant's world was not the village where he lived but the "marketing area" to which he was oriented.

Smith, Arthur. *Village Life in China*. Reprint, Boston: Little, Brown, 1970. An account by a nineteenth-century Protestant missionary of life in north China villages.

Watson, James L. *Class and Social Stratification in Post-Revolution China*. London: Cambridge University Press, 1984. These essays focus on aspects of the class structure from anthropological, sociological, and political perspectives.

Whyte, Martin King. *Small Groups and Political Ritual in China*. Berkeley: University of California Press, 1974. An important study of small groups (*xiaozu*)—their organization and the functions they play in political and social institutions.

Yang, Mayfair Mei-hui. *Gifts, Favors, and Banquets: The Art of Social Relationships in China*. Ithaca: Cornell University Press, 1994. A study of connections (*guanxi*) and their cultivation as essential linkages in Chinese society.

## SOCIAL DISLOCATION AND REBELLION

Billingsley, Philip. *Bandits in Republican China*. Stanford: Stanford University Press, 1988. Since the number of bandits at the time was an estimated twenty million, this analysis focuses on a major social and political problem.

Cohen, Paul. *History in Three Keys: The Boxers as Event, Experience, and Myth*. New York: Columbia University Press, 1997. A fascinating and award-winning meditation on the nature of history, historical writing, memory, and myth.

Esherick, Joseph W. *The Origins of the Boxer Uprising*. Berkeley: University of

California Press, 1987. This major study of the anti-Western Boxer movement focuses on its ecological and cultural foundations.

Jen Yu-wen. *The Taiping Revolutionary Movement*. New Haven: Yale University Press, 1973. The most complete account of this largest rebellion in history.

Kuhn, Philip A. *Soulstealers: The Chinese Sorcery Scare of 1768*. Cambridge: Harvard University Press, 1990. This analysis of the relationship of the Qianlong emperor to his bureaucracy uses social dislocation and fear as its entry point.

Lipman, Jonathan and Stevan Harrell. *Violence in China: Essays in Culture and Counterculture*. Albany: State University of New York Press, 1990. These essays explore the roles and import of violence from the Qing to the late twentieth century.

Michael, Franz. *The Taiping Rebellion: History and Documents*. Seattle: University of Washington Press, 1965–71. In 3 vols: vol. 1 is a narrative; vols. 2 and 3 offer documents from this social cataclysm.

Naquin, Susan. *Millenarian Rebellion in China: The Eight Trigrams Uprising of 1813*. New Haven: Yale University Press, 1976. A vivid depiction of a failed rebellion led by sectarian rebels.

Peck, Graham. *Two Kinds of Time*. Boston: Houghton Mifflin, 1950. A classic work on life and social dislocation in China in the 1940s.

Perry, Elizabeth J. *Rebels and Revolutionaries in North China, 1845–1945*. Stanford: Stanford University Press, 1980. Grounded in ecological realities of the Huaibei region of north central China, this analysis looks at rebellions from the Nian (1853–68) to the Red Spears of the early twentieth century.

## URBAN AND RURAL SOCIETY

Buck, David D. *Urban Change in China: Politics and Development in Tsinan, Shantung, 1890–1949*. Madison: University of Wisconsin Press, 1978. Traces the economic, political, and social development of the city.

Chan, Anita, Richard Madsen, and Jonathan Unger. *Chen Village Under Mao and Deng*. Berkeley: University of California Press, 1992. A dramatic account of change in a south China village.

Cochran, Sherman, Andrew C. K. Hsieh, and Janis Cochran, eds. *One Day in China: May 21, 1936*. New Haven: Yale University Press, 1983. A collection of reports submitted by people from all over China about their activities on this day.

Davis, Deborah, Richard Kraus, Barry Naughton, and Elizabeth Perry, eds. *Urban Spaces in Contemporary China: The Potential for Autonomy and Community in Post-Mao China*. Cambridge: Cambridge University Press, 1995. Significant and suggestive essays that focus on urban structures and identities.

Duara, Prasenjit. *Culture, Power, and the State: Rural North China, 1900–1942*. This analysis of state and society argues that changes in the early twentieth century worked to delegitimize the state in the localities, affecting what the author calls the traditional "cultural nexus."

Elvin, Mark and G. William Skinner, eds. *The Chinese City Between Two Worlds*.

Stanford: Stanford University Press, 1974. Important essays assessing change in urban structures from 1842 to 1949.

Fei Hsiao-t'ung (Fei Xiaotong). *Peasant Life in China: A Field Study of Country Life in the Yangtze Valley*. London: Routledge & Kegan Paul, 1939. A classic work by China's most famous sociologist, this book examines the transformation of rural life.

Gamble, Sidney. *Ting Hsien: A North China Rural Community*. New York: Institute of Pacific Relations, 1954. This survey, made in the late 1920s and early 1930s, focuses on Ding County, site of the famous experiment in rural reconstruction.

Goodman, Bryna. *Native Place, City, and Nation: Regional Networks and Identities in Shanghai, 1853–1937*. Berkeley: University of California Press, 1995. This study argues that strong local identity was not inimical to the development of national identity.

Hsiao Kung-chuan. *Rural China: Imperial Control in the Nineteenth Century*. Seattle: University of Washington Press, 1960. An encyclopedic description of local society and politics, with lengthy translations of source materials.

Hsu, Francis L. K. *Under the Ancestor's Shadow: Kinship, Personality, and Social Mobility in Village China*. New York: Columbia University Press, 1948. An important early study based on field work in "West Town" in Yunnan Province.

Huang Shumin. *The Spiral Road: Change in a Chinese Village Through the Eyes of a Communist Party Leader*. Boulder, Colo.: Westview Press, 1989. A rich account of the revolution in a village in Fujian Province.

Jankowiak, William R. *Sex, Death, and Hierarchy in a Chinese City: An Anthropological Perspective*. New York: Columbia University Press, 1993. An interpretation of urban culture in Huhhot, Inner Mongolia.

Madsen, Richard. *Morality and Power in a Chinese Village*. Berkeley: University of California Press, 1986. An examination of the morality of village life amid revolutionary change.

Rowe, William. *Hankow: Commerce and Society in a Chinese City, 1796–1889*. Stanford: Stanford University Press, 1984; *Hankow: Conflict and Community in a Chinese City, 1796–1895*. Stanford University Press, 1989. These two books constitute a major contribution to nineteenth-century urban history.

Skinner, G. William, ed. *The City in Late Imperial China*. Stanford: Stanford University Press, 1977. This collection of impressive essays includes Skinner's seminal work on macroregions, cores, and peripheries.

Strand, David. *Rickshaw Beijing: City People and Politics in the 1920s*. Berkeley: University of California Press, 1989. A suggestive social history of the capital.

Terrill, Ross. *Flowers on an Iron Tree: Five Cities of China*. Boston: Little, Brown, 1975. Essays on city life in the 1970s.

Wakeman, Frederic, Jr. *Policing Shanghai, 1927–1937*. Berkeley: University of California Press, 1995. A wide-ranging social history of governmental efforts to order and control the city.

## THE FAMILY

Chang Jung. *Wild Swans: Three Daughters of China*. New York: Simon & Schuster, 1991. Depicts the impacts of the revolution on a family.

Davis, Deborah and Stevan Harrell, eds. *Chinese Families in the Post-Mao Era*. Berkeley: University of California Press, 1993. Essays examining a wide range of family issues.

Ebrey, Patricia and James L. Watson, eds. *Kinship Organization in Late Imperial China, 1000–1940*. Berkeley: University of California Press, 1986. These essays probe many issues related to lineage, or "descent group."

Saari, Jon L. *Legacies of Childhood: Growing Up Chinese in a Time of Crisis, 1890–1920*. Cambridge: Harvard University Press, 1990. An examination of the psychology behind the personal development of adolescents grounded in the world of Confucianism but challenged by the modern West.

Stockard, Janice E. *Daughters of the Canton Delta: Marriage Patterns and Economic Strategies in South China, 1860–1930*. Stanford: Stanford University Press, 1989. A study of variant marital patterns growing out of female economic independence based on sericulture.

Waltner, Ann. *Getting an Heir: Adopting and the Construction of Kinship in Late Imperial China*. Honolulu: University of Hawaii Press, 1991. An examination of the important role of adoption in Ming and Qing China.

Watson, Rubie S. and Patricia Ebrey. *Marriage and Inequality in Chinese Society*. Berkeley: University of California Press, 1991. These essays explore topics dealing with marriage and gender inequality from very early Chinese history to the present.

Wolf, Arthur P. and Huang Chieh-shan. *Marriage and Adoption in China, 1845–1945*. Stanford: Stanford University Press, 1980. This work points to the array of marriage models, especially that of the adopted daughter-in-law.

Yang, C. K. *The Chinese Family in the Communist Revolution*. Cambridge: MIT Press, 1959. A study of the Chinese family in Guangdong Province in the early 1950s.

## WOMEN

Andors, Phyllis. *The Unfinished Liberation of Chinese Women, 1949–1980*. Bloomington: Indiana University Press, 1983. Argues that male family opposition and bureaucratic obstacles thwarted the intentions of leaders to effect female liberation.

Barlow, Tani, ed. *Gender Politics in Modern China: Writing and Feminism*. Durham: Duke University Press, 1993. Essays on issues of gender and modernist literature from the 1920s to the 1980s.

Croll, Elisabeth. *Feminism and Socialism in China*. London: Routledge & Kegan Paul, 1978. A survey of the interaction of these themes throughout the twentieth century.

Gilmartin, Christina, Gail Hershatter, Lisa Rofel, and Tyrene White, eds. *Engendering China: Women, Culture, and the State*. Cambridge: Harvard University Press, 1994.

A pathbreaking contribution to gender studies in China, these sixteen essays also contribute to our understanding of revolution and state/society relationships.

Johnson, Kay Ann. *Women, the Family, and Peasant Revolution in China*. Chicago: University of Chicago Press, 1983. A study of relevant policies from the 1940s to the 1970s, showing continuous subordination of women's issues to other priorities.

Judd, Ellen. *Gender and Power in Rural North China*. Stanford: Stanford University Press, 1994. A study of how the reforms of the 1980s affected family and gender relations.

Mann, Susan. *Precious Records: Women in China's Long Eighteenth Century*. Stanford: Stanford University Press, 1997. This important revisionist study argues that, in at least the eighteenth century, Lower Yangzi elite women were not oppressed and restrained but were actively negotiating gender roles in key arenas of the society and economy.

Pruitt, Ida. *Daughter of Han: The Autobiography of a Chinese Working Woman*. New Haven: Yale University Press, 1945. The story of Ning Lao T'ai-t'ai, this account touches on many of the social and family issues of women in traditional China.

Stacey, Judith. *Patriarchy and Socialist Revolution in China*. Berkeley: University of California Press, 1984. Suggests that the liberation of Chinese women failed because the course of the revolution was led by patriarchal community leaders.

Wolf, Margery and Roxane Witke. *Women in Chinese Society*. Stanford: Stanford University Press, 1975. An early important collection of essays on a variety of topics.

## EDUCATION AND STUDENTS

Ayers, William. *Chang Chih-tung and Educational Reform in China*. Cambridge: Harvard University Press, 1971. Describes Chang's educational reforms as part of his general self-strengthening program.

Bastid, Marianne. *Educational Reform in Early Twentieth Century China*. Trans. Paul Bailey. Ann Arbor: University of Michigan Press, 1988. Focuses on the educational reforms of important official Zhang Jian.

Chen, Theodore Hsi-en. *Chinese Education Since 1949: Academic and Revolutionary Models*. New York: Pergamon Press, 1981. The survey covers up to the Cultural Revolution; the models used are the Maoist populist and the professional.

Elman, Benjamin and Alexander Woodside, eds. *Education and Society in Late Imperial China, 1600–1900*. Berkeley: University of California Press, 1994. Analytical essays on social and intellectual developments relating to education.

Epstein, Irving, ed. *Chinese Education: Problems, Policies, and Prospects*. New York: Garland Press, 1991. Essays covering wide-ranging aspects of education up to the 1990s.

Hayhoe, Ruth. *China's Universities and the Open Door*. Armonk, N.Y.: M. E. Sharpe, 1989. A study of the impacts of the 1980s reforms on higher education.

——, ed. *Education and Modernization: The Chinese Experience*. Oxford: Pergamon

Press, 1992. Essays exploring wide-ranging topics from historical views to analysis of educational structures and issues.

Keenan, Barry C. *The Dewey Experiment in China: Educational Reform and Political Power in the Early Republic*. Cambridge: Harvard University Press, 1977. A study of the thought of John Dewey and its impact in China in the 1920s.

———. *Imperial China's Last Classical Academies: Social Change in the Lower Yangzi, 1864–1911*. Berkeley: University of California Press, 1994. A study of post-Taiping educational institutions in Jiangsu Province.

Lutz, Jessie Gregory. *China and the Christian Colleges, 1850–1950*. Ithaca: Cornell University Press, 1971. A study of the thirteen Protestant colleges, their educational developments and contributions, and their appeal to the Chinese.

Pepper, Suzanne. *China's Education Reform in the 1980s: Policies, Issues, and Historical Perspectives*. Berkeley: Institute of East Asian Studies, 1990. An analysis of the 1980s' reforms in historical context.

Seeberg, Vilma. *Literacy in China: The Effect of the National Development Context and Policy on Literacy Levels, 1949–1979*. Bochum, Germany: Brockmeyer, 1990. Seeberg argues that institutional problems, the Chinese writing system, lack of money, and the immensity of the problem prevented much improvement in literacy.

Shirk, Susan. *Competitive Comrades: Career Incentives and Student Strategies in China*. Berkeley: University of California Press, 1982. Studies urban middle schools and the competition that develops among students from the government's having control of career strategies and opportunities.

Wasserstrom, Jeffrey N. *Student Protests in Twentieth-Century China: The View from Shanghai*. Stanford: Stanford University Press, 1991. A history of students and their involvement in the revolution from 1911 into the 1980s.

White, Gordon. *Party and Professionals: The Political Role of Teachers in Contemporary China*. Armonk, N.Y.: M. E. Sharpe, 1989. Analysis of issues involving the changing status of teachers in Chinese society.

## ETHNIC MINORITIES

Crossley, Pamela Kyle. *Orphan Warriors: Three Manchu Generations and the End of the Qing World*. Princeton: Princeton University Press, 1990. Traces the construction and the waning of Manchu ethnic identity from the early Qing into the 1920s.

Dreyer, June Teufel. *China's Forty Millions: Minority Nationalities and National Integration in the People's Republic of China*. Cambridge: Harvard University Press, 1976. Primarily a study of the ethnic problem seen from the center.

Gladney, Dru C. *Making Majorities: Constituting the Nation in Japan, Korea, China, Malaysia, Fiji, Turkey, and the United States*. Stanford: Stanford University Press, 1998. The thrust of these essays is that societies make and recognize their majorities under specific evolving circumstances.

———. *Muslim Chinese: Ethnic Nationalism in the People's Republic*. Cambridge: Harvard University Press, 1991. A study of four Hui communities (the Hui are a state-recognized Muslim group) and their evolving ethnic identities.

Harrell, Stevan, ed. *Cultural Encounters on China's Ethnic Frontiers*. Seattle: University of Washington Press, 1995. Essays studying Han Chinese understanding and treatment of ethnic minorities.

Honig, Emily. *Creating Chinese Ethnicity: Subei People in Shanghai, 1850–1980*. New Haven: Yale University Press, 1992. A study of northern Jiangsu immigrants to Shanghai who are discriminated against for their alleged "backwardness."

Mackerras, Colin. *China's Minorities: Integration and Modernization in the Twentieth Century*. Hong Kong; New York: Oxford University Press, 1994. A study of the modern history of China's non-Han minorities.

### SEXUALITY

Dikotter, Frank. *Sex, Culture, and Modernity in China: Medical Science and the Construction of Sexual Identities in the Early Republican Period*. Honolulu: University of Hawaii Press, 1995. An exploration of sexual issues in the context of both traditional and modern Western categories.

Hershatter, Gail. *Dangerous Pleasures: Prostitution and Modernity in Twentieth-Century China*. Berkeley: University of California Press, 1997. A thorough study of aspects of Shanghai prostitution, showing among other things the substantial power attained by women in the brothels.

Hinsch, Bret. *Passions of the Cut Sleeve: The Male Homosexual Tradition in China*. Berkeley: University of California Press, 1990. A description of male homosexual love found in various literary and historical sources throughout Chinese history.

Levy, Howard S. *Chinese Footbinding: The History of a Curious Erotic Custom*. Reprint, New York: Bell, 1967. An exploration of various aspects of this disfiguring and crippling custom.

## The Economy

### THE ROLE OF THE STATE

Coble, Parks. *The Shanghai Capitalists and the Nationalist Government, 1927–1937*. Cambridge: Harvard University Press, 1980. This book argues that instead of the Nanjing government's having the bourgeoisie as a social base, it exploited this class.

Leonard, Jane Kate and John R. Watt. *To Achieve Wealth and Security: The Qing Imperial State and the Economy, 1644–1911*. Ithaca: Cornell University Press, 1993. Essays on the ways in which the state affected the economy: command, regulatory, and participatory.

Mann, Susan. *Local Merchants and the Chinese Bureaucracy, 1750–1950*. Stanford: Stanford University Press, 1987. An analysis of the relationship between merchants

and bureaucrats. Mann examines the assessment and collection of revenues, state
regulation, and how merchants performed public duties.

Perdue, Peter and R. Bin Wong, with James Lee. *Nourish the People: The State
Civilian Granary System in China, 1650–1850*. Ann Arbor: University of Michigan
Press, 1991. A study arguing that the state granary system was successful in dealing
with famine and in stabilizing local prices when supplies were low.

## AGRICULTURE

Bernhardt, Kathryn. *Rents, Taxes, and Peasant Resistance: The Lower Yangzi Region,
1840–1950*. Stanford: Stanford University Press, 1992. Bernhardt argues that landlordism after the Taiping Rebellion was in decline because of declining rents, rising taxes, and the rise of tenant associations.

Brandt, Loren. *Commercialization and Agricultural Development: Central and
Eastern China, 1870–1937*. Cambridge: Cambridge University Press, 1989. This
study concludes that commercialization supported and fostered agricultural development.

Chao Kang. *Man and Land in Chinese History: An Economic Analysis*. Stanford:
Stanford University Press, 1986. The author argues that the traditional economy,
despite significant limitations, functioned well under private landownership and
interregional markets supported by the state.

Gardella, Robert. *Harvesting Mountains: Fujian and the China Tea Trade, 1757–1937*.
Berkeley: University of California Press, 1994. A study of the tea trade in the context of increasing foreign trade and commercial capitalism.

Huang, Philip C. C. *The Peasant Economy and Social Change in North China*.
Stanford: Stanford University Press, 1985. An important study of basic agricultural
economic developments and trends from the seventeenth to the twentieth centuries.

——. *The Peasant Family and Rural Development in the Yangzi Delta, 1350–1988*.
Stanford: Stanford University Press, 1990. Huang argues that until the 1980s, peasants plowed any earnings back into the household economy, creating involutionary
growth but with no structural changes.

Lardy, Nicholas. *Agriculture in China's Modern Economic Development*. Cambridge:
Cambridge University Press, 1983. An economic analysis of agricultural development from the 1950s to the 1980s.

Little, Daniel. *Understanding Peasant China: Case Studies in the Philosophy of Social
Science*. New Haven: Yale University Press, 1989. This important book surveys various social science issues relating to the peasantry (e.g., the applicability of ration-
al-choice models and the moral economy debate and motives for peasant rebellion).

Myers, Ramon. *The Chinese Peasant Economy: Agricultural Development in Hopei
and Shantung, 1890–1949*. Cambridge: Harvard University Press, 1970. Myers (like
Brandt, above), finds positive relationships between foreign commercialization and
agricultural development.

Perdue, Peter. *Exhausting the Earth: State and Peasant in Hunan, 1500–1850.* Cambridge: Harvard University Press, 1987. This ecological history discovers cycles of agricultural development based upon commercialization and overpopulation.

## BUSINESS AND INDUSTRY

Bergère, Marie-Claire. *The Golden Age of the Chinese Bourgeoisie, 1911–1937.* Trans. Janet Lloyd. New York: Cambridge University Press, 1990. An examination of a period in which the urban elite that was "connected with business" had considerable autonomy and power.

Byrd, William A., ed. *Chinese Industrial Firms Under Reform.* New York: Oxford University Press, 1992. A study of seven firms as they came to face market mechanisms in the 1980s while still controlled by the bureaucracy.

Child, John. *Management in China During the Age of Reform.* Cambridge: Cambridge University Press, 1994. A study from theoretical and practical perspectives of Chinese management during the 1980s.

Cochran, Sherman. *Big Business in China: Sino-Foreign Rivalry in the Cigarette, 1890–1930.* Cambridge: Harvard University Press, 1980. A study of the competition between the Chinese Nanyang Brothers Tobacco Company and the British-American Tobacco Company.

Hueneman, Ralph William. *The Dragon and the Iron Horse: The Economics of Railroads in China, 1876–1937.* Cambridge: Harvard University Press, 1984. Discusses the development of railroads and related topics (e.g., economic benefit, economic harm, and foreign exploitation).

King, Frank H. H. *The History of the Hong Kong and Shanghai Banking Corporation.* Cambridge: Cambridge University Press, 1987–88. In 3 vols. Based on the bank's archives and records, this impressive study covers a crucial economic institution in China's past.

Li, Lillian M. *China's Silk Trade: Traditional Industry in the Modern World, 1842–1937.* Cambridge: Harvard University Press, 1981. An analysis of the important silk trade during challenges by commercial capitalism.

Rawski, Thomas. *China's Transition to Industrialism.* Ann Arbor: University of Michigan Press, 1980. Argues that China had constructed the important bases for industrial success before 1949.

Solinger, Dorothy. *Chinese Business Under Socialism: The Politics of Domestic Commerce, 1949–1980.* Berkeley: University of California Press, 1984. Solinger focuses on the pre-1978 period, when individual interests contended with state interests.

——. *From Lathes to Looms: China's Industrial Policy in Comparative Perspective, 1979–1982.* Stanford: Stanford University Press, 1991. Comparing China in the late 1970s with other former command economies, Solinger here examines decision-making policies and structures at national and local levels.

Walder, Andrew G. *Communist Neo-Traditionalism: Work and Authority in Chinese*

*Industry*. Berkeley: University of California Press, 1986. An important study that suggests that the party-state controls the lives of those involved in industrial institutions through "patrimonial," neotraditional structures.

## LABOR

Chesneaux, Jean. *The Chinese Labor Movement, 1919–1927.* Trans. H. M. Wright. Stanford: Stanford University Press, 1968. Wide-ranging in its coverage of industrial labor, Chesneaux's work describes the strikes and boycotts of the 1920s.

Hershatter, Gail. *The Workers of Tianjin, 1900–1949.* Stanford: Stanford University Press, 1986. This study shows that on the eve of the Communist takeover, most workers in this important city came from villages and worked in small workshops, not mechanized factories.

Honig, Emily. *Sisters and Strangers: Women in the Shanghai Cotton Mills, 1919–1949.* Stanford: Stanford University Press, 1986. A social history that rebuts many of the Communist myths about industrial workers on the eve of the Communist seizure of power.

Perry, Elizabeth. *Shanghai on Strike: The Politics of Chinese Labor.* Stanford: Stanford University Press, 1993. An important study of labor from the mid-nineteenth century to 1949, it has many suggestive comparisons to the situation in other areas and countries.

## ECONOMIC DEVELOPMENT

Elvin, Mark. *The Pattern of the Chinese Past.* Stanford: Stanford University Press, 1973. The most influential interpretation in this important book is that traditional China spurned technological change because of what the author called a "high-level equilibrium trap," a stasis reached because of a constellation in traditional society of high levels of commercialization, labor and technical proficiency, and effective merchant management of enterprises.

Hsueh Tien-tung, Li Qiang, and Liu Shucheng, eds. *China's Provincial Statistics, 1949–1989.* Boulder, Colo.: Westview Press, 1993. A compilation of important economic statistics from provinces, autonomous regions, and municipalities.

Naughton, Barry. *Growing Out of the Plan: Chinese Economic Reforms, 1978–1993.* Cambridge: Cambridge University Press, 1995. A thorough analysis of the backgrounds to the reforms and their execution.

Perkins, Dwight, ed. *China's Modern Economy in Historical Perspective.* Stanford: Stanford University Press, 1975. Essays on economic change that reflect on the role of tradition in economic development.

Rawski, Thomas. *Economic Growth in Pre-War China.* Berkeley: University of California Press, 1989. A revisionist study; among other things this analysis argues that the economy from the late Qing until 1937 did not suffer great harm from imperialism.

Riskin, Carl. *China's Political Economy: The Quest for Development Since 1949.* New

York: Oxford University Press, 1987. A fundamental account of economic development in the PRC.

Shue, Vivienne. *Peasant China in Transition: The Dynamics of Development Toward Socialism, 1949–1956.* Berkeley: University of California Press, 1980. Focusing on Hubei Province, the author analyzes peasant roles and responses to the early agricultural policies in the PRC.

White, Gordon. *Riding the Tiger: The Politics of Economic Reform in Post-Mao China.* Stanford: Stanford University Press, 1993. This analysis charts the political impacts of economic development.

Willmot, W. E., ed. *Economic Organization in Chinese Society.* Stanford: Stanford University Press, 1972. Essays focused on both traditional and modern economic organizations.

Xue Muqiao, ed. *Almanac of China's Economy, 1981: With Economic Statistics for 1949–1980.* Hong Kong: Ballinger Publishing, 1982. A compilation of statistics with relevant documents and articles.

## THE WEST AND INTERNATIONAL TRADE

Hao Yen-p'ing. *The Commercial Revolution in Nineteenth Century China: The Rise of Sino-Western Mercantile Capitalism.* Berkeley: University of California Press, 1986. This analysis of the growth of commerce from the 1830s to the 1880s argues that foreign trade was beneficial to China's economic growth.

Hou Chi-ming. *Foreign Investment and Economic Development in China, 1840–1937.* Cambridge: Harvard University Press, 1965. The author concludes that foreign trade, investment, and business were positive forces for China.

Lardy, Nicholas. *Foreign Trade and Economic Reform in China, 1978–1990.* Cambridge: Cambridge University Press, 1992. An analysis of the impacts of reform on trade and of trade on reform.

May, Ernest R. and John K. Fairbank, eds. *America's China Trade in Historical Perspective: The Chinese and American Performance.* Cambridge: Harvard University Press, 1986. Evaluates the records of each country and explores data on Chinese imports from and exports to the United States.

Pearson, Margaret. *Joint Venture in the People's Republic of China: The Control of Foreign Investment Under Socialism.* Princeton: Princeton University Press, 1991. An examination of the development and roles of business enterprises jointly undertaken by foreign and Chinese firms.

Seligman, Scott. *Dealing with the Chinese: A Practical Guide to Business Etiquette.* New York: Warner, 1989. An introduction to contemporary Chinese business and its culture.

Stross, Randall. *Bulls in the China Shop and Other Sino-American Business Encounters.* Honolulu: University of Hawaii Press, 1992. An account of many of the experiences of U.S. businesses in trying to achieve success in the China market in the 1980s.

Sung Yun-wing. *The China-Hong Kong Connection: The Key to China's Open-Door*

*Policy*. Cambridge: Cambridge University Press, 1991. An examination of the role Hong Kong played in China's development before the two were united.

Yeung Yue-man and Hu Xu-wei, eds. *China's Coastal Cities: Catalysts for Modernization*. Honolulu: University of Hawaii Press, 1992. These essays focus on issues relating to the Special Economic Zones established in the 1980s.

## THE ENVIRONMENT

Greer, Charles. *Water Management in the Yellow River Basin of China*. Austin: University of Texas Press, 1979. A study of nineteenth- and twentieth-century efforts at flood control and irrigation.

Luk Shiu-hung and Joseph Whitney. *Megaproject: A Case Study of China's Three Gorges Project*. Armonk, N.Y.: M. E. Sharpe, 1993. Essays by Chinese detailing the pros and cons of the gigantic dam project.

Pomeranz, Kenneth. *The Making of a Hinterland: State, Society, and Economy in Inland North China, 1853–1937*. Berkeley: University of California Press, 1993. An ecological and social study, this work also probes the effects of economic imperialism and the capacity of the Qing state for effective governance.

Ross, Lester. *Environmental Policy in China*. Bloomington: Indiana University Press, 1988. An important analysis of environmental policies and their implementation, this study focuses on policies in water conservancy, forestry, and pollution control.

Smil, Vaclav. *The Bad Earth: Environmental Degradation in China*. Armonk, N.Y.: M. E. Sharpe, 1984. A sharp critique of the destruction of the environment brought by industrial pollution and deforestation.

Van Slyke, Lyman P. *Yangtze: Nature, History, and the River*. Reading, Mass.: Addison-Wesley, 1988. An imaginative depiction of the roles played in the Chinese past by the Yangzi River.

## The World of Culture and Thought

### INTELLECTUAL CURRENTS

Chow Tse-tsung. *The May Fourth Movement: Intellectual Revolution in Modern China*. Cambridge: Harvard University Press, 1960. A pioneering overview of early twentieth-century China's crucial cultural and intellectual revolution.

Dikotter, Frank. *The Discourse of Race in Modern China*. Stanford: Stanford University Press, 1992. An analysis of the concept of race and its history in China in both traditional and modern times.

Elman, Benjamin A. *From Philosophy to Philology: Intellectual and Social Aspects of Change in Late Imperial China*. Cambridge: Harvard University Press, 1984. An important study that underscores the close relationship of economic and social change to intellectual developments.

Levenson, Joseph. *Confucian China and Its Modern Fate*. Berkeley: University of California Press, 1958, 1964, 1965. A highly significant cultural-intellectual history, in three volumes, by one of the early deans of China studies in the United States.

Link, Perry. *Evening Chats in Beijing: Probing China's Predicament*. New York: Norton, 1992. Sets forth the concerns of China's most important contemporary writers, professors, scientists, and dissidents.

Mao Tse-tung. *Selected Works of Mao Tse-tung*. Beijing: Foreign Languages Press, vols. 1–3, 1965, vol. 4, 1971, vol. 5, 1977. These volumes present the party's official choices among Mao's works, and their translation; they therefore offer clues to the party's intellectual milieu at the time of selection.

Schram, Stuart R. *The Thought of Mao Tse-tung*. Cambridge: Cambridge University Press, 1989. Analysis by the most important Western scholar on Mao's thought.

Schram, Stuart R. and Nancy J. Hodes, eds. *Mao's Road to Power: Revolutionary Writings, 1912–1949*. Armonk, N.Y.: M. E. Sharpe, 1994– . When completed, this series will be the most comprehensive collection of Mao's writings. The three volumes published in the 1990s include Mao's pre-1949 writings to 1930.

Schwarcz, Vera. *The Chinese Enlightenment: Intellectuals and the Legacy of the May Fourth Movement of 1919*. Berkeley: University of California Press, 1986. An important look at the May Fourth generation and the meaning of the movement's legacies for members of that generation in later periods.

Tu Wei-ming, ed. *China in Transformation*. Cambridge: Harvard University Press, 1994. Essays published first in the journal *Daedalus* (spring 1993) that discuss the crisis of cultural identity growing out of the 1989 Tian'anmen tragedy.

——. *The Living Tree: The Changing Meaning of Being Chinese Today*. Stanford: Stanford University Press, 1995. First published in *Daedalus* (spring 1991), these essays focus on issues relating to cultural, social, and political identity.

## POPULAR CULTURE

Brownell, Susan. *Training the Body for China: Sports in the Moral Order of the People's Republic*. Chicago: University of Chicago Press, 1995. This book examines competitive athletics and its political and social usage in the twentieth century.

Chang, K. C., ed. *Food in Chinese Culture: Anthropological and Historical Perspectives*. New Haven: Yale University Press, 1977. These essays examine changes in food and cooking from early times into the modern period.

Hung, Chang-tai. *Going to the People: Chinese Intellectuals and Folk Literature, 1918–1937*. Cambridge: Harvard University Press, 1985. This study not only tells the history of folk literature in the early twentieth century, it also examines Chinese attempts to collect the lore.

Johnson, David, Andrew Nathan, and Evelyn Rawski, eds. *Popular Culture in Late Imperial China*. Berkeley: University of California Press, 1985. These important essays examine the relationship of official elite culture with the culture of nonelites.

Su Xiaokang and Wang Luxiang. *Deathsong of the River: A Reader's Guide to the*

*Chinese TV Series* Heshang. Trans. Richard Bodman and Pin Wan. Ithaca: Cornell University Press, 1991. This translation of the controversial six-part television series shown in June 1988 is accompanied by interpretative essays and comments by Chinese historians.

Ting Lee-hsia Hsu. *Government Control of the Press in Modern China, 1900–1949*. Cambridge: Harvard University Press, 1974. A look at journalistic efforts to establish press freedoms and at government successes in controlling the press.

Zha Jianying. *China Pop: How Soap Operas, Tabloids, and Bestsellers Are Transforming a Culture*. New York: New Press, 1995. A breezily written account of the often startling changes in popular culture in the 1990s.

## BIOGRAPHIES

Alitto, Guy S. *The Last Confucian: Liang Shuming and the Chinese Dilemma of Modernity*. Berkeley: University of California, 1979. Biography of a Confucian who is best known for his running of a rural reconstruction project in Shandong Province in the 1930s.

Arkush, R. David. *Fei Xiaotong and Sociology in Revolutionary China*. Cambridge: Harvard University Press, 1981. Standard biography of China's most famous anthropologist.

Chang Hao. *Liang Ch'i-ch'ao and Intellectual Transition in China, 1890–1907*. Cambridge: Harvard University Press, 1971. This biography argues that many of Liang's general views grew from Qing dynasty thought rather than the impact of the West.

Cohen, Paul. *Between Tradition and Modernity: Wang T'ao and Reform in Late Ch'ing China*. Cambridge: Harvard University Press, 1974. An account of one of nineteenth-century China's important reformers. Cohen notes the difference in the rate of development between "littoral" regions and "inland" China.

Dennerline, Jerry. *Qian Mu and the World of Seven Mansions*. New Haven: Yale University Press, 1988. An inventive biography of a Confucian scholar (1895–1990) and aspects of his "world," his ancestral home in Jiangsu Province.

Grieder, Jerome B. *Hu Shih and the Chinese Renaissance: Liberalism in the Chinese Revolution, 1917–1937*. Cambridge: Harvard University Press, 1970. A standard biography of this liberal pragmatist who played important cultural, educational, and diplomatic roles.

Hsiao Kung-ch'uan. *A Modern China and New World: K'ang Yu-wei, Reformer, and Utopian, 1858–1927*. Seattle: University of Washington Press, 1975. This biography centers on the thought of this protean thinker and reformer.

Meisner, Maurice. *Li Ta-chao and the Origins of Chinese Marxism*. Cambridge: Harvard University Press, 1967. This important work argues that Li sinicized Marxism well before Mao set forth his own thoughts.

Schwartz, Benjamin. *In Search of Wealth and Power: Yen Fu and the West*. Cambridge: Harvard University Press, 1964. This important book explores not only the translations of Yen, but also Yen's interpretation about the nature of Western civilization as it applied to the remaking of China.

## RELIGION

Dean, Kenneth. *Taoist Ritual and Popular Cults of Southeast China*. Princeton: Princeton University Press, 1993. This study points to the revival in Fujian Province of a wide range of Daoist practices in Dengist China.

Hunter, Alan and Kim-kwong Chan. *Protestantism in Contemporary China*. Cambridge: Cambridge University Press, 1993. A survey of Protestant activity beginning in the relative freedom of the 1980s, including discussion of Protestant relations with other religious groups and the context of Chinese religious culture in general.

Kohn, Livia, ed. *The Taoist Experience: An Anthology*. Albany: State University of New York Press, 1993. Texts, with introductions, that serve as a good starting point for understanding the major Daoist schools from early China to the present.

Naquin, Susan and Chun-fang Yu, eds. *Pilgrims and Sacred Sites in China*. Berkeley: University of California Press, 1993. Essays on pilgrimages, including those to the five sacred mountains.

Overmyer, Daniel L. *Folk Buddhist Religion: Dissenting Sects in Late Traditional China*. Cambridge: Harvard University Press, 1976. A discussion of the beliefs, structures, and practices of popular Buddhist sects.

Pas, Julian F., ed. *The Turning of the Tide: Religion in China Today*. Hong Kong: Oxford University Press, 1989. These essays underscore the revival and liveliness of religious diversity.

Tang, Edmond and Jean-Paul Wiest, eds. *The Catholic Church in Modern China: Perspectives*. Maryknoll, N.Y.: Orbis Books, 1993. Papers and interviews on the role and status of the Roman Catholic Church in China after the establishment of the PRC.

Weber, Max. *The Religions of China: Confucianism and Taoism*. Trans. Hans H. Gerth. Glencoe, Ill.: Free Press, 1964. Though outdated, this work remains important for Weber's suggestiveness about China as well as the West.

Watson, James L. and Evelyn Rawski, eds. *Death Ritual in Late Imperial and Modern China*. Berkeley: University of California Press, 1988. Essays that examine practices and beliefs associated with funerals, mourning, memorials, and other such rituals, noting changes over time.

Welch, Holmes. *The Practice of Chinese Buddhism, 1900–1950*. Cambridge: Harvard University Press, 1967. A history of the adaptations of Buddhist organizations to the changes in early twentieth-century life.

Wolf, Arthur P., ed. *Religion and Ritual in Chinese Society*. Stanford: Stanford University Press, 1974. Essays focused on local folk beliefs and practices.

Yang, C. K. *Religion in Chinese Society: A Study of Contemporary Social Functions of Religion and Some of Their Historical Factors*. Berkeley: University of California

Press, 1961; reprint, Prospect Heights, Ill.: Waveland, 1991. Yang's survey examines many aspects of Chinese society that are impacted by religion.

## LANGUAGE AND LITERATURE

Anderson, Marston. *The Limits of Realism: Chinese Fiction in the Revolutionary Period.* Berkeley: University of California Press, 1990. Literary criticism focusing on the concept of realism in writings from 1915–1942.

Ba Jin. *Cold Nights.* Trans. Nathan K. Mao and Liu Ts'un-yan. Seattle: University of Washington Press, 1978. This novel captures the corruption of the Chongqing government during the war.

——. *Family.* Trans. Olga Lang. New York: Anchor Books, 1972. Ba Jin's most famous novel details the travails of three brothers trying to make lives of their own in the midst of the power of traditional family values.

Bei Dao. *Old Snow.* Trans. Bonnie S. McDougall and Chen Maiping. New York: New Directions, 1991. Poetry by one of China's most important contemporary poets.

Birch, Cyril, ed. *Anthology of Chinese Literature*, vol. 2: *From the Fourteenth Century to the Present Day.* New York: Grove Press, 1972. An anthology that includes poetry, fiction, and drama.

Chang, Eileen. *The Rice-Sprout Song.* New York: Scribners, 1955. A novel about young Chinese forced into cruelty by the political realities in villages in the early 1950s.

Chen Jo-hsi. *The Execution of Mayor Yin and Other Stories from the Great Proletarian Cultural Revolution.* Trans. Nancy Ing and Howard Goldblatt. Bloomington: Indiana University Press, 1979. Stories depicting the bitter realities of the Cultural Revolution.

De Francis, John. *Nationalism and Language Reform in China.* Princeton: Princeton University Press, 1950. An account of the debate over whether to do away with Chinese characters and install some alphabetic system.

Ding Ling. *I Myself Am a Woman: Selected Writings of Ding Ling.* Ed. Tani E. Barlow. Boston: Beacon Press, 1989. Twelve short stories by China's most famous female writer.

——. *The Sun Shines Over the Sanggan River.* Trans. Yang Hsien-yi and Gladys Yang. Beijing: Foreign Languages Press, 1954. Ding Ling's famous novel focused on land reform in North China won the Stalin Prize in 1951.

Eoyang, Eugene Chen. *The Transparent Eye: Reflections on Translation, Chinese Literature, and Comparative Poetics.* Honolulu: University of Hawaii Press, 1993. Essays relating to theoretical and practical issues of translating Chinese into English.

Goldman, Merle, ed. *Modern Chinese Literature in the May Fourth Era.* Cambridge: Harvard University Press, 1977. These conference essays examine, among other things, the relation of May Fourth writings to tradition and to Western approaches.

Gunn, Edward M., Jr. *The Unwelcome Muse: Chinese Literature in Shanghai and*

*Peking, 1937–1945*. New York: Columbia University Press, 1980. An examination of literature written in cities occupied by Japan during the war.

Hsia, C. T. *A History of Modern Chinese Fiction, 1917–1957*. New Haven: Yale University Press, 1971. The standard history of modern Chinese fiction in these forty years.

Hsu Kai-yu and Ting Wang, eds. *Literature of the People's Republic of China*. Bloomington: Indiana University Press, 1980. A translation of some two hundred selections from different literary genres—essays, poems, excerpts from novels, and short stories.

Lao She. *Cat Country*. Trans. William A. Lyell Jr. Columbus: Ohio State University Press, 1970. First published in 1932, this novel satirizes Chinese political culture in the wake of Japan's seizure of Manchuria.

——. *Rickshaw: The Novel* Lo-t'o Hsiang Tzu *by Lao She*. Trans. Jean James. Honolulu: University of Hawaii Press, 1979. Lao She's most famous novel. The bleak, Dickensian story describes the life of a Beijing ricksha puller.

Larson, Wendy. *Literary Authority and the Modern Chinese Writer*. Durham: Duke University Press, 1991. Using autobiographies and novels from the early twentieth century, Larson describes activities that five authors suggested increased their stature at a time when fiction writing was looked down on.

Lee, Leo Ou-fan. *The Romantic Generation of Chinese Modern Writers*. Cambridge: Harvard University Press, 1973. A study of a generation of writers that espoused romantic literature and lifestyles as a reaction against Chinese tradition.

——. *Voices from the Iron House: A Study of Lu Xun*. Bloomington: Indiana University Press, 1987. An important biography of China's most famous modern writer (1881–1936).

Link, Perry. *Mandarin Ducks and Butterflies: Popular Fiction in Early Twentieth-Century Chinese Cities*. Berkeley: University of California Press, 1981. This study examines fiction that was popular among the new urban middle class, especially detective stories, love stories, and martial-arts tales.

——, ed. *Stubborn Weeds: Popular and Controversial Chinese Literature After the Cultural Revolution*. Bloomington: Indiana University Press, 1983. Short stories, poetry, a drama, and short selections from the popular performing arts, all from 1979 and 1980.

Liu, Lydia H. *Translingual Practice: Literature, National Culture, and Translated Modernity—China 1900–1937*. Stanford: Stanford University Press, 1995. An important book that focuses on the issues of language in studies across cultures.

Lu Xun. *Lu Xun: Selected Works*. Trans. Yang Xianyi and Gladys Yang. Beijing: Foreign Languages Press, 1980. In 4 vols. Stories, essays, and poetry by China's most important twentieth-century writer.

Mair, Victor, ed. *The Columbia Anthology of Traditional Chinese Literature*. New York: Columbia University Press, 1994. The more than thirteen hundred pages of this anthology include poetry, nonfiction, fiction, and oral and performing arts from early times to the twentieth century.

Mao Dun. *Midnight*. Trans. Xu Mengxiong and A. C. Barnes. Beijing: Foreign

Languages Press, 1957. Mao Dun depicts the morally corrupt capitalist class in Shanghai.

——. *Rainbow*. Trans. Madeleine Zelin. Berkeley: University of California Press, 1992. Focusing on a young woman, this novel captures the important historical shift from May Fourth individualism to revolutionary nationalism.

Mo Yan. *Red Sorghum: A Family Chronicle*. Trans. Howard Goldblatt. New York: Viking Penguin, 1993. A fascinating story of the local dynamics of war and revolution from the 1930s to the 1950s, set in Shandong Province.

Norman, Jerry. *Chinese*. Cambridge: Cambridge University Press, 1988. An important description of the nature of written and spoken Chinese.

Pickowicz, Paul G. *Marxist Literary Thought in China: The Influence of Ch'u Ch'iu-pai*. Berkeley: University of California Press, 1981. A study that emphasizes Qu Qiubai's life and the increasing importance of Marxist literary theory as opposed to other Western approaches in the 1920s and 1930s.

Shen Congwen. *Imperfect Paradise: Stories by Shen Congwen*. Trans. Jeffrey Kinkley. Honolulu: University of Hawaii Press, 1994. A basic collection by one of the major authors in the period before 1949. Many of his stories use material from his military experiences among the Miao minority in western Hunan.

Siu, Helen, comp. and trans. *Furrows: Peasants, Intellectuals, and the State: Stories and Histories from Modern China*. Stanford: Stanford University Press, 1990. Stories and personal histories that document the changing construction of the idea of the peasantry from the 1930s to the 1980s.

Wang Meng. *Selected Works of Wang Meng*. Trans. Denis Mair et al. Beijing: Foreign Languages Press, 1989— . In 2 vols. Wang was denounced in the Anti-Rightist Campaign of 1957 for his work; rehabilitated in 1979, he served as minister of culture from 1986 to 1989.

Wang Ruowang. *Hunger Trilogy*. Trans. Kyna Rubin with Ira Kasoff. Armonk, N.Y.: M. E. Sharpe, 1991. A short novel, detailing three periods in the author's life when he went through deprivation and starvation.

Wen I-to. *Red Candle: Selected Poems*. Trans. Tao Tao Sanders. London: Cape, 1972. Poetry by a leading intellectual, assassinated in 1946 for his involvement with the Democratic League.

Widmer, Ellen and David Der-wei Wang, eds. *From May Fourth to June Fourth: Fiction and Film in Twentieth-Century China*. Cambridge: Harvard University Press, 1993. These essays explore similarities between the literature of the 1920s and that after the Cultural Revolution.

Yeh, Michelle, ed. and trans. *Anthology of Modern Chinese Poetry*. New Haven: Yale University Press, 1992. More than three hundred poems by twentieth-century writers. A basic compilation.

Yin Binyong and John S. Rohsenow. *Modern Chinese Characters*. San Francisco: China Books, 1994. Comprehensive coverage includes pronunciation, meaning, stroke order, synonyms and antonyms, and dictionaries.

## FINE ARTS AND PERFORMING ARTS

Andrews, Julia F. *Painters and Politics in the People's Republic of China, 1949–1979*. Berkeley: University of California Press, 1994. A significant book that studies the impacts of changing ideas of political correctness on artists as they strive for artistic development.

Crozier, Ralph. *Art and Revolution in Modern China: The Lingnan (Cantonese) School of Painting, 1906–1951*. Berkeley: University of California Press, 1988. An analysis of the history and development of style and content of art that was both modern and yet distinctively Chinese.

Gunn, Edward M., Jr., ed. *Twentieth Century Chinese Drama: An Anthology*. Bloomington: Indiana University Press, 1983. Includes the texts of sixteen dramas, among them Cao Yu's *Thunderstorm*, Lao She's *Teahouse*, and Wu Han's *Hai Rui Dismissed from Office*.

Harbsmeier, Christopher. *The Cartoonist Feng Zikai: Social Realism with a Buddhist Face*. New York: Columbia University Press, 1984. Biography of an important artist and writer.

Keswick, Maggie. *The Chinese Garden: History, Art, and Architecture*. New York: Rizzoli, 1978. A general history covering many aspects of the traditional garden.

Kraus, Richard Kurt. *Brushes with Power: Modern Politics and the Chinese Art of Calligraphy*. Berkeley: University of California Press, 1991. A study of the uses of calligraphy in the traditional and modern state.

———. *Pianos and Politics in China: Middle-Class Ambitions and the Struggle Over Western Music*. New York: Oxford University Press, 1989. This interesting study analyzes the meaning of piano music to various groups as a prelude to its sketches of the lives of four pianists.

Liang, Sicheng. *A Pictorial History of Chinese Architecture*. Ed. Wilma Fairbank. Cambridge: MIT Press, 1984. Photographs taken in the 1930s by the son of Liang Qichao.

Mackerras, Colin, ed. *The Chinese Theater from Its Origins to the Present Day*. Honolulu: University of Hawaii Press, 1983. A standard survey.

———. *The Performing Arts in Contemporary China*. London: Routledge & Kegan Paul, 1981. Covers the period from 1976 on. Examines theater, cinema, traditional performing arts, and music.

McDougall, Bonnie S., ed. *Popular Chinese Literature and Performing Arts in the People's Republic of China, 1949–1979*. Berkeley: University of California Press, 1984. Conference essays. The editor writes an overview of developments in these three decades.

Sullivan, Michael. *The Arts of China*. Berkeley: University of California Press, 1984. A standard treatment written for the layman.

———. *The Meeting of Eastern and Western Art: From the Sixteenth Century to the Present Day*. Berkeley: University of California Press, 1989. A study of the exchanges in technique and approaches between the European and East Asian art worlds.

Tung, Constantine, and Colin Mackerras, eds. *Drama in the People's Republic*. Albany: State University of New York Press, 1987. Conference essays on aspects of drama.

## FILM

Berry, Chris. *Perspectives on Chinese Cinema*. Bloomington: Indiana University Press, 1991. Essays that introduce film in both the People's Republic and Taiwan.

Browne, Nick, Paul Pickowicz, Vivian Sobchak, and Esther Yau, eds. *New Chinese Cinemas: Forms, Identities, Politics*. Cambridge: Cambridge University Press, 1994. These essays analyze films, film theory, and the relationship of film to the power of the state.

Clark, Paul. *Chinese Cinema: Culture and Politics Since 1949*. New York: Cambridge University Press, 1987. Focuses especially on blatantly political films from the 1930s to the mid-1980s.

## MEDICINE AND HEALTH

Crozier, Ralph. *Traditional Medicine in Modern China: Science, Nationalism, and the Tensions of Cultural Change*. Cambridge: Harvard University Press, 1968. Explores the debate in the Republican period and early years of the PRC over whether the practice of traditional medicine was congruent with modern science and how its future fit into the reality of nationalism.

Farquhar, Judith. *Knowing Practice: The Clinical Encounter of Chinese Medicine*. Boulder, Colo.: Westview Press, 1994. An anthropological analysis of the relationship between theory and practice in traditional Chinese medicine.

Hsu, Francis L. K. *Religion, Science, and Human Crises: A Study of China in Transition and Its Implications for the West*. London: Routledge & Kegan Paul, 1952. A field study of a cholera epidemic during World War II, used by Hsu as a vehicle to raise questions about traditional Chinese medical approaches and those of the modern West.

Kleinman, Arthur. *Social Origins of Distress and Disease: Depression, Neurasthenia, and Pain in Modern China*. New Haven: Yale University Press, 1986. An important exploration into the nonphysical sources of both physical and psychological illness.

Kleinman, Arthur and Lin Tsung-yi, eds. *Normal and Abnormal Behavior in Chinese Culture*. Dordrecht, Netherlands: Reidel, 1981. This collection looks at, among other things, the manifestation of mental illness at particular times and places.

Lampton, David M. *The Politics of Medicine in China: The Policy Process, 1949–1977*. Boulder, Colo.: Westview Press, 1977. Analyzes the struggle in the medical profession between the Maoists, who called for ideological correctness, and the Liu-Deng group, who called for professionalism.

Unschild, Paul U. *Medicine in China: A History of Ideas*. Berkeley: University of California Press, 1985. Discusses theory, not practice, commenting on the theoretical texts that Unschild himself translates.

SCIENCE AND TECHNOLOGY

Orleans, Leo, ed. *Science in Contemporary China*. Stanford: Stanford University Press, 1980. Essentially an encyclopedia cataloging aspects of science and scientific techniques, approaches, and structures.

Reardon-Anderson, James. *The Study of Change: Chemistry in China, 1840–1949*. Cambridge: Cambridge University Press, 1991. Discusses the development of chemistry as a profession, its relation to state and society, and the growth of chemical industries.

Saich, Tony. *China's Science Policy in the 1980s*. Manchester, England: Manchester University Press, 1989. Discusses organizational and financial strategies and the role of the larger economic reforms in the derivation of science policies.

Suttmeier, Richard P. *Research and Revolution: Science Policy and Societal Change in China*. Lexington, Mass.: Lexington Books, 1974. Analyzes the relationship of science policy to the state and society into the Cultural Revolution.

## Relations with the Outside World

CULTURAL RELATIONS WITH THE WEST AND WESTERNERS

Butterfield, Fox. *Alive in the Bitter Sea*. New York: Times Books, 1982. A trenchant account of Chinese society and culture in the early 1980s by a U.S. journalist.

Ch'en, Jerome. *China and the West: Society and Culture, 1815–1937*. Bloomington: Indiana University Press, 1979. An overview of various kinds of contact between China and the West.

Cohen, Paul A. *China and Christianity: The Missionary Movement and the Growth of Chinese Anti-foreignism, 1860–1870*. Cambridge: Harvard University Press, 1963. A study of the roles of Christian missionaries, the impacts they had on the Chinese, and the Chinese reactions.

Espey, John. *Minor Heresies, Major Departures: A China Mission Boyhood*. Berkeley: University of California Press, 1994. A missionary memoir.

Evans, Paul M. *John Fairbank and the American Understanding of Modern China*. Oxford: Basil Blackwell, 1988. This biography of the distinguished U.S. scholar probes Fairbank's concepts about China and its relations with the West.

Fairbank, John K., ed. *The Missionary Enterprise in China and America*. Cambridge: Harvard University Press, 1974. Important essays that analyze the mission effort from two perspectives—that of the home boards as well as that of proselytizing in China.

Fogel, Joshua A. *Nakae Ushikichi in China: The Mourning of the Spirit*. Cambridge: Harvard University Press, 1989. A biography of a scholar who, although an expatriate from 1911 until his death in 1942, played a role in China.

Hersey, John. *The Call*. New York: Knopf, 1985. A novel about a Protestant missionary; Hersey reportedly based the fictional character on five actual missionaries, one of whom was his father.

Hunter, Jane. *The Gospel of Gentility: American Women Missionaries in Turn-of-the-Century China*. New Haven: Yale University Press, 1984. Using letters and diaries, the author describes the missionary experience and the cultural and personal issues missionaries had to face.

Hyatt, Irwin. *Our Ordered Lives Confess: Three Nineteenth-Century American Missionaries in East Shantung*. Cambridge: Harvard University Press, 1976. Three interconnected biographies (of two men and one woman, two Baptists and one Presbyterian) reveal the varied experiences of late nineteenth-century missionaries.

Mahoney, Rosemary. *The Early Arrival of Dreams: A Year in China*. New York: Ballantine, 1990. Sometimes embittered but always thoughtful reactions to Chinese and Chinese culture by an American teacher.

Price, Eva Jane. *China Journal, 1889–1900: An American Missionary Family During the Boxer Rebellion*. New York: Scribner's, 1989. An interesting account by the wife of a missionary who served in Shanxi Province. She and her husband were killed in the Boxer disturbances.

Salzman, Mark. *Iron and Silk*. New York: Random House, 1986. Lighter than Mahoney's memoir, Salzman's is equally thoughtful and insightful about Chinese culture.

Service, Grace. *Golden Inches: The China Memoir of Grace Service*. Ed. John Service. Berkeley: University of California Press, 1989. A missionary account.

Shaw, Yu-ming. *An American Missionary in China: John Leighton Stuart and Chinese-American Relations*. Cambridge: Harvard University Press, 1992. A biography of the missionary who became president of Yenching University and U.S. ambassador to China.

Spence, Jonathan. *To Change China: Western Advisors in China, 1620–1960*. Boston: Little, Brown, 1969. Brief depictions of the roles of sixteen men who brought ideas, expertise, technology, or military prowess to their attempts to change China.

Stross, Randall E. *The Stubborn Earth: American Agriculturalists on Chinese Soil, 1898–1937*. Berkeley: University of California Press, 1986. Chronicles the cultural and agricultural experiences of specialists who worked in China, trying to "reconstruct" Chinese farming.

Thomson, James C. *While China Faced West: American Reformers in Nationalist China, 1928–1937*. Cambridge: Harvard University Press, 1969. A study of the rural reconstruction work supported by the Rockefeller Foundation and progressive missionaries.

## IMPERIALISM

Duus, Peter, Ramon Myers, and Mark Peattie, eds. *The Japanese Informal Empire in China, 1895–1937*. Princeton: Princeton University Press, 1989. Conference essays on aspects of Japanese imperialism before the Sino-Japanese War.

Hu Sheng. *Imperialism and Chinese Politics, 1840–1925*. Beijing: Foreign Languages Press, 1981. The standard Communist interpretation of the impact of imperialism on China.

Schrecker, John. *Imperialism and Chinese Nationalism: Germany in Shantung*. Cambridge: Harvard University Press, 1971. A study of imperialism from 1894 to 1914, examining elements ranging from diplomacy to military, political, and economic pressures.

Coble, Parks M. *Facing Japan: Chinese Politics and Japanese Imperialism, 1931–1937*. Cambridge: Harvard University Press, 1991. An important study of the interrelationship of Japanese imperialism and the realities and intricacies of Chinese domestic politics.

## DIPLOMATIC RELATIONS

Boyle, John Hunter. *China and Japan at War: The Politics of Collaboration, 1937–1945*. Stanford: Stanford University Press, 1972. An account of the decisions and process by which Wang Jingwei agreed to collaborate with the Japanese.

Chang, Gordon H. *Friends and Enemies: The United States, China, and the Soviet Union, 1948–1972*. Stanford: Stanford University Press, 1990. In a broadly revisionist study, Chang finds that, among other things, U.S. policy makers held ignorant, stereotypical views of East Asia.

Cohen, Warren. *America's Response to China: An Interpretive History of Sino-American Relations*. New York: Columbia University Press, 1990. A standard survey.

——, ed. *Pacific Passage: The Study of American-East Asian Relations on the Eve of the Twenty-first Century*. New York: Columbia University Press, 1995. Important essays offering the latest interpretations on relations between the U.S. and all East Asian nations.

Dittmer, Lowell. *Sino-Soviet Normalization and Its International Implications, 1945–1990*. Seattle: University of Washington Press, 1992. A solid history of the alliance, the breakup, and the restoration of relations in the thirteen years after Mao's death.

Fairbank, John K. *Trade and Diplomacy on the China Coast: The Opening of the Treaty Ports, 1842–1854*. Cambridge: Harvard University Press, 1953. A basic study of the period of the Opium Wars and the establishment of the "unequal" trading system.

Garver, John W. *Chinese-Soviet Relations, 1937–1945: The Diplomacy of Chinese Nationalism*. New York: Oxford University Press, 1988. As suggested by the title, Garver finds nationalism and national interests to be the main dynamics of the period's diplomacy between Mao, Chiang, and Stalin.

Goncharov, Sergei, John Lewis, and Xue Litai. *Uncertain Partners: Stalin, Mao, and the Korean War*. Stanford: Stanford University Press, 1994. This analysis of the dynamics of the relations between Stalin and Mao over Korea concludes that Stalin was able to manipulate China into carrying out Stalin's desired policies.

Harding, Harry. *A Fragile Relationship: The United States and China Since 1972*. Washington, D.C.: Brookings Institution, 1992. A basic study of the relationship that has lurched between periods of hostility and cooperation.

Hevia, James L. *Cherishing Men from Afar: Qing Guest Ritual and the Macartney Embassy of 1793*. Durham: Duke University Press, 1995. A revisionist interpretation of the Macartney Mission, focusing on the rituals by which each side dealt with the other.

Hunt, Michael. *The Making of a Special Relationship: The United States and China to 1914*. New York: Columbia University Press, 1983. Discusses the years when Americans came to have the pretension that they were a benevolent patron of China.

Iriye, Akira. *Across the Pacific: An Inner History of American-East Asian Relations*. New York: Harcourt, Brace, & World, 1967. An important early survey of U.S. relations with China and Japan from the late eighteenth century to the 1960s.

———. *After Imperialism: The Search for a New Order in the Far East, 1921–1931*. Cambridge: Harvard University Press, 1965. Analyzes the system of internationalism operative from the end of World War I to the Japanese seizure of Manchuria.

———, ed. *The Chinese and the Japanese: Essays in Political and Cultural Interactions*. Princeton: Princeton University Press, 1979. Iriye's essays cover a wide range of topics, all of which shed light on political and cultural relationships.

Kirby, William. *Germany and Republican China*. Stanford: Stanford University Press, 1984. This study shows that Chiang Kai-shek utilized the German model for industrialization as well as for mobilization of the populace.

Robinson, Thomas W. and David Shambaugh, eds. *Chinese Foreign Policy: Theory and Practice*. Oxford: Oxford University Press, 1994. A thorough study of the nature, structures, patterns, and contexts of the making of foreign policy.

Ross, Robert. *The Indochina Tangle: China's Vietnam Policy, 1975–1979*. New York: Columbia University Press, 1988. A basic study of the policies that led to the war in early 1979.

Shambaugh, David. *Beautiful Imperialist: China Perceives America, 1972–1990*. Princeton: Princeton University Press, 1991. This analysis finds great diversity in views and interpretations among America-watchers in China.

Tsou, Tang. *America's Failure in China, 1941–1950*. Chicago: University of Chicago Press, 1963. An analysis of this failure, growing out of the inability of the United States to utilize strategies that might bring success or to give up its pretentious goals.

Tucker, Nancy Bernkopf. *Taiwan, Hong Kong, and the United States, 1945–1992*. New York: Twayne, 1994. An analysis that goes beyond diplomacy to include a variety of cultural relations. This study finds that United States China policy was deeply affected by U.S. relations with Taiwan and Hong Kong.

Westad, Odd Arne. *Cold War and Revolution: Soviet-American Rivalry and the Origins of the Chinese Civil War, 1944–1946*. New York: Columbia University Press, 1993. This study underscores the complexity of the relations between the Soviet Union, the United States, Chiang, and Mao.

## WARS

Chang Hsin-pao. *Commissioner Lin and the Opium War*. Cambridge: Harvard University Press, 1964. Studies the role of Lin Zexu at Canton, finding a source of the war in Lin's misunderstanding of the nature of the Western threat.

Eastman, Lloyd. *Seeds of Destruction: Nationalist China in War and Revolution, 1937–1949.* Cambridge: Harvard University Press, 1984. An analysis of a variety of political issues that set the stage for the Nationalist defeat in the civil war.

Fay, Peter Ward. *The Opium War, 1840–1842.* Chapel Hill: University of North Carolina Press, 1975. A readable narrative of the war.

Fu, Poshek. *Passivity, Resistance, and Collaboration: Intellectual Choices in Occupied Shanghai, 1937–1945.* Stanford: Stanford University Press, 1993. Studies the strategies of Shanghai intellectuals in dealing with life under Japanese occupation.

Hsiung, James C. and Steven Levine, eds. *China's Bitter Victory: The War with Japan.* Armonk, N.Y.: M. E. Sharpe, 1992. These essays provide basic interpretations about the war but do not break much new ground.

Hung, Chang-tai. *War and Popular Culture: Resistance in Modern China, 1937–1945.* Berkeley: University of California Press, 1994. An analysis of the variety of cultural efforts undertaken to mobilize the masses for resistance against Japan.

Pepper, Suzanne. *Civil War in China: The Political Struggle, 1945–1949.* Berkeley: University of California Press, 1978. A basic political history.

Polachek, James M. *The Inner Opium War.* Cambridge: Harvard University Press, 1992. An analysis of court factions and intrigue that, the author argues, were one reason for Commissioner Lin's actions at Canton.

Wakeman, Frederic, Jr. *Strangers at the Gate: Social Disorder in South China, 1839–1861.* Berkeley: University of California Press, 1966. Sees the Opium War in the context of Guangdong society and notes the effects that the loss of the war had on south China localities.

White, Theodore and Annalee Jacoby. *Thunder Out of China.* New York: William Sloane, 1946. White and Jacoby present a vivid picture of wartime China; their work is well-deservedly called a classic.

## DOCUMENTARIES AND FEATURE FILMS

### *Documentaries*

*China: A Century of Revolution.* Excellent documentary film of Chinese history since 1911. Excellent footage and telling interviews with people who participated in the events described. Three one-hour videocassettes. 1: China in Revolution: 1911–1949; 2: The Mao Years: 1949–1976; 3: Born Under the Red Flag: 1976–1997. By Ambrica Productions in association with WGBH Boston (1994–97). Distributed by WinStar Home Entertainment.

*China After Tiananmen.* An excellent film that looks at China three years after the Beijing Spring of 1989, detailing the conflicting realities of liberal economic reform and continuing political repression. A strength of the documentary is its interviews with Chinese. Videocassette (88 minutes). Produced for the Documentary

Consortium by WGBH Boston; a Drasnin Production for *Frontline* (1992). Distributed by PBS Video.

*The China Call*. A critical examination of the history of the U.S. missionary movement in China during the nineteenth and twentieth centuries. Videocassette (60 minutes). Part of the series *The Dragon and the Eagle*. Produced by James Culp Productions (1994). Distributed by the University of California Center for Media and Independent Learning, Berkeley, Calif.

*The Emperor's Eye: Art and Power in Imperial China*. An interesting film detailing the Qianlong emperor's patronage of art as a way of establishing legitimacy for his Manchu rule. The film uses art works at the National Palace Museum in Taipei. Videocassette (60 minutes). Produced by Alvin H. Perlmutter (1989).

*The Gate of Heavenly Peace*. The best film on the 1989 demonstrations in Tian'anmen Square, it captures the complexity of the student movement and the controversial reality of what occurred. Two videocassettes (189 minutes). A production of the Long Bow group, produced in association with WGBH/*Frontline* and the Independent Television Service (1996). Distributed by NAATA/CrossCurrent Media.

*The Genius That Was China*. An excellent four-part series examining the role of science and technology from the eleventh century to the present and the clash between East and West. Four videocassettes (232 minutes). 1: *Rise of the Dragon*; 2: *Empires in Collision*; 3: *The Threat from Japan*; 4: *Will the Dragon Rise Again?* A production of Film Australia in association with WGBH for *NOVA* (1990). Distributed by Coronet Film and Video.

*Heart of the Dragon*. Excellent twelve-part series capturing various aspects of Chinese life in the mid-1980s. The programs, in order, are entitled *Remembering, Eating, Living, Believing, Caring, Marrying, Mediating, Working, Correcting, Creating, Understanding*, and *Trading*. Twelve videocassettes (684 minutes). Produced by Time-Life Video (1985). Distributed by Time-Life Video.

*Moving the Mountain*. A very fine film capturing the power and especially the passion of the 1989 demonstrations in Tian'anmen Square. Newsreel footage, dramatic reenactments, and interviews with student participants. Videocassette (83 minutes). A joint October/Xingu Films production (1994). Distributed by Hallmark Home Entertainment.

*One Village in China*. An interesting and enlightening exploration of daily life in Long Bow (four hundred miles southwest of Beijing) in the mid-1980s before effects of the economic reforms were felt. Four videocassettes. 1: *All Under Heaven*—an intimate look at daily life (58 minutes); 2: *Small Happiness*—an exploration of gender and sexual politics (58 minutes); 3: *To Taste a Hundred Herbs*—an exploration of traditional medicine and beliefs about healing (60 minutes); 4: *First Moon*—an examination of New Year's celebrations (37 minutes). The first three cassettes distributed by the Long Bow Group, Philadelphia, 1984; #4 by New Day Films, New York. 1987.

*Presenting "River Elegy."* Excerpts from a controversial six-part Chinese documentary series broadcast in 1988. It condemned Chinese tradition as it openly embraced Western capitalism. The series was subsequently banned. Videocassette (58 minutes). A production of Central Chinese Television and Video Asia (1992?). Distributed by Video Asia, New York.

*Red Capitalism.* This fine documentary focuses on the municipality of Shenzhen, the most significant of the Special Economic Zones established in the 1980s. Videocassette (60 minutes). Produced by the Canadian Broadcasting Corporation (1995?). Distributed by Filmmakers Library.

*Tragedy at Tiananmen.* A very good, shorter look at the dynamics and events of the democracy movement and its climactic tragedy in the spring of 1989, produced within three weeks of the event. Videocassette (48 minutes). Produced by Koppel Communications in association with ABC News (1989). Distributed by Coronet Film and Video.

*Unleashing the Dragon.* An excellent documentary that shows the effects of the economic reforms of the 1980s and 1990s on the lives of individuals. Four videocassettes (200 minutes). 1: *Deng's Legacy*; 2: *The Fragile Rice Bowl*; 3: *The Soul of the Master*; 4: *Hong Kong and the Boom Towns.* Produced by Miracle Films (1995). Distributed by First Run/Icarus Films.

## Feature Films

*The Blue Kite.* Told from the perspective of a young boy, this film traces the fate of a Beijing family and their neighbors through the political and social upheavals in the 1950s and 1960s. Longwick Film Studio. Suitable for college-level and above.

*Eat, Drink, Man, Woman.* A retired master chef and widower is concerned about the future of his three single daughters; in the meantime, he carries on a secret affair with a much younger woman. Made in Taiwan. Central Motion Pictures in association with Ang Lee Productions and Good Machine (1994). High school and above.

*City of Sadness.* One of the Taiwan trilogy of director Hou Hsiao-hsien, this film looks at a family's experiences in the period 1945–49, from Japanese rule to Nationalist rule and the February Incident (1947). ERA International and 3-H Films (1989). High school and above.

*Farewell My Concubine.* Winner of the 1993 Palme d'Or Award at the Cannes Film Festival, this often violent film spans more than fifty years in the lives of two men at the Beijing Opera and the woman who comes between them. In the process of telling its tale, it incorporates history from the warlord period through the Cultural Revolution. Miramax Films in association with Maverick Picture Company and Tomson Film Company (1993). College and above.

*Iron and Silk.* An account of Mark Salzman, who taught English and practiced martial arts in China in the 1980s. The film introduces key general elements of Chinese culture and specific aspects of Chinese political culture from the mid-1980s. Produced by Prestige in association with Tokyo Broadcast System International, (1990). General audiences.

*Girl from Hunan.* Based on a story by Shen Congwen, this film captures central China early in the century as change begins to alter relationships and perceptions; it recounts the story of a child bride who raises her illegitimate son as her husband's younger brother. Youth Film Studio of the Beijing Film Academy (1986). High school and above.

*The Go Masters.* The first coproduction of China and Japan, this film details the story of a Chinese master of the game of Go who defeats the Japanese master. When Japan invades China in 1937, he has to decide whether to renounce his Chinese citizenship so that he can stay in Japan to keep his title. Toko Tokuma and Beijing Film Studio (1982). High school and above.

*Good Men, Good Women.* The third in Hou Hsiao-hsien's Taiwan trilogy, this film looks at the 1950s White Terror of the Nationalist government, recounting the story of a contemporary actress starring in a movie that was based on lives of leftists targeted in the terror. 3-H Productions (1995). High school and above.

*The Horse Thief.* Documentary in style, this film tells the story of a Tibetan whose theft of horses leads to his family's expulsion from their clan and to his own death. Produced by Xi'an Film Studio (1987). College and above.

*Ju Dou.* A story of doomed love couched as a struggle between generations. The film underscores the oppression of the social order. China Film Co-Production and Xi'an Film Studio (1990). College and above.

*The Last Emperor.* An Academy Award winner (Best Picture, 1988), this is the story of Puyi, the last Qing emperor, enthroned at the age of three and deposed three years later. He served under the Japanese as puppet ruler in Manchukuo. Puyi died in 1967 as a gardener in Beijing. Produced by Hemdale Film (1987). High school and above.

*Life on a String.* A blind child is told that his sight will be restored if he devotes his life to music; a critic described the film as "a timeless allegory of a master musician and his disciple." Serene Productions. Beijing Film Studio/China Film Co-Production (1991). High school and above.

*The Puppetmaster.* The second film in Hou Hsiao-hsien's Taiwan trilogy looks at the Japanese occupation (1895–1945) through an "anecdotal biography" of Taiwan master puppeteer Li T'ien-lu. ERA International presentation of a City Films production (1993). High school and above.

*Raise the Red Lantern.* In the 1920s, a nineteen-year-old woman comes to be the fourth wife of her husband, setting the stage for sometimes violent competition between the wives for his attention. Explores the position of women in late traditional society. ERA International (1991). College and above.

*Red Sorghum.* Winner of the Golden Bear Award at the Berlin Film Festival, this earthy and violent tale of rural life ends as a heroic drama of partisan resistance during the Japanese occupation. A critic saw it as "an allegory of an empowered masculinity freed from age-old repression." Produced by the Xi'an Film Studio (1988). College and above.

*Shanghai Triad.* Marked by massacres and carnage, the story is told through the eyes of a fourteen-year-old boy who serves the mistress of a gangster boss. Many die, including the mistress, but the power of the gangster remains unshaken. Shanghai Film Studio, Alpha-films, UGC Images and La Sept Cinema (1995). College and above.

*The Story of Qiu Ju.* A farmer's wife seeks justice for her husband, who has been kicked in the groin by the local Communist cadre village chief. Set in contemporary China with an almost documentary sense. SIL-Metropole Organisation and the Youth Film Studio of the Beijing Film Academy (1993). High school and above.

*To Live.* Winner of the Jury Prize at the Cannes Film Festival, this film covers the span of Communist rule to the end of the Cultural Revolution. A story of the effect of the political and social upheavals on the lives of one family. ERA International. College and above.

*The Wedding Banquet.* A Taiwanese man in a gay relationship tries to get his parents to stop their matchmaking efforts, using the excuse that he is already engaged, but they still go to New York to help make the marriage arrangements. Central Motion Pictures (1993). High school and above.

*Yellow Earth.* A poor peasant daughter falls in love with a Communist soldier sent to the countryside before the Sino-Japanese War to collect folk songs for the party; her yearning to escape an arranged marriage, however, ends tragically. Guangxi Film Studio (1984). High school and above.


## ELECTRONIC RESOURCES


### *Library Catalogs*

Harvard University
  telnet://hollis.harvard.edu
University of California, Berkeley
  telnet://gopac.berkeley edu
University of Michigan
  http//asia.lib.umich.edu/china/index.htm
Library of Congress
  telnet://locis.loc.gov


### *WWW Gateways to Information on China*

The Internet Guide for China Studies and the Asian Studies WWW Virtual Library

Thirty-eight links to electronic bibliographies of reference works, history, religion and philosophy, art, medicine, women in Chinese history, education, and more.
http://www.unive.it/~Edsie/vl/biblio.html

The Chinese Embassy, Washington, D.C.

A guide organized into more than twenty broad topics. Includes press releases and political, economic, and cultural information.
http://www.china-embassy.org

The Chinese Information and Culture Center

Information about Taiwan from the Taipei Economic and Cultural Office in New York.
http://www.taipei.org

## Government Links

The following URL offers links to the permanent mission of the People's Republic to the United Nations, to China's Foreign Ministry, to the U.S. State Department China Homepage, to the U.S. embassy in China.
http://freenet.buffalo.edu/~Ecb863/china.html

## Other News on China

*China Daily*—the official English-language newspaper in the People's Republic.
http://www.chinadaily.net/

*Inside China Today*—an English-language newspaper
http://www.insidechina.com/

*China Times*—an English-language newspaper in Taiwan.
http://www.chinatimes.com.tw/english/english.htm

# PART IV

## Appendices

The materials in the appendices supplement themes and points in other sections of the guide. Appendix 1 offers a chronology of crucial events from 1780 to the present. Appendix 2 contains passages from twenty key documents from modern Chinese history. Appendix 3 provides data on the major party congresses of the Nationalist Party and the Communist Party. Tables and charts in Appendix 4 supply key twentieth-century social and economic data.

# Chronology of Key Events
## 1780 to the Present

| | | |
|---|---|---|
| 1793 | September | Macartney Mission |
| 1796–1804 | | White Lotus Rebellion |
| 1839 | March | Commissioner Lin appointed to deal with opium problem |
| 1839–42 | | Opium War |
| 1842 | August 29 | Sino-British Treaty of Nanjing; beginning of unequal treaty system |
| 1844 | July 3 | Sino-American Treaty of Wangxia |
| 1851 | January | Hong Xiuquan declares the Heavenly Kingdom of Great Peace |
| 1851–64 | | Taiping Rebellion |
| 1853–68 | | Nian Rebellion |
| 1855–73 | | Muslim Rebellion in southwest China |
| 1856–60 | | Arrow War |
| 1858 | May | Treaty of Aigun cedes the north bank of the Amur River to Russia |
| | June | Treaty of Tianjin allows permanent foreign ambassadors in Beijing |
| 1860 | October | British and French troops sack and burn Summer Palace |
| | November | China cedes all territory east of the Ussuri River to Russia |
| 1861 | March 11 | Establishment of the Zongli Yamen |
| | August | Emergence of Cixi, the Empress Dowager |
| 1862–73 | | Muslim Rebellion in northwest China |
| 1865 | September | Establishment of the Jiangnan Arsenal |
| 1867 | November | Departure of the Burlingame mission, the first Chinese mission abroad |
| 1868 | January | Establishment of the Fuzhou Shipyard |
| 1870 | June 21 | Tianjin Massacre |
| 1873 | June 14 | Li Hongzhang establishes the China Merchants' Steamship Navigation Company |
| 1883–85 | | Sino-French War |
| 1884 | August 23 | France destroys the Fuzhou fleet and shipyard |

| | | |
|---|---|---|
| 1894–95 | | Sino-Japanese War |
| 1895 | April 17 | Treaty of Shimonoseki |
| | May 2 | Kang Youwei presents his 10,000-word memorial |
| 1897–98 | | Western powers demand leaseholds in the "Scramble for Concessions" |
| 1898 | June–Sept. | The Hundred Days of institutional reforms prompted by Kang Youwei |
| 1899–1900 | | The Boxer Uprising |
| 1901 | September 7 | The Boxer Protocol |
| 1905 | | Abolition of the civil service examination |
| | July | Formation of Sun Yat-sen's Revolutionary Alliance in Tokyo |
| 1906 | September | Manchu court announces decision for constitutional system |
| 1908 | November | Deaths of Cixi and the Guangxu emperor; three-year-old Puyi ascends throne |
| 1909 | | Convening of provisional provincial assemblies |
| 1910 | October | Convening of provisional national assembly |
| 1911 | October 10 | Revolution breaks out in Wuhan |
| 1912 | January 1 | The Republic of China is established |
| | February 12 | Manchus abdicate the throne |
| | August | High point of democracy in twentieth-century China elections for National Assembly lead to Nationalist Party (Guomindang) victory |
| 1912–16 | | Presidency of Yuan Shikai |
| 1913 | July–Sept. | "Second Revolution" directed against Yuan fails |
| | November 4 | Yuan outlaws Nationalist party (Guomindang) |
| 1914 | February | Yuan abolishes constitutional bodies at all levels |
| 1915 | January 20 | Japan presents the Twenty-One Demands |
| | | Chen Duxiu's important journal, *New Youth*, begins the May Fourth Movement |
| 1916 | June 6 | Death of Yuan Shikai |
| | December 26 | Cai Yuanpei appointed chancellor of Beijing University |
| 1917 | August 14 | China enters World War I on the side of the Allied Powers |
| 1919 | May 4 | May Fourth incident protesting Versailles conference decision allowing Japan to retain control of Shandong province |
| | May–June | John Dewey lectures in China |
| | July 25 | Soviet Union issues the Karakhan Declaration |
| 1920 | March | Ministry of Education announces that textbooks will be printed in the vernacular (*baihua*) |
| 1921 | July | Founding and First Congress of the Chinese Communist Party |

| 1923 | October | Mikhail Borodin arrives to serve as Comintern adviser to the Guomindang |
|---|---|---|
| 1924 | January | First Congress of the Nationalist Party (Guomindang) |
| | May | Establishment of Whampoa Military Academy with Chiang Kai-shek as commandant |
| 1925 | March 12 | Death of Sun Yat-sen |
| | May 30 | May Thirtieth Incident gives rise to mass movement |
| 1926–28 | | Northern Expedition |
| 1927–28 | | White Terror of Chiang Kai-shek targets Communists and left-wing Guomindang members; Communist party decimated |
| 1927 | September | Autumn Harvest Uprisings |
| 1929 | February | Mao Zedong and Zhu De begin to build Jiangxi base |
| 1930–34 | | Chiang Kai-shek's five "extermination" campaigns against the Communists in Jiangxi |
| 1931 | September 18 | Manchurian "incident" inaugurates Japanese military aggression |
| | November | Formal establishment of the Chinese Soviet Republic (the Jiangxi Soviet) |
| | Autumn | Anti-Japanese boycott |
| 1932 | Jan.–March | Japanese attack Shanghai in retaliation for boycott |
| | March | Japanese puppet state of Manchukuo established |
| 1933–36 | | Japanese military aggression continues in Inner Mongolia and North China |
| 1934 | February | Chiang Kai-shek launches the New Life Movement |
| 1934–35 | Oct.–Oct. | The Long March |
| 1935 | January 15–18 | Zunyi Conference brings Mao Zedong to CCP leadership |
| 1936 | December | Xi'an Incident |
| 1937 | July 7 | Marco Polo Bridge Incident leads to general war with Japan |
| 1937–45 | | Sino-Japanese War |
| 1937 | December | Rape of Nanjing |
| 1938 | June | Chiang blasts open Yellow River dikes to try to halt Japanese advance |
| | October | Canton and Wuhan fall to the Japanese |
| 1940 | August | The Communists' Hundred Regiments Offensive begins |
| 1941 | January 4 | New Fourth Army Incident |
| | May | Rectification Movement begins in Yan'an |
| | December 7 | China becomes an Allied power with Japan's attack on Pearl Harbor |
| 1942 | May | Yan'an Forum on Art and Literature |

| | | |
|---|---|---|
| 1942–44 | | Joseph Stilwell serves as chief of staff of the China theater |
| 1943 | January | Treaties abolish extraterritoriality |
| 1945 | August 15 | Japan surrenders; World War II ends |
| 1945–47 | | Marshall mission |
| 1946–48 | | Land reform campaign in north China |
| 1947–49 | | Civil War between the Communists and Nationalists |
| 1947 | February 28 | Brutal suppression of Taiwanese protests by Nationalists |
| 1949 | October 1 | Establishment of the People's Republic of China |
| | December | Chiang Kai-shek retreats to Taiwan |
| 1950 | February 14 | Treaty of friendship signed with the Soviet Union |
| | May 1 | Marriage Law announced |
| | June 25 | Korean War begins |
| | November | China enters the Korean War against UN forces |
| 1951 | February | Resist America–Aid Korea campaign |
| | September | Chinese troops to Tibet |
| 1951–52 | Aug.–July | Three-Anti campaign |
| 1952 | Feb.–May | Five-Anti campaign |
| 1955 | April | Bandung Conference of Asian and African nations |
| 1957 | May–June | Hundred Flowers Movement |
| | June | Anti-Rightist Campaign begins |
| 1958 | April | Establishment of the first People's Commune |
| 1958–61 | | Great Leap Forward |
| 1959 | March | China puts down Tibetan uprising; Dalai Lama flees |
| | August 12–16 | Lushan conference; ouster of Peng Dehuai |
| 1959–61 | | Great Famine |
| 1960 | July | Sino-Soviet Split; Soviet advisers and technicians pulled out |
| 1962 | Oct.–Dec. | Sino-Indian border war |
| 1963–64 | | Socialist Education campaign |
| 1964 | October | China's first nuclear test |
| 1966 | August 5 | Mao's big character poster, "Bombard the Headquarters," published |
| | August 20 | Red Guards launch campaign against the Four Olds |
| 1966–76 | | The Great Proletarian Cultural Revolution |
| 1967 | | Factional fighting reaches civil war proportions |
| | June | China's first hydrogen bomb |
| 1968 | October | Liu Shaoqi expelled from CCP |
| 1969 | March, summer | Sino-Soviet fighting on the Amur River and in Xinjiang |
| 1970 | April | China's first satellite in orbit |
| 1971 | September | Lin Biao plot to assassinate Mao; Lin killed in plane crash |
| | October 25 | The PRC admitted into United Nations |

| | | |
|---|---|---|
| 1972 | February | Nixon visits China; the Shanghai Communiqué |
| 1973–74 | | Anti-Lin (Biao), anti-Confucius campaign |
| 1975 | April 5 | Death of Chiang Kai-shek |
| 1976 | January 8 | Death of Zhou En-lai |
| | April 4–5 | Tian'anmen demonstration and incident |
| | July 28 | Tangshan earthquake casualties total up to 660,000 |
| | September 9 | Death of Mao Zedong |
| | October 6 | Arrest of the Gang of Four |
| 1978 | July | Emergence of Deng Xiaoping |
| | December | Third plenum of the Eleventh Central Committee adopts Deng's reform program |
| 1978–79 | | |
| | Nov.–Dec. | Democracy Wall |
| 1979 | January 1 | U.S.-China relations normalized |
| | Feb.–March | Sino-Vietnamese War |
| | July | Four Special Economic Zones opened; fourteen more added in 1986 |
| 1979–84 | | Agricultural reforms include the "responsibility system" and the ending of agricultural communes |
| 1980–81 | Nov.–Jan. | Trial of the Gang of Four |
| 1983 | | Campaign against "spiritual pollution" |
| 1986 | December | Student demonstrations call for political reform |
| 1987 | January | General Secretary Hu Yaobang ousted |
| | September | Armed rebellion in Tibet suppressed |
| 1989 | Apr.–June | Pro-democracy demonstrations |
| | May | Rapprochement with Soviet Union |
| | June 4 | Bloody crackdown on demonstrators by People's Liberation Army |
| | June | Zhao Ziyang ousted as CCP General Secretary |
| 1992 | January | In trip to Shenzhen, Deng Xiaoping gives go-ahead to economic reforms |
| | spring | National People's Congress approves construction of Three Gorges Dam |
| 1993 | | Party General Secretary Jiang Zemin becomes President of the PRC |
| 1997 | February 19 | Death of Deng Xiaoping |
| | July 1 | Hong Kong reverts to Chinese control |
| 1998–99 | | U.S.-China relations deteriorate over China-spying allegations, accusations of Chinese illegal campaign contributions, and NATO bombing of Chinese embassy in Yugoslavia |
| 1999 | December 20 | Macao reverts to Chinese control |

# Documents

## I. LETTER OF COMMISSIONER LIN TO QUEEN VICTORIA (AUGUST 1839)

This letter of Lin Zexu, the Imperial Commissioner dispatched to deal with the opium problem in Guangdong province, was sent to Queen Victoria shortly before the Opium War began. It reveals the Chinese self-conception and relationship with foreigners and foreign nations. It also expresses consternation and incredulity about Britain's continuing to smuggle opium into China even though well aware of its tragic consequences.

His Majesty the Emperor comforts and cherishes foreigners as well as Chinese; he loves all the people in the world without discrimination. Whenever profit is found, he wishes to share it with all men; whenever harm appears, he likewise will eliminate it on behalf of all of mankind. His heart is in fact the heart of the whole universe.

Generally speaking, the succeeding rulers of your honorable country have been respectful and obedient. . . . [T]he Celestial Empire, following its traditional policy of treating foreigners with kindness, has been doubly considerate towards the people from England. You have traded in China for almost 200 years, and as a result your country has become wealthy and prosperous.

As this trade has lasted for a long time, there are bound to be unscrupulous as well as honest traders. Among the unscrupulous are those who bring opium to China to harm the Chinese: they succeed so well that this poison has spread far and wide in all the provinces. You, I hope, will certainly agree that people who pursue material gains to the great detriment of the welfare of others can be neither tolerated by Heaven nor endured by men. Having learned about this deadly poison, His Majesty the Emperor was furious with anger; he dispatched me to Guangdong Province to examine the situation more thoroughly and, in consultation with the governor-general and the governor, to adopt necessary remedial measures. It is hoped that you, admiring China and the Chinese civilization as the ruler of England, will instruct your subjects to be diligent in observing the Chinese law. Emphatically you should let them know how grave the consequences will be if they choose not to observe it. Under no circumstances will we allow foreigners in China to violate the Chinese law.

Your country is more than 60,000 li from China. The purpose of your ships in coming to China is to realize a large profit. Since this profit is realized in China and is in fact taken away from the Chinese people, how can foreigners return injury for the benefit they have received by sending this poison to harm their benefactors? They may not intend to harm others on purpose, but the fact remains that they are so obsessed with material gain that they have no concern whatever for the harm they can cause to others. Have they no conscience? I have heard that you strictly prohibit opium in your own country, indicating unmistakably that you know how harmful opium is. You do not wish opium to harm your own country, but you choose to bring that harm to other countries such as China. Why?

Our Celestial Empire towers over all other countries in virtue and possesses a power great and awesome enough to carry out its wishes. . . . You, as the ruler of your honorable country, should do your part to uncover the hidden and unmask the wicked. . . .

It is further hoped that once you receive this letter, you will immediately convey the reasons behind the prohibition of opium to all who need to know them.

Dun Jen Li, *China in Transition, 1517–1911* (New York: Van Nostrand Reinhold, 1969), pp. 64–67.

## 2. THE TAIPING PLAN FOR REORGANIZING CHINESE SOCIETY FROM *THE LAND SYSTEM OF THE HEAVENLY DYNASTY* (1853)

This document points to various important features of Taiping rule as it was intended by the leadership: the primitive economic communism, the emphasis upon equality, the military organization, the favorable stance toward women, the sexual segregation (here mentioned in regard to church services), an authoritarian attention to details, and the stress placed upon church worship.

The division of land must be according to the number of individuals, whether male or female; calculating upon the number of individuals in a household, if they be numerous, then the amount of land will be larger, and if few, smaller. . . . All the fields in the empire are to be cultivated by all the people alike. If the land is deficient in one place, then the people must be removed to another. . . . Thus, all the people in the empire may together enjoy the abundant happiness of the Heavenly Father, Supreme Lord and Great God. There being fields, let all cultivate them; there being food, let all eat; there being clothes, let all be dressed; there being money, let all use it, so that nowhere does inequality exist, and no man is not well fed and clothed.

All men and women, every individual of sixteen years and upwards, shall receive land, twice as much as those of fifteen years of age and under. . . .Throughout the empire the mulberry tree is to be planted close to every wall, so that all women may engage in rearing silkworms, spinning the silk, and making garments. Throughout the empire every family should keep five hens and two sows. . . . At the time of the harvest, every sergeant shall direct the corporals to see to it that of the twenty-five families under his charge each individual has a sufficient supply of food, and aside from the new grain each may receive, the remainder must be deposited in the public granary . . . for the whole empire is the universal family of our Heavenly Father, the Supreme Lord and Great God. When all the people in the empire will not take anything as their own but submit all things to the Supreme Lord, then the Lord will make use of them, and in the universal family of the empire, every place will be equal and every individual well fed and clothed. This is the intent of our Heavenly Father, the Supreme Lord and Great God, in specially commanding the true Sovereign of Taiping to save the world.

However, the sergeant must keep an account of money and grain figures in a record book. . . . For every twenty-five families there must be established one public granary, and one church where the sergeant must reside. Whenever there are marriages, or births, or funerals, all may go to the public granary; but a limit must be observed, and not a cash be used beyond what is necessary. Thus, every family which celebrates a marriage or a birth will be given one thousand cash and a hundred catties of grain. This one rule is applicable throughout the empire. In the use of all things let there be economy, to provide against war and famine. As for marriages in the empire, wealth should not be a consideration. . . . In every circle of twenty-five families, all young boys must go to church every day, where the sergeant is to teach them to read the Old Testament and the New Testament, as well as the book of proclamations of the true ordained Sovereign. Every Sabbath the corporals must lead the men and women to the church, where the males and females are to sit in separate rows. There they will listen to sermons, sing praises, and offer sacrifices to our Heavenly Father, the Supreme Lord and Great God.

J. Mason Gentzler, *Changing China: Readings in the History of China from the Opium War to the Present* (New York: Praeger, 1977), pp. 54–58.

## 3. MEMORIAL OF KANG YOUWEI TO THE GUANGXU EMPEROR (1898)

This memorial submitted in late January 1898, less than five months before the launching of the Hundred Days, attempts to persuade the Guangxu emperor that he must take an active role in initiating major institutional reform. It points out the necessity of reform for China's survival; counters the argument that the institutions of the ancestors cannot be changed (because change would suggest a lack of filial reverence for the ancestors); and talks about the proper foreign models to be followed.

A survey of all states in the world will show that those states which undertook reforms became strong while those states which clung to the past perished. The consequences of clinging to the past and the effects of opening up new ways are thus obvious. If Your Majesty, with your discerning brilliance, observes the trends in other countries, you will see that if we can change, we can preserve ourselves; but if we cannot change, we shall perish. Indeed, if we can make a complete change, we shall become strong, but if we only make limited changes, we shall still perish. If Your Majesty and his ministers investigate the source of the disease, you will know that this is the right prescription.

Our present trouble lies in our clinging to old institutions without knowing how to change. In an age of competition between states, to put into effect methods appropriate to an era of universal unification and laissez-faire is like wearing heavy furs in summer or riding a high carriage across a river. This can only result in having a fever or getting oneself drowned.

It is a principle of things that the new is strong but the old weak; that new things are fresh but old things rotten; that new things are active but old things static. If the institutions are old, defects will develop. Therefore there are no institutions that should remain unchanged for a hundred years. Moreover, our present institutions are but unworthy vestiges of the Han, Tang, Yuan, and Ming dynasties; they are not even the institutions of the [Manchu] ancestors. In fact, they are the products of the fancy writing and corrupt dealing of the petty officials rather than the original ideas of the ancestors. To say that they are the ancestral institutions is an insult to the ancestors. Furthermore, institutions are for the purpose of preserving one's territories. Now that the ancestral territory cannot be preserved, what good is it to maintain the ancestral institutions? . . .

Although there is a desire for reform, yet if the national policy is not fixed and public opinion not united, it will be impossible for us to give up the old and adopt the new. The national policy is to the state just as the rudder is to the boat or the pointer is to the compass. It determines the direction of the state and shapes the public opinion of the country.

Nowadays the court has been undertaking some reforms, but the action of the emperor is obstructed by the ministers, and the recommendations of the able scholars are attacked by old-fashioned bureaucrats. If the charge is not "using barbarian ways to change China," then it is "upsetting the ancestral institutions." Rumors and scandals are rampant, and people fight each other like fire and water. A reform in this way is as ineffective as attempting a forward march by walking backward. It will inevitably result in failure. Your Majesty knows that under the present circumstances reforms are imperative and old institutions must be abolished. I beg Your Majesty to make up your mind and to decide on the national policy. After the fundamental policy is determined, the methods of implementation must vary according to what is primary and what is secondary, what is important and what is insignificant, what is strong and what is weak, what is urgent and what can wait. . . . If anything goes wrong, no success can be achieved.

. . . . As to the republican governments of the United States and France and the constitutional governments of Britain and Germany, these countries are far away and their customs are different from ours. Their changes occurred a long time ago and can no longer be traced. Consequently I beg Your Majesty to adopt the purpose of Peter the Great of Russia as our purpose and to take the Meiji Reform of Japan as the model of our reform. The time and place of Japan's reform are not remote and her religion and customs are somewhat similar to ours. Her success is manifest; her example can easily be followed.

J. Mason Gentzler, *Changing China: Readings in the History of China from the Opium War to the Present* (New York: Praeger, 1977), pp. 86–87.

# 4. THE BOXER PROTOCOL (1901)

Often seen as the low point of China's relations with the West, this protocol was forced on the Chinese government in the wake of its tacit support of the Boxer Uprising. Most destructive was Article VI, which forced an already all but bankrupt China to pay an enormous sum as an indemnity. Other details were humiliating and reflective of the Western powers' drive for vengeance.

### ARTICLE IA

[An apology from the Chinese government to the German government for the killing of German minister von Ketteler in Beijing in June 1900]

### ARTICLE IB

[A commemorative monument for von Ketteler to be built on the spot of the assassination]

### ARTICLE IIA

[High-ranking Chinese officials], the principal authors of the outrages and crimes committed against the foreign Governments and their nationals, are to be to be condemned to death by execution, death by committing suicide, "posthumous degradation," etc.

### ARTICLE IIB

The suspension of official examinations for five years in all cities where foreigners were massacred or submitted to cruel treatment.

### ARTICLE III

[An apology for the assassination of Mr. Sugiyama, chancellor of the Japanese legation]

### ARTICLE IV

The Chinese Government has agreed to erect an expiatory monument in each of the foreign or international cemeteries which were desecrated and in which the tombs were destroyed.

It has been agreed with the Representatives of the Powers that the legations interested shall settle the details for the erection of these monuments, China bearing all the expenses thereof, estimated at ten thousand taels for the cemeteries at Peking and within its neighborhood, and at five thousand taels for the cemeteries in the provinces. The amounts have been paid and the list of these cemeteries is enclosed herewith.

ARTICLE V

China has agreed to prohibit the importation into its territory of arms and ammunition, as well as of materials exclusively used for the manufacture of arms and ammunition.

An Imperial Edict has been issued on the 25th of August, 1901 forbidding said importation for a term of two years. New Edicts may be issued subsequently extending this by other successive terms of two years in case of necessity recognized by the Powers.

ARTICLE VI

By an Imperial Edict dated the 29th of May, 1901, His Majesty the Emperor of China agreed to pay the Powers an indemnity of four hundred and fifty millions of Haikwan Taels. This sum represents the total amount of the indemnities for States, companies or societies, [and] private individuals. . . .

ARTICLE VII

The Chinese Government has agreed that the quarter occupied by the legations shall be considered as one specially reserved for their use and placed under their exclusive control, in which Chinese shall not have the right to reside and which may be made defensible. . . .

ARTICLE VIII

The Chinese Government has consented to raze the forts of [Dagu] and those which might impede free communication between Peking and the sea; steps have been taken for carrying this out.

ARTICLE IX

The Chinese Government has conceded the right to the Powers in the protocol annexed to the letter of the 16th of January, 1901, to occupy certain points, to be determined by an agreement between them, for the maintenance of open communication between the capital and the sea. The points occupied by the powers are [then named].

ARTICLE X

The Chinese Government has agreed to post and to have published during two years in all district cities the following Imperial Edicts:

    a. Edict of the 1st of February, prohibiting forever, under pain of death, membership in any antiforeign society.

b. Edicts of the 13th and 21st February, 29th April, and 19th August, enumerating the punishments inflicted on the guilty.

c. Edict of the 19th of August, 1901, prohibiting examinations in all cities where foreigners were massacred or subjected to cruel treatment.

d. Edict of the 1st of February, 1901, declaring all governors-general, governors, and provincial or local officials responsible for order in their respective districts, and that in case of new antiforeign troubles or other infractions of the treaties which shall not be immediately repressed and the authors of which shall not have been punished, these officials shall be immediately dismissed, without possibility of being given new functions or new honors.

The posting of these edicts is being carried on throughout the Empire.

## ARTICLE XI

The Chinese Government has agreed to negotiate the amendments deemed necessary by the foreign Governments to the treaties of commerce and navigation and other subjects concerning commercial relations, with the object of facilitating them. . . .

## ARTICLE XII

An Imperial Edict of the 24th of July, 1901 reformed the Office of Foreign Affairs [Zongli Yamen], on the lines indicated by the Powers, that is to say, transformed it into a Ministry of Foreign Affairs (Wai-wu Bu), which takes precedence over the six other Ministries of State. The same edict appointed the principal members of this Ministry.

An agreement has also been reached concerning the modification of Court ceremonial as regards the reception of foreign Representatives and has been the subject of several notes from the Chinese Plenipotentiaries, the substance of which is embodied in a memorandum herewith annexed. . . .

The present final Protocol has been drawn up in twelve identical copies and signed by all the Plenipotentiaries of the Contracting Countries. One copy shall be given to each of the foreign Plenipotentiaries, and one copy shall be given to the Chinese Plenipotentiaries.

Peking, 7th September, 1901

Dun Jen Li, *China in Transition, 1517–1911* (New York: Van Nostrand Reinhold, 1969), pp. 288–291.

## 5. THE MANIFESTO OF THE REVOLUTIONARY ALLIANCE (*TONGMENGHUI*) (1905)

Issued in Tokyo at the founding of Sun Yat-sen's Revolutionary Alliance, this manifesto represented the first revolutionary organization's attempt in that period to set forth a program beyond ousting the Manchus. The first two goals uphold nationalism; the third, republicanism; and the fourth, a somewhat ambiguous "people's livelihood." Sun took the idea about the state's seizing the unearned increment on land values from the American economist Henry George.

> We recall that, since the beginning of our nation the Chinese have always ruled China; although at times alien peoples have usurped the rule, yet our ancestors were able to drive them out and restore Chinese sovereignty so that they could hand down the nation to posterity. Now the men of Han [i.e., the Chinese] have raised a righteous [or patriotic] army to exterminate the northern barbarians. This is a . . . great righteous cause, . . . a national revolution. . . . [We] proclaim to the world in utmost sincerity the outline of the present revolution and the fundamental plan for the future administration of the nation.
>
> 1. Drive out the Tartars: The Manchus [in the seventeenth century] . . . conquered China, and enslaved our Chinese people. Those who opposed them were killed by the hundreds of thousands, and our Chinese have been a people without a nation for two hundred and sixty years. The extreme cruelties and tyrannies of the Manchu government have now reached their limit. With the righteous army poised against them, we will overthrow that government, and restore our sovereign rights. . . .
> 2. Restore China: China is the China of the Chinese. The government of China should be in the hands of the Chinese. After driving out the Tartars we must restore our national state.
> 3. Establish the Republic: Now our revolution is based on equality, in order to establish a republican government. All our people are equal and all enjoy political rights; the president will be publicly chosen by the people of the country. The parliament will be made up of members publicly chosen by the people of the country. A constitution of the Chinese Republic will be enacted, and every person must abide by it. . . .
> 4. Equalize land ownership: The good fortune of civilization is to be shared equally by all the people of the nation. We should improve our

social and economic organization, and assess the value of all the land in the country. Its present price shall be received by the owner, but all increases in value resulting from reform and social improvements after the revolution shall belong to the state, to be shared by all the people, in order to create a socialist state, where each family within the empire can be well supported, each person satisfied, and no one fail to secure employment. . . .

The above four points will be carried out in three steps in due order. . . . Of these three periods the first is the period in which the Military Government leads the people in eradicating all traditional evils and abuses; the second is the period in which the Military Government gives the power of local self-government to the people while retaining general control over national affairs; the third is the period in which the Military Government is divested of its powers, and the government will by itself manage the national affairs under the constitution. It is hoped that our people will proceed in due order and cultivate their free and equal status; the foundation of the Chinese Republic will be entirely based on this.

J. Mason Gentzler, *Changing China: Readings in the History of China from the Opium War to the Present* (New York: Praeger, 1977), pp. 134–136.

## 6. CHEN DUXIU'S "CALL TO YOUTH" FROM *NEW YOUTH* (1915)

The importance of the journal *New Youth* in awakening students and intellectuals in the May Fourth movement cannot be exaggerated. Here the founder of the journal challenges Chinese youth to be aggressive in efforts to change China. Above all, in the face of enormous difficulties and challenges, Chen calls for practicality and the use of science in solving problems.

The Chinese compliment others by saying, "He acts like an old man although still young." Englishmen and Americans encourage one another by saying, "Keep young while growing old." Such is one respect in which the different ways of thought of the East and West are manifested. Youth is like early spring, like the rising sun, like trees and grass in bud, like a newly sharpened blade. It is the most valuable period of life. The function of youth in society is the same as that of a fresh and vital cell in a human body. In the processes of metabolism, the old and the rotten are incessantly eliminated to be replaced by the fresh and living. . . . [I] place my plea before the young and vital youth, in the hope that they will achieve self-awareness, and begin to struggle. What is this self-awareness? It is to be conscious of the value and responsibility of one's young life and vitality, to maintain one's self-respect, which should not be lowered. What is the struggle? It is to exert one's intellect, discard resolutely the old and the rotten, regard them as enemies and as the flood or savage beasts, keep away from their neighborhood and refuse to be contaminated by their poisonous germs. . . . O youth, is there anyone who takes upon himself such responsibilities? As for understanding what is right and wrong, in order that you may make your choice, I carefully propose the following six principles, and hope you will give them your calm consideration.

1) Be independent, not servile.

. . . . Emancipation means freeing oneself from the bondage of slavery and achieving a completely independent and free personality. I have hands and feet, and I can earn my own living. I have a mouth and a tongue, and I can voice my own likes and dislikes. I have a mind, and I can determine my own beliefs. I will absolutely not let others do these things in my behalf, nor should I assume an overlordship and enslave others. For once the independent personality is recognized, all matters of conduct, all rights and privileges, and all belief should be left to the natural ability of each person; there is definitely no reason why one should blindly follow others. . . . [It should be clear that] loyalty, filial piety, chastity and righteousness are a slavish morality.

2) Be progressive, not conservative.

Now our country still has not awakened from its long dream, and isolates itself by going down the old rut. . . . All our traditional ethics, law, scholarship, rites and customs are survivals of feudalism. When compared with the achievement of the white race, there is a difference of a thousand years in thought, although we live in the same period. Revering only the history of the twenty-four dynasties and making no plans for progress and improvement, our people will be turned out of this twentieth-century world, and be lodged in the dark ditches fit only for slaves, cattle, and horses. . . . The progress of the world is like that of a fleet horse, galloping and galloping onward. Whatever cannot skillfully change itself and progress along with the world will find itself eliminated by natural selection because of failure to adapt to the environment. Then what can be said to defend conservatism!

3) Be aggressive, not retiring.

. . . . It is impossible to avoid the struggle for survival, and so long as one draws breath there can be no place where one can retire for a tranquil hermit's life. It is our natural obligation in life to advance in spite of numerous difficulties. . . .

4) Be cosmopolitan, not isolationist.

. . . . The prosperity or decline, rise or fall of a nation of today depends half on domestic administration, and half on influences from outside the country. . . . If at this point one still raises a particularist theory of history and of national circumstances and hopes thereby to resist the current, then this still indicates the spirit of an isolationist country and a lack of knowledge of the world. When its citizens lack knowledge of the world, how can a nation expect to survive in it?

5) Be utilitarian, not formalistic.

. . . . The age-long precepts of ethical convention, the hopes and purposes of the people—there is nothing which does not run counter to the practical life of society today. If we do not re-string our bow and renew our effort, there will be no way to revive the strength of our nation, and our society will never see a peaceful day. . . . Though a thing is of gold or of jade, if it is of no practical use, then it is of less value than coarse cloth, grain, manure, or dirt. That which brings no benefit to the practical life of an individual or of society is all empty formalism and the stuff of cheats. And even though it were bequeathed to us by our ancestors, taught by the sages, advocated by the government and worshipped by society, the stuff of cheats is still not worth one cent.

6) Be scientific, not imaginative.

What is science? It is our general conception of matter which, being the sum of objective phenomena as analyzed by subjective reason, contains no contradiction within itself. What is imagination? It first oversteps the realm of objective phenomena, and then discards reason itself; it is something constructed out of thin air, consisting of hypotheses without proof, and all the existing wisdom of mankind cannot be made to find reason in it or explain its laws and principles. . . . To explain truth by science means proving everything with fact. Although the process is slower than that of imagination and arbitrary decision, yet every step taken is on firm ground; it is different from those imaginative flights which eventually cannot advance even one inch. The amount of truth in the universe is boundless, and the fertile areas in the realm of science awaiting the pioneer are immense! Youth, take up the task!

Ssu-yu Teng and John K. Fairbank, *China's Response to the West: A Documentary Survey, 1839–1923* (Cambridge: Harvard University Press, 1954), pp. 240–246.

## 7. THE THREE PRINCIPLES OF THE PEOPLE, SUN YAT-SEN (1924)

The "Three Principles of the People" is the basic ideology of the Nationalist Party (Guomindang), set forth by Sun and later championed by Chiang Kai-shek. It reveals a strong animus against the actions of Western nations in China as it reflects knowledge about and sometimes appreciation of some aspects of the Western political system. In its analysis of the Chinese economy, it breaks sharply with the Marxist view in its claim that the root problem in China is poverty and not the uneven distribution of wealth.

### NATIONALISM

. . . . In view of the ruthless exploitation of China by foreign powers, China is in fact a subcolony, a status that is much worse than that of a colony. Korea is a colony of Japan and Annam is a colony of France; the Koreans and the Annamese are the slaves of Japan and France respectively. Though we often use the terms "slaves without a country" to describe them, do we realize that our position is really much worse than theirs? China has concluded unequal treaties with many countries all of whom, because of the existence of these treaties, are China's masters. In fact China has become a colony of all these countries to whom the Chinese are merely slaves. Which one is better, to be slaves to one country or to be slaves to many countries?
. . . Today our urgent task is to restore our lost nationalism and to use the combined force of our 400 million people to avenge the wrongs of the world. . . . Only when imperialism is eliminated can there be peace for all mankind. To achieve this goal, we should first rejuvenate Chinese nationalism and restore China's position as a sovereign state.

### DEMOCRACY

There is a difference between the European and Chinese concept of freedom. While the Europeans struggle for personal freedom, we struggle for national freedom. As far as we are concerned, personal freedom should never be too excessive. In fact, in order to win national freedom, we should not hesitate to sacrifice our personal freedom. . . . The revolutionaries in Europe and America are fond of saying that men are born equal, and this concept of the natural equality of men was incorporated into such documents as the Declaration of Independence during the American Revolution. . . . But is it really true that men are born equal? No stretch of land is completely level; nor are there two flowers exactly identical. Since there is no such thing as equality in the sphere of nature, how can there be equality among men? True equality . . . has nothing to do with equality in achievement; it merely means that all people in a democratic society should enjoy the same political rights.

Among the popular rights in a democracy the foremost is the right to vote . . . ; besides the right to vote for officials, the people should also have the right to recall them.

Insofar as the enactment of legislation is concerned, the people should have the right of initiative as well as the right of referendum. Only when the people have these four rights (election, recall, initiative, and referendum) can they be said to have direct control over their government or to enjoy full democracy. . . .

Now that the people have four rights to control their government, what powers should the government have so that it can function like a piece of well-oiled machinery and serve the interests of the people? . . . I believe that we should establish a five-power government in which the traditional Chinese powers of censorship and examination would be merged with the executive, legislative, and judiciary powers of the West; . . . [such a] government, once established, would be the most advanced, most progressive in the world.

## PEOPLE'S LIVELIHOOD

The purpose of social progress cannot be more than the realization of the utmost good for the largest number of people in the society, and such realization lies in the harmonization, rather than conflict, between different economic interests . . . the law of social progress is man's continuous struggle for existence rather than class struggle as enunciated by Karl Marx.

What is the basic fact about China? It is the grinding poverty of the Chinese people. A privileged class of the extremely wealthy does not exist in China; instead, there is such a thing as universal poverty. The so-called disparity in wealth is really a disparity between the poor and the extremely poor, since all Chinese are undeniably poor.

Different countries have different ways of solving their land problem. . . . The true solution of our land problem is to make sure that farmers own the land which they till; land ownership by tillers is in fact the final goal of the principle of people's livelihood. Though China does not have "great land-lords" in the Western sense, more than 90 percent of the farmers till land they do not own. This is a serious problem. Unless this problem is solved, it is senseless to talk about the principle of people's livelihood. According to our investigation, a landlord usually receives 60 percent of the crops as rent, leaving only 40 percent to be retained by the tillers. How can a situation be more unfair? . . .

To solve the problem of people's livelihood, we should [also] have the political power to protect our native industry so that it will not be encroached upon by foreign powers. Enchained by unequal treaties, China today not only cannot protect her own industry but is also forced to protect foreign industry at her own expense. . . . In short, we must adopt the political means to abolish the unequal treaties so that we ourselves can control our own customs.

Dun Jen Li, *The Road to Communism: China Since 1912* (New York: Van Nostrand Reinhold, 1969), pp. 115–125.

## 8. FUNDAMENTALS OF NATIONAL RECONSTRUCTION, SUN YAT-SEN (1924)

Sun here sets forth his vision of the path toward constitutional government and of the eventual government structure. The central structure was realized with the establishment of Chiang Kai-shek's government in 1928, but the Republic of China remained in the period of political tutelage until the late 1980s when Lee Teng-hui lifted martial law and opened up the political system to greater competition.

The order of national reconstruction shall be divided into three stages: first, the stage of military rule; second, the stage of political tutelage; third, the stage of constitutional government.

In the stage of military rule, the whole administrative system shall be placed under military rule. The government on the one hand should employ its armed forces to eradicate all internal obstacles and, on the other, disseminate its principles so that the people may be enlightened and national unification hastened.

As soon as a province is completely restored to order, the stage of political tutelage shall commence and the military stage shall come to an end. In the stage of political tutelage, the government should send persons, trained and qualified through examination, to various counties (*xian*) to assist the people in the preparation of self-government. . . . A census of the whole county must be properly taken; a survey of its land must be completed; its police and local defense forces must be satisfactorily maintained; road-building and repairing within its boundaries must be successfully carried out; and its people must receive training on the exercise of the four powers [suffrage, recall, initiative, and referendum], fulfill their duties as citizens, and pledge themselves to carry out the revolutionary principles.

The stage of constitutional government will commence in a province when all the counties of the province have attained complete self-government. . . . In this stage, the principle of equilibrium shall be adopted in reference to the powers of the central and the provincial government. Matters which, by nature, require uniform action on the part of the nation shall be assigned to the central government; matters which, by nature, should be dealt with locally shall be assigned to the local government. There shall be no inclination to either centralization or decentralization of power.

At the beginning of constitutional government, the central government should complete the formation of the five yuan to [create] a five-power government. The five yuan are named in the following order: the Executive Yuan, the Legislative Yuan, the Judicial Yuan, the Examination Yuan, and the Censor Yuan. . . . A Draft Constitution should be prepared by the Legislative Yuan in accordance with the *Fundamentals of National Reconstruction* and the experiences gained in the stages of political tutelage and constitutional government. . . . When more than one half of the provinces in the country have reached the constitutional stage, i.e., when they have completely adopted local self-government, the People's Congress shall be convened to decide on and promulgate the Constitution. After the promulgation of the Constitution, the administrative power of the central government shall be vested in the People's Congress.

Dun Jen Li, *The Road to Communism: China Since 1912* (New York: Van Nostrand Reinhold, 1969), pp. 125–128.

## 9. REPORT ON AN INVESTIGATION OF THE PEASANT
## MOVEMENT IN HUNAN, MAO ZEDONG (1927)

In this report Mao departs from the orthodox Marxist-Leninist line that the vanguard of the revolution must be the urban proletariat; he describes the explosive power of the peasantry that he found while organizing peasant associations in the Hunan countryside. Mao's apocalyptic language and readiness to embrace violence and terror in the cause of revolution are note-worthy.

### THE IMPORTANCE OF THE PEASANT PROBLEM

During my recent visit to Hunan I made a first-hand investigation of con-ditions in the five districts of Xiangtan, Xiangxiang, Hengshan, Liling, and Changsha. In the thirty-two days from January 4 to February 5, I called together fact-finding conferences in villages and county seats, which were attended by experienced peasants and by comrades working in the peasant movement, and I listened attentively to their reports and collected a great deal of material.

The present upsurge of the peasant movement is a colossal event. In a very short time, in China's central, southern and northern provinces, sever-al hundred million peasants will rise like a mighty storm, like a hurricane, a force so swift and violent that no power, however great, will be able to hold it back. They will smash all the shackles that bind them and rush forward along the road to liberation. They will sweep all the imperialists, warlords, corrupt officials, local tyrants and evil gentry into their graves.

### DOWN WITH THE LOCAL TYRANTS AND EVIL GENTRY!
### ALL POWER TO THE PEASANT ASSOCIATIONS!

The main targets of attack by the peasants are the local tyrants, the evil gen-try and the lawless landlords, but in passing they also hit out against patri-archal ideas and institutions, against the corrupt officials in the cities and against bad practices and customs in the rural areas. In force and momen-tum the attack is tempestuous; those who bow before it survive and those who resist perish. As a result, the privileges which the feudal landlords enjoyed for thousands of years are being shattered to pieces. Every bit of the dignity and prestige built up by the landlords is being swept into the dust. With the collapse of the power of the landlords, the peasant associations have now become the sole organs of authority and the popular slogan "All power to the peasant associations" has become a reality.

## "IT'S TERRIBLE!" OR "IT'S FINE!"

The peasants' revolt disturbed the gentry's sweet dreams. When the news from the countryside reached the cities, it caused an immediate uproar among the gentry. Soon after my arrival in Changsha, I met all sorts of people and picked up a good deal of gossip. From the middle social strata upwards to the Guomindang right-wingers, there was not a single person who did not sum up the whole business in the phrase, "It's terrible!" . . . But, as already mentioned, the fact is that the great peasant masses have risen to fulfill their historic mission and that the forces of rural democracy have risen to overthrow the forces of rural feudalism. . . . This is a marvelous feat never before achieved, not just in forty, but in thousands of years. It's fine. It is not "terrible" at all. . . . What the peasants are doing is absolutely right; what they are doing is fine! "It's fine!"

## THE QUESTION OF "GOING TOO FAR"

Then there is another section of people who say, "Yes, peasant associations are necessary, but they are going rather too far." This is the opinion of the middle-of-the-roaders. But what is the actual situation? True, the peasants are in a sense "unruly" in the countryside. . . . At the slightest provocation they make arrests, crown the arrested with tall paper hats, and parade them through the villages, saying, "You dirty landlords, now you know who we are." Doing whatever they like and turning everything upside down, they have created a kind of terror in the countryside. This is what some people call "going too far," or "exceeding the proper limits in righting a wrong," or "really too much."

Such talk may seem plausible, but in fact it is wrong. . . . A revolution is not a dinner party, or writing an essay, or painting a picture, or doing embroidery; it cannot be so refined, so leisurely and gentle, so temperate, kind, courteous, restrained and magnanimous. A revolution is an insurrection, an act of violence by which one class overthrows another. A rural revolution is a revolution by which the peasantry overthrows the power of the feudal landlord class.

J. Mason Gentzler, *Changing China: Readings in the History of China from the Opium War to the Present* (New York: Praeger, 1977), pp. 217–222.

## 10. THE JIANGXI SOVIET LAND LAW OF 1932

This law produced the first Chinese Communist land reform effort; it also produced such social unrest and violence that it was halted and replaced by the Guomindang land law that simply limited rent to $37\frac{1}{2}$ percent of the harvest. This law raised the thorny issue of categorizing peasants as rich, middle, and poor and the ensuing reality of class struggle. Note the degree of detail, the various loopholes in the redistribution regulations, the antibourgeois and antireligion stipulations, and evidence of ways that rural elites tried to evade the redistribution.

A. WHOSE LAND SHOULD BE CONFISCATED?

1. Land (including land rented to tenants), houses, and all other forms of property, including household items, that belonged to members of the gentry and landlords are to be confiscated.
2. Land, houses, and all other forms of property, including household items, that belong to family shrines, Buddhist or Daoist temples, clan or social organizations are to be confiscated.
3. Land owned by rich peasants should be confiscated.

B. WHO SHOULD RECEIVE LAND?

1. The amount of land to be distributed is the same for all tenant farmers and poor peasants. Whether the land of the middle peasants should be redistributed so as to assure that they have the same amount as that of tenant farmers and poor peasants depends upon the decision to be made by the middle peasants themselves. If the majority of them so desires, the land of the middle peasants will be redistributed, even though the minority does not agree. If the majority of the middle peasants does not want its land to be redistributed, its land will not be redistributed and it can keep the land it presently has; but its decision, in this case, does not bind the minority of the middle peasants which, if it so chooses, can participate in the redistribution program. This provision, however, does not affect land distribution among the middle peasants that had been completed before December 31, 1931. The completed distribution should remain effective and should not be altered in any fashion.
2. The relatives of a farm laborer shall receive land. He himself should also receive land if he is unemployed. (By unemployment is meant the lack of employment for most of the year. It does not include temporary unemployment that lasts only a short period of time.)
3. Independent artisans (including artisans who have apprentices working for them but excluding those who have hired workers), physicians, and teachers are to receive land if they have been unemployed for six months or longer.

4. Shop owners and their relatives shall not receive any land.

5. Rich peasants will receive poor land in accordance with the size of their respective households as well as the number of able-bodied workers in them. If a rich peasant household has able-bodied workers, each of them will receive a certain amount of poor land as his share. If none of its members can work, a subsidy in the form of poor land will be provided, but this subsidy shall not be more than two-thirds of the land granted to others.

6. Beginning with the operation of this statute, members of the gentry, landlords, and members of counterrevolutionary organizations will not be entitled to land distribution.

7. There are cases in which members of the gentry, landlords, and counterrevolutionary rich peasants have adopted the method of "invitation marriage" by marrying their wives or daughters to farm laborers, tenant farmers, poor or middle peasants for the sole purpose of preserving their own properties. The properties in question, including houses, shall be confiscated by the government forthwith. However, the farm laborers, tenant farmers, poor or middle peasants who have been thus married will receive their fair share when the confiscated properties, including houses, are redistributed.

8. As for the adopted sons or daughters of members of the gentry, landlords, and those rich peasants who have in the past been members of counterrevolutionary organizations, they are not entitled to land distribution if they have lived the same kind of life and have had the same kind of education as their foster parents. If on the other hand they have been treated like slaves even though they are adopted sons or daughters, they are entitled to land distribution.

9. As for Buddhist monks and nuns, Taoist priests, magicians and sorcerers, fortunetellers, geomancers, and other feudal remnants as well as Protestant ministers and Catholic priests, they are not entitled to land distribution if religion is their main means of earning a livelihood. If land has been granted to them, it should be returned. If on the other hand religion is only their avocation and farming is in fact their main occupation, they are entitled to land distribution if people in their respective communities approve.

10. Beginning with the operation of this statute, the sons or daughters of the members of the gentry or landlords are no longer entitled to land distribution even though they have been adopted by poor laborers or peasants as their own children.

11. Members of the gentry, landlords, and those rich peasants who have in the past assumed the leadership in opposing land distribution of their own accord, together with all of their relatives, are not entitled to land distribution. If land has been granted to them, it shall be returned to the government.

12. Rural merchants who, prior to the revolution, had been able to support their families through trade and commerce are not entitled to land distribution. If land has been granted to them, it shall be returned to the government. They will be granted land in the same fashion as independent artisans, however, had they become unemployed after the revolution.

13. Unemployed peddlers are entitled to land distribution.

14. A woman can dispose of her land the way she wishes when she is married.

Dun Jen Li, *The Road to Communism: China Since 1912* (New York: Van Nostrand Reinhold, 1969), pp. 143–148.

## 11. TALKS AT THE YAN'AN FORUM ON LITERATURE AND ART, MAO ZEDONG (1942)

At the Yan'an forum, Mao laid down his dictum that literature and art must serve the state and the "people" as defined by the Party. In general, the policies set forth in this short excerpt set the stage for the contentious and often violent relationship between the CCP and intellectuals. The forum took place in the context of the rectification movement and writings by authors like Ding Ling and Wang Shiwei.

The first problem is: For whom are our art and literature intended?

This problem, as a matter of fact, was solved long ago by Marxists, and especially by Lenin. As far back as 1905 Lenin emphatically pointed out that our art and literature should "serve the millions upon millions of working people." . . .Who, then, are the people? The overwhelming majority, constituting more than 90 percent of our total population, are the workers, peasants, soldiers and the urban petty bourgeoisie. . . . Our art and literature should be intended for these four kinds of people. To serve them we must take the standpoint of the proletariat instead of that of the petty-bourgeoisie. Today writers and artists who cling to their individualistic petty-bourgeois standpoint cannot truly serve the mass of revolutionary workers, peasants and soldiers, but will be interested mainly in the small number of petty-bourgeois intellectuals. . . .

A complete solution of this problem will require a long time, maybe eight or ten years. But, no matter how long it takes, we must find the solution, and it must be unequivocal and complete. Our artists and writers must fulfill this task; they must gradually shift their standpoint over to the side of the workers, peasants and soldiers, to the side of the proletariat, by going into their midst and plunging into the actual struggle and by studying Marxism and society. Only in this way can we have art and literature that are genuinely for the workers, peasants and soldiers, and genuinely proletarian. . . .

. . . . In the world today all culture, all art and literature belong to definite classes and follow definite political lines. There is in fact no such thing as art for art's sake, art which stands above classes or art which runs parallel to or remains independent of politics. Proletarian art and literature are part of the whole cause of the proletarian revolution, in the words of Lenin, "cog and wheel" of a single mechanism. Therefore the Party's artistic and literary activity occupies a definite and assigned position in the Party's total revolutionary work and is subordinated to the prescribed revolutionary task of the Party in a given revolutionary period.

J. Mason Gentzler, *Changing China: Readings in the History of China from the Opium War to the Present* (New York: Praeger, 1977), pp. 230–233.

## 12. ON THE PEOPLE'S DEMOCRATIC DICTATORSHIP, MAO ZEDONG (1949)

In this famous essay, Mao explains the juxtaposition of democracy and dictatorship that was at the root of the so-called New Democracy at the beginning of the People's Republic. Though he talks of people who can be defined as "not people," the general tone of the piece is of inclusion, coalition, united front, and moderation; the vision is of a long gradual process culminating in the "Great Harmony" of a classless society.

Twenty-four years have passed since Sun Yat-sen's death, and the Chinese revolution, led by the Communist Party of China, has made tremendous advances both in theory and practice and has radically changed the face of China. Up to now the principal and fundamental experience the Chinese people have gained is twofold:

1.  Internally, arouse the masses of the people. That is, unite the working class, the peasantry, the urban petty bourgeoisie and the national bourgeoisie, form a domestic united front under the leadership of the working class, and advance from this to the establishment of a state which is a people's democratic dictatorship under the leadership of the working class and based on the alliance of workers and peasants.

2.  Externally, unite in a common struggle with those nations of the world which treat us as equals and unite with the peoples of all countries. That is, ally ourselves with the Soviet Union, with the People's Democracies and with the proletariat and the broad masses of the people in all other countries, and form an international united front.

"You are leaning to one side." Exactly. The forty years' experience of Sun Yat-sen and the twenty-eight years' experience of the Communist Party have taught us to lean to one side, and we are firmly convinced that in order to win victory and consolidate it we must lean to one side. In the light of the experiences accumulated in these forty years and these twenty-eight years, all Chinese without exception must lean either to the side of imperialism or to the side of socialism. Sitting on the fence will not do, nor is there a third road. We oppose the Chiang Kai-shek reactionaries who lean to the side of imperialism, and we also oppose the illusions about a third road.

"You are dictatorial." My dear sirs, you are right, that is just what we are. All the experience the Chinese people have accumulated through several decades teaches us to enforce the people's democratic dictatorship, that is, to deprive the reactionaries of the right to speak and let the people alone have that right.

Who are the people? At the present stage in China, they are the working class, the peasantry, the urban petty bourgeoisie and the national bourgeoisie. These classes, led by the working class and the Communist Party, unite to form their own state and elect their own government; they enforce their dictatorship over the running dogs of imperialism—the landlord class and bureaucrat bourgeoisie, as well as the representatives of those classes, the Guomindang reactionaries and their accomplices—suppress them, allow them only to behave themselves and not to be unruly in word or deed. If they speak or act in an unruly way, they will be promptly stopped and punished. Democracy is practiced within the ranks of the people, who enjoy the rights of freedom of speech, assembly, association and so on. The right to vote belongs only to the people, not to the reactionaries. The combination of these two aspects, democracy for the people and dictatorship over the reactionaries, is the people's democratic dictatorship.

"Don't you want to abolish state power?" Yes, we do, but not right now; we cannot do it yet. Why? Because imperialism still exists, because domestic reaction still exists, because classes still exist in our country. Our present task is to strengthen the people's state apparatus—mainly the people's army, the people's police and the people's courts—in order to consolidate national defense and protect the people's interests. Given this condition, China can develop steadily, under the leadership of the working class and the Communist Party, from an agricultural into an industrial country and from a new-democratic into a socialist and communist society, can abolish classes and realize the Great Harmony.

J. Mason Gentzler, *Changing China: Readings in the History of China from the Opium War to the Present* (New York: Praeger, 1977), pp. 242–246.

# 13. THE MARRIAGE LAW OF THE PEOPLE'S REPUBLIC OF CHINA (1950)

This law was the logical conclusion to the May Fourth period's drive to destroy patriarchal, parental, and age dominance in the family system. Women hereby gained at least legal equality with men; betrothed marriages, male dominance in family affairs, and such evils as infanticide were outlawed. This law followed an earlier one set forth during the Jiangxi Soviet period; it was further elaborated upon by a law in 1980.

CHAPTER 1: GENERAL PRINCIPLES

ARTICLE 1. The feudal marriage system which is based on arbitrary and compulsory arrangement and the superiority of man over woman and ignores the children's interests shall be abolished.

The New-Democratic marriage system, which is based on the free choice of partners, on monogamy, on equal rights for both sexes, and on the protection of the lawful interests of women and children, shall be put into effect.

ARTICLE 2. Bigamy, concubinage, child betrothal, interference with the remarriage of widows, and the exaction of money or gifts in connection with marriages, shall be prohibited.

## CHAPTER 2: THE MARRIAGE CONTRACT

ARTICLE 3. Marriage shall be based upon the complete willingness of the two partners. Neither party shall use compulsion and no third party shall be allowed to interfere.

ARTICLE 4. A marriage can be contracted only after the man has reached 20 years of age and the woman 18 years of age.

## CHAPTER 3: RIGHTS AND DUTIES OF HUSBAND AND WIFE

ARTICLE 7. Husband and wife are companions living together and shall enjoy equal status in the home.

ARTICLE 8. Husband and wife are in duty bound to love, respect, assist and look after each other, to live in harmony, to engage in productive work, to care for the children and to strive jointly for the welfare of the family and for the building up of the new society.

ARTICLE 9. Both husband and wife shall have the right to free choice of occupation and free participation in work or in social activities.

ARTICLE 10. Both husband and wife shall have equal rights in the possession and management of family property.

ARTICLE 11. Both husband and wife shall have the right to use his or her own family name.

ARTICLE 12. Both husband and wife shall have the right to inherit each other's property.

## CHAPTER 4: RELATIONS BETWEEN PARENTS AND CHILDREN

ARTICLE 13. Parents have the duty to rear and to educate their children; the children have the duty to support and assist their parents. Neither the parents nor the children shall maltreat or desert one another.

The foregoing provision also applies to foster-parents and foster-children. Infanticide by drowning and similar criminal acts are strictly prohibited.

ARTICLE 14. Parents and children shall have the right to inherit one another's property.

ARTICLE 15. Children born out of wedlock shall enjoy the same rights as children born in lawful wedlock. No person shall be allowed to harm them or discriminate against them. . . .

ARTICLE 16. Husband or wife shall not maltreat or discriminate against children born of a previous marriage.

## CHAPTER 5: DIVORCE

ARTICLE 17. Divorce shall be granted when husband and wife both desire it. In the event of either the husband or the wife alone insisting upon divorce, it may be granted only when mediation by the district people's government and the judicial organ has failed to bring about a reconciliation. . . .

ARTICLE 18. The husband shall not apply for a divorce when his wife is with child. He may apply for divorce only one year after the birth of the child. In the case of a woman applying for divorce, this restriction does not apply.

ARTICLE 19. The consent of a member of the revolutionary army on active service who maintains correspondence with his or her family must first be obtained before his or her spouse can apply for divorce. . . .

## CHAPTER 6: MAINTENANCE AND EDUCATION OF CHILDREN AFTER DIVORCE

ARTICLE 20. The blood ties between parents and children do not end with the divorce of the parents. No matter whether the father or the mother acts as guardian of the children, they still remain the children of both parties. After divorce, both parents still have the duty to support and educate their children. After divorce, the guiding principle is to allow the mother to have custody of a baby still being breast-fed. After the weaning of the child, if a dispute arises between the two parties over the guardianship and an agreement cannot be reached, the people's court shall render a decision in accordance with the interests of the child.

ARTICLE 21. If, after divorce, the mother is given custody of a child, the father shall be responsible for the whole or part of the necessary cost of the maintenance and education of the child. Both parties shall reach an agreement regarding the amount and the duration of such maintenance and education. In the case where the two parties fail to reach an agreement, the people's court shall render a decision. . . .

J. Mason Gentzler, *Changing China: Readings in the History of China from the Opium War to the Present* (New York: Praeger, 1977), pp. 268–272.

## 14. DECISION OF THE CENTRAL COMMITTEE OF THE CCP CONCERNING THE GREAT PROLETARIAN CULTURAL REVOLUTION (1966)

Published in August 1966, this document sets forth the general players and techniques in the tragic drama that unfolded from 1966 to 1976. Mao's effort to destroy the party he built was based both upon policies (which path toward socialism China would take) and personal power considerations (eliminating the perceived challenges of Liu Shaoqi and Deng Xiaoping). The emphasis on Mao's thought reflects the cult that had grown up around him, a result in part of the efforts of Lin Biao and the People's Liberation Army.

The great proletarian cultural revolution now unfolding is a great revolution that touches people to their very souls and constitutes a new stage in the development of the socialist revolution in our country, a stage which is both broader and deeper. . . . Although the bourgeoisie has been overthrown, it is still trying to use the old ideas, culture, customs, and habits of the exploiting classes to corrupt the masses, capture their minds and endeavor to stage a come-back. The proletariat must do the exact opposite: it must meet head-on every challenge of the bourgeoisie in the ideological field and use the new ideas, culture, customs and habits of the proletariat to change the mental outlook of the whole of society. At present, our objective is to struggle against and overthrow these persons in authority who are taking the capitalist road, to criticize and repudiate the reactionary bourgeoisie and all other exploiting classes and to transform education, literature and art and all other parts of the superstructure not in correspondence with the socialist economic base, so as to facilitate the consolidation and development of the socialist system.

The masses of the workers, peasants, soldiers, revolutionary intellectuals and revolutionary cadres form the main force in this great cultural revolution. Large numbers of revolutionary young people, previously unknown, have become courageous and daring pathbreakers. They are vigorous in action and intelligent. Through the media of big-character posters and great debates, they argue things out, expose and criticize thoroughly, and launch resolute attacks on the open and hidden representatives of the bourgeoisie. In such a great revolutionary movement, it is hardly avoidable that they should show short-comings of one kind or another; however, their general revolutionary orientation has been correct from the beginning. This is the main current in the great proletarian cultural revolution.

In the great proletarian cultural revolution, the only method is for the masses to liberate themselves, and any method of doing things in their stead must not be used.

Trust the masses, rely on them and respect their initiative. Cast out fear. Don't be afraid of disturbances. Chairman Mao has often told us that revolution cannot be so very refined, so gentle, so temperate, kind, courteous, restrained and magnanimous. Let the masses educate themselves in this great revolutionary movement and learn to distinguish between right and wrong and between correct and incorrect ways of doing things. Make the fullest use of big-character posters and great debates to argue matters out, so that the masses can clarify the correct views, criticize the wrong views and expose all the ghosts and monsters. In this way the masses will be able to raise their political consciousness in the course of the struggle, enhance their abilities and talents, distinguish right from wrong and draw a clear line between ourselves and the enemy.

In the great proletarian cultural revolution, it is imperative to hold aloft the great red banner of Mao Zedong's thought and put proletarian politics in command. The movement for the creative study and application of Chairman Mao Zedong's works should be carried forward among the masses of the workers, peasants and soldiers, the cadres and the intellectuals, and Mao Zedong's thought should be taken as the guide to action in the cultural revolution. In this complex great cultural revolution, Party committees at all levels must study and apply Chairman Mao's works all the more conscientiously and in a creative way. In particular, they must study over and over again Chairman Mao's writings on the cultural revolution and on the Party's methods of leadership. . . . Party committees at all levels must abide by the directions given by Chairman Mao over the years, namely that they should thoroughly apply the mass line of "from the masses, to the masses" and that they should be pupils before they become teachers. They should try to avoid being one-sided or narrow. They should foster materialistic dialectics and oppose metaphysics and scholasticism. The great proletarian cultural revolution is bound to achieve brilliant victory under the leadership of the Central Committee of the Party headed by Comrade Mao Zedong.

J. Mason Gentzler, *Changing China: Readings in the History of China from the Opium War to the Present* (New York: Praeger, 1977), pp. 343–351.

## 15. BIG CHARACTER POSTER, "BOMBARD THE HEADQUARTERS," MAO ZEDONG (1966)

In this poster, Mao initiated open warfare on the Chinese Communist Party and its leadership. In the months following, hundreds of thousands of Red Guards flocked to Beijing to get a view of the man they knew as the Red Sun and the Great Helmsman.

> China's first Marxist-Leninist big-character poster [a reference to the poster by Nie Yuanzi, a philosophy instructor at Beijing University] and commentator's article on it in the *People's Daily* [*Renmin ribao*] are indeed superbly written! Comrades, please read them again. But in the last fifty days or so some leading comrades from the central down to the local levels have acted in a diametrically opposite way. Adopting the reactionary stand of the bourgeoisie, they have enforced a bourgeois dictatorship and struck down the surging movement of the great cultural revolution of the proletariat. They have stood facts on their head and juggled black and white, encircled and suppressed revolutionaries, stifled opinions differing from their own, imposed a white terror, and felt very pleased with themselves. They have puffed up the arrogance of the bourgeoisie and deflated the morale of the proletariat. How poisonous! Viewed in connection with the Right deviation in 1962 and the wrong tendency of 1964 which was "Left" in form but Right in essence, shouldn't this make one wide awake?

> Gregor Benton and Alan Hunter, eds., *Wild Lily, Prairie Fire: China's Road to Democracy, Yan'an to Tian'anmen, 1942–1989* (Princeton: Princeton University Press, 1995), p. 121.

## 16. "DEMOCRACY OR A NEW DICTATORSHIP," WEI JINGSHENG, PUBLISHED IN *EXPLORATIONS* (1979)

This excerpt from an essay by China's most famous dissident in the last quarter of the twentieth century expressed the desire for what he called in another context the Fifth Modernization, i.e., democracy. The essay was written as Democracy Wall, which had initially been allowed by Deng Xiaoping, was being closed. In Wei's trial, "Democracy or a New Dictatorship" was used against him as evidence of "counter-revolutionary agitation and propaganda" and of Wei's "incitement to overthrow the dictatorship of the proletariat."

EVERYONE in China knows that the Chinese social system is not democratic and that this lack of democracy has severely stunted every aspect of the country's social development over the past thirty years. In the face of this hard fact there are two choices before the Chinese people. Either to reform the social system if they want to develop their society and seek a swift increase in prosperity and economic resources; or, if they are content with a continuation of the Mao Zedong brand of proletarian dictatorship, then they cannot even talk of democracy, nor will they be able to realize the modernization of their lives and resources.

Where is China heading and in what sort of society do the people hope to live and work? The answer can be seen in the mood of the majority. It is this mood that brought about the present democratic movement. With the denial of Mao Zedong's style of dictatorship as its very prerequisite, the aim of this movement is to reform the social system and thereby enable the Chinese people to increase production and develop their lives to the full in a democratic social environment. This aim is not just the aim of a few isolated individuals but represents a whole trend in the development of Chinese society. Those who doubt this need only recall the April Fifth Movement in 1976 [the Tiananmen disturbances over the memorializing of Zhou Enlai], for those who were judged by the court in the minds of the people then, even when they were some of the most powerful in the country, have not escaped its ultimate verdict. . . .

Does Deng Xiaoping want democracy? No, he does not. He is unwilling to comprehend the misery of the common people. He is unwilling to allow the people to regain those powers usurped by ambitious careerists. He describes the struggle for democratic rights—a movement launched spontaneously by the people—as the actions of troublemakers who must be repressed. To resort to such measures to deal with people who criticize mistaken policies and demand social development shows that the government is very afraid of this popular movement. . . .

After [Deng] was reinstated in 1975, it seemed he was unwilling to follow Mao Zedong's dictatorial system and would instead care for the interests of the people. So the people eagerly looked up to him in the hope that he would realize their aspirations. They were even ready to shed their blood for him—as the Tiananmen Square incident showed. But was such support vested in his person alone? Certainly not. If he now wants to discard his mask and take steps to suppress the democratic movement then he certainly does not merit the people's trust and support. From his behavior it is clear that he is neither concerned with democracy nor does he any longer protect the people's interests. By deceiving the people to win their confidence he is following the path to dictatorship.

It has been demonstrated countless times throughout China's history that once the confidence of the people has been gained by deception, the dictators work without restraint—for as the ancients said: "He who can win the people's minds, can win the empire." Once masters of the nation, their private interests inevitably conflict with those of the people, and they must use repression against those who are struggling for the interests of the people themselves. So the crux of the matter is not who becomes master of the nation, but rather that the people must maintain firm control over their own nation, for this is the very essence of democracy. . . .

Furthering reforms within the social system and moving Chinese politics toward democracy are prerequisites for solving the social and economic problems that confront China today. Only through elections can the leadership gain the people's voluntary cooperation and bring their initiative into play. Only when the people enjoy complete freedom and expression can they help their leaders to analyze and solve problems. Cooperation, together with policies formulated and carried out by the people, are necessary for the highest degree of working efficiency and the achievement of ideal results.

This is the only road along which China can make progress. Under present-day conditions, it is an extremely difficult path.

Gregor Benton and Alan Hunter, eds., *Wild Lily, Prairie Fire: China's Road to Democracy, Yan'an to Tian'anmen, 1942–1989* (Princeton: Princeton University Press, 1995), pp. 180–184.


## 17. PROPOSALS FOR THE REFORM OF THE POLITICAL STRUCTURE, SU SHAOZHI (1986)

Su was director of the Institute of Marxism-Leninism-Mao Zedong Thought at the Chinese Academy of Social Sciences until early 1987. A proponent of political liberalization, he set down these ideas shortly before the outburst of student demonstrations in December 1986–January 1987. He went abroad after the June 4, 1989 massacre.

The ongoing economic structural reform urgently calls for the simultaneous reform of the political structure and the regeneration of ideology. We began to reform the economic structure after the Third Plenary Session of the Eleventh Central Committee. The reform has been carried out step by step and is successful. But the economic reform has not been combined with political, social, and cultural reforms. The new economic system and the old one are at present in a state of equilibrium and deadlock. The measures adopted to tackle problems that have cropped up in the course of the reform are basically those of the old system. The political structure and ideology are unprepared and offer no guarantee for in-depth reform. The economic reform is increasingly becoming more than an "economic" question. It is being obstructed by political, social, and psychological factors. Modernization is not limited to the "four modernizations" [Deng's program announced in 1978 to modernize agriculture, industry, national defense, and science and technology], which modernize the material world.

Modernization should include modernization of the political structure, social and cultural modernization, and ideological modernization. True modernization means the simultaneous modernization of the structures and the man himself. China needs modernization, but not only the "four modernizations."

The influence of the vestiges of feudal autocracy in the ideological and political fields is the principal obstruction to China's reform and modernization today. . . .

Democratization is our political ideal; it should be guaranteed by our political system and elucidated in our political philosophy and political culture. Only the interests of the people are above all else. Party leadership means leadership in the political line, principles, and policies. It does not mean the Party running everything.

First of all, the Party and the government should not be combined into one, turning government authorities into Party authorities. . . . Second, the relationship between the Party and the law should be made clear. Which comes first? The law or the Party? There can be only one first. It cannot be a case of both the law and the Party coming first. The Constitution and the laws are formulated by the people's deputies. The Party is to serve the people. Therefore, the Party should conduct its activities within the bounds of the law and the Constitution. Nobody is permitted to overstep the Constitution and the laws. It is therefore self-evident that the legislative organs and judicial organs should be independent. This is a topic in the reform of the political structure. Third, the relationship between the Party and the mass organizations is not one between the "prime mover" and the "conveyor belt." The mass organizations are links between the Party and the masses. But "links" are not "conveyor belts." They are not part of the machine. They can only be understood as bridges between the Party and the masses, otherwise the mass organizations will become part of the Party organization. The mass organizations should represent the interests of their masses and should have independent rights. The relationship between the Party and the mass organizations should be one of mutual cooperation, supervision, coordination, and promotion. . . .

Marxist methodology also needs to absorb critically the methods of modern systems theory and other scientific methods. Only then can it help us to grasp the progress of reform in all its complexity and variety and understand the constantly changing external world. Marxism also needs to develop its theories of the state, classes, and nationalities. Under new conditions, it is necessary to study not only the class nature of the state, but also its social character. In the new society, the old exploiting classes have disappeared and new social strata have emerged. The classical definition of "classes" has to be reconsidered. Only by developing Marxism can we persist in Marxism. . . .

The Constitution has made extensive stipulations concerning people's democracy. We should strive to turn into reality the rights to democracy and freedom given by the Constitution and correct and eliminate all factors that are not consistent with the spirit of the Constitution. We cannot expect to have all our wishes realized overnight; we can only promote the political reform in firm and steady steps. We are heading toward modernization and democratization. The two cannot be separated. . . .

Gregor Benton and Alan Hunter, eds., *Wild Lily, Prairie Fire: China's Road to Democracy, Yan'an to Tian'anmen, 1942–1989* (Princeton: Princeton University Press, 1995), pp. 298–305.


## 18. WALL POSTER, BEIJING SPRING (1989)

This poster was put up at People's University on April 28, 1989, two days after a *People's Daily* editorial had condemned student demonstrations as "turmoil." This reaction was echoed in countless posters around the capital.

Comrade Party Members:
    According to the analysis of the commentator in the *People's Daily* and to the general position of the Central Committee as transmitted by a meeting of Party members, the Central Committee has already adopted a tough

position: "Only sixty thousand of Beijing's students are boycotting classes while a hundred thousand have not acted. We have three million troops. What do we have to be afraid of?" (Deng Xiaoping said this.) This shows that it is highly likely that the government will use armed force to suppress the democracy movement. Tomorrow's demonstration may well be the occasion of another bloody massacre!

We have only two choices: to be a Chinese with conscience, a Party member with conscience, and to fight to make China democratic, prosperous, and strong; or to act as a qualified "Party member" and actively respond to the Central Committee's call in order to stay in the Party and assure one's future. Which should we choose? I remember Comrade Zhou Enlai once said in reply to a foreign friend, "I am first a Chinese and only then a Party member." Some people are even prepared to shed their blood for democracy, freedom, and the promotion of reforms. For what is Party membership and one's future compared with these things? Actually, this decision by the Central Committee cannot represent the true feelings of Party members. We must cry out in the true voice of a Communist with conscience!

Just consider! Three student representatives kneel under China's solemn national emblem on the steps of the Great Hall of the People with a letter of petition, but no one pays the slightest attention to them. Where is the Party spirit of the leaders of the Central Committee? Does the Party speak for the people? Who is destroying the Party?

The government wants to use the three-million-strong armed forces — those protectors of the people — against the students and their campaign for democracy and freedom. Is this not a case of dictatorship against the people? As a Party member, I no longer want to shed tears on account of the corruption of the state and the apathy of the people. All I want is to be a true Communist, and to fight and shed blood for democracy and freedom!

History will prove me right! History will remember us as fighters for democracy: true Communists who fight for the prosperity and strength of the nation!

A student Party member of People's University

Gregor Benton and Alan Hunter, eds., *Wild Lily, Prairie Fire: China's Road to Democracy, Yan'an to Tian'anmen, 1942–1989* (Princeton: Princeton University Press, 1995), pp. 270–271.

## 19. MAIN POINTS OF DENG XIAOPING'S TALKS IN SHENZHEN (1992)

In these remarks, Deng discusses the relationship between capitalism and socialism in the economic reforms he introduced in the 1980s. Noteworthy here is the emphasis upon speed in carrying out economic modernization. His remarks at Shenzhen, the most famous of the new economic zone cities, gave the green light to rapid economic expansion in the 1990s.

We should be bolder in carrying out reforms and opening up to the outside world and in making experimentations; we should not act like a woman with bound feet. For what we regard as correct, just try it and go ahead daringly. Shenzhen's experience means daring to break through. One just cannot blaze a trail, a new trail, and accomplish a new undertaking without the spirit of daring to break through, the spirit of taking a risk, and without some spirit and vigor. Who can say that everything is 100 percent sure of success with no risk at all? One should not consider oneself always in the right—there is no such thing. I never think so myself. Leaders should sum up experiences every year. They should persist in what is right and promptly correct what is not. New problems should be immediately solved whenever they emerge. It may take thirty more years for us to institute a whole set of more mature and complete systems in various fields. Under this set of systems, our principles and policies will fall more into a pattern. Now we are better experienced with each passing day in building socialism of the Chinese type. . . .

Failing to take bigger steps and break through in carrying out reforms and opening to the outside world is essentially for fear that there may be too much capitalism or that the capitalist road is followed. The question of whether a move is socialist or capitalist is crucial. The criterion for judging this can only be whether or not a move is conducive to developing the productive forces in socialist society, increasing the comprehensive strength of the country, and improving the people's living standards. There were differing views on setting up special economic zones from the beginning, and people feared that they might involve the practice of capitalism. The achievements made in the construction of Shenzhen provide clear answers to people with various misgivings. The special economic zones are socialist, not capitalist. Judging from Shenzhen's situation, public ownership is the main system of ownership, and the investment by foreign businessmen accounts for only one-fourth of the total amount of investment in the zone.

As for foreign investment, we can also benefit from it through taxation and by providing labor services. . . .

Whether the emphasis is on planning or market is not the essential distinction between socialism and capitalism. A planned economy is not socialism—there is planning under capitalism, too; and a market economy is not capitalism—there is market regulation under socialism, too. Planning and market are both economic means. The essence of socialism is to liberate and develop productive forces, to eliminate exploitation and polarization, and to finally realize common prosperity. . . .

In short, in order to win a relative edge of socialism over capitalism, we must boldly absorb and draw on all fruits of civilization created by the society of mankind, as well as all advanced management and operational methods and modes reflecting the law on modern socialized production in various countries of the world today, including developed capitalist countries.

Lawrence R. Sullivan, ed., *China Since Tiananmen: Political, Economic, and Social Conflicts* (Armonk, N.Y.: M. E. Sharpe, 1995), pp. 151–153.

## 20. EXCERPT FROM *DECISION OF THE CENTRAL COMMITTEE ON SOME ISSUES CONCERNING THE ESTABLISHMENT OF A SOCIALIST MARKET ECONOMIC STRUCTURE* (1993)

This brief excerpt from the opening of the report offers a view of the tremendous breadth of reform activities as well as the depth of their impact on the Chinese economic, social, political, and cultural scenes. It points out the clear relationship between domestic reform and opening to the world, and suggests the revolutionary nature of the reforms relative to the situation inherited from Maoist China.

Great changes have occurred in China's economic structure through reforms over the past 10-odd years guided by the theory of building socialism with Chinese characteristics put forward by Comrade Deng Xiaoping. A situation with the publicly owned economic sector constituting the mainstay while various other economic sectors develop simultaneously has taken initial shape. The economic restructuring in the rural areas continues to develop in depth; state-owned enterprises are shifting to new management mechanisms; the role of the market in the allocation of resources is rapidly expanding; economic and technological exchanges and cooperation with other countries are conducted widely; and the structure of a planned economy is gradually being replaced by the socialist market economic structure. Reform has emancipated and developed the social productive forces, and promoted to a new height the country's economic construction, the people's living standards and overall national strength. China's socialist system has shown great vitality in a situation marked by abrupt changes in the international arena. The reform and opening to the outside world which have been adopted by the Party and people on the basis of a conscientious summing up of historical experiences constitute a strategic policy decision that conforms with the law of social and economic development and is the necessary path for China to achieve modernization.

. . . The 14th National Congress [in October 1992] explicitly laid down the task of establishing a socialist market economic structure, which is an important component of the theory of building socialism with Chinese characteristics and is of profound and far-reaching significance for China's modernization drive. To establish a new economic structure by the end of this century is a great historic task of the whole Party and people of all nationalities in China during the new period. . . .

Attention should be paid to the following points:

—Emancipating the mind and seeking truth from facts. It is necessary to change the traditional concepts of planned economy and advocate active exploration and bold experiment. Therefore, it is necessary, on the one hand, to inherit our fine traditions and, on the other, to break away from outmoded conventions and, proceeding from the realities of China, learn from those experiences of all countries, including the developed capitalist countries, that reflect the general laws of social production and market economy. It is necessary to be on the alert against Right tendencies, but mainly to guard against "Left" tendencies.

—With economic construction as the central link, reform and opening to the outside world, economic development and social stability promote one another and form a single entity. Development is an essential criterion. Only by seizing the favorable opportunities, conducting reform in depth, expanding the opening to the outside world and accelerating the pace of development, can we consolidate China's political stability and unity. . . .

—Respecting the pioneering spirit of the masses and attaching importance to their personal interests. It is necessary to sum up in time the experience the masses create in practice, show respect for the wishes of the people and to properly guide and protect their initiative so as to give it full play. . . .

— Combining package reform with breakthroughs in key areas. It is a correct policy decision conforming to China's realities to start the reform from the countryside and gradually extend it to the cities, to combine urban reform with rural reform, keep micro-economic reform in step with macro-economic reform, and ensure that the enlivening of the domestic economy and the opening to the outside world are closely related to and promote each other. . . .

Kenneth Lieberthal, *Governing China* (New York: Norton, 1995), pp. 419–421.

# Major Party Congresses

## CHINESE COMMUNIST PARTY (CCP)

**First:** July 1921, Shanghai

Set forth general political program; elected Chen Duxiu general secretary and Central Bureau of three; thirteen attended.

**Second:** July 1922, Shanghai

Elected Central Executive Committee; voted to join the Comintern; adopted concept of democratic centralism; agreed in principle to adopt tactic of a united front with the Guomindang to fight the warlords and imperialists.

**Third:** June 1923, Guangzhou

Formally agreed—with pressure from the Comintern—to the policy of the "bloc within" whereby individual CCP members could join the Guomindang.

**Fourth:** January 1925, Shanghai

Established Secretariat to deal with communications and documentation. In context of CCP's role in labor and peasant organizing, tensions increased within the united front.

**Fifth:** April–May 1927, Wuhan

Established Party's first Political Bureau. After inauguration of Chiang Kai-shek's purge, Party abandoned united front policy. In early August an Emergency Conference elected Qu Qiubai as secretary general, stressed tight party discipline, and advocated armed resistance against the Guomindang.

**Sixth:** June–July 1928, Moscow

Party dominated by Li Lisan until ousted in 1930 after failure of Changsha uprising; from 1932–1935 party head was Bo Gu, one of the "returned Bolsheviks." During this period the conflict over an urban or rural strategy grew as Mao Zedong established the Jiangxi Soviet. The sixth plenum in Yan'an in October 1938 was the first chaired by Mao, who had risen to power on the Long March at the Zunyi conference in January 1935. At the seventh in April 1945, Mao Zedong Thought was formally adopted.

**Seventh:** April–June 1945, Yan'an

Adopted Party constitution that stressed greater central control. Over the course of the other six plenary meetings (stretching to September 1956), the focus shifted to economic reconstruction and development even as the Party still concentrated on rectification, mass campaigns, and indoctrination.

**Eighth:** September 1956, Beijing

This congress had two sessions and ten other plenary sessions (stretching to October 1968); thus this momentous period featured the Hundred Flowers Movement, the Anti-Rightist Campaign, the Great Leap Forward, and the violent beginning of the Cultural Revolution. In short, the generalized struggle between two lines was being waged. The two most momentous plenums were the eighth, the Lushan conference in August 1959 when Peng Dehuai was ousted, and the eleventh in August 1966 at the inauguration of the Cultural Revolution.

**Ninth:** April 1969, Beijing

Lin Biao was named as Mao's successor by the new constitution; delegates were mainly military and those who had risen in the Cultural Revolution's Revolutionary Committees; and Mao Zedong Thought was glorified. As evidence of how the military emerged the winner of the Cultural Revolution, 45 percent of the new Central Committee as opposed to 27 percent of the Eighth Central Committee were from the military. Their influence was lessened after Lin Biao's failed 1971 coup.

**Tenth:** August 1973, Beijing

The rehabilitation of purged leaders, especially Deng Xiaoping, was initiated at the Congress. At the third and last plenum under the Tenth Committee in July 1977, Deng reclaimed all his posts. In between was the traumatic year of 1976 with Zhou's, Zhu's, and Mao's deaths and the arrest of the Gang of Four.

**Eleventh:** August 1977, Beijing

The Party constitution of 1977 was approved as Hua Guofeng continued as Party chair. The most important meeting following the Eleventh Congress was the Third Plenum, which met in December 1978: it committed the Party to economic reforms espoused by Deng. In the early 1980s, Deng chose protégés Hu Yaobang and Zhao Ziyang to head reform efforts. Hu became party chair and secretary general. At the fifth plenum in February 1980, Liu Shaoqi was rehabilitated. At the sixth plenum in June 1981, the Party agreed on the definitive assessment of Mao: "his merits are primary and his errors secondary" and thus his contributions far outweighed his mistakes.

**Twelfth:** September 1982, Beijing

Deng strengthened his position and that of reforms by various high-level appointments and the retirement of older Party leaders to the Central Advisory Commission. The 1982 Party constitution eliminated the position of party chair in favor of collective leadership. Party rectification and urban economic reforms were important foci.

**Thirteenth:** October–November 1987, Beijing

Zhao Ziyang was confirmed as general secretary of the Party, following the ouster of Hu in January. Party leadership produced an ideological rationalization for economic reforms. Half of the Politburo and over half of the old Central Committee stepped down; the new Politburo and its Standing Committee contained no open critics of reform. The average age of members of the Central Committee dropped about four years to 55.2 in the Party's apparent effort to build a new generation of leadership. There was a further decline of the military membership on the Committee, receding from its high (of almost half the committee) in 1969.

At the third plenum in September–October 1988, Zhao faced criticism for his management of the reforms: he was forced to write a self-criticism and his role in economic matters was curtailed. Decisions were made to postpone price reform, to sharply cut back capital construction, and to push "ideological rectification and administrative recentralization."

At the fourth plenum in June 1989, after the crackdown on democracy protesters, Zhao was expelled from all positions in party and government.

At the fifth plenum in November 1989, Deng Xiaoping formally retired from party and government posts but remained the key figure in China until his death in February 1997.

**Fourteenth:** October 1992, Beijing

Congress confirmed rapid economic market reforms following Deng's trip to Shenzhen earlier that year and his remarks equivalent to "full steam ahead."

Reformer Zhu Rongji elevated to Standing Committee.

**Fifteenth:** September 1997, Beijing

Congress confirmed once again Deng's ideology of reform and agreed to maintain the leadership Deng had installed. General Secretary Jiang

Zemin strengthened his position as the Congress accepted his program, which included restructuring state-owned enterprises, reducing the size of the army, strengthening the legal system, increasing attempts to reduce corruption, and rejecting ideas of Western-style democracy.

## GUOMINDANG (NATIONALIST PARTY)

**First:** January 1924, Guangzhou
Adopted policy of cooperation with the Soviet Union and the Chinese
    Communist Party.
**Second:** January 1926, Guangzhou
Adopted policy of continuing cooperation with Borodin and other Soviet
    advisers and the CCP; censured the alleged right-wing Western Hills fac-
    tion, which then held its own Congress in March 1926 in Shanghai.
**Third:** March 1929, Nanjing
Continuing problem with party and government; lack of control a major
    issue. Guidelines for important administrative measures of the political
    tutelage period set. In the third plenum (June 1929), the decision was
    made that the period of tutelage would last from 1930 to 1935. This deci-
    sion became a dead letter.
**Fourth:** November 1930, Nanjing
Organic law of the National Government was revised; the central govern-
    ment and the national army were reorganized; and the National People's
    convention met on May 5, 1931.
**Fifth:** November 1935, Nanjing
Chiang Kai-shek consolidated his power.
**Extraordinary:** March 1938, Wuhan
The party constitution was modified so that Chiang could be ranked as pres-
    ident or director (*zongcai*) equivalent to Sun Yat-sen's rank of president
    (*zongli*). In that capacity Chiang retained veto power over all party deci-
    sions. The Congress adopted the program of National Resistance to serve
    as a framework for government policy during the Japanese invasion.
    The People's Political Council was established to give representation
    to all active political groups in China.
**Sixth:** May 1945, Chongqing
Chiang was reelected president; the Central Executive Committee was
    enlarged to gain support for Chiang's political cause from non-
    Communist political figures and peripheral power centers. The Party

Manifesto called for realizing the goals of the Three People's Principles, for decisively defeating Japan and strengthening ties to the Allies, and for securing independence for China and equality for China's racial groups.

**Seventh:** October 1952, Taipei

Chiang elected president. Accepted principle that opposition to Communism and resistance against Russia were basic to all other party missions. Party goals set forth in the "oppose Communists, resist Russia period" to make Taiwan a model province of the Three People's Principles.

**Eighth:** October 1957, Taipei

Chiang reelected president. Adopted a more detailed and substantial platform than at the Seventh Congress. Central foci were three: realization of the Three People's Principles, the reconstruction of Taiwan, and the recovery of the mainland.

**Ninth:** November 1963, Taipei

Chiang reelected president. A platform of thirty-five articles set forth concerning general policies, mostly a restatement of the Eighth Congress's goals.

**Tenth:** March–April 1969, Taipei

Acceleration of process of transferring power to Chiang's son, Chiang Ching-kuo. Ching-kuo received the most votes to serve on the Central Committee and was later named vice premier.

**Eleventh:** November 1976, Taipei

First party congress after the death of Chiang Kai-shek in April 1975. Party constitution revised to limit the title of *zongcai* to Chiang Kai-shek.

Chiang Ching-kuo elected party chair. All advisors, Central Committee, and Standing Committee members who had been approved by Chiang Kai-shek were retained. The Executive Committee was enlarged, permitting the new chair to appoint both younger mainlanders and Taiwanese, if he so chose.

**Twelfth:** March–April 1981, Taipei

No change of course. First time anyone not associated with military or political circles was elected to the Central Committee.

**Thirteenth:** July 1988, Taipei

First congress after the death of Chiang Ching-kuo in January 1988. The most open Guomindang congress in history. Of the delegates, 36 percent were chosen by the party's members. Of the 180 Central Committee members, 65 percent were new; the average age dropped from 70 in the preceding committee to 59; the numbers of Taiwanese rose from 20 to 45 percent.

**Fourteenth:**  August 1993, Taipei

After having lifted martial law, Taiwanese president Lee Teng-hui consoli-
    dated his power at this congress. He was the first Guomindang leader
    ever to be elected by secret ballot; he received 82.5 percent of the vote.

By the middle of the 1990s there were at least two other parties vying for power
in what had become a democratic Taiwan. The Democratic Progressive Party
formed in the 1980s and the New Party were having their own congresses. In
the presidential election of 1996, there were in fact four slates of candidates
vying for election victory. In such circumstances, it is appropriate to cease coverage of Guomindang congresses since the situation of one party constituting
in essence the state had changed dramatically.

# Tables and Figures on Trends and Developments

*Table 1*

Selected Development and Demographic Trends, 1950–90

|  | 1950 | 1960 | 1970 | 1980 | 1990 |
|---|---|---|---|---|---|
| Total population (in millions) | 552.00 | 662.00 | 830.00 | 987.00 | 1,120.00 |
| GNP per capita (US$) | — | — | — | 290.00 | 370.00 |
| % urban | 11.20 | 19.70 | 17.40 | 19.40 | 26.00 |
| Infant mortality per 100 births | 13.80 | 8.56 | 5.15 | 3.76 | 3.70 |
| Crude birth rate (% increase) | 3.70 | 2.09 | 3.34 | 1.82 | 2.10 |
| Crude death rate (% decrease) | 1.80 | 2.54 | 0.76 | 0.63 | 0.63 |
| Rate of population growth (%) | 1.90 | -0.45 | 2.58 | 1.19 | 1.47 |
| Total fertility rate per childbearer | 5.80 | 3.30 | 5.80 | 2.20 | 2.30 |
| Life expectancy (female) | 49.20 | 58.00 | 63.20 | 69.20 | 71.10 |
| Life expectancy (male) | 46.70 | 56.00 | 61.10 | 66.20 | 67.80 |

Robert E. Gamer, ed., *Understanding Contemporary China* (Boulder: Lynne Rienner, 1999), p. 217.

## Table 2

### Regional Variation in Demographic Indicators

| REGION | CRUDE BIRTH RATE (% INCREASE) | | | CRUDE DEATH RATE (% INCREASE) | | |
|---|---|---|---|---|---|---|
| | 1970 | 1980 | 1990 | 1970 | 1980 | 1990 |
| Tibet | 1.94 | 2.24 | 2.76 | 0.76 | 0.82 | 0.92 |
| Xinjiang | 3.67 | 2.18 | 2.47 | 0.82 | 0.77 | 0.64 |
| Guangdong | 2.96 | 2.07 | 2.40 | 0.60 | 0.54 | 0.53 |
| Jiangsu | 3.07 | 1.47 | 2.05 | 0.69 | 0.66 | 0.61 |
| Inner Mongolia | 2.89 | 1.85 | 2.01 | 0.58 | 0.55 | 0.58 |
| Sichuan | 5.27 | 1.19 | 1.78 | 1.26 | 0.68 | 0.71 |
| Heilongjiang | 3.48 | 2.36 | 1.75 | 0.58 | 0.72 | 0.53 |
| Beijing | 2.07 | 1.56 | 1.34 | 0.64 | 0.63 | 0.54 |
| Shanghai | 1.38 | 1.26 | 1.13 | 0.50 | 0.65 | 0.64 |
| China as a whole | 3.34 | 1.82 | 2.10 | 0.76 | 0.63 | 0.63 |

Robert E. Gamer, ed., *Understanding Contemporary China* (Boulder: Lynne Rienner, 1999), p. 213.

## Table 3

### Ethnic Minorities with Populations Over Four Million

| ETHNIC MINORITIES | 1982 | 1990 | GROWTH (%) | ANNUAL GROWTH RATE (%) |
|---|---|---|---|---|
| Zhuang | 13.38 | 15.49 | 15.7 | 1.8 |
| Manchu | 4.30 | 9.82 | 128.2 | 10.9 |
| Hui | 7.23 | 8.60 | 19.0 | 2.2 |
| Miao | 5.02 | 7.40 | 46.9 | 5.0 |
| Uygur | 5.96 | 7.21 | 21.0 | 2.4 |
| Yi | 5.45 | 6.57 | 20.4 | 2.4 |
| Tujia | 2.83 | 5.70 | 101.2 | 9.1 |
| Mongolian | 3.41 | 4.81 | 40.7 | 4.4 |
| Tibetan | 3.85 | 4.59 | 18.6 | 2.2 |

Robert E. Gamer, ed., *Understanding Contemporary China* (Boulder: Lynne Rienner, 1999), p. 231.

## Table 4

### Basic Indicators for Greater China, 1995

| INDICATORS | HONG KONG | TAIWAN | MACAO | CHINA | GUANG-DONG | FUJIAN |
|---|---|---|---|---|---|---|
| Area (square kilometers) | 1,068 | 35,961 | 19 | 960,000 | 177,901 | 121,400 |
| Population (millions) | 6.2 | 21.3 | 0.4 | 1,211.2 | 66.7 | 32.3 |
| GDP (US$ billions) | 142.0 | 257.2 | 6.5 | 691.4 | 65.1 | 26.3 |
| Per capita GDP (US$) | 23,019 | 12,490 | 15,878 | 571 | 949 | 814 |
| GDP growth rate (percent) | 4.6 | 6.3 | 4.0 | 10.2 | 15 | 15 |
| Exports (US$ billions) | 172.3 | 111.7 | 1.87 | 148.8 | 56.6 | 7.9 |

Barry Naughton, ed., *The China Circle* (Washington, D.C.: The Brookings Institution, 1997), p. 42.

## Table 5

### Indicators of Economic Development Level in Taiwan, 1952–90

|  | 1952 | 1958 | 1962 | 1968 | 1973 | 1978 | 1983 | 1988 | 1990 |
|---|---|---|---|---|---|---|---|---|---|
| Population (millions) | 8.1 | 10.0 | 11.5 | 13.7 | 15.6 | 17.1 | 18.7 | 19.9 | 20.4 |
| GNP per capita (NT$1,000) | 2.0 | 4.3 | 6.5 | 12.2 | 26.6 | 58.3 | 113.1 | 181.2 | 215.0 |
| GNP per capita (US$) | 153 | 173 | 162 | 304 | 695 | 1,577 | 2,823 | 6,333 | 7,997 |
| Manufacturing % GDP | 12.9 | 16.8 | 20.0 | 26.5 | 36.8 | 35.6 | 36.0 | 37.8 | 34.1 |
| Agriculture % GDP | 32.2 | 26.8 | 25.0 | 19.0 | 12.1 | 9.4 | 7.3 | 5.0 | 4.2 |
| Agriculture % employment | 56.1 | 51.1 | 49.7 | 40.8 | 30.5 | 24.9 | 18.6 | 13.7 | 12.9 |
| Export % GDP | 8.5 | 8.6 | 11.3 | 18.6 | 41.6 | 47.4 | 48.5 | 50.5 | 41.4 |
| % Industrial exports | 8.1 | 14.0 | 50.5 | 68.4 | 84.6 | 89.2 | 93.1 | 94.5 | 95.5 |
| Trade balance (US$ mil.) | -71 | -70 | -86 | -114 | 691 | 1,660 | 4,836 | 10,994 | 12,498 |
| % Exports to U.S. | 3.5 | 6.2 | 24.4 | 35.3 | 37.4 | 39.5 | 45.1 | 38.7 | 32.4 |
| Foreign reserve (US$ bil.) | — | — | 0.1 | 0.3 | 1.0 | 1.4 | 11.9 | 79.0 | — |
| Inflation (%) | 18.8 | 1.3 | 2.3 | 7.9 | 8.2 | 5.8 | 1.4 | 1.3 | 4.1 |
| Savings % GNP | 9.2 | 9.9 | 12.4 | 22.1 | 34.6 | 34.9 | 32.1 | 34.4 | 29.7 |
| Investment % GNP | 15.3 | 16.6 | 17.8 | 25.1 | 29.1 | 28.2 | 23.5 | 23.3 | 22.2 |
| U.S. aid % investment | 45.5 | 37.3 | 20.2 | 0.6 | 0.0 | 0.0 | 0.0 | 0.0 | 0.0 |
| Foreign investment % investment | 0.5 | 0.8 | 1.5 | 8.4 | 7.9 | 2.8 | 3.5 | 4.2 | 6.6 |
| Unemployment rate (%) | 4.6 | 4.0 | 4.3 | 1.8 | 1.3 | 1.7 | 2.7 | 1.7 | 1.7 |

Bih-jaw Lin and James T. Myers, eds., *Contemporary China in the Post-Cold War Era* (Columbia: University of South Carolina Press, 1996), p. 171.

## Table 6

### China's Trade with Selected Countries and Regions, 1970, 1979–85

Millions of current U.S. dollars and, in parentheses, percentage of total trade

| TRADING PARTNERS | 1970 | 1979 | 1982 | 1985 |
|---|---|---|---|---|
| Total trade | 4,200 | 28,224.3 | 39,586.0 | 70,804.1 |
| | (100) | | | |
| Developed countries | 2,030 | 15,811.3 | 21,028.5 | 38,203.3 |
| | (48.3) | (56.0) | (53.1) | (54.0) |
| East Asia and Pacific | 984 | 7,532.3 | 9,888.7 | 20,153.6 |
| | (23.4) | (26.7) | (25.0) | (28.5) |
| Australia | 164 | 942.4 | 1,157.1 | 1,157.0 |
| | (3.9) | (3.3) | (2.9) | (1.6) |
| Japan | 811 | 6,466.8 | 8,583.4 | 18,812.4 |
| | (19.3) | (22.9) | (21.7) | (26.7) |
| North America | 153 | 2,968.2 | 6,357.4 | 8,921.2 |
| | (3.6) | (10.5) | (16.1) | (12.6) |
| Canada | 153 | 649.5 | 1,170.5 | 1,225.3 |
| | (3.6) | (2.3) | (2.3) | (1.7) |
| United States | 0 | 2,318.7 | 5,186.9 | 7,695.9 |
| | (0.0) | (8.2) | (13.1) | (10.9) |
| Western Europe | 892 | 5,310.8 | 4,782.4 | 9,128.5 |
| | (21.2) | (18.8) | (12.1) | (12.9) |
| Less developed countries | 1,301 | 8,715.2 | 15,862.8 | 27,733.0 |
| | (31.0) | (30.9) | (40.1) | (39.2) |
| Southeast Asia | 770 | 5,153.9 | 10,537.0 | 20,449.5 |
| | (18.3) | (18.3) | (26.6) | (28.9) |
| Hong Kong | 477 | 3,403.0 | 7,384.9 | 15,425.6 |
| | (11.4) | (12.1) | (18.7) | (21.8) |
| ASEAN | 267 | 1,560.3 | 2,533.4 | 4,008.0 |
| | (6.4) | (5.5) | (6.4) | (5.7) |
| South Asia and Middle East | 258 | 1,348.9 | 3,394.0 | 3,318.9 |
| | (6.1) | (4.8) | (8.6) | (4.7) |
| Latin America | 11 | 1,088.1 | 1,096.8 | 2,243.9 |
| | (0.3) | (3.9) | (2.8) | (3.2) |
| Africa | 260 | 1,124.4 | 943.9 | 1,720.7 |

## Table 6 *(continued)*

### China's Trade with Selected Countries and Regions, 1970, 1979–85
Millions of current U.S. dollars and, in parentheses, percentage of total trade

| | | | | |
|---|---|---|---|---|
| | (6.2) | (4.0) | (2.4) | (2.4) |
| Communist bloc | 869 | 3,697.8 | 2,991.4 | 4,867.8 |
| | (20.7) | (13.1) | (7.6) | (6.9) |
| USSR | 47 | 508.8 | 307.8 | 1,931.4 |
| | (1.1) | (1.8) | (0.8) | (2.7) |
| Eastern Europe | 480 | 2,335.4 | 1,701.1 | 2,213.0 |
| | (11.4) | (8.3) | (4.3) | (3.1) |
| Other communist | 342 | 853.5 | 982.5 | 722.5 |
| | (8.1) | (3.0) | (2.5) | (1.0) |

Harry Harding, *China's Second Revolution* (Washington, D.C.: The Brookings Institution, 1987), pp. 146–147.

## Table 7

### United States Trade with China, 1978–93

| YEAR | EXPORTS | IMPORTS | BALANCE |
|---|---|---|---|
| 1978 | 821 | 324 | +497 |
| 1979 | 1,724 | 592 | +1,132 |
| 1980 | 3,754 | 1,058 | +2,696 |
| 1981 | 3,603 | 1,865 | +1,726 |
| 1982 | 2,912 | 2,284 | +628 |
| 1983 | 2,173 | 2,244 | -68 |
| 1984 | 3,004 | 3,065 | -61 |
| 1985 | 3,856 | 3,862 | -10 |
| 1986 | 3,106 | 4,771 | -1,665 |
| 1987 | 3,497 | 6,293 | -2,776 |
| 1988 | 5,021 | 8,511 | -3,490 |
| 1989 | 5,775 | 11,990 | -6,235 |
| 1990 | 4,806 | 15,237 | -10,431 |
| 1991 | 6,278 | 18,969 | -12,691 |
| 1992 | 7,418 | 25,728 | -18,309 |
| 1993 | 6,318 | 23,013 | -16,695 |

Nicholas R. Lardy, *China in the World Economy* (Washington, D.C.: Institute for International Economics, 1994), p. 74.

## Table 8

United States Direct Foreign Investment in
China, 1983–93

| YEAR | CONTRACTED | ACTUAL |
|------|-----------|--------|
| 1983 | 477.52 | n.a. |
| 1984 | 165.18 | 256.25 |
| 1985 | 1,152.02 | 357.19 |
| 1986 | 527.35 | 314.90 |
| 1987 | 432.19 | 262.80 |
| 1988 | 235.96 | 235.96 |
| 1989 | 640.52 | 284.27 |
| 1990 | 357.82 | 455.99 |
| 1991 | 548.08 | 323.20 |
| 1992 | 3,121.25 | 511.05 |
| 1993 | n.a. | 280.00 |

Nicholas R. Lardy, *China in the World Economy* (Washington,
D.C.: Institute for International Economics, 1994), p. 119.

## Table 9

Agricultural Performance, 1957–78 and 1978–84
Per capita output in kilograms[*]

| YEAR | GRAINS | COTTON | EDIBLE OILS | MEAT (PORK, BEEF, MUTTON) | AQUATIC PRODUCTS (FISH, SEAFOOD) |
|------|--------|--------|-------------|---------------------------|----------------------------------|
| 1957 | 306 | 2.5 | 6.6 | 6.3 | 4.9 |
| 1978 | 319 | 2.3 | 5.5 | 9.0 | 4.9 |
| 1984 | 397 | 5.9 | 11.6 | 14.9 | 5.9 |

Average annual growth rates in percent
(per capita annual growth rates in parentheses)

| | | | | | |
|------|--------|--------|-------------|---------------------------|----------------------------------|
| 1957–78 | 2.1 (0.2) | 1.3 (-0.6) | 1.0 (-0.9) | 3.7 (1.7) | 1.9 (0) |
| 1978–84 | 4.9 (3.8) | 18.7 (17.5) | 14.6 (14.0) | 10.1 (9.0) | 4.6 (3.3) |

[*]Per capita refers to the national population.
Mark Selden, *The Political Economy of Chinese Development* (Armonk, N.Y.: M.E. Sharpe, 1993), p. 30.

## Table 10

### State Budgets with Reference to Defense and Other Expenditures, 1978–94
#### (billion RMB)

| | DEFENSE | | | CULTURE/HEALTH EDUCATION/S & T | | |
|---|---|---|---|---|---|---|
| | | % change | % state budget | | % change | % state budget |
| 1978 | 16.8 | | n.a. | n.a. | | |
| 1979 | 20.2 | 20.2 | n.a. | n.a. | | — |
| 1980 | 19.38 | -4.1 | 16.0 | 15.63 | — | 12.88 |
| 1981 | 16.8 | -13.3 | 15.1 | 17.14 | 9.7 | 15.34 |
| 1982 | 17.87 | 6.4 | 15.5 | 19.7 | 14.9 | 17.08 |
| 1983 | 17.64 | -1.3 | 13.97 | 20.4 | 3.5 | 16.16 |
| 1984 | 18.07 | 2.4 | 11.76 | 26.34 | 29.1 | 17.14 |
| 1985 | 19.15 | 6.0 | 10.49 | 31.72 | 20.4 | 17.37 |
| 1986 | 20.13 | 5.1 | 8.79 | 38.0 | 20.0 | 16.58 |
| 1987 | 20.97 | 4.2 | 8.64 | 40.56 | 6.7 | 16.71 |
| 1988 | 21.8 | 4.0 | 8.17 | 47.9 | 18.1 | 17.95 |
| 1989 | 25.1 | 12.6 | 8.56 | 51.39 | 7.3 | 17.53 |
| 1990 | 29.03 | 15.6 | 8.98 | 61.6 | 19.9 | 19.06 |
| 1991 | 33.03 | 13.8 | 8.7 | 69.9 | 13.5 | 18.42 |
| 1992 | 37.78 | 14.4 | 8.53 | 78.95 | 12.9 | 17.83 |
| 1993 | 43.2 | 14.3 | 7.52 | 96.0 | 21.6 | 16.7 |
| 1994 | 52.0 | 20.4 | 8.57 | 113.3 | 18.0 | 18.67 |
| | Increase 1985–94 = 171.5% | | | Increase 1985–94 = 257.2% | | |

Gerald Segal and Richard H. Yang, eds., *Chinese Economic Reform* (London: Routledge, 1996), p. 63.

## Table 11

### Indicators of Social Development, 1952–90

| | 1952 | 1958 | 1962 | 1968 | 1973 | 1978 | 1983 | 1988 | 1990 |
|---|---|---|---|---|---|---|---|---|---|
| Population growth (%) | 3.3 | 3.6 | 3.3 | 2.7 | 1.8 | 1.9 | 1.5 | 1.2 | 1.3 |
| People per family | — | — | 5.6 | — | 5.2 | 5.0 | 4.5 | 4.1 | — |
| Literacy rate (%) | 57.9 | 69.1 | 75.2 | 83.6 | 86.2 | 88.8 | 90.9 | 92.6 | 93.2 |
| % Population with secondary education | 10.2 | 13.0 | 15.7 | 22.1 | 32.2 | 41.0 | 48.4 | 54.3 | — |
| % Primary graduates to junior high school | 34.9 | 51.1 | 55.1 | 74.2 | 83.7 | 94.1 | 98.0 | 99.1 | 99.1 |
| College students % population | 0.1 | 0.3 | 0.4 | 1.2 | 1.7 | 1.8 | 2.1 | 2.5 | — |
| % College students in humanities | 22 | — | 21 | 12 | 14 | 12 | 9 | 9 | — |
| % College students in science and engineering | 33 | — | 29 | 30 | 35 | 30 | 39 | 41 | — |
| Real expenditure/ primary student (1981 NT$) | 3,296 | 2,784 | 3,501 | 4,781 | 7,861 | 13,002 | 18,927 | 20,224 | — |
| % Homes self-owned | — | — | — | — | 67 | 70 | 75 | 78 | — |
| Average space per home (p'ing) | — | — | — | — | 23 | 24 | 29 | 32 | — |
| % Population with electricity | — | — | 77 | 94 | 98 | 99 | 99 | 99 | 99 |
| % Population with tap water | 29 | 29 | 31 | 41 | 46 | 62 | 75 | 82 | — |
| % Homes with refrigerator | — | — | — | — | 74 | 86 | 95 | 98 | — |

## Table 11 (continued)

### Indicators of Social Development, 1952–90

| | 1952 | 1958 | 1962 | 1968 | 1973 | 1978 | 1983 | 1988 | 1990 |
|---|---|---|---|---|---|---|---|---|---|
| % Homes with washing machine | — | — | — | — | 39 | 54 | 74 | 84 | — |
| % Homes with air conditioning | — | — | — | — | 4 | 9 | 20 | 34 | — |
| % Homes with color TV | — | — | — | — | 23 | 47 | 88 | 97 | — |
| % Homes with VCR | — | — | — | — | 0 | 0 | 9 | 51 | — |

Bih-jaw Lin and James T. Myers, eds., *Contemporary China in the Post-Cold War Era* (Columbia: University of South Carolina Press, 1996), p. 186.

## Table 12

### Number of Schools, 1952–91

| YEAR | JUNIOR PRIMARY | SENIOR SECONDARY | SECONDARY |
|---|---|---|---|
| 1952 | 526,964 | 3,117 | 1,181 |
| 1965 | 681,939 | 13,990 | 4,112 |
| 1977 | 982,291 | 136,365 | 64,903 |
| 1978 | 949,323 | 113,130 | 49,215 |
| 1979 | 923,532 | 103,944 | 40,289 |
| 1980 | 917,316 | 87,077 | 31,300 |
| 1981 | 894,074 | 82,271 | 24,447 |
| 1982 | 880,516 | 80,775 | 20,874 |
| 1983 | 862,165 | 77,598 | 18,876 |
| 1984 | 853,740 | 75,867 | 17,847 |
| 1985 | 832,309 | 75,903 | 17,318 |
| 1986 | 820,846 | 75,856 | 17,111 |
| 1987 | 807,406 | 75,927 | 16,930 |
| 1988 | 793,261 | 74,968 | 16,524 |
| 1989 | 777,244 | 73,525 | 16,050 |
| 1990 | 766,072 | 71,953 | 15,678 |
| 1991 | 729,158 | 70,608 | 15,243 |

Colin Mackerras, Pradeep Taneja, and Graham Young, eds., *China Since 1978* (Melbourne: Longman, Cheshire, 1994), p. 175.

## Table 13

### Number of Students, 1950–91
### (in millions)

| YEAR | PRIMARY | SECONDARY | TERTIARY |
|------|---------|-----------|----------|
| 1950 | 28.924 | 1.57 | 0.14 |
| 1965 | 116.21 | 14.32 | 0.67 |
| 1978 | 146.24 | 66.37 | 0.86 |
| 1980 | 146.27 | 56.78 | 1.14 |
| 1981 | 143.33 | 50.15 | 1.28 |
| 1982 | 139.72 | 47.03 | 1.15 |
| 1983 | 135.78 | 46.35 | 1.21 |
| 1984 | 135.57 | 48.61 | 1.40 |
| 1985 | 133.70 | 50.93 | 1.70 |
| 1986 | 131.83 | 53.22 | 1.88 |
| 1987 | 128.36 | 54.03 | 1.96 |
| 1988 | 125.36 | 52.46 | 2.07 |
| 1989 | 123.73 | 50.54 | 2.08 |
| 1990 | 122.41 | 51.05 | 2.06 |
| 1991 | 121.64 | 52.27 | 2.04 |

Colin Mackerras, Pradeep Taneja, and Graham Young, eds., *China Since 1978* (Mel-bourne: Longman, Cheshire, 1994), p. 174.

Table 14

Changes in Aspects of Freedom of Mate Choice, 1900–82

YEAR OF MARRIAGE

| Mate-Choice Patterns | 1900–1938 | 1939–1945 | 1946–1949 | 1950–1953 | 1954–1957 | 1958–1965 | 1966–1976 | 1977–1982 |
|---|---|---|---|---|---|---|---|---|
| Parental arrangement (%) | 53.9 | 36.3 | 30.6 | 19.8 | 11.2 | 3.1 | 0.8 | 0.9 |
| Introduction by relatives (%) | 24.0 | 27.2 | 25.9 | 25.7 | 24.1 | 21.2 | 17.8 | 15.2 |
| Introduction by friends (%) | 15.1 | 23.3 | 24.4 | 29.9 | 34.3 | 42.3 | 44.2 | 48.3 |
| Own effort (%) | 5.0 | 9.8 | 14.5 | 18.5 | 25.7 | 26.4 | 33.5 | 31.7 |
| Others (%) | 0.5 | 1.0 | 0.4 | 1.9 | 0.6 | 1.4 | 0.6 | 0.1 |
| N.A. (%) | 1.6 | 2.4 | 4.5 | 4.2 | 4.0 | 5.6 | 3.1 | 3.8 |
| Number of cases | 570 | 622 | 468 | 475 | 498 | 641 | 877 | 889 |

Robert E. Gamer, ed., *Understanding Contemporary China* (Boulder: Lynne Rienner, 1999), p. 278.

Table 15

Bride Age at First Marriage, 1900–82

YEAR OF MARRIAGE

| Age at First Marriage | 1900–1938 | 1939–1945 | 1946–1949 | 1950–1953 | 1954–1957 | 1958–1965 | 1966–1976 | 1977–1982 |
|---|---|---|---|---|---|---|---|---|
| 15 and under (%) | 9.5 | 4.3 | 3.0 | 1.7 | 0.2 | 0.5 | 0.0 | 0.0 |
| 16–17 | 26.3 | 19.3 | 18.6 | 15.2 | 4.6 | 2.4 | 0.0 | 0.0 |
| 18–20 | 40.9 | 37.9 | 37.2 | 40.0 | 36.6 | 19.3 | 3.8 | 0.2 |
| 21–24 | 17.9 | 26.5 | 26.3 | 26.5 | 36.6 | 40.9 | 35.0 | 14.2 |
| 25–29 | 4.7 | 7.9 | 11.1 | 11.6 | 15.9 | 29.0 | 53.9 | 72.4 |
| 30–35 | 0.4 | 3.2 | 2.6 | 3.8 | 4.8 | 4.8 | 4.9 | 10.9 |
| 36–40 | 0.0 | 0.8 | 1.3 | 1.3 | 1.4 | 2.1 | 0.5 | 0.3 |
| 41 and over | 0.05 | 0.0 | 0.05 | 0.0 | 0.0 | 1.1 | 1.9 | 1.9 |
| N.A. | .25 | .1 | 2.80 | — | .8 | — | — | — |
| Number of cases | 570 | 622 | 468 | 475 | 498 | 641 | 877 | 889 |

Robert E. Gamer, ed., *Understanding Contemporary China* (Boulder: Lynne Rienner, 1999), p. 277.

Table 16

Groom Age at First Marriage, 1900–82

| Age at First Marriage | YEAR OF MARRIAGE | | | | | | | |
|---|---|---|---|---|---|---|---|---|
|  | 1900–1938 | 1939–1945 | 1946–1949 | 1950–1953 | 1954–1957 | 1958–1965 | 1966–1976 | 1977–1982 |
| 15 and under (%) | 5.5 | 2.6 | 2.4 | 0.2 | 0.2 | 0.0 | 0.0 | 0.0 |
| 16–17 | 8.0 | 5.6 | 5.2 | 3.2 | 0.4 | 0.2 | 0.0 | 0.0 |
| 18–20 | 21.0 | 21.6 | 16.3 | 21.8 | 9.3 | 2.4 | 0.8 | 0.0 |
| 21–24 | 30.9 | 29.4 | 30.3 | 30.7 | 36.9 | 24.5 | 8.9 | 2.8 |
| 25–29 | 22.0 | 24.0 | 29.2 | 27.7 | 35.2 | 47.1 | 58.2 | 59.2 |
| 30–35 | 8.9 | 10.8 | 11.8 | 11.4 | 23.4 | 19.6 | 27.3 | 33.5 |
| 36–40 | 2.0 | 2.6 | 2.4 | 2.7 | 2.6 | 3.5 | 2.8 | 2.5 |
| 41 and over | 1.1 | 2.9 | 1.7 | 1.9 | 2.0 | 2.9 | 2.1 | 2.1 |
| N.A. | 0.7 | 0.5 | 0.7 | 0.4 | — | — | — | — |
| Number of cases | 563 | 612 | 465 | 473 | 493 | 629 | 869 | 879 |

Robert E. Garner, ed., *Understanding Contemporary China* (Boulder: Lynne Rienner, 1999), p. 276.

## Figure 1

Urban Residents' Income and Living Expenditures, 1995

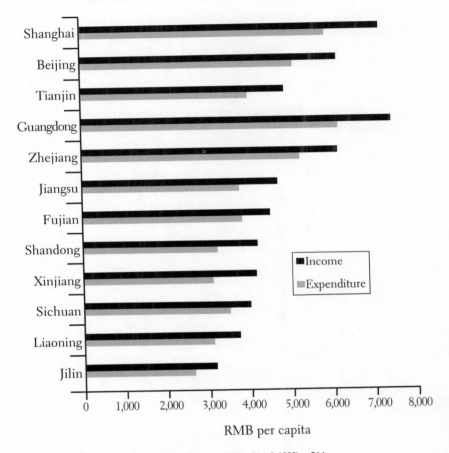

RMB per capita

Conghua Li, *China: The Consumer Revolution* (Singapore: Wiley [Asia], 1998), p. 214.

*Figure 2*

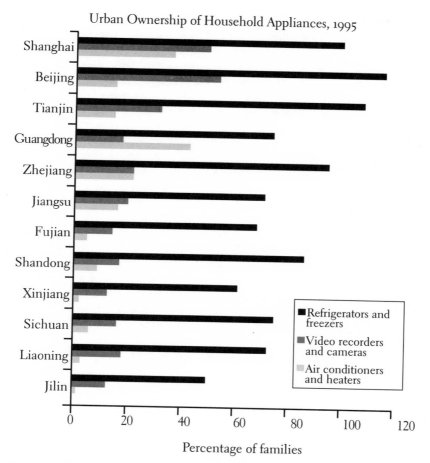

Urban Ownership of Household Appliances, 1995

Percentage of families

Conghua Li, *China: The Consumer Revolution* (Singapore: Wiley [Asia], 1998), p. 215.

# INDEX

Page numbers in **bold** refer to entries in the Compendium.